The Enlightenment values of individual autonomy, democracy, and secularizing reason appear to conflict with the religious traditions of community, authority, and traditional learning. Yet in American history the two heritages have been intertwined since the colonial era: The development of the Enlightenment has been influenced by community-based thinking, and religious institutions have adopted to some extent critical methods and a democratic ethos even within their own walls.

This volume brings together the work of a distinguished group of theologians, intellectual historians, literary critics, and philosophers to explore the interaction between Enlightenment ideals and American religion. The Enlightenment's effect on the major religious traditions, including the Catholic Church, evangelical Protestantism, and Judaism, is examined. Also highlighted is religion in the thinking of such representative figures as Edwards, Franklin, Emerson, Lincoln, Santayana and the pragmatists, Stevens, and Eliot. The collection concludes with a three-part discussion of the nature of the "post-Enlightenment."

WOODROW WILSON CENTER SERIES

Knowledge and belief in America

Other books in the series

Michael J. Lacey, editor, *Religion and Twentieth-Century American Intellectual Life*

Michael J. Lacey, editor, *The Truman Presidency*

Joseph Kruzel and Michael H. Haltzel, editors, *Between the Blocs: Problems and Prospects for Europe's Neutral and Nonaligned States*

William C. Brumfield, editor, *Reshaping Russian Architecture: Western Technology, Utopian Dreams*

Mark N. Katz, editor, *The USSR and Marxist Revolutions in the Third World*

Walter Reich, editor, *Origins of Terrorism: Psychologies, Ideologies, Theologies, States of Mind*

Mary O. Furner and Barry Supple, editors, *The State and Economic Knowledge: The American and British Experiences*

Michael J. Lacey and Knud Haakonssen, editors, *A Culture of Rights: The Bill of Rights in Philosophy, Politics, and Law—1791 and 1991*

Robert J. Donovan and Ray Scherer, *Unsilent Revolution: Television News and American Public Life, 1948–1991*

Nelson Lichtenstein and Howell John Harris, editors, *Industrial Democracy in America: The Ambiguous Promise*

William Craft Brumfield and Blair A. Ruble, editors, *Russian Housing in the Modern Age: Design and Social History*

Michael J. Lacey and Mary O. Furner, editors, *The State and Social Investigation in Britain and the United States*

Hugh Ragsdale, editor and translator, *Imperial Russian Foreign Policy*

Dermot Keogh and Michael H. Haltzel, editors, *Northern Ireland and the Politics of Reconciliation*

Joseph Klaits and Michael H. Haltzel, editors, *The Global Ramifications of the French Revolution*

René Lemarchand, *Burundi: Ethnocide as Discourse and Practice*

James R. Millar and Sharon L. Wolchik, editors, *The Social Legacy of Communism*

James M. Morris, editor, *On Mozart*

Blair A. Ruble, *Money Sings: The Changing Politics of Urban Space in Post-Soviet Yaroslavl*

Theodore Taranovski, editor, *Reform in Modern Russian History: Progress or Cycle?*

Deborah S. Davis, Richard Kraus, Barry Naughton, and Elizabeth J. Perry, editors, *Urban Spaces in Contemporary China: The Potential for Autonomy and Community in Post-Mao China*

Knowledge and belief in America

Enlightenment traditions and modern religious thought

Edited by
WILLIAM M. SHEA
and
PETER A. HUFF

WOODROW WILSON CENTER PRESS

AND

Published by the Press Syndicate of the University of Cambridge
The Pitt Building, Trumpington Street, Cambridge CB2 1RP
40 West 20th Street, New York, NY 10011–4211, USA
10 Stamford Road, Oakleigh, Melbourne 3166, Australia

First published 1995

"Enamored against Thee by These Strange Minds," by Giles Gunn, was first published in *Thinking across the American Grain: Ideology, Intellect, and the New Pragmatism*, ed. Giles Gunn (Chicago: University of Chicago Press), 119–151.

"Sunday Morning" and *Notes toward a Supreme Fiction* from *Collected Poems* by Wallace Stevens. Copyright © 1954 by Wallace Stevens. Reprinted by permission of Alfred A. Knopf, Inc., and Faber & Faber Ltd.

Excerpts from "East Coker" and "Burnt Norton" from *Four Quartets* by T. S. Eliot. Copyright © 1943 by T. S. Eliot and renewed 1971 by Esme Valerie Eliot. Reprinted by permission of Harcourt Brace & Company and Faber & Faber Ltd.

"Millennium" by Jonathan Edwards from the Jonathan Edwards manuscript collection, Beinecke Rare Book and Manuscript Library, Yale University. Reprinted by permission of Yale University.

Printed in the United States of America

Library of Congress Cataloging-in-Publication Data
Knowlege and belief in America: enlightenment traditions and modern
religious thought / edited by William M. Shea and Peter A. Huff.
p. cm. — (Woodrow Wilson Center series)
Includes index.
ISBN 0-521-55011-4
1. United States—Religion. 2. Enlightenment—Influence.
I. Shea, William M., 1935– . II. Huff, Peter A. III. Series.
BL2525.K66 1995
277.3—dc20   95-6531
                         CIP

A catalog record for this book is available from the British Library.

ISBN 0–521–55011–4 hardback

Contents

Foreword   *page* ix
   Michael J. Lacey

Introduction   1
   William M. Shea and Peter A. Huff

PART I. ENLIGHTENMENT AND RELIGIOUS TRADITIONS

1 Knowledge and belief in American public life   27
   James T. Kloppenberg
2 Enamored against thee by these strange minds:
  Recovering the relations between religion and the
  Enlightenment in nineteenth- and twentieth-century
  American literary culture   52
   Giles Gunn
3 The rise and long life of the Protestant
  Enlightenment in America   88
   Mark A. Noll
4 American Catholicism and the Enlightenment ethos   125
   Patrick W. Carey
5 Organizing the past   165
   Jacob Neusner

PART II. ENLIGHTENMENT AND REPRESENTATIVE FIGURES

6 Puritanism and Enlightenment: Edwards and
  Franklin   195
   John E. Smith
7 Emerson's constitutional amending: Reading "Fate"   227
   Stanley Cavell

8 Lincoln and modernity 247
  Andrew Delbanco
9 Stuck between debility and demand: Religion and
  Enlightenment traditions among the pragmatists 270
  Henry Samuel Levinson
10 Wallace Stevens, T. S. Eliot, and the space between
   them 299
   Denis Donoghue

PART III. THE END OF THE ENLIGHTENMENT?

11 The Enlightenment is not over 321
   Schubert M. Ogden
12 Modernity, antimodernity, and postmodernity in the
   American setting 328
   David Tracy
13 Are we beyond the Enlightenment horizon? 335
   Richard J. Bernstein

List of contributors 347
Index 349

Foreword

This book is the result of a Woodrow Wilson Center project on the place of religion in modern American culture and intellectual life. Thanks are due to many whose patient cooperation made possible the completion of this volume—first among them the scholarly contributors. A planning committee composed of Richard J. Bernstein, James T. Kloppenberg, William M. Shea, John E. Smith, and David Tracy sketched out the basic rationale and terms of reference for the collaborative effort. The Center is pleased to acknowledge the support of the Exxon Education Fund, without which the undertaking of the project would not have been possible. Finally, a special word of gratitude is due to William M. Shea, the senior editor of this book. He had more to do with bringing it into being than anyone else, and when occasionally the project faltered, he steadied it. The volume's writers and readers equally are in his debt.

MICHAEL J. LACEY
Director, Division of United States Studies,
Woodrow Wilson Center

Introduction

WILLIAM M. SHEA

and

PETER A. HUFF

ORIGINS AND CONTEXT

This volume is a result of a Woodrow Wilson Center project on the place of religious thought, and thought about religion, within the broad field of American intellectual history. It is the companion book to *Religion and Twentieth-Century American Intellectual Life*, edited by Michael J. Lacey, which comprised a selection of essays originally presented at a Wilson Center symposium by prominent authors from sectors of the academy normally aloof from one another and seldom engaged in public conversation. The participants were, on the one hand, cultural and intellectual historians from university departments of history and American studies and, on the other hand, theologians, church historians, and philosophers of religion from the seminaries, divinity schools, and those curious academic hybrids, departments of religious studies.

That prior volume was concerned with scholarship on elites and religion, particularly with how to make sense, in terms of both continuity and change, of the ethos of the higher learning in America that had developed under the influence of the rise of the modern research university beginning in the late nineteenth century and at the expense of the displacement of the clerical elites and theologically informed styles of thought that had dominated higher education from its colonial beginnings through the early part of the present century. The essays were attempts to trace the outlines of an appropriately complex picture of the contemporary situation.

The collection was intended to raise new questions about the lack of strong historical evidence for what was generally presumed to be a thoroughgoing secularization of academic culture, and to shed new

1

light both on the dominant naturalist tradition of thought, which finds itself opposed in principle to all forms of thought that assert the existence of a supernatural or transcendental realm of being, and on neglected forms of religious modernism. The essays dealt, among other topics, with the history, achievements, and problems of the academic study of religion in American universities over the past century; with the cultural and institutional roots that contributed to the intellectual marginalization of American Protestant theology; with the search for objectivity and the corresponding ethics of belief that inspired the scientific challenge to religion in modern America; with John Dewey and the Niebuhr brothers as different but broadly representative types of intellectual aspiration; and with the reasons why, for those who concede its legitimacy (a problem here for naturalists), the practice of theology is necessarily so different from the practice of other scholarly disciplines.

Discussions that occurred during the project's first conference made clear the need for another one to pursue with more focus and in more depth some of the subjects that emerged as neglected but especially promising. First among these was the historical dynamism of the exchange between inherited secular and religious traditions of thought; it virtually suggested itself as a multifaceted theme rich in implications for deeper understanding of contemporary culture that merited rethinking. The roots of American naturalism and the interplay between different forms of naturalism and forms of religious modernism also surfaced as topics requiring fresh scholarly attention.

These were the origins of the present book. To establish a framework for reconsideration of the variable but dynamic interplay of secular and religious thought in the American heritage, we chose as a convenient starting point the concerns manifest in the pervasive contemporary critique of reason and rationalism—that is, the widespread sense of disappointment regarding yesterday's naive dreams of reason (so prominent in the cultural debates of recent years)—and attempted to deepen and extend its range of reference by some historical probing and recollection. Such probing might reach back indefinitely, but the Enlightenment of the eighteenth century provided a familiar and conventional context in which to begin. For although the Enlightenment, at least in its American guise, cannot be said to have inaugurated secularity of a naturalist type (the radical skepticism of the eighteenth century was notoriously feeble in America, and even Tom Paine and Thomas Jefferson were devout in the rather old-fashioned manner permitted by their deism), it *did* register a new cosmopolitanism that brought into prominence those forms of natural theology from which the systematic philosophical naturalism of the post-Darwinian period would descend. Accordingly the 1990 symposium—from which most of the chapters that follow are derived (two of the chapters were designed subsequently to round out the coverage of the volume)—was addressed to the relations between knowledge and belief in America, where, with a necessary minimum of ambiguity, the term *knowledge* encapsulates the challenge presented by the secularizing cosmopolitanism of the Enlightenment and where the term *belief*, despite its cognitive elements, symbolizes religion.[1]

Taken together, the two volumes constitute an original contribution to the interdisciplinary study of American religion and intellectual life. This book gathers for the first time a variety of scholarly approaches to the relationship between the Enlightenment and the religious heritages, and in doing so presents new questions and perspectives. Note should be taken of the particular timeliness of this effort. In the first place, the end of the Enlightenment has been announced by some prominent critics who consider rationalism a failing foundation for modern morals,[2] yet we have here a set of authors from distinct and even opposed viewpoints who conclude that the announcement is premature. This pronouncement is nearly parallel to the frequent declaration of the deterioration of religion over the past two centuries and even the occasional eulogy; yet we find religious activity flourishing everywhere we turn. It is so evident in the fundamentalist resurgence in the politics of nations that even the most cloistered academics have been unable to ignore it any longer.[3] The

---

[1]The essays solicited after the conference are those by Henry Samuel Levinson and Jacob Neusner. Although pragmatism was a concern of several of the contributors to the first volume, we could not skip by the movement which in both its naturalist (Dewey and Santayana) and its supernaturalist (James and Royce) sides brilliantly displays currents of our concern with knowledge and belief, and thus Levinson's essay. Nor could we ignore the overriding importance of the Jewish contribution to the practice and assessment of the Enlightenment, and thus Neusner's piece on Enlightenment historicism.

[2]Richard Bernstein, ed., *Habermas and Modernity* (Cambridge, Mass.: MIT Press, 1985). See also Alasdair C. MacIntyre, *After Virtue: A Study in Moral Theory* (Notre Dame, Ind.: University of Notre Dame Press, 1984).

[3]See the first volume of the University of Chicago's Fundamentalist Project, *Fundamentalisms Observed*, ed. Martin Marty and R. Scott Appleby (Chicago: University of Chicago Press, 1991); there are five more volumes in the series. See also William M. Shea, ed., *The Struggle over the Past: Fundamentalism in the Modern World* (Lanham, Md.: Uni-

Enlightenment persists and religion persists, and nowhere more than in the United States, that most religious and most modern of nations.[4]

A second oddity is that we read complaints in books that are read widely and hear in loud voices that can scarcely be said to cry out from the wilderness that religion has been denied a place in the public forum.[5] The "resurgence" of evangelicals in American politics, the beginnings of a "return" of religious intellectuals to the academy, and the "rebirth" of religion in the public forum now seem in continuity with the historical experience of the American people, who, with varying emphases, have managed to keep the Enlightenment heritage and the religious heritage in relation to one another. Here we present a collection of scholarly essays that bear the conviction that the heritages have been intertwined since the colonial period; evidently, neither has flagged.

The scholarly nature of the chapters, however, should not hide the fact that in dealing with the relations between knowledge and religious belief our authors are handling hot wires. Whereas on the campus of the research university the most radical political and philosophical views have become so familiar and conventional as to attract little notice, the acknowledgment of even the most orthodox religious views sometimes seems to require an attitude of cultural daring. Live currents are involved. We are dealing with one of those complexes of issues that call on the deepest intellectual and spiritual convictions of scholars, and debate over the ethics of belief can engage serious personal and professional commitments that appear as much in carefully maintained silences as in vigorous exchange. Our intellectual culture remains profoundly divided over what responsibilities are attached to the intellectual life, what to believe and what is believable, how belief is or is not knowledge, what is and is not fruitful subject matter for public discourse, and what the future ought to bring to reason and faith.

The gaps that divide religious and secularist academics are wide indeed. Although little is known about the religious views of modern ac-

---

versity Press of America, 1993) for studies of fundamentalism in world religions, in American Protestantism, and in American Catholicism.

[4]See Andrew Greeley and Gregory Baum, eds., *The Persistence of Religion* (New York: Herder and Herder, 1973), and Andrew Greeley, *American Catholics since the Council: An Unauthorized Report* (Chicago: Thomas More Press, 1985); see also George Gallup, *The People's Religion: American Faith in the 90's* (New York: Macmillan, 1989), and idem, *Religion in America: 1990* (Princeton: Princeton University Press, 1990).

[5]Richard J. Neuhaus, *The Naked Public Square* (Grand Rapids, Mich.: Eerdmans, 1984). See also Stephen L. Carter, *The Culture of Disbelief: How American Law and Politics Trivialize Religious Devotion* (New York: Basic Books, 1993).

ademic scholars in the social sciences and the humanities (far less, for example, than is known about their political orientations), it is nonetheless broadly evident that religious and secularist scholars do constitute two easily distinguished communities in the academy, that the two factions rarely communicate directly and publicly, and that, in spite of their obvious relish in discussion at the occasional symposium, inertia may outweigh even the joys of new communication. The communities of religious faith have made a return to the academy of late, but the academy is still marked by a profound suspicion of the role of religion in scholarly and scientific life and the place of the religious intellectual in the academy.[6]

Part I of this volume surveys the relationship of the Enlightenment and religious traditions in America. In Chapter 1, James T. Kloppenberg, a leading authority in the field of American intellectual history, surveys recent historical literature on connections between the secular and religious in the nation's public life from the colonial era to the present. He traces the development of an American style of postfoundationalism in the writings of William James and John Dewey and argues that both the secular and the religious are compatible with the uncertainties and sense of limits that followed this tradition of thought. In Chapter 2, Giles Gunn examines the interplay of the legacies of Enlightenment secularism and religious conviction in American literature. He traces the fading of both, but particularly the decline or increasing opacity of Enlightenment motifs, associated with liberal republican ideals of freedom, autonomy, individualism, and rationalism—all of which have fared badly under the gaze of twentieth-century criticism, wherein they came to be seen as elements in the apparatus of cultural complacency.

Chapters 3, 4, and 5 take up the historical relations between the Enlightenment and the nation's three main religious traditions—Protes-

[6]See George M. Marsden and Bradley J. Longfield, eds., *The Secularization of the Academy* (New York: Oxford University Press, 1992); George M. Marsden, *The Soul of the American University* (New York: Oxford University Press, 1994); and Mark R. Schwehn, *Exiles from Eden: Religion and the Academic Vocation in America* (New York: Oxford University Press, 1992). The argument in the American Academy of Religion (AAR) between scholars of religious studies and scholars of theological studies over the place of theology in the study of religion in the American university and over the theologians' active participation in the AAR continues unabated, with periodic reheatings. There are currently substantial numbers of Catholic and evangelical scholars who form interest groups under AAR auspices. In 1992 the presidential address defended the presence of theologians while several other AAR members questioned it. See Ray Hart, "Theological Studies in American Higher Education: A Pilot Study," *Journal of the American Academy of Religion* 59 (Winter 1991): 715–827.

tantism, Catholicism, and Judaism. In Chapter 3, Mark Noll, a leading authority on the history of American religion, reviews in succinct form the best known of these histories, the trajectory of American Protestantism, and does so from the point of view of critical evangelical Protestantism. He examines the Protestant embrace in all its complexity of many of the procedures and assumptions of eighteenth-century rationalism and traces out many of the cultural ironies—secularism with a lack of confidence—that followed the consequent blurring of distinctions between Enlightenment and religion. Patrick Carey presents a lesser-known history, the story of American Catholicism's encounter with the Enlightenment ethos, and provides an essay that opens up the subject for new consideration. Carey offers an account of Catholic attempts to struggle with their own selective appropriations of Enlightenment values and emphases from the apologetics of the early eighteenth century through the phased and multilayered elaboration of the twentieth century's neo-Thomist revival. In Chapter 5, one of this century's greatest scholars of Judaism, Jacob Neusner, examines the conflict between the secular and religious senses of time and treats the Enlightenment's secular rationality, with its reading of time as linear, cumulative, and progressive, as a substitute for the time sense inherent in the teleology of revealed religion. Although Neusner does not address the particular historical experience of American Judaism, he confronts a problem common to all religions in their relations to secularity, and from his thirty-year immersion in the sources he offers a recovery of the Talmudic sense of time as something quite distinct from the time sense of the Enlightenment historian.

Part II turns to selected thinkers, writers, and shapers of the American cultural tradition, from Jonathan Edwards and Benjamin Franklin through Wallace Stevens and T. S. Eliot. In Chapter 6, John E. Smith, one of the nation's most distinguished philosophers of religion and the editor of the papers of Jonathan Edwards, conveys the complexity and surprising freshness, when properly formulated, of the two poles by treating Edwards and Franklin as representative figures. Stanley Cavell, an influential master of Emerson studies, approaches one aspect of the troubling legacy of the Enlightenment by taking a new look at Emerson's paradoxical statement that freedom is necessary, and he elicits some of the implications of the fact that Emerson's key essay on freedom— "Fate"—which makes no reference to slavery, appeared just months before the Fugitive Slave Law. In speculating deeply and connectively on the ironies involved in this juxtaposition, Cavell provides an exemplary postmodernist rendering of an outstanding Enlightenment figure.

In the next chapter, the relation Lincoln had to both secular and religious currents of thought and his attempt to meld them into a faith are treated by Andrew Delbanco, a distinguished student of the Puritan heritage and its aftermath. Henry Levinson places three of the great originators of and contributors to American pragmatism, William James, George Santayana, and John Dewey, in a critical relation to the Enlightenment via comparison with the thought of perhaps its most influential philosopher, Immanuel Kant. Finally, in Chapter 10, literary critic Denis Donoghue continues exploration of the theme by asking again whether Christianity is compatible with Enlightenment thinking, and, if it is, or might be, whether it is still Christianity. Not likely, it seems to Donoghue; he develops his response by comparing two representative figures of the twentieth century, T. S. Eliot and Wallace Stevens.

Part III differs in character and tone from the previous sections of the book. Its chapters are brief and schematic, not scholarly essays in the traditional sense. They are derived from the 1990 symposium, where each played a specific, preassigned role. The authors, two of the nation's most distinguished theologians and one of its most prominent neopragmatist philosophers (Schubert Ogden, David Tracy, and Richard Bernstein, respectively), were asked to provide the systematic outlines for discussion of the question—posed for them with an eye to the efforts in recent years to find a common term for what some critics believe to be a new cultural era—of whether in any deep sense the Enlightenment can be considered to be superseded or over. What can be said in contemporary terms of the living elements in the Enlightenment heritage, particularly with reference to their relation to the living elements in modernist religious thought? The authors' answers provide thoughtful, carefully measured insights into the balance among the traditions and the ongoing interplay between them.

To provide a more precise sense of context for reading the chapters that follow and to draw out some of the interrelations among them, we next comment on the terms of reference for the conference from which the chapters were derived. The conference was organized around three questions: What is the Enlightenment in America? Is it over, and if so, what now? What have been and are the relations between religious belief and the Enlightenment in America? The conference papers and the present book reflect the controlling position of these questions, and although the papers are organized differently in this volume, we follow the three questions in our introduction.

WHAT IS THE ENLIGHTENMENT IN AMERICA?

The authors were asked not to stray from the subject of the Enlightenment and religion in America. No one was asked to take on the systematic task of defining the Enlightenment or religion, but the first term was discussed ad hoc by most and the latter by a few. Renderings and emphases differ. While Peter Gay's Enlightenment makes its appearance, so too does Carl Becker's; Ernst Cassirer and Isaiah Berlin enter the discussion as well. If any one view dominates the discussion it is clearly Henry May's, for his helpful distinctions with regard to the identifiable strands and phases of the American Enlightenment tradition seem to have become close to common property.[7] Most of the many available options in interpretation and definition of the Enlightenment are present: the rise of individual autonomy over traditional community, the rise of secularizing reason over inherited authority, the disengagement of nature from a supernatural worldview, the rise of methodical and institutionalized criticism, the rise of science as both technique and worldview, the rise of historical consciousness and the practice of historical method, and the establishment of bourgeois institutions and a democratic ethos in public life.[8]

Each contributor takes one or another of these options, more or less nuanced, and proceeds to work with it. Some authors, however, hold that the tale of the Enlightenment as a historical movement is so complex as to defy normative definition, whereas others either argue or lean toward the view that the Enlightenment is essentially a matter of affirming the role of critical intelligence in evaluating the evidential basis of all claims to truth. Ogden states the case for criticism in this way:

How, in a normative sense, is the Enlightenment to be understood? My answer to this question, which I consider crucial to my argument, is this: the Enlight-

---

[7]Henry F. May, *The Enlightenment in America* (New York: Oxford University Press, 1976).

[8]For a discussion of many attempts at definition, see Robert A. Ferguson, " 'What is Enlightenment?': Some American Answers," *American Literary History* 1 (Summer 1989): 245–72. For an excellent survey of the Enlightenment in America and its impact on religion, see John Corrigan, "The Enlightenment," in *Encyclopedia of the American Religious Experience*, ed. Charles H. Lippy and Peter W. Williams, 3 vols. (New York: Charles Scribner's Sons, 1988), 2:1089–102.

enment is to be understood normatively as the consistent affirmation of the unique authority of human reason over all other putative authorities. By *human reason* I mean our capacity not only to make or imply various kinds of claims to validity but also, and above all, to validate critically all such claims as and when they become problematic by appropriate kinds of discourse or argument involving appeal in one way or another to common human experience.

The sharp edge of this view allows Ogden to do what the views of others—though they tend toward his own analysis—do not permit, namely, to count the more ambiguous features of the Enlightenment as adventitious or merely descriptive rather than normative. Richard Bernstein, for example, agrees that the Enlightenment is criticism and that the Enlightenment is not what its current enemies claim it to be (totalism, universalism, voluntarism), warning against questionable definitions that ignore the internal ambiguities of the Enlightenment. In contrast David Tracy and Patrick Carey, although they acknowledge the primacy of what Kant called the "critical path," also recognize the factors that make the Enlightenment a multifaceted cultural force—an ethos shaping a host of ideas, prejudices, assumptions, and practices. Mark Noll affirms the Enlightenment to be a methodology, an epistemology, rather than merely an ethos. John Smith's careful evaluation allows him at once to set up an essential contrast between the Enlightenment heritage and the religious heritage on the nature of evil and to find that aspect of the religious heritage—a concern with the reality of evil—present in the views of Franklin, Peirce, and James, as well as in the representative of the religious heritage, Jonathan Edwards. Smith also locates the Enlightenment heritage in the attitude of Dewey and the Enlightenment "belief in the salutary effects of the diffusion of knowledge to all mankind," a view as central to the "cosmopolitan" character he discovers in the thought of Jonathan Edwards as it is to Dewey's faith in education.

Stanley Cavell, though the only participant who does not address the topic of the Enlightenment as such, offers Emerson as a representative type of it; this "founder of American thinking" by his "performance" defines the American Enlightenment for us as freedom grounded in a thinking that is "on the side of God" and no other side, a partisan of itself alone. Perhaps we can take that as Cavell's definition of enlightened reason. Cavell worries at length over the ambiguity of reason in its performance: Are there matters over which reason cannot remain "on the side of God" but must become partisan? Could truth require taking sides? If so, then Emerson may also be an "ideal type" of the moral collapse of the Enlightenment understanding of reason, for Cavell is troubled by Emerson's silence regarding the Fugitive Slave Law in the essay "Fate." He wonders whether Emerson's philosophical flight beyond human squabbles is an evasion of moral responsibility, and he is clearly troubled by the possibility that textual evidence links Emerson, through Nietzsche, to Heidegger, casting a shadow over Emerson's achievement. Whatever may be the case, it seems that Cavell himself stands on a side, namely, that enlightened intelligence is autonomous reason, freed from the chains of traditional beliefs and practices, as displayed in Emerson's "Divinity School Address."

The list continues. No matter whether the author finds that the Enlightenment is fatally flawed (as do Donoghue and Neusner), or in need of significant pruning (as Carey, Noll, Smith, and Tracy suggest), or in need of internal correction (as Bernstein, Gunn, and Levinson maintain), nearly all the participants find the Enlightenment to be a passel of interrelated and overlapping, but distinguishable and even separable, concerns, interests, assumptions, and conclusions.[9]

It remains that Ogden's articulation of the Enlightenment's normative principle as the insistence that authorities support their claims with evidence, and the recognition that reason finds itself obliged to assess that evidence and live by its conclusions, is the best and clearest statement of the intellectual achievement of the Enlightenment and the point at which its failures begin to become evident.

The institutionalization of that principle of criticism in science, in universities, and in public life and the espousal of it by religious communities mark the vast cultural changes that have occurred in the West since the late seventeenth century. Of course, human beings have always questioned—else nothing would have changed—yet now change runs on before method. Peirce uttered a version of the imperative of the Enlightenment: "Do not block the path of inquiry."[10] Likewise, Bernard Lonergan argued an even broader version of it in his transcendental imperatives: "Be attentive! Be intelligent! Be reasonable! Be

---

[9]Perhaps Isaiah Berlin, as Gunn suggests, said it best. See Giles Gunn's essay herein (Chapter 2), particularly note 10, where he discusses the special merits of Berlin's recent essay on Joseph de Maistre. In his discussion of the bitter contempt felt by de Maistre for the bland, naturalistic optimism of the philosophes, Berlin has summarized cogently the basic elements and connectives of the Enlightenment worldview that sparked such hostility in one of its preeminent adversaries. Berlin's presentation of the underlying credo of the philosophes, which Gunn quotes at length, is the finest in recent literature.

[10]C. S. Peirce, *Philosophical Writings of Peirce*, ed. J. Buchler (New York: Doubleday, 1955), 54.

responsible!"[11] Ogden, then, is correct when he insists that there is nothing in the religious heritage normatively considered that runs contrary to the Enlightenment heritage normatively considered. But still we are left with the massive debris of over two centuries of strife between the two heritages.

IS IT OVER?

If we are to trust our authors, there is no "what then?" because the Enlightenment is not over. None of them believes that the Enlightenment project is completely finished. Though some might think it *ought* to be over, even they provide no term for its possible successor (postmodernism will not do). One critic of the Enlightenment, Denis Donoghue, looks to Jürgen Habermas and Emmanuel Levinas for a way out of it, whereas Jacob Neusner sees the vigorous revival of religion worldwide as a clue to the waning influence of the Enlightenment. The author who comes closest to offering a eulogy is Donoghue, and he says only that the Enlightenment is "bankrupt."

The majority think that not only the Enlightenment is not over but also that it should not be. Each response is qualified by the contributor's quite distinct perspective. James Kloppenberg was asked to provide a general historical perspective of the relations between religion and the Enlightenment in American public life. His narrative, tracing both the religious motivations for social reform movements aimed toward Enlightenment goals and the lively interchange between religion and politics in the United States, supposes that the relation continues into the present, and he gives not a hint that the Enlightenment is over. Pragmatism, which he regards as the reigning American voice on the subject and as a descendant of the Enlightenment, not its replacement, is counseled to avoid excluding the religious voice (perhaps even the reflective religious voice in theology).

Levinson's essay on the golden age of American philosophy indicates the ways in which the Enlightenment has continued to shape the American mind in the twentieth century. It explores the continuities and discontinuities between the Enlightenment heritage and the pragmatist religious thought of James, Santayana, and Dewey. Challenging the

[11]Bernard Lonergan, *Method in Theology* (New York: Seabury Press, 1972), 52–55, 231–33.

view—influential in the field of American intellectual history—of Murray Murphey and Bruce Kuklick, which portrays the originating pragmatists as "Kant's children," Levinson detects signs of unrest in the Kantian family of Enlightenment thinkers. He employs the term *post-Enlightenment* to designate the significant ways in which the pragmatists departed from the classical consciousness of Kant's Enlightenment while retaining much of the Enlightenment's distinctive spirit. In other words, Levinson says that we are correct to point out both the filial rebellion and the family resemblance. Drawing on Gordon Michalson's reinterpretation of Kant, he suggests that the first generation of American pragmatists made decisive judgments regarding the true nature of the Enlightenment, precisely at those points where Kant and an earlier generation of Enlightenment figures had been paralyzed by ambivalence.

Giles Gunn is acutely aware of the role of postfoundationalism and postmodernism in American literary culture. Taking Richard Rorty and Stanley Cavell to be chief figures in these movements, he makes a case for their continuities with the Enlightenment. If he sees an end to the Enlightenment at all, it is an end to Henry May's didactic Enlightenment, with its reasonable moderation and complacency. Principally, Gunn argues for the rediscovery at long last of the influence of the skeptical Enlightenment in American letters. According to him, a modernist "narrative" of literary history, curiously privileging New England's Puritan intellectual legacy, is now being replaced by a new pragmatist "narrative," which continues the antidogmatic and critical lines of the modernist pragmatism but corrects them with an elimination of the modernist and Enlightenment longing for transcendentals and universals. Like Kloppenberg, he counsels the neopragmatists of postfoundationalism and postmodernism to remain "open to experience" and to the voice even of religion. And so the Enlightenment lives on in a new phase.

It is not clear just what Andrew Delbanco thinks has ended. In contrast to Jon Butler, whose *Awash in a Sea of Faith* identifies Lincoln's religious heterodoxy as representative of the American past rather than the future,[12] Delbanco locates Lincoln at a critical juncture in American history. His riveting account of Lincoln's struggle to revive American faith at the crucial moment when the nation's founding experience and insights were fading from memory seems to be drawn as a parallel to

---

[12]Jon Butler, *Awash in a Sea of Faith: Christianizing the American People* (Cambridge, Mass.: Harvard University Press, 1990), 295.

his view of our own times and their need for revival. Insofar as Enlightenment is the content of the founding experience and insights, and so of our "civil religion," Delbanco could be seen as mourning the passing of the Enlightenment—lamenting, for different reasons, the state of Robert Bellah's "broken covenant." Clearly, though, he sees it as possible and even necessary to revive. Like Alasdair MacIntyre scanning the cultural horizon for a new Saint Benedict, Delbanco seems to be waiting for an enlightened revivalist capable of speaking to those whose memories are gone, renewing their faith in the national experience, facing the reality of human evil without resort to devils—a Lincoln, perhaps, with Lincoln's faith but without the supernaturalism and fatalism of his theistic beliefs.

Smith, Carey, and Noll tell tales of the intersections of Enlightenment and religion, supposing the continuance of the tensions between the living heritages. None of them displays any sympathy for the current brand of pragmatist antifoundationalism. In fact, Smith indicates strong antipathy for it, climaxing his essay with a sharp homily on the moral problems of postmodernism; for him, the fashionable postmodernist looks disturbingly like the devious and elusive title character of Malcolm Bradbury's recent novel *Doctor Criminale*.[13] Smith, however, has a decidedly more sanguine view of the Enlightenment heritage than does either Noll or Carey. Although he marks the failure of that heritage (in figures such as Dewey) to deal seriously with radical evil, he nonetheless sees its strengths in knowledge and freedom that make it worth continuance. Even with the tensions that Noll and Carey find between the two heritages, Noll seeks an evangelical critical engagement with the Enlightenment, and Carey sees the two-century-old struggle of American Catholics with the Enlightenment still actively displayed in the varieties of U.S. Catholic theological endeavor.

None of the commentators to whom the question "Is it over?" was explicitly put—namely Richard Bernstein, Schubert Ogden, and David Tracy—seemed surprised at the question, but none could manage much suspense over an answer. Tracy and Bernstein sharply criticize excess in the Enlightenment heritage, but neither would deny the correctness of Ogden's remark that "the struggle over it still goes on," and that is proof of its liveliness.

If it is not over, then what are we to make of its obituaries, both in

---

[13] Malcolm Bradbury, *Doctor Criminale* (New York: Viking, 1992).

the United States and abroad? Perhaps the same thing many Christians did at the announcement of the death of the Christian age: draw a deep breath and have patience. The three "posts" so prominent in contemporary cultural criticism (foundationalism, modernism, Enlightenment) are clearly misnomers if they are taken to mean that the vast stream of Western culture-creating and -informing active and critical intelligence has come to an end. Rather, the three "posts" can be taken as an attempt on the part of some critics to correct shortcomings of the culture, perhaps indicating no more than an important step in Reason recognizing its weaknesses. Here, Gunn may have the best analysis: He suggests that the two "posts" of the American situation (foundationalism and modernism) may represent the recovery of the subversive skeptical Enlightenment. Likewise, Levinson suggests that the pragmatist project overhauls the Enlightenment, "snipping the scientistic, representationalist, foundationalist, essentialist, and existentialist growths . . . eating away at Enlightenment gains from the inside out."

HOW DO THE HERITAGES INTERSECT?

We had several serious, if not especially systematic, attempts to articulate the Enlightenment heritage; we now have several serious, if not especially systematic, attempts to articulate the religious heritage. To repeat, no one was given either assignment, and the persons best able by academic vocation to articulate the religious heritage—systematic theologians Schubert Ogden and David Tracy—were asked to address not this subject but rather the "end of the Enlightenment." But by the dialectical nature of the conference plan—knowledge and belief—articulations abound, and it is to these we now turn.

Among the positions taken on the religious heritage, the following range of possibilities seems most important:

1. The religious heritage is fundamentally incompatible with the Enlightenment—and so much the worse for the Enlightenment.
2. The religious heritage of memory and hope carried in a community has suffered at the hands of distorted elements in the Enlightenment heritage.
3. The religious heritage in America engaged the Enlightenment with quite distinct community strategies and quite different outcomes.

4. The religious heritage has appeared within persons otherwise placed as Enlightenment figures.
5. The religious heritage and the Enlightenment heritage are fundamentally compatible.

The old chestnut theodicy, or the problem of evil, returns in several essays as a key issue between the religious heritage and the Enlightenment heritage. Indeed, Smith, Delbanco, Gunn, Levinson, Donoghue, and Tracy all see the issue as a measure of continuity, not discrepancy, between religion and the Enlightenment.

Although there is silence on the part of several participants on the matter of the religious heritage (Bernstein, Delbanco, and Cavell), no one supposes or argues what would have been a commonplace half a century ago, namely, that the religious heritage has perished or is soon to do so; nor do any argue that it should perish or be ignored as a partner in public discourse. All regard the secularization thesis of days gone by as confounded by the obvious vitality of religion in the late twentieth century.

We are concerned here with three issues among the many that attract comment: What sort of evaluation does the religious heritage deliver of the Enlightenment? What sorts of strategies have religious communities devised for dealing with the Enlightenment? What are the prospects of the religious heritage in an intellectual culture still seemingly dominated by the naturalism that grew out of the Enlightenment heritage and took root in the modern university?

The response of religious people to the Enlightenment is polymorphous. The simplest, most direct, and long-lived of them all is the response examined by Carey: that generated by the administrative and intellectual leaders of the Catholic Church. Catholics have a history of profoundly anti-Enlightenment rhetoric and action, especially when the Enlightenment ethos has impinged on Catholic belief and practice and on the Catholic communitarian ethos. Carey makes the important point that the opposition to the Enlightenment is not simply a matter of theory, but very much a matter of incompatibility of practices:

For most members of the church, Catholic sensibilities on these issues flowed not so much from papal statements, rational argumentation, or intellectual and theological defenses, as important as these were, but from their personal and communal involvement in the signs and symbols of public worship, the sacramental system, pious practices of prayer and cult of the saints, catechetical training in the fundamentals of a creedal tradition, parish life, and their voluntary participation in building up a free institutional church in a free society.

Carey also points out that Catholic opposition to the Enlightenment, especially in the United States, has been selective, and the elements approved of have been validated by this or that piece of previous Catholic practice. There have been phases and developments in the centuries of Catholic response, and there have been groups and individuals who have periodically modulated the church's central negation of the Enlightenment. For example, the Americanist bishops of the late nineteenth century, lay intellectuals such as the editors of *Commonweal* in the twentieth, and contemporary theologians such as Avery Dulles and David Tracy have all attempted to mediate between Catholic traditions and Enlightenment traditions in America. Moreover, the American Catholic experience has offered an alternative to the traditional, Continental Catholic stance toward the Enlightenment's political and social elements. Throughout its history the American church has harbored few Catholic monarchists; indeed, since the days of John Carroll, and especially since the Second Vatican Council's endorsement of American-style views of political liberty and religious pluralism, American Catholicism has rarely opposed and frequently celebrated the republican form of democracy.

Where the Enlightenment tradition has been judged less benign, the Catholic practice has been to build community identity through intense sacramental and spiritual practice, to erect its own educational system, to develop theoretic criticisms where possible, and to inculcate in the education of its clergy and through them of the laity the views taught by the popes and their schools of theology. The rhetorical tradition of anti-Enlightenment discourse within the Vatican began in reaction to the French Revolution and its public displacement of the church. It was intensified in the mid-nineteenth century by Pope Gregory XVI in *Mirari vos* (1832) and Pius IX in *Quanta cura* and *Syllabus errorum* (1864), and it came to a climax in the early twentieth century in the antimodernist pronouncements of Pius X in *Pascendi dominici gregis* and *Lamentabili sane exitu* (1907).

Catholics in the United States developed their own accompanying theologies both to mirror and to modulate the papal critique. In the nineteenth century the chief intellectual water was carried by Orestes Brownson and Isaac Hecker, two converts. Hecker and Brownson loom large as representative of the currents then flowing through American Catholicism precisely because of their status as converts, and because (unlike lay Catholics in their day) they were so careful in articulating the grounds for their opposition to the growth of secular individualism and the attractions of communitarian solidarity. In the twentieth century the focus of attention shifted to a reborn Thomist "synthesis" flourishing in the seminaries and the Catholic literary community. The massive change in attitude and action initiated by Pope John XXIII and the Second Vatican Council should not be taken to have cleared the slate, for the criticisms by past popes and other Catholic leaders continue in the evaluation of Western culture consistently given throughout the reign of John Paul II. One suspects that such criticisms lie behind the wholesale rejection of the Enlightenment in Donoghue's essay in this volume.

At the conclusion to his sketch of the history of American Catholic reactions to the Enlightenment, Carey offers us examples of three distinct current Catholic responses—namely, those of James Hitchcock, the "activist conservative" historian of Saint Louis University; Avery Dulles, S.J., of Fordham University, whose moderation in all things theological is legendary in Catholic theological circles; and David Tracy of the University of Chicago, a Catholic "revisionist." Although the three differ on the relationship between the Catholic community and the Enlightenment, together they continue the Catholic tradition of critical evaluation of it. Tracy, for example, in his chapter in this volume, writes:

For modernity for some thinkers has become what modernity seemed most to oppose and fear—one more tradition. The honest concern of many modern thinkers can reveal a general pathos, namely, that the forces for emancipation (and surely such emancipatory forces were set loose by the Enlightenment in the great modern bourgeois revolutions) may now seem to be entrapped in purely technical notions of reason from which there can seem no honorable exit: no exit and no ethics; above all, no genuine politics; and, just as tellingly for the concerns of this volume, no genuine conversation on religion that could be called reasonable. This surely would be a pathetic end to the American practical experiment in relating the Enlightenment and religion.

Mark Noll, concentrating on the reformed tradition in American Protestantism, tells a quite different tale. Aside from lingering suspicions of reason unaided by revelation in the Protestant imagination, the reaction of American Protestantism to the Enlightenment was rarely negative until the rise of fundamentalist rejection of modernism at the beginning of the twentieth century. Agreeing with the substance of Smith's treatment of Jonathan Edwards, Noll maintains that the discriminating adaptation of selected elements of the early Enlightenment by Edwards, bolstered by a brilliant rewriting of its classicist psychology and anthropology, was soon abandoned for a blanket acceptance of the didactic Enlightenment of the Scottish Common Sense philosophers. Drawing from James Turner's thesis regarding the ironic nature of Protestantism's adoption of the didactic Enlightenment for apologetic reasons and its unwitting contribution to the rise of unbelief in American culture,[14] Noll narrates the virtual wedding of mainline Protestantism and Enlightenment tradition and its unexpected secularizing consequences. The fusion was so complete that one has difficulty distinguishing Christian belief from Enlightenment belief in the nineteenth-century churches and educational institutions. The essay invites research into the suggestion that the lack of any significant critique of the Enlightenment in the liberal, modernizing Protestant heritage must have played a role in the rise of both countercultural religions and fundamentalist opposition.

Noll emphasizes the epistemological problems set for evangelical thinkers by the Enlightenment to which those thinkers made no adequate address. He agrees that the Enlightenment is criticism, but, aside from Edwards, finds no evangelical critical evaluation of and response to Enlightenment criticism, and an all too easy acceptance of the Enlightenment as a public Christian philosophy of the American republic. Echoing the sentiments of Robert Jenson's recent recommendation of Edwards,[15] Noll advocates the retrieval of an Edwardsean approach to theological heritage and Enlightenment values in contemporary American culture.

Jacob Neusner emerges as the volume's chief and unrelieved critic of the Enlightenment from the point of view of the religious heritage. Unlike Donoghue, whose criticism is broad, Neusner holds the Enlightenment to one crucial mistake: It has defined its views of history and time, and of historical method, as the only ones intellectually viable. The dominance of "historicism," the premier intellectual legacy of the Enlightenment in Neusner's view, has effected a distorted and tortured religious consciousness in the West by undercutting the legitimacy and practice of a millennium and a half of Jewish and Christian understanding of God's presence in events and texts. Neusner, interpreter of the Judaism of the Mishnah and the Talmud and an accomplished practitioner of contemporary historical method and textual criticism, details the differ-

---

[14]James Turner, *Without God, without Creed: The Origins of Unbelief in America* (Baltimore: Johns Hopkins University Press, 1985).

[15]Robert W. Jenson, *America's Theologian: A Recommendation of Jonathan Edwards* (New York: Oxford University Press, 1988).

ences between conceptions of time and history in the two heritages, religious and Enlightenment. The product is a critical performance worth comparing to Hans Frei's analysis of the demise of precritical Christian hermeneutics in *The Eclipse of Biblical Narrative*.[16] Arguing for the rights of religious consciousness, Neusner drafts historical method into the service of his argument to indict the Enlightenment ideology of history for making it nearly impossible for students to read sacred literature as their ancestors did.

In addition, Neusner, like Donoghue, indirectly assaults the views of other authors. Donoghue's interpretation of Wallace Stevens, for example, implies rejection of Levinson's hope for a naturalist/pragmatist spirituality and of Gunn's hope for conversation between the traditions. Similarly, Neusner attacks what may well be fundamental assumptions of most of our contributors—namely, that despite all admissions of its shortcomings, the modern historical method is reliable in the long run, that one apprehends the truth through historical method, that one can come to know "what really happened," and that when one cannot do so, one knows nothing worthwhile.

In fact, on one level, Neusner may suggest just the opposite: that religious readings of the text deliver the meaning of the text and that meaning is true and basic to any historical meaning arrived at by critical history. To put Neusner's question in our own terms, if "historical method" were to disappear, would we still have humanity whole? Yes. If "historical method" is successful in eliminating religious reading of texts and so religious life, do we have humanity whole? No, we have a distortion of humanity, a crippled humanity. One might suggest that at several points Neusner's view is identical with the Catholic criticism of the Enlightenment priorities of theory over practice and the individual over the community. It shares very little of the liberal and modernist Protestant and Catholic tendencies to construct mediating positions. What Neusner practices as a historian and textual critic he refuses to accord primacy for life as it is lived.

Our second question is, What sorts of strategies has the religious heritage evolved to cope with what Walter Lippmann called the "acids of modernity"? The first strategy is, of course, to take one's place within the current or a past version of the naturalist/pragmatist interpretation

---

[16]Hans W. Frei, *The Eclipse of Biblical Narrative: A Study in Eighteenth and Nineteenth Century Hermeneutics* (New Haven: Yale University Press, 1974).

of the Enlightenment and its benefits, and go on to redefine the religious heritage so far as possible to fit that interpretation. Dewey, on the American scene, would be the outstanding example of this approach, along with Sidney Hook and Felix Adler. Some of our contributors articulate a stand that can be considered only marginally, if at all, within the religious but chiefly or exclusively within the Enlightenment heritage. The essays of Bernstein, Cavell, Delbanco, Gunn, and Levinson represent diverse appropriations of this intellectual legacy. Interestingly enough, no one comments on the "secular humanists," including most prominently those "children of the Enlightenment" who signed the Humanist Manifestos of 1933 and 1973.[17]

The second strategy is fundamentalism, a form of militant separatism that will have none of the reigning intellectual positions and attempts to construct an alternate culture, worried all the time that even a dialectical critique of the intellectual culture means infidelity to the religious heritage. One recalls that Karl Barth was regarded as a modernist by American Christian fundamentalists.[18] Because no representative of fundamentalism was present at the conference, the claims to intellectual legitimacy by fundamentalists receive little attention and no respect in the essays in this volume. With the exception of Noll, none of the contributors investigates fundamentalism's intricate relationship to the Enlightenment—the delicate "cognitive bargaining" that George M. Marsden observed when he spoke of the "evangelical love affair with Enlightenment science."[19]

The third approach is orthodoxy, which we might regard as a slow and critical sifting of the implications of the Enlightenment for the religious heritage, for which traditional texts and authorities remain the norm. Sharing the liabilities of all projects in "neo-orthodoxy" or "postliberalism," such an approach seeks to protect the integrity of the religious community and the survival of its distinctive language and set of values while cautiously engaging intellectual movements outside the community. Edwards, as sketched by Noll, is the historical model for

---

[17]Paul Kurtz, ed., *The Humanist Manifestos I and II* (Buffalo: Prometheus Books, 1973), and Howard B. Radest, *The Devil and Secular Humanism: The Children of the Enlightenment* (New York: Praeger, 1990). Also see Stephen L. Carter, *The Culture of Disbelief.*

[18]Cornelius Van Til, *The New Modernism: An Appraisal of the Theology of Barth and Brunner* (Philadelphia: Presbyterian and Reformed Publishing Company, 1946).

[19]George M. Marsden, *Understanding Fundamentalism and Evangelicalism* (Grand Rapids, Mich.: Eerdmans, 1991), 122–52. See also Ronald L. Numbers, *The Creationists* (Berkeley: University of California Press, 1992).

this strategy. Historians Noll and Carey and literary critic Donoghue share an affinity with this approach to the Enlightenment.

And finally, there is the complex of positions that might be named mediating theologies, or accelerated orthodoxy. They are varieties of religious modernism that include liberal, modernist, and revisionist theologies which profess loyalty to both heritages and attempt to stake out reasonable and fresh positions in the center, mediating one heritage to the other. Individual versions of "rational Christianity," the early Christian Unitarian tradition, classic Protestant liberals like Horace Bushnell, and the American Protestant modernists would fall here, along with philosophers Charles S. Peirce, William James, and Josiah Royce. Among the contributors, Kloppenberg, Ogden, and Tracy argue for the viability of such projects. Likewise, Smith, objecting to the trite polarization of Edwards and Franklin as well as to the irresponsible "presentism" that would draft them as partisans in contemporary arguments between evangelicals and "secular humanists," reopens the perennial debate over Edwards's modernity, defending Perry Miller's "modernist" Edwards.[20]

Prospects for the relation between the religious and the Enlightenment heritages foreseen by our contributors vary, as do the authors' stances. They range from that of Donoghue, who sees no traffic between the two without the abandonment of Christianity, to that of Ogden, who sees no contradiction between the heritages on the normative Enlightenment imperative that the truth of claims be validated in terms of evidence for them. Cavell does not seem to see an issue or, if he does, chooses not to speak of it. For him the issue is between freedom and bondage, and thinking leads to the former. The postmodernists and postfoundationalists (Delbanco, Gunn, and Levinson) see the need for retention of the religious heritage in one form or another.

---

[20]For a discussion of the debate over the "modernity" of Jonathan Edwards, see Donald Weber, "Perry Miller and the Recovery of Jonathan Edwards," introduction to Perry Miller, *Jonathan Edwards* (Amherst: University of Massachusetts Press, 1981), v–xxv, and Donald Weber, "The Recovery of Jonathan Edwards," in *Jonathan Edwards and the American Experience,* ed. Nathan O. Hatch and Harry S. Stout (New York: Oxford University Press, 1988), 50–70. Also see Sang Hyun Lee, *The Philosophical Theology of Jonathan Edwards* (Princeton: Princeton University Press, 1988). An early critique of Miller's "modernist" rendering of Edwards is Vincent Tomas, "The Modernity of Jonathan Edwards," *New England Quarterly* 25 (March 1952): 60–84. The discussion was continued in John Opie, ed., *Jonathan Edwards and the Enlightenment* (Lexington, Mass.: D. C. Heath, 1969). Two recent critiques of the "modernist" interpretation of Edwards are Samuel Storms, *Tragedy in Eden: Original Sin in the Theology of Jonathan Edwards* (Lanham, Md.: University Press of America, 1985), and R. C. De Prospo, *Theism in the Discourse of Jonathan Edwards* (Newark: University of Delaware Press, 1985).

FURTHER QUESTIONS

These essays come at a critical moment in the life of the American academy and the history of religion in the United States. Addressing the issues of knowledge and belief from a variety of perspectives and with a variety of intentions, they come to grips with points driving the debates in the contemporary disciplines of intellectual history, literary criticism, philosophy, religious studies, and theology. They answer many questions but, as they were intended to do, pose many others.

First, "Is it over?" appears to have been an unhelpful phrasing of an important question. Perhaps its intention can be better put, "In what condition is the Enlightenment?" This seems closer to the way our participants approach the issue. Each author has an estimate of that condition and everyone seems to agree that Enlightenment traditions are in need of critical scrutiny and correction, but no one here thinks it is over.

Second, since the Enlightenment continues to shape American thought and religion, it is important that we understand the fissures and oppositions within the Enlightenment heritage. The Enlightenment figures loved to shape things into periods in order to highlight the *novus ordo* and so relegate its critics to a benighted past. That same experience of exile to the past is now being imposed on the enlightened, the foundationalists, and the modernists. Perhaps, for more adequate categories than the "posts" provide, we should distinguish (with Bernard Lonergan) between a First and a Second Enlightenment, and anticipate an alternation between constructive and skeptical phases in each.[21] Without introducing the dreaded notion of a historical dialectic, we might suggest an instability within the Enlightenment tradition that repeatedly pits close-to-the-bone empiricists or relativists such as David Hume, John Stuart Mill, Bertrand Russell, Alfred Ayer, and Richard Rorty against synthesizers (Rorty's philosophers) such as Kant, Hegel, Marx, Royce, and Dewey. In such a view the Enlightenment "turn to the subject" goes through two phases, the second of which dismantles the vestiges of the inherited classicist formulations of the First Enlightenment while continuing the subject-centered, analytic anthropological work of the first. The Second Enlightenment would include "all the usual suspects" of the later nineteenth century from Ludwig Feuerbach, Nietzsche, and Marx

---

[21]See Bernard Lonergan, "Prolegomena to the Study of the Emerging Religious Consciousness of Our Time," in *A Third Collection: Papers by Bernard J. F. Lonergan, S.J.*, ed. Frederick E. Crowe, S.J. (Mahwah, N.J.: Paulist Press, 1985), 55–99, esp. 63–65.

through the psychoanalytic movement of this century and on to Heidegger and the "posts."[22]

A distinction of this sort, combined with an expectation of alternation between constructive and skeptical positions within the two phases,[23] seems to accommodate the fact that the Enlightenment is in constant motion and yet never seems weaker, not to say dead and gone. It accounts for the fact that the Enlightenment seems to feed on itself or perhaps, like Freud's primal horde, to engage in forbidden acts of occasional patricide.

Third, some of our contributors make a case for a reappraisal of Carl Becker's argument in *The Heavenly City of the Eighteenth-Century Philosophers* (1932).[24] Have we adequately investigated the subtle points of continuity linking the Enlightenment heritage at its origins with the religious heritage? One recent approach to the same question is displayed by Trutz Rendtorff in "The Modern Age as a Chapter in the History of Christianity; or, the Legacy of Historical Consciousness."[25] His thesis is that the Enlightenment represents one stage of the West's ongoing struggle to come to terms with its Christian origins and its religious identity. Is our current and conventional distinction between the heritages the product of unexamined prejudices affecting both sides? Despite claims and some evidence to the contrary, do we see signs of a repristinated and vigorous Christianity emerging from the ashes of its classicist ancestors?

Fourth, what about the new American religious traditions that bypassed and ignored the Enlightenment? And the survival of pre-Enlightenment popular traditions in and outside of Christianity? Engaging these often neglected elements of the American religious heritage would significantly transform any discussion of knowledge and belief, vigorously

---

[22]The impact of the new biology on this Second Enlightenment in its American stream, sketched by Dewey, retold decades later by his student John Randall, and mentioned in this volume by Levinson, should not be overlooked. See John Dewey, "The Influence of Darwin on Philosophy," in *The Influence of Darwin on Philosophy and Other Essays in Contemporary Thought* (Bloomington: Indiana University Press, 1965), and John Herman Randall, Jr., "The Changing Influence of Darwin on Philosophy," *Journal of the History of Ideas* 22 (October–December 1961): 435–62.

[23]Lonergan would explain the alternation in terms of shifts in cognitional theory involving what he calls counterpositions. See Bernard Lonergan, *Insight: A Study of Human Understanding* (New York: Philosophical Library, 1957), 385–430, 458–87.

[24]Carl Becker, *The Heavenly City of the Eighteenth-Century Philosophers* (New Haven: Yale University Press, 1932).

[25]Trutz Rendtorff, "The Modern Age as a Chapter in the History of Christianity; or, The Legacy of Historical Consciousness," *Journal of Religion* 65 (October 1985): 478–99.

challenging the assumption that the United States is the Enlightenment's nation.[26]

Fifth, we do not have a comprehensive book on the religious heritage and the Enlightenment in America to parallel May's classic on the American Enlightenment.[27] At what stage of scholarly development are we on this? What have the individual authors whose work appears in this volume accomplished toward an interdisciplinary understanding of the American Enlightenment, religion, and the relations between them?

Finally, our hot wires. Are we to expect a continuation of the culture wars between the representatives of the two heritages? One senses in these chapters and in their predecessor volume that a century of antagonism could give way to something else. As difficult as the conversation sometimes proved to be at the conferences, has it provided an example worth following? Was it "more of the same," or could it be one moment in an expanding dialogue? Even were we to agree with Gunn that the naturalist-supernaturalist distinction constitutes the distance between the groups, is it not evident that this distance, too, merits reappraisal of its sources, meanings, and implications, and perhaps, in pragmatic fashion, with an eye to its consequences? Perhaps naturalists and religious thinkers still have something to learn from one another.

[26]On one important religious tradition see Richard Bushman, *Joseph Smith and the Beginnings of Mormonism* (Urbana: University of Illinois Press, 1984), and D. Michael Quinn, *Early Mormonism and the Magic World View* (Salt Lake City: Signature Books, 1987). See also Howard Kerr and Charles L. Crow, eds., *The Occult in America: New Historical Perspectives* (Urbana: University of Illinois Press, 1983), and R. Laurence Moore, *In Search of White Crows: Spiritualism, Parapsychology, and American Culture* (New York: Oxford University Press, 1977).

[27]May himself invites such a project in Henry F. May, *The Divided Heart: Essays on Protestants and the Enlightenment in America* (New York: Oxford University Press, 1991).

Part I

Enlightenment and religious traditions

1

Knowledge and belief in American public life

JAMES T. KLOPPENBERG

Knowledge is not what it used to be. Almost three decades have passed since Thomas Kuhn rocked the confidence of the scientific community by explaining scientific revolutions in terms of paradigm shifts rather than straightforward advances in knowledge. Since that time, as students of the *Geisteswissenschaften* have followed Kuhn's lead, we have learned to speak less of progress than of historicity, forms of life, thick descriptions, communities of discourse, archaeologies of knowledge, undecidability, prejudices, and life worlds. Foundations have evaporated across the disciplines; establishing authoritative claims has grown increasingly problematical as all knowledge has fallen under the scrutiny of a hermeneutics of suspicion. An erstwhile Kantian such as John Rawls can join hands with a former Marxist such as Alasdair MacIntyre in denying even the possibility of disclosing timeless truths; postfoundationalists turn instead toward a choice among competing traditions, whose claims "for us" should not be confused with any pretense to transcendental status. Where once the human sciences as fervently as the natural sciences aspired to certainty, we can now only watch as knowledge appears to recede beyond the horizon of inquiry.[1]

Belief, by contrast, may be making a modest comeback. The popular press mirrors the scholarly community in paying renewed and even respectful attention to the claims of faith of intellectuals as well as nonintellectuals. Divinity schools are flourishing, courses and books dealing with all sorts of religion proliferate, and even religious observance ap-

---

[1] An extended discussion of recent developments in social theory, philosophy of science, and epistemology is beyond the scope of this chapter. I discuss these matters in greater detail in "Pragmatism: An Old Name for Some New Ways of Thinking?" *Journal of American History* (in press).

pears to be slowly increasing in some denominations.² In this chapter, I discuss three sets of issues. First, I briefly review recent historical literature on the relation between knowledge and belief in American public life from the eighteenth century to the present. Second, I discuss the origins of postfoundationalism in the writings of William James and John Dewey, and I examine their rather different ideas concerning the role of faith in pragmatic conceptions of truth. Finally, I reflect on the continuing attractiveness of a particular, historically rooted conception of the proper relation between rationalism and religion in American culture. Since much recent poststructuralist thought challenges the very possibility of knowledge conceived within the framework of Enlightenment rationalism, it might seem self-evident that religion, the philosophes' whipping boy, would be increasingly implausible. Perhaps paradoxically, that is not the case, for reasons I suggest later.

HISTORICAL PERSPECTIVES

In his contribution to this book's companion volume, *Religion and Twentieth-Century American Intellectual Life*, David Tracy contrasts "the two classic traditions of the American experiment." He characterizes the Enlightenment tradition as "fundamentally a tradition of reason based on argument." The other tradition, "the Puritan covenantal tradition, is, like all religious traditions, grounded in conversation with particular religious classics."³ Tracy argues that in America's public sphere both traditions mingled, and he calls for the continuation of exchanges between the community of inquiry pursuing the Enlightenment tradition of knowledge and the community of interpretation pursuing the religious tradition of belief. This formulation, although sensible, does not go far enough: until quite recently, it has been all but impossible to separate, even for purposes of analysis, the strands of rationalism and

²For recent developments in American religion, see the following: "Church Membership Statistics, 1940–1985, for Selected U.S. Denominations," in *Yearbook of American and Canadian Churches 1987*, ed. Constant H. Jacquet (Nashville: Abington Press, 1987); Andrew M. Greeley, *American Catholics since the Council: An Unauthorized Report* (Chicago: Thomas More Press, 1985); Robert Wuthnow, *The Restructuring of American Religion: Society and Faith since World War II* (Princeton: Princeton University Press, 1988); and George M. Marsden, *Religion and American Culture* (New York: Harcourt Brace Jovanovich, 1990).

³David Tracy, "Afterword: Theology, Public Discourse, and the American Tradition," in *Religion and Twentieth-Century American Intellectual Life*, ed. Michael J. Lacey (Cambridge: Cambridge University Press, 1989), 201.

religion in American thought or American politics. "Our tradition," to invoke the phrase favored by postfoundationalists such as Richard Rorty, has been formed by continuously intertwined communities of inquiry and communities of interpretation.

For much of the twentieth century, prevailing historical interpretations of America emphasized either the progressive view of economic conflict or the consensus view of substantial agreement on the principles of liberal individualism. In either case, historians tended to assume that economic self-interest was the bedrock of American culture. When the new social history emerged in the 1960s to challenge prevailing conceptions, historians' focus shifted from elites to previously ignored groups. For a time the emphasis on economic questions persisted, but in the last two decades historians have gradually altered their perspective. Taking their cues increasingly from cultural anthropology and philosophical hermeneutics, historians have become more concerned with the phenomenology of historical experience. As they have sought to understand the past as it was lived, in addition to continuing their efforts to explain how the present emerged from it, historians have found themselves confronting everywhere the clear evidence of religiosity. As history has become increasingly a quest for meanings as well as structures and causes, the role of religion has become more central, because it is impossible to interpret accurately the experience of earlier Americans unless we attend to religion as well as economics, politics, and society.[4] Paradoxically, now that philosophers and political theorists are turning deliberately to the American cultural tradition to inform a self-consciously hardheaded, skeptical, and postfoundationalist approach to knowledge, they are learning from historians that the heart of their tradition is both rationalistic and religious. As I suggest in my conclusion, this realization poses awkward problems for both champions of Enlightenment and champions of religion.

The absence of an established church in America has made the clean separation of rationalist and religious traditions impossible. The proliferation of religious denominations has of course prevented the identification of faith with authority or autocracy that sparked Enlightenment anticlericalism in Europe. It has also meant, just as crucially, that all

---

[4]For further discussion of these trends, see Joyce Appleby, Lynn Hunt, and Margaret Jacob, *Telling the Truth about History* (New York: W. W. Norton, 1994); Peter Novick, *That Noble Dream: The "Objectivity Question" and the American Historical Profession* (Cambridge: Cambridge University Press, 1988); and James T. Kloppenberg, "Objectivity and Historicism: A Century of American Historical Writing," *American Historical Review* 94 (1989): 1011–30.

challenges to established ways of thinking or forms of social organization have attracted explicitly religious allies, whose participation sprang
from their faith and manifested itself in spirited political action. In the
quick survey of American reform that follows, I mean only to suggest
the pivotal importance of religion in effecting social change. It goes without saying that the opposition also deployed religious arguments in every
case; clearly, neither progressives nor conservatives, radicals nor reactionaries have had any persistent monopoly over religious convictions or
rhetoric. Tories, proslavery Southerners, laissez-faire capitalists, imperialists, fascists, racists, and cold warriors all believed God was on their
side, and all attracted followers who invoked their faith to justify their
commitments. What may be somewhat more surprising, or at least deserves to be emphasized, is the extent to which those who carried forward the Enlightenment principles of liberty, equality, and fraternity—
or sought to universalize the American rights to life, liberty, and the
pursuit of happiness—were motivated explicitly by, and understood
their activity primarily in terms of, their commitment to religious principles.

In *Albion's Seed*, the recently published first volume of his ambitious
cultural history of America, David Hackett Fischer writes, "Of all the
determinants which shaped the cultural character of British America, the
most powerful was religion. During the seventeenth century, the English-
speaking people were deeply divided by the great questions of the Protestant Reformation. These divisions in turn created a broad spectrum of
English denominations in the New World."[5] Beneath the umbrella of
Protestantism, various groups set off in various directions socially and
politically, and trying to arrange them on a single spectrum distorts the
multidimensional complexity of their variations. In the words of David
Hall, when studying colonial America the "imperative task is to detach
religion from a backward-looking communalism," because "modes of
belief" changed along with American society. "But we should not say
that emerging capitalism determined the path of religious development.
Though it was conditioned by social change and social forces, religion
retained important powers of autonomy; religion was a mediating
force."[6]

[5] David Hackett Fischer, *Albion's Seed: Four British Folkways in America* (New York:
Oxford University Press, 1989), 795.
[6] David D. Hall, "Religion and Society: Problems and Reconsiderations," in *Colonial Brit-*

Although American partisans of Enlightenment in the eighteenth century shared their European counterparts' confidence in reason, in the New World Christianity provided the framework within which, rather than against which, the Enlightenment emerged. The pervasiveness of religion, whether manifested in varieties of orthodox or dissenting Protestantism or, in a few notable instances, reformulated by deists, conditioned the reception of European ideas in America. Locke, Newton, Pope, and Montesquieu were especially revered, as were spokesmen for the radical Whig tradition, such as Algernon Sidney, and Scottish moral philosophers who followed Francis Hutcheson and Adam Ferguson. Skeptics such as Voltaire and Hume, and free thinkers such as Thomas Paine (in his later years), exerted less widespread influence. Regardless of the tension between Enlightenment rationalism and Protestant Christianity, which seemed as undeniable to many philosophes as it seems to many critics today, in America the Age of Reason was nevertheless also an age of belief.

Despite some variations within each region, distinguishable forms of Enlightenment emerged in New England, the Middle Atlantic, and the South. In all three regions faith mediated the claims of reason. In New England, the tension between Calvinists' convictions regarding humanity's depravity and the experience of democracy, heightened by the Great Awakening of the mid-eighteenth century, could be eased if not altogether resolved through the idea of the moral sense. This innate capacity, according to Charles Chauncy and Jonathan Mayhew, enabled human beings, though flawed by sin, to discern the difference between right and wrong. Calm confidence in the human ability to identify and comply with the demands of morality, while hardly consistent with Puritan doctrine, became the backbone of the Scottish-inspired and New England–dominated genteel tradition that was to emerge in the early nineteenth century. Although Jonathan Edwards sympathized with some of the central efforts of the Enlightenment, as John Smith and Mark Noll emphasize in their essays in this volume, he nevertheless denied the adequacy of reason to penetrate the mysterious depths of being revealed by God. By resisting the most expansive claims of reason, and by insisting on the reality of evil, Edwards counterposed themes from Augustinian Chris-

ish America: Essays in the New History of the Early Modern Era, ed. Jack P. Greene and J. R. Pole (Baltimore: Johns Hopkins University Press, 1984), 336.

tianity to the domesticated religiosity that began making its peace with science through the efforts of Americans such as Benjamin Franklin. In Franklin's more heterogeneous, commercial, and urban Middle Atlantic region, such accommodations with the Arminian ideas of free will and perfectibility came more easily. Franklin scorned the Puritan divines' otherworldly fatalism, declaring, with Montesquieu, that we best serve God by serving his children. Franklin's fellow Philadelphians Benjamin Rush and James Wilson espoused a similar eclectic faith in divine providence, human reason, the moral sense of sympathy, and progressive social reform through education and democratic politics. In the South, champions of the Enlightenment were members of the planter oligarchy whose religious views were generally unconventional forms of Anglicanism.[7]

These regional and denominational differences mattered profoundly to Americans, but their significance shrank after 1763. J. C. D. Clark recently demonstrated how the conflicts among American denominations and the common mistrust of Anglicanism helped unify the colonists against England. In an essay surveying recent literature on religion and the Revolution, Ruth Bloch writes, "Far from having become secularized by the eighteenth century, the religious preoccupations that had always informed political ideology remained vitally important to Americans of the Revolutionary generation." During these crucial years, "ideological change occurred within a symbolic structure largely defined by the Calvinist experiential approach to salvation and providential understanding of the collective experience of God's people on earth."[8] Forced by the

[7]See Henry F. May, *The Enlightenment in America* (New York: Oxford University Press, 1976); Donald H. Meyer, *The Democratic Enlightenment* (New York: G. P. Putnam's Sons, 1976); and J. R. Pole, "Enlightenment and the Politics of American Nature," in *The Enlightenment in National Context,* ed. R. Porter and M. Teich (Cambridge: Cambridge University Press, 1981). See also the essays by John E. Smith and Mark Noll in this volume.

[8]J. C. D. Clark, *The Language of Liberty, 1660–1832: Political Discourse and Social Dynamics in the Anglo-American World* (Cambridge: Cambridge University Press, 1994); Ruth H. Bloch, "Religion and Ideological Change in the American Revolution," in *Religion and American Politics from the Colonial Period to the 1980s,* ed. Mark A. Noll (New York: Oxford University Press, 1990), 47. This splendid collection of essays, which provides up-to-date discussions by leading historians of American religion, has been immensely useful in preparing this chapter. Other discussions of the central role of religion in the Revolution include Ruth H. Bloch, *Visionary Republic: Millennial Themes in American Thought, 1756–1800* (New York: Cambridge University Press, 1985); Nathan O. Hatch, *The Sacred Cause of Liberty: Republican Thought and the Millennium in Revolutionary New England* (New Haven: Yale University Press, 1977); Patricia Bonomi, *Under the Cope of Heaven: Religion, Society, and Politics in Colonial America* (New York: Oxford University Press, 1986); and James T. Kloppenberg, "The Virtues of Liberalism:

pressure of war to create a new language for a new nation, colonial Americans refashioned and wove together the quite different vocabularies of Protestant Christianity, classical republicanism, and Scottish Common Sense philosophy to form a powerful, if ambiguous, discourse of virtue that served their purposes well. America's revolutionaries used religious, civic, and ethical conceptions of duty to express the commitments that sustained them until they had secured their independence and established a constitution for their new republic. Unfortunately, their new language could not contain the rapidly changing shape of the democratic and commercial culture that was beginning to develop.

Yet perhaps the loose weave of the American language of politics explains both its initial success and its survival in the Constitution. The "multiple meanings" of the key words in the American lexicon, according to Harry Stout, enabled different Americans to read what they wanted into the language of the founding documents; that ambiguity helped keep the genuine conflicts among changing and competing social groups from ripping the nation apart.[9] Moreover, the provision for amending the Constitution not only sealed the doctrine of popular sovereignty by preserving the people's effective power to shape their laws, it further testified to the founders' willingness to admit their own limitations. Whereas the French Revolution would seek to fix forever the luminous principles of government disclosed by reason, the U.S. Constitution provided explicitly for the corrections that would inevitably be required. Although the nature of the religiosity of James Madison in particular, and the founders in general, remains an open question, it is arguable that their faith in reason was bounded by their awareness of their finitude. Thus the Bill of Rights in general reflects the Federalists' shrewd political instincts, which enabled them to allay the Antifederalists' fears, and also their piety. The First Amendment in particular, which guaranteed the separation of church and state, rested on a combination of calculation and sobriety. The First Amendment neither explicitly prevented any government involvement with religion nor authorized the promotion by government of a vague, nondenominational Christianity. The aim of the amendment, according to John F. Wilson, was simply to

---

Christianity, Republicanism, and Ethics in Early American Political Discourse," *Journal of American History* 74 (1987): 9–33.
[9]Harry S. Stout, "Rhetoric and Reality in the Early Republic: The Case of the Federalist Clergy," in Noll, *Religion and American Politics*, 62–76.

"neutralize religion as a factor that might jeopardize the achievement of a federal government."[10] Not because faith was flagging, then, but precisely because it remained so powerful—and so protean—was the exclusion of government from religion, and vice versa, of such importance to the new republic.[11]

When the volatile blend of faith, civic virtue, and enlightened self-interest that had fueled the Revolution began to run out, the role of religion in American culture changed. *The Federalist*, the writings of John Adams on the Constitution, and the efforts of evangelical denominations and the New England clergy represent alternate strategies designed to solve a widely perceived problem: the virtue of individual citizens might no longer be adequate to sustain the public life of the republic after the crises of the Revolution and founding had passed. As hierarchies fell and economic opportunities rose, a new species of individualism began to appear throughout America. Harnessing that new energy, finding ways to turn it to the public interest, was a project shared by religious and political elites of various persuasions.[12]

The dramatic rise of evangelical Christianity accompanied the transformation of American culture from the 1770s through the 1930s. Civic virtue no longer seemed adequate to religious leaders, and they began calling Americans away from economic and political diversions to confront their sinfulness. Whereas historians twenty years ago routinely characterized early nineteenth-century Americans as "unchurched," and implied that they were increasingly irreligious as well, recent interpretations stress the persistent religiosity of the new nation. Americans were, to use the title of Jon Butler's recent study, floating into a new world of democracy and capitalism "awash in a sea of faith."[13] They

---

[10]John F. Wilson, "Religion, Government, and Power in the New Nation," in Noll, *Religion and American Politics*, 77–91.

[11]Guyora Binder, "Revolution as a Constitutional Concept," paper delivered at the Annual Meeting of the American Society for Legal History, February 1990, copy in my possession.

[12]In addition to Gordon Wood, *The Creation of the American Republic, 1776–1878* (New York: Norton, 1969), see Robert E. Shalhope, *The Roots of Democracy: American Thought and Culture 1760–1800* (Boston: Twayne, 1990); the fine, brief discussion in Daniel Walker Howe, "Anti-Federalist/Federalist Dialogue and Its Implications for Constitutional Understanding," *Northwestern University Law Review* 84 (1989): 1–11; and John L. Brooke, *The Heart of the Commonwealth: Society and Political Culture in Worcester County, Massachusetts, 1731–1861* (Cambridge: Cambridge University Press, 1989).

[13]Jon Butler, *Awash in a Sea of Faith: Christianizing the American People* (Cambridge, Mass.: Harvard University Press, 1990).

were confident that the exercise of reason would enable them to fulfill their divinely ordained historical mission. Christianity provided the frame of reference for worldly forms of political, economic, and scientific activity. Rationalism and religion seemed fully compatible. "Educated Evangelicals," James Turner argues, "no less than the eighteenth century infidels they abhorred, hitched their wagon to the rising star of science." In the estimation of Lyman Beecher, evangelicalism was "eminently a rational system"; by that he meant, Turner notes, "nothing more nor less than the rationality of science."[14]

As American political life became increasingly boisterous in the 1820s and 1830s, religious issues remained central to debates about rational policy choices. The democratization of American culture proceeded within the dual contexts of enthusiasm for science and enthusiasm for evangelical Christianity, and the various reformist crusades of the antebellum years thus cannot be understood in narrowly secular terms. They manifested neither merely elitist attempts to impose order on unruly multitudes nor merely the efforts of ambitious and uncultivated Americans to remove the last vestiges of privilege. In the words of Daniel Walker Howe: "It was the explosive combination of humanitarianism plus Christianity that gave the world the evangelical movement and its attendant reforms." In antebellum America, "it was the institutional and emotional resources of Christianity that typically empowered humanitarian reform."[15] Criticism of all these reforms as veiled efforts to achieve social control confuses their effect with their cause and neglects the widespread support from all classes for measures such as temperance and antislavery. Opponents of Indian removal and champions of compulsory education and penal reform shared a commitment to positive freedom; only by ignoring the Whigs' greater sympathy for the causes of feminism and abolitionism can their politics of self-control be judged more coercive than the laissez-faire politics of Jacksonians.[16] The cultural

[14]James Turner, *Without God, without Creed: The Origins of Unbelief in America* (Baltimore: Johns Hopkins University Press, 1985), 100–101; see also Nathan O. Hatch, "The Democratization of Christianity and the Character of American Politics," in Noll, *Religion and American Politics*, 92–120; Gordon Wood, "Ideology and the Origins of a Liberal America," *William and Mary Quarterly*, 3d ser., 44 (1987): 628–40; and R. Laurence Moore, "Religion, Secularization, and the Shaping of the Culture Industry in Antebellum America," *American Quarterly* 41 (1989): 216–42.
[15]Daniel Walker Howe, "Religion and Politics in the Antebellum North," in Noll, *Religion and American Politics*, 130, and Daniel Walker Howe, *The Political Culture of the American Whigs* (Chicago: University of Chicago Press, 1979).
[16]Martin J. Wiener, ed., "Humanitarianism or Control? A Symposium on Aspects of Nineteenth-Century Social Reform in Britain and America," *Rice University Studies* 67

and economic conflicts of these years were real enough, but only if we view the Whigs' crusades through the prism of their Christianity can we move beyond easy cynicism toward an understanding of their motivation. It is not enough to affirm, as the ethnocultural interpretation of American politics enables us to do, that political affiliation was tied to ethnicity and religion. We must also stop assuming that the hidden economic dimensions of these conflicts were somehow more "real" than the surface moral and religious issues. Democracy, Alexis de Tocqueville wrote, throws the individual back forever upon himself alone, and "there is danger that he may be shut up in the solitude of his own heart."[17] Without the resources provided by religion, Tocqueville argued, democratic individuals find themselves damned to a civic hell. He believed that the process of democratization he witnessed, and chronicled, skirted that inferno precisely because Americans' worldviews were not so much comfortably capitalist as they were uncomfortably Christian. The transformation of American society during these years of rapid economic change is clear, but its meaning for those who experienced it will remain opaque unless we acknowledge the importance of religion as well as science in their conception of progress.

The centrality of religion likewise explains Lincoln's commanding power for his contemporaries and his uniquely enduring stature. Although his own religiosity was as idiosyncratic as Jefferson's, Lincoln became increasingly drawn to a profound, heterodoxically Christian supernaturalism during the final decade of his life. His responses to Stephen Douglas in their debates, as J. David Greenstone and John Diggins have argued in very different ways, and as Andrew Delbanco confirms in his essay in this volume, derive their moral authority from biblical injunctions as much as from political principles.[18] Lincoln's writings and speeches, both before and after his election as president, carried forward another set of themes in addition to the classical emphasis on civic duty and the liberal emphasis on individual rights. Lincoln expressed as well

(1981): 1–84; Lois Banner, "Religious Benevolence as Social Control: A Critique of an Interpretation," *Journal of American History* 60 (1973): 34–41; and Joan Williams, "Domesticity as the Dangerous Supplement of Liberalism," *Journal of Women's History* 2 (1991): 69–88.
[17]Alexis de Tocqueville, *Democracy in America*, ed. J. P. Mayer (Garden City, N.Y.: Anchor Books, 1969), 508.
[18]J. David Greenstone, *The Lincoln Persuasion: Remaking American Liberalism* (Princeton: Princeton University Press, 1993); and John P. Diggins, *The Lost Soul of American Politics: Virtue, Self-Interest, and the Foundations of Liberalism* (New York: Basic Books, 1984), 277–333.

an Augustinian awareness of the human capacity for evil and the possibility of redemption. As was true in the eighteenth century, the most powerful arguments in American public discourse during the nineteenth century were those grounded on both faith and reason. Commitments to the Union (and the Confederacy) were inspired by, and justified in terms of, a cosmology of sacred sacrifice and salvation rather than either republican sacrifice and glory or calculating sacrifice and personal profit. The horror of slavery for Lincoln extended beyond its "monstrous injustice" for slaves and beyond its threat to the Union, to the fundamental challenge slavery represented to the sanctity of all human life. Yet again as was true in the eighteenth century, Lincoln's deepest convictions were chastened by his acknowledgment, in the Second Inaugural Address, that "the Almighty has His own purposes." Thus not only his resolve to fight but also his commitment to reconciliation drew on his unconventional but unmistakable Christian faith.[19]

In the Gilded Age, not only did ethnocultural identity continue to be among the most important determinants of political partisanship, but religious principles continued to undergird the efforts of many reformers. Leon Fink has pointed out that the Knights of Labor used religious as well as economic arguments to mobilize workers.[20] The religious imagery of the populists is familiar. The social gospel moved gradually from the periphery to the center of American Protestantism, and by the first decade of the twentieth century the commitment to progressive reform had become orthodox in many denominations. Moreover, the pre–World War I alliance between such partisans of the social gospel as Walter Rauschenbusch and such social scientists as Richard T. Ely suggested that scholarship, faith, and political activism were natural partners. If social problems are rooted in the sin of greed, as Rauschenbusch argued in *A Theology for the Social Gospel*, then progress toward their solution would require repentance in addition to institutional reform.[21] To achieve the latter, the work of professional organizations such as the American Economic Association, which Ely helped to establish and tried unsuccessfully to steer toward social activism, should be directed toward helping scholars bring knowledge to bear on questions of justice. Both

---

[19]Reinhold Niebuhr, *The Irony of American History* (New York: Charles Scribner's Sons, 1952), 171–74.
[20]Leon Fink, *Workingmen's Democracy: The Knights of Labor and American Politics* (Urbana: University of Illinois Press, 1983).
[21]Walter Rauschenbusch, *A Theology for the Social Gospel* (New York: Macmillan, 1918).

Rauschenbusch and Ely sought to shift their contemporaries' attention away from the fixation on inevitability that they thought incapacitated too many laissez-faire economists and mainstream Protestants, who interpreted the social scientific and sacred scriptures as authorizing the quiet acceptance of conditions that could not be changed. During the 1920s both social science and fundamentalism seemed to move, in oddly opposite ways, toward newer versions of orthodoxy that sought to freeze the present into the eternal, but it is important to keep in mind the more fluid condition of both knowledge and belief in the climate of American progressivism before World War I. Interpretations that would collapse all of American progressivism into Protestantism seem to me overdrawn, but the centrality of religion to certain varieties of progressive reform, such as the work of social settlements and the efforts to regulate economic activity and working conditions, is undeniable.[22]

The years since World War I have witnessed the partial unraveling of the ties that bound much of progressivism to religious commitment. Two parallel trends—the rise of a self-conscious devotion to objectivity among social scientists and the rise of an equally self-conscious aspiration to realism among political liberals—combined with the resurgence of religious fundamentalism to weaken the links between religion and reform. Paradoxically, this transformation of American academic and political culture may have been responsible for both the short-term successes of the moderate New Deal and the long-term failures of the truncated American welfare state. The sobering experiences of the Depression and two global wars intensified the commitments of many American intellectuals and politicians to resisting naïveté in both its religious and ideological forms. Although this realism could take the shape

[22]This analysis draws on a wide variety of materials, including the rapidly proliferating secondary literatures on academic professionalization and twentieth-century politics that are impossible to discuss adequately here. For especially useful treatments of these related phenomena, see Bruce Kuklick, *Churchmen and Philosophers: From Jonathan Edwards to John Dewey* (New Haven: Yale University Press, 1985); Julie A. Reuben, "In Search of Truth: Scientific Inquiry, Religion, and the Development of the American University, 1870–1920," Ph.D. dissertation, Stanford University, 1990; Edward A. Purcell, *The Crisis of Democratic Theory: Scientific Naturalism and the Problem of Value* (Lexington: University Press of Kentucky, 1973); and Richard Wightman Fox and T. J. Jackson Lears, eds., *The Culture of Consumption: Critical Essays in American History, 1880–1980* (New York: Pantheon, 1983). I explore the political dimension of these developments in two recent essays: "Who's Afraid of the Welfare State," *Reviews in American History* 18 (1990): 395–405, and "Elusive Consensus: Shaping the Welfare States in Britain, France, and the United States since World War II" (paper delivered at a meeting of the American Historical Association, December 30, 1989).

of Reinhold Niebuhr's austere neo-orthodoxy, it more often manifested itself in smug dismissals of faith and celebrations of science. Scholars who had learned to examine the functional role of religion from a variety of psychological, sociological, or anthropological perspectives frequently assumed that regardless of its therapeutic value, its social utility, or its meaning-giving quality, religion is illusory. Secular cultural critics emerged to play the part often filled in the nineteenth century by theologians, explaining to the educated bourgeoisie what is to be done and what is to be thought about matters of ultimate concern.

At the same time, both liberal and conservative politicians nevertheless continued to rely, with increasing sophistication (and at times with quite unnerving cynicism), on appeals to the millions of Americans who still conceived of their public commitments in terms of their religious faith. As the separation of knowledge from belief has become more and more apparent in the American academic community, equally deep rifts have emerged within most religious denominations concerning social and political issues. Progressive Protestants tracing their lineage from Rauschenbusch make common cause with Catholics descended from Dorothy Day, while conservatives invoke different but equally lively traditions grounded in their favorite biblical commands. Thus despite the apparent acceleration of the secularization process in the last fifty years, religion remains an inextricable part of public life in late twentieth-century America. It is as impossible to understand the civil rights movement without Martin Luther King, Jr., the antiwar movement without William Sloane Coffin, the farm workers' movement without Cesar Chavez, or the Rainbow Coalition of the late 1980s without Jesse Jackson as it is to understand earlier American reform movements in isolation from the religious activists who helped give them their shape and their energy. By itself religion does not explain American politics, especially now that electoral politics appears to be devolving into a species of marketing that competes in banality, if not imagination, with the advertising of athletic shoes. But American politics can be neither understood nor explained without attending to the persistence as well as the transformation of religious belief.[23]

[23]Recent discussions of religion and politics in contemporary America include Taylor Branch, *Parting the Waters: America in the King Years, 1954–63* (New York: Simon and Schuster, 1988); Richard H. King, *Civil Rights and the Idea of Freedom* (New York: Oxford University Press, 1992); James E. Findlay, "Religion and Politics in the Sixties: The Churches and the Civil Rights Act of 1964," *Journal of American History* 77 (1990): 66–92; Doug Rossinow, " 'The Break-through to New Life': Christianity and the Emer-

PRAGMATIC TRUTH AND RELIGIOUS FAITH

Viewed strictly as an empirical question, then, it is clear that knowledge and belief have been inseparable in American public life from the colonial period through the present. The second question I want to raise, however, is more difficult to answer: Is the postfoundationalism that attracts the allegiance of many contemporary scholars compatible with religious faith? I approach this question by concentrating on the answers given by two twentieth-century American thinkers, William James and John Dewey, postfoundationalists *avant la lettre*. The choice of James and Dewey is hardly arbitrary, since their writings are central to the renewed interest in pragmatism apparent in much contemporary American philosophy, cultural criticism, and political theory.

James's ideas about religion have two different aspects, the phenomenological and the pragmatic. The pragmatic dimensions are familiar from James's *Will to Believe* and *The Varieties of Religious Experience*. James argued that religious questions, like other questions that cannot be answered by empirical tests, should be addressed from a particular perspective: we should inquire what practical difference the answers to such questions make. His investigations into the consequences of religious beliefs revealed that faith can have a profound influence on individual lives, and that influence itself seemed to James worth emphasizing. But beyond and beneath the invocation of the pragmatic test lay James's own personal crisis and his recovery through an act of will. That familiar incident provided the experiential ground for James's lifelong quest to understand the multiple dimensions of consciousness. From his *Principles of Psychology* to his *Pluralistic Universe*, James consistently opposed all dualisms and all dogmatisms. He understood that separations between mind and body, subject and object, fact and value, knowledge and action, and natural and supernatural conformed only to the conventional categories of Western thought. Experience, amorphous, plastic, shimmering, and slippery as it was, escaped whatever conceptual nets philosophers and psychologists might devise to capture it.

gence of the New Left in Austin, Texas, 1956–64," *American Quarterly* 46 (1994): 309–40; Marsden, *Religion and American Culture*, 167–278; the essays by Martin Marty, Robert Wuthnow, and George Marsden in Noll, *Religion and American Politics*; and the wide-ranging article by Patrick McCormick, "That They May Converse: Voices of Catholic Social Thought," *Cross Currents* 42 (1992): 521–27. I discuss these issues further in my essay "Political Ideas," in *Encyclopedia of the United States in the Twentieth Century*, ed. Stanley I. Kutler (New York: Charles Scribner's Sons, 1995).

James's own quirky religiosity was consistent with his conception of immediate experience as the intersection of self with nonself in the fluid and ever-changing encounters of an attending individual consciousness. Just as his ethics stood not on bedrock but rather on his preference for a "strenuous" rather than an "easygoing" morality, a preference based on pragmatic judgment rather than logical demonstration of its superiority, so his faith stood on a felt fact, which he described in the conclusion of *The Varieties of Religious Experience* as "*the fact that the conscious person is continuous with a wider self through which saving experiences come.*" The impulse toward something beyond the self, something "more" with which we seek union, the desire for consolation in the face of persistent feelings that the self and its limits do not circumscribe the realm of the possible, were for James adequate warrants for belief. As an empirical scientist he was sensitive to charges that his " 'piecemeal' supernaturalism" lacked substance, but he responded without apology: "Humbug is humbug, even though it bear the scientific name, and the total expression of human experience, as I view it objectively, [that is, as a scientific naturalist] invincibly urges me beyond the narrow 'scientific bounds.' Assuredly, the real world is of a different temperament—more intricately built than physical science allows."[24] For James, the claims of knowledge could not topple the fact of belief, because the latter was rooted in the mysterious court of last appeal, the phenomenology of personal experience. A truly radical empiricism, James insisted, must leave open the possibility of faith, and also the possibility that the object of that faith might exist.[25] In his sensitivity to the inadequacy of language to express the depth and breadth of experience, in his resolute refusal to admit the possibility of closure for any knowledge claims, and in his resistance to the grander claims of scientific rationality, James stands as a champion of ideas cherished by many contemporary dissident intellectuals.

In James's writings, the relation between religion and knowledge is never quite clear, possibly because his ideas always seem to slide just out-

[24]William James, *The Varieties of Religious Experience* (1902; New York: Modern Library, 1929), 505, 509.
[25]Gerald E. Myers, *William James: His Life and Thought* (New Haven: Yale University Press, 1986), 446–80; John E. Smith, *Purpose and Thought: The Meaning of Pragmatism* (New Haven: Yale University Press, 1978), 159–66; William A. Clebsch, *American Religious Thought: A History* (Chicago: University of Chicago Press, 1973), 125–70; and James T. Kloppenberg, *Uncertain Victory: Social Democracy and Progressivism in ·European and American Thought, 1870–1920* (New York: Oxford University Press, 1986), chaps. 1–5, on James's epistemology and his ethics.

side the frame of his texts. That deliberate elusiveness was a matter of principle for James; it accounts in part for both his charm and his continuing significance. "It is perhaps an advantage," Alfred North Whitehead wrote of James, "that his system of philosophy remained so incomplete. To fill it out would necessarily have made it smaller." By contrast, Whitehead wrote, we should consider the work of John Dewey: "In carrying out the philosophy of William James, I think he enormously narrowed it. With James the consciousness of the ever present complexity and possibility in human experience is always implicit in his writing. Dewey is without it."[26] From the perspective of some commentators, Dewey appeared to lack that consciousness precisely because, after he shifted from his early Congregationalist faith to his mature naturalism, he seemed to rule out the possibility of unscientific discourse, unconventional modes of experience, and traditional forms of religiosity. James and Dewey thus apparently offered two alternative judgments concerning the compatibility of knowledge and belief. But that appearance is illusory.

Like James, Dewey believed we should begin thinking about religion by reflecting on its concrete consequences, and he argued that those consequences, not any theological or metaphysical claims, constitute its importance. So troubled was Dewey by doctrine that he refused even to use the word "religion," preferring instead the adjective "religious" to express his conception of an attitude that always springs from human experience and should never be allowed to settle into institutionalized form. In his most sustained discussion of the religious, *A Common Faith*, Dewey insisted that "it denotes nothing in the way of a specifiable entity, either institutional or as a system of beliefs." The religious was not limited to mystical or supernatural faith; on the contrary, Dewey defined religious belief as "the unification of the self through allegiance to inclusive ideal ends."[27] These ideal ends can be aesthetic, scientific, political, or moral; they can relate to any realm in which the individual seeks to relieve experienced tension through unification with an ideal. For Dewey, such ideals are not necessarily associated with any deity; the decision to seek harmony with them springs from individual choice rather than from achieving any mystical union with, or dispensation of grace from, something supernatural. In the words of John E. Smith, for

[26]*Dialogues of Alfred North Whitehead: As Recorded by Lucien Price* (Boston: Little, Brown, 1954), 337–38, quoted in Myers, *William James*, 614 n. 82.
[27]John Dewey, *A Common Faith*, in Dewey, *The Later Works, 1925–1953*, vol. 9, *1933–1934*, ed. Jo Ann Boydston (Carbondale: Southern Illinois University Press, 1986), 8, 23.

Dewey "God is the *function* which this active union of ideal and actual performs in human experience as it develops against the background of a natural environment."[28] Religion has no existence independent of the human community's struggle to achieve what Dewey called "the democratic idea."

For Dewey, democracy embodies the religious; efforts to realize "the great community," to use his phrase from *The Public and Its Problems*, constitute the most sublime religious project. Whereas James conceptualized such struggles for unity as quests for some mysterious beyond, Dewey explicitly rejected such notions as distractions from the hard work of aesthetic, scientific, political, or moral praxis. The young Dewey's antidualistic Hegelianism carried over into his mature naturalism. The passionate commitment to overcoming dualisms persisted, but in place of *Geist* Dewey invoked science. The community of inquiry, extended to politics and society through the diffusion of democratic principles, took over for abstract reason as the motor driving history. For Dewey, the religious originated in human striving, and its proper target remained the sanctification of this world rather than the achievement of salvation in another. If Dewey's mysticism remained earthbound, however, it was not without romantic, or even unconventionally religious, aspirations. As the ideals of democratic intelligence and instrumentalism "find adequate expression in social life," Dewey wrote in *Reconstruction in Philosophy*, they will

color the imagination and temper the desires and affections. . . . Then they will take on religious value. The religious spirit will be revivified because it will be in harmony with men's unquestioned scientific beliefs and their ordinary day-by-day activities. . . . And when the emotional force, the mystic force one might say, of communication, of the miracle of shared life and shared experience is spontaneously felt, the hardness and crudeness of contemporary life will be bathed in the light that never was on land or sea.[29]

Neither James nor Dewey, then, saw a necessary conflict between knowledge and the authentically religious—at least as they understood

[28]Smith, *Purpose and Thought*, 191. Steven C. Rockefeller, *John Dewey: Religious Faith and Democratic Humanism* (New York: Columbia University Press, 1991), provides an incisive and comprehensive analysis of Dewey's ideas on religious faith.

[29]John Dewey, *Reconstruction in Philosophy*, in Dewey, *The Middle Works, 1899–1924*, vol. 12, *1920*, ed. Jo Ann Boydston (Carbondale: Southern Illinois University Press, 1982), 200–201. See also Kuklick, *Churchmen and Philosophers*; Bruce Kuklick, "John Dewey, American Theology, and Scientific Politics," in Lacey, *Religion and Twentieth-Century American Intellectual Life*, 78–93; and Kloppenberg, *Uncertain Victory*, 43–46, 76, 140–42.

the latter in their quite different ways. Yet both men distrusted institutionalized religion, and both detested dogmatism. James was willing to entertain the possibility that some realm beyond our own might exist, whereas Dewey's conception of religious ideals generated by human striving evidently did not admit that possibility. Important as that difference is, it seems equally important to acknowledge that both James and Dewey deployed their religious ideas, just as they deployed all pragmatic knowledge, for ethical purposes. Both faith and reason were part of the pragmatic project, and both were to be judged by their consequences.

If pragmatism need not necessarily rule out undogmatic varieties of religious belief, however, as the writings of James and Dewey suggest, what might be the consequences of such belief for politics? If our ideals are to derive from experience rather than dogma or metaphysics, if we are to learn from "our tradition" rather than from abstract principles (as some neopragmatists such as Richard Rorty advise), what are we to make of a tradition that has been marked, as I have indicated, by the deep penetration into public life of religious doctrines and rationalist principles of just the sort we are urged to discard? "Strong poets," to use the term Rorty borrows from Harold Bloom, might respond by changing the subject. In *Contingency, Irony, and Solidarity*, Rorty calls for the creation of a culture that would be "enlightened, secular, through and through. It would be one in which no trace of divinity remained, either in the form of a divinized world or a divinized self. Such a culture would have no room for the notion that there are nonhuman forces to which human beings should be responsible."[30] Having discussed his recent writings elsewhere, I will not elaborate here the reasons why Rorty's liberal utopia seems to me neither liberal, utopian, nor consistent with the ethics of pragmatism as conceived by James or Dewey. Instead I want merely to suggest that Rorty's recent proclamations of contingency and irony seem to me incapable of yielding the solidarity he seeks, because by authorizing the narcissistic self-absorption of strong poets he en-

---

[30]Richard Rorty, *Contingency, Irony, and Solidarity* (Cambridge: Cambridge University Press, 1989), 45. In "Pragmatism without Method," an essay first published in 1983 and reprinted in Rorty, *Objectivism, Relativism, and Truth: Philosophical Papers*, vol. 1 (Cambridge: Cambridge University Press, 1991), 63, 66-70, and 76, Rorty contrasted the pugnaciously antireligious naturalism of Sidney Hook with the quite different sensibility manifested in Dewey's *Common Faith*, a sensibility Rorty found indistinguishable from that of Paul Tillich.

courages precisely the cultivation of inwardness that James and Dewey rejected.[31]

In his contribution to this volume, Giles Gunn points out that nothing other than the creativity of isolated individuals remains when postmodernists declare the death of Enlightenment rationality and religious faith. Although both James and Dewey likewise appreciated the artificiality of language as a system of signs, they also believed that interpersonal communication nevertheless remains a possibility. In James's words, "All human thinking gets discursified; we exchange ideas; we lend and borrow verifications, get them from one another by means of social intercourse. All truth thus gets verbally built out, sorted up, and made available for everyone. Hence, we must *talk* consistently just as we must think consistently: for both in talk and in thought we deal with kinds. Names are arbitrary, but once understood they must be kept to."[32] We can acknowledge the arbitrariness of signifiers, James insisted, without being incapacitated by that knowledge or freed from our responsibility to communicate with each other. Likewise Dewey recognized the instability of language without denying its pragmatic potential.

Symbols in turn depend upon and promote communication. The results of conjoint experience are considered and transmitted. Events cannot be passed from one to another, but meanings may be shared by means of signs. Wants and impulses are then attached to common meanings. They are thereby transformed into desires and purposes, which, since they implicate a common or mutually understood meaning, present new ties, converting a conjoining activity into a community of interest and endeavor. Thus there is generated what, metaphorically, may be termed a general will and social consciousness: desire and choice on the part of individuals in behalf of activities that, by means of symbols, are communicable and shared by all concerned. A community thus presents an order of energies transmuted into one of meanings which are appreciated and mutually

---

[31]See James T. Kloppenberg, "Democracy and Disenchantment: From Weber and Dewey to Habermas and Rorty," and Richard Rorty, "Dewey between Hegel and Darwin," in *Modernist Impulses in the Human Sciences, 1870–1930,* ed. Dorothy Ross (Baltimore: Johns Hopkins University Press, 1994), 69–90, 54–68; Richard J. Bernstein, "One Step Forward, Two Steps Back: Richard Rorty on Liberal Democracy and Philosophy," and "Rorty's Liberal Utopia," in *The New Constellation: The Ethical-Political Horizons of Modernity/Postmodernity* (Cambridge, Mass.: MIT Press, 1992), 230–92; Nancy Fraser, "Solidarity or Singularity: Richard Rorty between Romanticism and Technocracy," in *Unruly Practices: Power, Discourse, and Gender in Contemporary Social Theory* (Minneapolis: University of Minnesota Press, 1989), 93–110; and Cornel West, *The American Evasion of Philosophy* (Madison: University of Wisconsin Press, 1989), 194–210.

[32]William James, *Pragmatism,* in *The Works of William James,* ed. Frederick Burkhardt (Cambridge, Mass.: Harvard University Press, 1975), 102–3.

referred by each to every other on the part of those engaged in combined action.[33]

Dewey appreciated the difficulty of such "communicative action," to use the phrase Jürgen Habermas applies to this process. Dewey admitted that the emergence of "mutual interest in shared meanings . . . does not occur all at once nor completely. At any given time, it sets a problem rather than marks a settled achievement."[34] Solving such problems, moreover, is a continuing process, never ending in the closure postmodernists dread but instead forever opening up new possibilities—and new problems to be discussed and addressed. In marked contrast to the social tests of truth emphasized by James and Dewey, celebrations of ironic subjectivity not only beg the questions raised by James's strenuous ethics and Dewey's democratic community, they concede the political field to those with power who would shape public opinion by cynically manipulating a kinder and gentler imagery.[35]

Yet the solvent of historical criticism is indeed corrosive, and it is not clear that a faith chastened by its awareness of contingency can still have the consequences James and Dewey respected. Nietzsche reflected on this difficulty with some satisfaction. Historical study reduced faith to "pure knowledge about Christianity, and so has annihilated it." All living things need "to be surrounded by an atmosphere, a mysterious circle of mist: if one robs it of this veil, if one condemns a religion, an art, a genius to orbit as a star without an atmosphere: then one should not wonder about its rapidly becoming withered, hard and barren."[36] Santayana put the point more succinctly: The pragmatists' gods are demonstrable only as hypotheses, but as hypotheses they are no longer gods. What sustenance can a culture take from its traditions once they have been dissected? As I suggest briefly in my conclusion, one possible response to that challenge can be drawn from a strand of the discourse of

[33]John Dewey, *The Public and Its Problems*, in *The Later Works*, vol. 2, *1925–1927*, ed. Jo Ann Boydston (Carbondale: Southern Illinois University Press, 1984), 331.
[34]Ibid.
[35]See Robert B. Westbrook, "Politics as Consumption: Managing the Modern American Election," in Fox and Lears, *Culture of Consumption*, 143–73; Thomas Byrne Edsall, "The Changing Shape of Power: A Realignment in Public Policy," in *The Rise and Fall of the New Deal Order, 1930–1980*, ed. Steve Fraser and Gary Gerstle (Princeton: Princeton University Press, 1989), 269–93; and Kathleen Hall Jamieson, *Eloquence in an Electronic Age: The Transformation of Political Speechmaking* (New York: Oxford University Press, 1988).
[36]Friedrich Nietzsche, *On the Advantage and Disadvantage of History for Life*, trans. Peter Preuss (Indianapolis: Hackett, 1980), 40.

American public life as it has developed from Edwards and Madison to James and Dewey.

RETHINKING KNOWLEDGE AND BELIEF

In the bracing climate of postfoundationalist criticism, several strategies have been suggested to protect faith from skepticism. To those for whom religion is not, in James's phrase, a live option, and to those whose faith remains solid, such discussions may seem pointless; others face these questions with attitudes that range from idle curiosity to urgency. If faith has indeed died for us, can we will it back to life by pretending ourselves back to innocence? This is the counsel of Daniel Bell in *The Cultural Contradictions of Capitalism*, but such a functionalist appeal seems born of desperation rather than conviction. Can we select a therapeutic religion from a faith court of congregations marketing sin-free affirmations of the self? To pose the question is to answer it, since such transparent consumerism parodies religious faith rather than expressing it. Can we instead deepen and redeem our dominant cultural norms of utilitarian and expressive self-interest by recovering submerged but still vital traditions of civic republicanism and religion? In *Habits of the Heart*, Robert Bellah and his associates recommend that project, arguing that the republican and biblical communities of memory can deliver us from our culture's individualist excesses. While that might seem an attractive prospect, even roughly consistent with the account of the shaping of American political culture I have sketched, there are reasons to resist its powerful appeal, because as H. Richard Niebuhr periodically reminded his brother, Reinhold, that strategy compromises religion without sanctifying politics.[37]

Politics has suffered as much as religion from the disenchantment the twentieth century has brought. In contrast to Dewey's hope that secularization would lead to the transfer of religious energies into political

[37]Daniel Bell, *The Cultural Contradictions of Capitalism* (New York: Basic Books, 1976), and Robert Bellah et al., *Habits of the Heart: Individualism and Commitment in American Life* (Berkeley: University of California Press, 1985). See also two fine studies: Jeffrey Stout, *Ethics after Babel: The Languages of Morals and Their Discontents* (Boston: Beacon Press, 1988), and George Armstrong Kelly, *Politics and Religious Consciousness in America* (New Brunswick, N.J.: Transaction Books, 1984), 258, 261. On the Niebuhrs, see Richard Wightman Fox, "The Niebuhr Brothers and the Liberal Protestant Heritage," in Lacey, ed., *Religion and Twentieth-Century American Intellectual Life*, 94–115, and Richard Wightman Fox, "H. Richard Niebuhr's Divided Kingdom," *American Quarterly* 42 (March 1990): 93–101.

action, these energies have either dissipated or been directed toward private pleasures. The citizen as well as the believer has tended to disappear, as the secular state finds itself staggering under the weight of what Habermas calls the "legitimation crisis." Welfare states can generate loyalty only by using instrumental rationality to achieve economic prosperity. Although technical considerations alone are permitted to influence decision making in such a depoliticized culture, the persistence of other norms and goals leads to resistance by dissident groups whose aspirations cannot be reconciled with those of the state system. According to Habermas, such efforts to combat the "colonization of the life world" make use of cultural resources inherited from traditional, noninstrumental forms of reasoning and interaction.[38] This much of Habermas's critique, which I find persuasive as an updating of Max Weber's analysis of democratic culture under conditions of disenchantment and rationalization, illuminates the inadequacy of Bellah's solution. Merging the vocabularies of religion, republicanism, and individual expressiveness cannot be achieved, since the forms of reasoning—and just as important, the conceptions of the capacity of reason—are irreconcilable. When the demands of religious faith and the demands of instrumental rationality collide, as they inevitably do now that religion does not provide, as it did in the eighteenth century, the context surrounding the exercise of reason, something must give way. For Bellah, presumably, religious commitments would triumph, but only at the cost of sacrificing individuals' responsibilities as republican citizens and their desire to achieve personal fulfillment as they conceive it for themselves.

Instead we must be content to hold in suspension, and resist efforts to unite, the claims of faith and the claims of reason, because both the public and the religious communities of discourse are diminished when they collapse into one another. In the pluralistic and contentious culture that America has always been, the commitment to the separation of church and state has been grounded and validated in experience. A faith deep enough to have consequences is fierce enough to need restraint. That realization, as old as Montaigne's *Essays* and Locke's *Essay Concerning Toleration*, is fundamental to the American tradition, and it con-

---

[38]The most comprehensive presentation of this analysis is Jürgen Habermas, *The Theory of Communicative Action*, trans. Thomas McCarthy, 2 vols. (Boston: Beacon Press, 1984; 1987); among the many discussions of Habermas, see especially Stephen K. White, *The Recent Work of Jürgen Habermas: Reason, Justice, and Modernity* (Cambridge: Cambridge University Press, 1988).

tinues to offer the strongest response to urgings from across the political spectrum to bring the full force of religious fervor to the debates of the public sphere.

This tradition of endorsing restraint in the face of diversity has characterized the thinking of those whose contributions to American public discourse I emphasized in the first section of this chapter. Jefferson and Madison differed on important issues, but they shared the commitment that manifested itself in the Virginia Statute for Religious Freedom. Their passion for the principles embodied in the founding documents, on the one hand, and for the separation of religion from politics, on the other, likewise animated Lincoln's condemnation of slavery as the denial of everything for which he and his nation claimed to stand. Although Lincoln understood the force of the arguments from expediency that had bolstered defenses of slavery, he responded in a vocabulary altogether different from that of the rational pursuit of self-interest. The language of the Enlightenment seemed to Lincoln inadequate to the task facing him: the consecration of great sacrifice for the sake not of material advantage but of universal principles. A faith such as Lincoln's, alert to the perils of expecting too much from politics, and perched between skepticism and fanaticism, is sturdy enough to survive the toxin of instrumental rationality.

The faith of William James was similarly immune to disenchantment. James perceived clearly what Charles Taylor has made the central theme of his brilliant *Sources of the Self*: all the choices that confront us in the modern era exact a price.[39] The conflict between the insistent demands of Enlightenment rationality and the persistent yearnings for a source of values beyond our subjectivity does not disappear simply because reason cannot yield answers to all our questions. Although an "irremediable flatness" appeared to James to be replacing "the rare old flavors" of life, he remained committed to the possibility that something lay beyond the thin and tasteless broth of modernity. As Taylor points out, the Enlightenment drew on the accumulated resources of the Judeo-Christian conception of *agape* to fund its commitments to autonomy, equality, and benevolence. As I have tried to indicate here, voices in the American tradition have sought to keep alive both the discourse of religion and the discourse of reason, and to keep them distinct, so that the conver-

[39]Charles Taylor, *Sources of the Self: The Making of the Modern Identity* (Cambridge, Mass.: Harvard University Press, 1989).

sation between them can continue, so that faith and knowledge can engage each other in spirited disagreement as well as forge the occasional fertile alliance. For individuals the "solid meaning of life is always the same eternal thing," James claimed, "the marriage, namely, of some unhabitual ideal, however special, with some fidelity, courage, and endurance; with some man's or woman's pains."[40]

For the public culture, however, collapsing the ideal into the everyday, or defining the everyday as the ideal, risks confusing our aspirations with our achievements. By identifying his democratic goal with the process of inquiry itself, Dewey sometimes slipped into that confusion; by advocating the fusion of religious and political commitments, or the erasure of religion to clear the field for secular rationality, contemporary critics run a similar risk. The cost of silencing the claims of reason can be enormous, as the most cursory glance at religious oppression indicates. But the cost of denying what Taylor calls "the deepest and most powerful spiritual aspirations that humans have conceived" may be even higher.[41] A better strategy can be derived from the experience of our tradition and the commitment to tolerance expressed in sermonic terms by Madison after he retired from the presidency:

> Ye States of America, which retain in your Constitutions or Codes, any aberration from the sacred principle of religious liberty, by giving to Caesar what belongs to God, or joining together what God has put asunder, hasten to revise and purify your systems, and make the example of your Country as pure and compleat, in what relates to the freedom of the mind and its allegiance to its maker, as in what belongs to the legitimate objects of political and civil institutions.[42]

The contributions of both reason and faith to American public life have been, and continue to be, as crucial as they are disconcerting to those who believe that one or the other of them threatens to undermine all that is precious. Yet both the insistence on tolerating religion and the insistence on restraining it are necessary for precisely the same reasons

---

[40]William James, "What Makes a Life Significant?" in *Talks to Teachers on Psychology and to Students on Some of Life's Ideals*, in James, *Writings 1878–1899*, ed. Gerald E. Myers (New York: Library of America, 1992), 878.
[41]Taylor, *Sources of the Self*, 520.
[42]The passage from Madison's "Detached Memoranda," originally published in the *William and Mary Quarterly*, 3d ser., 3 (1946): 555, is quoted in a thoughtful essay by Leo Pfeffer, "Madison's 'Detached Memoranda': Then and Now," in *The Virginia Statute for Religious Freedom: Its Evolution and Consequences in American History*, ed. Merrill D. Peterson and Robert C. Vaughan, Cambridge Studies in Religion and American Public Life (Cambridge: Cambridge University Press, 1988), 307.

they are painful.[43] Champions of religion and Enlightenment rationality should acknowledge that their cultural tradition has been shaped by the constant interaction of religious and secular passions and ideals. Skeptical rationalists should be chastened by the knowledge that reason itself is a blunt instrument, incapable of prying open the recesses of experience and aspiration. Fervent believers should remember the injunctions of Saint Paul and Saint Augustine concerning the folly of trying to leap the gulf dividing the city of man from the city of God. Both such a skepticism and such a faith, sensitive to the limits of human knowledge and to the inaccessibility of divine wisdom, are potentially compatible with the uncertainties of postfoundationalism. Whether these delicately balanced perspectives can still inspire action, or whether they can even survive in a culture impatient with the notion of finitude and quick to greet all yearnings with the promise of instant gratification, remains to be seen.

[43]The view of the relation between postfoundationalism, faith, and political action that I am suggesting thus differs in its insistence on circumspection from the views recommended in recent studies that are somewhat more optimistic than I am about the consequences of forging a strong union between religion and politics. See Glenn Tinder, *The Political Meaning of Christianity: An Interpretation* (Baton Rouge: Louisiana State University Press, 1989), and West, *The American Evasion of Philosophy*, 226–39. West recommends a "prophetic pragmatism" balanced "on the tightrope between Promethean romanticism and Augustinian pessimism," a position I consider attractive but precarious. Much as I admire West's ambitions in that book, I believe his enthusiasm for the potential of organic intellectuals such as those described by Antonio Gramsci needs to be tempered not only by the counsel of Augustine but also by the wisdom, if not the patience, of Job.

2

Enamored against thee by these strange minds:
Recovering the relations between religion and
the Enlightenment in nineteenth- and twentieth-
century American literary culture

GILES GUNN

We thank thee, Father, for these strange minds that enamor us against thee.
        Emily Dickinson, *The Letters of Emily Dickinson*

I feel along the edges of life for a way that leads to open land.
        David Ignatow, *The One in Many*

The story I wish to tell about religion and the Enlightenment in American literature of the last two centuries is a fairly familiar one, although it has never been told, so far as I know, from the point of view I wish to present. This is the point of view predominantly, but not exclusively, of the American Enlightenment, or at least of certain selective and extended emphases within it. Like all narratives, mine is a distortion, but a distortion created not to deform the truth so much as to try to divine a portion of it that has been obscured. While mine is not the perspective from which this story is usually told, the traditional perspective itself has been recently challenged by an important set of counternarratives constructed by feminist and African-American critics.

My own narrative reflects the ambivalence sedimented in both of my epigraphs, as well as the tension between them. Like the Dickinson passage, those thinkers who seek to challenge the religious legacy in America also testify to the power that once gave it life by virtue of the terms in which they cast their spiritual rebellion, as though in that act of resistance, to borrow some lines of Robert Frost, "regret were in it / And were sacred."[1] As in the passage from Ignatow, those persons released from love for the conventional source or sources of religious devotion who set off on their antinomian quests for a new life can only imagine it in terms of the limitations they must overcome, the boundaries they must cross, to find what is yet unbounded, limitless, free. There is, moreover, the tension between the retrospective, nostalgic echo of the first epigraph—who can fail to hear the note of remorse in Ahab's curses?—and the wariness of the prospective outlook of the second—who isn't afraid of the open independence of one's own sea? As John Berryman ruefully remarks for the pessimists in both camps, the American soul is divided, "headed both fore & aft and guess which soul will swamp & lose: / that hoping forward, brisk & vivid one / of which nothing will ever be heard again."

Of course, something always is heard of that other soul again because even its own darkness is double, paradoxical, mixed. So Henry can do no less than split the difference by urging an "Advance into the past!" Thus the poem ends where so many American journeys, like the narrative I shall try to tell, seem to begin: "Henry made lists of his surviving friends / & of the vanished on their uncanny errands / and took a deep breath."[2]

DIFFICULTIES IN DISTINGUISHING BETWEEN RELIGION AND THE ENLIGHTENMENT

Such a narrative must begin with the difficulty of beginning itself, or at least with beginning here. There are, in fact, two such difficulties. The first concerns the reference of the two constitutive terms of this inquiry, religion and the Enlightenment. Even if we confine religion to the basic tenets of American Protestantism in the first two centuries of colonial settlement and restrict our understanding of the Enlightenment to the core of epistemological, anthropological, and cosmological ideas shared by the founding fathers, there is considerable variation in the way such principles and axioms were interpreted by representative figures of each so-called camp.[3] For example, the theological affirmations of the Synod

---

[1]Robert Frost, *Collected Poems of Robert Frost* (New York: Henry Holt, 1936), 329.
[2]John Berryman, "Dream Song #29," *The Dream Songs* (New York: Farrar, Straus and Giroux, 1969), 33.
[3]There is, of course, considerable historical inaccuracy in so selective a procedure. Even if one grants the dominance of Protestantism in early American Christianity, Roman Catholicism was not an inconsequential presence in some of the colonies, and by the time

of Dort—unconditional election, limited atonement, total depravity, irresistible grace, and the perseverance of the saints—were by no means accepted by all Protestant Christians in the seventeenth and eighteenth centuries, any more than Voltaire's cynicism, David Hume's skepticism, or Dugald Stewart's Common Sense can be flattened out into a characterization of all members of the Enlightenment. Just as colonial Christians differed greatly over their views on everything from the nature of God, the ineradicability of sin, and the universality of redemption to the order of worship and the organization of the church, so the American Enlightenment, as Henry F. May has shown, was composed of at least four discriminable traditions that ranged in ethos and method from the moderation, rationality, and balance of figures such as John Locke, Isaac Newton, and Benjamin Franklin, through the skepticism and critique of Voltaire, Hume, and the Baron d'Holbach, to the utopian optimism and revolutionary millennialism that begins in Rousseau and continues through Thomas Jefferson, Thomas Paine, and William Godwin, to, finally, the didacticism of Scottish Common Sense philosophy associated with Thomas Reid and Dugald Stewart.[4]

In addition, it must be noted that the Enlightenment did not constitute itself as a historical movement in reaction to religion and thus by nature opposed to religion, but rather, as Crane Brinton was among the first to note, as itself an alternative to or substitute for religion.[5] Hence religion and reason, belief and doubt, faith and freedom are never opposed, or at least opposed as absolutes, in the writings of the founding fathers, but are opposed instead, particularly as one moves closer to the American Revolution, to what Jonathan Mayhew described as "Tyranny, PRIEST-CRAFT, and Nonsense."[6] This opposition should scarcely be surprising, because so much of the concern about liberty and democracy in the eighteenth century, as well as suspicions of authoritarianism, originated in debates about explicitly theological issues and were nourished

of the American Revolution Judaism had established a modest foothold in Rhode Island and South Carolina.

[4]Henry F. May, *The Enlightenment in America* (New York: Oxford University Press, 1976).

[5]See Crane Brinton, *Ideas and Men* (Englewood Cliffs, N.J.: Prentice-Hall, 1950), 369–408, and idem, *A History of Western Morals* (New York: Harcourt, Brace, 1959), 297–98, 306–7, 374–75, 450–79.

[6]Jonathan Mayhew, "A Discourse Concerning Unlimited Submission," in *Pamphlets of the American Revolution, 1750–1765,* ed. Bernard Bailyn (Cambridge, Mass.: Harvard University Press, 1965), 1:213.

by evangelical interests.[7] The founders came by their ability to mix secular and religious rhetoric in their writing naturally, and they exploited that ability for reasons other than political expediency. As in the changes the signers of the Declaration of Independence made to Jefferson's initial draft, the founders felt that they could not convey their theological sense of the cosmic significance of the events in which they were participating unless they added to the phrase about "the laws of nature and of nature's God" an appeal "to the supreme judge of the world for the rectitude of our intentions." One can try to discount this kind of appeal as merely the hegemonic effort of a dominant group to appropriate the theological language of its residual precursor, but as Robert A. Ferguson (whose reflections on these matters I have been following) has noted, the founders' need for such discourse was anything but disingenuous or simply calculating:

Irrespective of belief, the frame of mind within which the Founders operated has a vital religious component, and that component is richly connotative. "In God we trust" is more than just the motto of American republicanism; it points back in time to a central promise in the language of national creation.[8]

Nevertheless, there are important distinctions to be made between the spiritual legacy associated with the Protestant tradition of thought and feeling in America and that associated with the American Enlightenment. For purposes of this discussion, *religion* shall mean the disposition to view all human problems not traceable to natural accidents as reducible to the perfidiousness of human nature; to view the perfidiousness of human nature as unamenable to satisfactory redress by any agencies such as reason, will, or feeling intrinsic to human nature itself; and to view access to any agencies of empowerment transcendent to human nature as possible only through faith rather than works, including the efforts of the human mind to secure through analysis, criticism, or imaginative projection relief from such problems. By *the Enlightenment* I shall mean the disposition to view all human problems amenable to any kind of redress, whether they derive from human nature or not, as dependent for their relief on the human capacity to think about them crit-

---

[7]Alan Heimert, *Religion and the American Mind from the Great Awakening to the Revolution* (Cambridge, Mass.: Harvard University Press, 1966).
[8]Robert A. Ferguson, "We Hold These Truths," in *Reconstructing American Literary History*, ed. Sacvan Bercovitch (Cambridge, Mass.: Harvard University Press, 1986), 24.

ically and to critically validate the insights achieved by the intellect through appeal to human experience.[9]

These provisional definitions can carry with them—though not necessarily always—certain other associations: religion is often linked with belief in a sovereign God, dependence on a personal savior, the existence of original sin, the treachery of reason, the need for justification and absolution, the intercession of the sanctified, or the immortality of the soul; the Enlightenment is frequently related to convictions about historical progress, the beneficence of nature, the reliability of ordinary human understanding, the salience of criticism, the existence of inalienable rights, the virtues of free inquiry, and the pursuit of happiness. But the key to the difference between Protestant Christianity and the Enlightenment, as I am defining them here, is the question of whether relief of the human estate is dependent on powers that originate in, and derive their authority from, realms of experience beyond the boundaries of its own agencies and capacities or, rather, from realms of experience within them.[10]

[9]For this formulation of the innermost assumption of Enlightenment belief, I am indebted to remarks made by Schubert M. Ogden at the symposium "Knowledge and Belief in America," sponsored by the Woodrow Wilson Center for International Scholars at the Smithsonian Institution, 18–20 April 1990. This formulation also possesses a distant relation to Henry May's association of Enlightenment faith with all those who believe the following two propositions: "first, that the present age is more enlightened than the past; and second, that we understand nature and man best through the use of our natural faculties" (May, *The Enlightenment in America*, xiv).

[10]Of the two, the Enlightenment is probably the easier to define simply because the historical movement to which it refers, however various its expressions, was confined to a much smaller group of people who were far narrower in interests and enjoyed such dominion as they achieved for a decisively shorter period of time. Thinking of a collection of intellectuals that included Voltaire, Locke, Hume, Moses Mendelssohn, Montesquieu, Rousseau, Diderot, Turgot, Helvetius, Condorcet, Adam Smith, Jefferson, and Paine, Isaiah Berlin has provided perhaps the most satisfactory summary of the consensus that linked their diverse views in the following statement, which must be quoted in its entirety ("Joseph de Maistre and the Origins of Fascism," *New York Review of Books*, 27 September 1990, 60):

"But sharp as the genuine differences between these thinkers were, there were certain beliefs that they held in common. They believed in varying measure that men were, by nature, rational and sociable; or at least understood their own and others' best interests when they were not being bamboozled by knaves or misled by fools; that, if only they were taught to see them, they would follow the rules of conduct discoverable by the use of the ordinary human understanding; that there existed laws which govern nature, both animate and inanimate, and that these laws, whether empirically discoverable or not, were equally evident whether one looked within oneself or at the world outside. They believed that the discovery of such laws, and knowledge of them, if it were spread widely enough, would of itself tend to promote a stable harmony both between individuals and associations, and within the individual himself.

"Most of them believed in the maximum degree of individual freedom and the mini-

The second difficulty that attends the problem of beginning an inquiry into the relations between religion and the Enlightenment in nineteenth- and twentieth-century American literature has to do with the state of late twentieth-century scholarship. The problem can be put simply. While elements of religion and the Enlightenment have both exerted a measurable—in fact, significant—cultural pressure on the shape of literary life in the United States during the last two centuries, their mutual presence has not been equally assessed. Indeed, the pressures exerted by the Enlightenment, no less than a sense of the tension between Enlightenment and Protestant pressures, have grown more and more invisible, or at least opaque, to recent generations of literary historians. This phenomenon is the more surprising because traces of the passage of that tension beyond the confines of the eighteenth century are everywhere evident in subsequent American writing.

Evidence of those pressures and the tension between them can be seen readily, for example, in Edgar Allan Poe's vacillation between experiments with the associationist psychology of David Hartley in nature poems like "Tamerlane," or his more radical commitment to reason in such "tales of ratiocination" as "The Murders in the Rue Morgue," "A Descent into the Maelstrom," and "The Gold Bug," and the residual religious Gothicism of other tales like "The Fall of the House of Usher" or "The Cask of Amontillado" and poems such as "The Raven," "Ulalume," and "Annabel Lee." Traces of this tension between Enlightenment interests in reason, freedom, and individual fulfillment and Christian, really Protestant, commitments to faith, obedience, and self-renunciation are even more apparent in Nathaniel Hawthorne. So often and correctly acknowledged as our best historian of American Puritanism, Hawthorne

mum of government—at least after men had been suitably reeducated. They thought that education and legislation founded upon the 'precepts of nature' could right almost every wrong; that nature was but reason in action, and its workings therefore were in principle deducible from a set of ultimate truths like the theorems of geometry, and latterly of physics, chemistry, and biology.

"They believed that all good and desirable things were necessarily compatible, and some maintained more than this—that all true values were interconnected by a network of indestructible, logically interlocking relationships. The more empirically minded among them were sure that a science of human nature could be developed no less than a science of inanimate things, and that ethical and political questions, provided that they were genuine, could in principle be answered with no less certainty than those of mathematics and astronomy. A life founded upon these answers would be free, secure, happy, virtuous, and wise. In short they saw no reason why the millennium should not be reached by the use of faculties and the practice of methods that had for over a century, in the sphere of the sciences of nature, led to triumphs more magnificent than any hitherto attained in the history of human thought."

was also a child of the eighteenth century who, for all of his anguished misgivings about the rights and responsibilities of the detached observer, was incapable of subordinating his quasi-scientific interest in the psychological complexities of human nature to any residual religious scruples about their moral impropriety or experiential belatedness. Employing ethical and religious allegory in his best work only to suspend and often to deconstruct it, Hawthorne risked the "specular gaze," as we have come to call it, because in the last analysis he was as convinced as any of his Enlightenment forebears that the only way we could see at all was first by looking at the empirical facts of human behavior themselves intently, remorselessly—even if, in a reflex action deferential to his own conscience, he quickly added that the act of looking out and looking at required the ironic correction of an equally unforgiving look within.

In a different and less tortured form, this tension is also present in the writings of the "autocrat of the breakfast-table," Oliver Wendell Holmes. An early imitator of Laurence Sterne and a devoted scientist as well as distinguished physician, Holmes could be adamant in his opposition to the harshness of Calvinist doctrines such as predestination in *Elsie Venner*, and yet indulge in playful satire on the logic of Jonathan Edwards in "The Deacon's Masterpiece; or, The Wonderful 'One-Hoss Shay.' " Holmes's more characteristic stance is expressed in poems like "The Chambered Nautilus" and "The Secret of Stars," where science and faith are shown to be perfectly compatible, where religious and Enlightenment concerns can, like the lamb and lion of Revelations, lie down together.

This more irenic position sometimes found a corresponding resonance in the work of several of Holmes's other nearly forgotten contemporaries, such as Henry Wadsworth Longfellow and John Greenleaf Whittier, but it was not until after the Civil War that strong Enlightenment concerns, still colored by religious ideality but also chastened with a strong dose of Scottish Common Sense, found their way back into the center of literary culture and seemed to displace religion, or at least the religion of American Protestantism, altogether. The route back for the Enlightenment was mapped by a disparate group of writers that included the poet Edmund Clarence Stedman, novelist-editors like Thomas Bailey Aldrich and Charles Dudley Warner, and better-known figures such as William Dean Howells and even Henry James—men of letters who for all their diversity of talents and accomplishments helped create, in the second half of the nineteenth century, what Richard Brodhead has recently described as perhaps the closest thing the United States has ever achieved to "a coherent national literary culture."[11] Easily dismissed for its sometimes tepid spirituality, its latent didacticism, and its reliance, at least in writers like Howells, on Common Sense, the Genteel tradition not only gave new life to Enlightenment perspectives and postures but extended deep into the present century. Its descendants include the New Humanists of the 1920s, many of the Southern Agrarians and New Critics of the 1930s and 1940s, and even several of the more prominent cultural critics of the 1940s and 1950s who, like Edmund Wilson and Lionel Trilling, were deeply suspicious of the Genteel tradition's optimistic assessment of human nature but were no less indebted to some of the consistently emphasized Enlightenment values of balance, variousness, complexity, possibility, modulation, and mind.

Other major writers in the later nineteenth century, however, worked to one side of the Genteel tradition and expended much of their energy puncturing its pretensions. In these writers—particularly Mark Twain and Henry Adams—the dialogue between what still existed of the Calvinist roots of American religion and what remained of the Enlightenment origins of American skepticism left an indelible imprint on later nineteenth-century American literary culture. Think only of *The Adventures of Huckleberry Finn*, which reduced the posturings of a sentimentalized Calvinism to "soul butter and hogwash," or Mark Twain's most enigmatic novel, *Pudd'nhead Wilson*, in which he mounted a withering satire against the emergent religion of Jim Crowism through a defense of the empirical temper. All the more interesting, if not surprising, that in his last years the Calvinism that Mark Twain had earlier spurned in its specious versions of racist sentimentality and spiritual soporifics tended to turn against him by darkening his view of humanity and generating the quiet but corrosive bitterness of "The War Prayer" and *The Mysterious Stranger*.

In Adams, it could be said, the Enlightenment confronted its old Calvinist antagonist more directly than it had for an entire century. But it was a confrontation that took place not in the realm of ideas so much as in the medium of temperament, when a child of New England resistance—"the atmosphere of education in which he lived was colonial,

---

[11]Richard Brodhead, "Literature and Culture," in *The Columbia Literary History of the United States*, ed. Emory Elliott (New York: Columbia University Press, 1988), 472–73.

revolutionary, almost Cromwellian, as though he were steeped, from his greatest grandmother's birth, in the odor of political crime"—sought to measure the value of an eighteenth-century education for living in a nineteenth-century world.[12] *The Education of Henry Adams* is simultaneously one of the genuine masterworks of American literature and one of the few fully self-conscious assessments of the two moral, intellectual, and spiritual legacies that have shaped its past. In this, the *Education* not only sums up a century but also seeks to rescue a divided past, or at least to assess what has been irretrievably lost to it.

Mention of Adams's central achievement in the *Education* returns us again to the paradox with which we began: Why has the Enlightenment disappeared so quickly and, seemingly, so irretrievably from our modern calculus of the religious meanings of nineteenth- and twentieth-century literary culture? Why has the Enlightenment been so singularly effaced in modern literary historiography, even when critics and scholars have continued to employ distinctions that reflect the difference between the American religious heritage and the American Enlightenment heritage, distinctions between piety and rationalism, or enthusiasm and skepticism, or sense and sensibility, to structure their understanding of the past?

THE ERASURE OF THE ENLIGHTENMENT
IN MODERN LITERARY HISTORIOGRAPHY

Looming above all other reasons for this critical disjuncture has to be the primacy we have given to New England and to the experience of its seventeenth-century Protestant spokesmen in American literary history. Ever since the appearance in 1939 of the first volume of Perry Miller's *New England Mind*, American literary historians have maintained, often in the face of considerable counterevidence, that European colonization of America took most fateful root around Massachusetts Bay and that the most socially significant and intellectually articulate colonists spoke, thought, and felt almost exclusively in the language of a selective kind of Christian theology. Moreover, by the time Miller had published the second volume of *The New England Mind* in 1953 and complemented it in 1956 with the enormously influential collection of essays that made his view of this "errand into the wilderness" fully accessible to literary

---

[12]Henry Adams, *The Education of Henry Adams* (Boston: Houghton Mifflin, 1961), 7.

scholars, it had become possible to see how this significant immigration of peoples and ideas across the Atlantic had made its way not only spatially across the water but also temporally across the centuries.

Miller's case for the existence of Puritan continuities of experience capable of surviving the successive articulation of ideas for three centuries owed its credibility to the brilliant intellectual and cultural links that he forged between, say, "the marrow of Puritan Divinity," or the federal theology of the seventeenth century, and the eighteenth-century metaphysics of Jonathan Edwards, or between Jonathan Edwards's latter-day Puritanism and the nineteenth-century transcendentalism of Ralph Waldo Emerson, or between Emerson's conversion of America into the trope of "Nature's nation" and modern millennialist expectations exacerbated by the threat of nuclear apocalypse in the cold-war era.

Now it seems to matter little or not at all that critics have shown many of these associations to have been more rhetorical than historical, or that numerous later students of the period have found Miller's view of Puritanism, indeed his interpretation of the whole legacy of early American spirituality, to be highly intellectualistic and selective.[13] Seventeenth-century New England, and the theological precepts for which it became known, has continued to hold priority of place and exert hegemonic authority at every turn. Listen to the way Kenneth Murdock, one of American Puritanism's first great modern students and one of Miller's predecessors at Harvard University, dissmisses the Enlightenment, even as he truncates it, in his discussion of the "Puritan legacy" in his 1949 study, *Literature and Theology in Colonial New England*:

If . . . the phenomenon of religious experience is still real for some men; if there is a place for a faith transcending what unaided reason, logic, or science can supply; if there is still value in the prayer and worship which proceed from deep inward emotion, then scientific manuals, polite moral essays, and popular novels will not suffice. There will be need for more intellectually incisive and more

---

[13]Serious objections to the primacy Miller accords the mind and the role of cognition generally in Puritan spirituality begin with Alan Simpson's *Puritanism in Old and New England* (Chicago: University of Chicago Press, 1955) and continue to the present day in Andrew Delbanco's *The Puritan Ordeal* (Cambridge, Mass.: Harvard University Press, 1989). Important challenges to Miller's focus on New England in early American cultural settlement can be found in several studies, from Daniel J. Boorstin's *The Americans: The Colonial Experience* (New York: Random House, 1958) to Jack P. Greene, *Pursuits of Happiness: The Social Development of Early Modern British Colonies and the Formation of American Culture* (Chapel Hill: University of North Carolina Press, 1989), and David Hackett Fischer, *Albion's Seed: Four British Folkways in America* (New York: Oxford University Press, 1989).

emotionally effective expression of contemporary religious life; there will be need for some myth in which to symbolize and concretize its values.[14]

With its grand themes of creation, damnation, election, and sanctification, seventeenth-century American Protestantism clearly lent itself to the provision of such a myth "to symbolize and concretize its values" in a way that the Enlightenment's eighteenth-century preoccupation with rights, reasons, and rectitude never could. Just as important, the central tenets of early American religion were far more susceptible to demythologization than those of the American Enlightenment in terms consonant with the modernist-existentialist spirit of the immediate postwar age. To reduce Franklin's beliefs about a divine providence whose rule guarantees the immortality of the soul, and whose service is to be found in doing good to others, to any set of precepts or prescriptions more elemental than the terms in which they were expressed in Franklin's own prose was to risk caricaturing them as wholly prudential and self-serving, or as what Van Wyck Brooks and D. H. Lawrence called, respectively, "catchpenny realities" and moral machinery.[15] By contrast, Miller's identification of the whole of seventeenth-century religion with what he called the "Augustinian strain of piety" and his translation of that characterization into what he described as a subjective mood or frame of mind—that which in the first chapter of *The New England Mind* converted Puritan metaphysics into a prefiguration of romantic metaphysics and which in his intellectual biography of Jonathan Edwards made Puritanism sound instead like a metaphysical precursor of modernism—only succeeded in rendering Puritan spirituality more intellectually attractive rather than less in the postwar cultural climate. One could, of course, merely conclude that Puritanism has been better served than the Enlightenment by its modern interpreters, but this would be to gloss several other factors that have delimited our historical ability to perceive the Enlightenment's aftereffects in the last two centuries of literary expression.

One of these factors derives from the assessment literary and cultural historians have made about the different spiritual legacies that each of

[14]Kenneth Murdock, *Literature and Theology in Colonial New England* (New York: Harper and Row, 1949; 1963), 208.
[15]Van Wyck Brooks, *America's Coming-of-Age* (Garden City, N.Y.: Doubleday Anchor, 1958), 3, and D. H. Lawrence, *Studies in Classic American Literature* (Garden City, N.Y.: Doubleday Anchor, 1951), 26.

these traditions left to subsequent centuries. It is generally assumed, for example, that American Protestantism, at least in its Calvinist form, has left as its chief legacy in America something like an inherited penchant for self-criticism that is at its best capable of correcting even its own excesses. This assessment of the spiritual legacy of American Protestantism is often explained by reference to Herman Melville's famous review of Hawthorne's *Mosses from an Old Manse*, where Melville attributes the force of Hawthorne's appeal to "a blackness, ten times black" that shrouds, or at least casts into deep shadow, the "Indian-summer sunlight" of Hawthorne's historical romances. Melville is not prepared to say whether Hawthorne has availed himself of this "mystic blackness" merely to secure his marvelous chiaroscuro effects or is really afflicted with a "touch of Puritanic gloom," but he is convinced that the power of this blackness in Hawthorne ultimately derives from its reference to an intuition that no deeply feeling, thoughtful person who attempts to "weigh this world" and "strike an uneven balance" can for long do without. This is an intuition of "something, somehow" like "that Calvinistic sense of Innate Depravity and Original Sin, from whose visitations, in some shape or other, no deeply thinking mind is always and wholly free."[16]

Melville's emphasis on the indefinite pronouns—"something, somehow"—is what makes all the difference in the way this statement has offered itself to later generations. Although it permits him to appropriate a sense of evil as a principle of moral and spiritual correction, it enables him at the same time to dissociate this sense from the necessity of any conscious assent to the theological doctrine in which it was first expressed. The cultural utility of the principle continues to engender respect for the tradition which generated it without requiring that anyone believe in the specific tenets of that tradition itself. Thus Melville and his cultural heirs can remain, and have remained, Puritans in spirit while spurning Puritanism as dogma.

By comparison, the cultural heirs of the Enlightenment have not been similarly favored. To embrace the Enlightenment in almost any form during the postwar period has been tantamount to affirming virtually all of the liberal republican ideals, from freedom, autonomy, individualism, and rationalism to the self-reliance, democracy, and free-market

---

[16]Herman Melville, "Hawthorne and His Mosses," in *Moby-Dick*, ed. Harrison Hayford (New York: Norton, 1967), 540.

capitalism from which they have been thought to issue. But to affirm as diverse, vague, and potentially conflicting a set of ideals as these has been to advocate something much like what America's editorial pundits, no less than historical scholars on the extreme Right and Left, take to be America's official ideological version of itself. Thus where the Calvinist legacy has frequently been interpreted as the intellectual and spiritual source of whatever real cultural criticism has been produced in America, the Enlightenment legacy has as readily been dismissed as the moral and philosophical source of American cultural consensus and complacency.

Yet another factor contributing to the increasing opaqueness of the Enlightenment in twentieth-century literary scholarship is the fairly widespread conviction that its chief aesthetic assumptions exerted an influence on subsequent literary practice in the United States that was essentially negative. Their influence is held to have been basically negative because it is still supposed generally that they derived from those Scottish Common Sense philosophers who restricted the creative arts, and particularly the writing of fiction, to the provision of moral exempla.[17] As the story goes, the effect of such strictures was to compel gifted young antebellum writers like Hawthorne and William Gilmore Simms to abandon the writing of novels altogether in favor of creating an alternative fictive form in reaction to the restraints of eighteenth-century Common Sense. This fictive form is known as the romance and came in time to be defined as a kind of counteraesthetic to the Enlightenment. This development would have made little difference, however, if the romance had not in turn, after World War II, come to be regarded as the only authentic fictive form in America. The key text was no doubt Richard Chase's *The American Novel and Its Tradition*, published in 1957, but it was supported by countless other studies that not only defined the romance aesthetically as a form antagonistic to the Enlightenment but also helped transform postwar nineteenth- and twentieth-century literary history into an outright repudiation of Enlightenment values.[18]

---

[17]Terrence Martin, *The Instructed Vision: Scottish Common Sense Philosophy and the Origins of American Fiction* (Bloomington: Indiana University Press, 1961), 60–76.

[18]Richard Chase, *The American Novel and Its Tradition* (Garden City, N.Y.: Doubleday Anchor, 1957). This trend has beginnings as early as F. O. Matthiessen's *American Renaissance: Art and Expression in the Age of Emerson and Whitman* (New York: Oxford University Press, 1941) and its persistence can be seen even in works that problematize the understanding of the form, such as Michael Davitt Bell's *The Development of American Romance* (Chicago: University of Chicago Press, 1980), or that seemingly address

Finally, there is the historical prescience of the Enlightenment's last great representative in the nineteenth century and the accuracy of his diagnosis about the ways experience was to change in the twentieth. I am referring once more to Henry Adams and to the book he pointedly did not wish to refer to as his autobiography, where the reader is forced to contemplate something far more shattering than the discovery that an eighteenth-century education, however painstakingly acquired and brilliantly adapted, no longer prepares a person to live a life of useful and productive service in the nineteenth century. What breaks Adams's historical neck at the Great Exposition of 1900 in Paris as he looks up at the forty-foot dynamos in the Gallery of Machines is the discovery of an "irruption of forces totally new" that plunges him into what one of his later chapters calls an "abyss of ignorance." What was once a carefully ordered universe has become a haphazard and chaotic multiverse, and when Adams tries to imagine what kind of new education would suit this New World, he is confounded:

He found himself in a land where no one had ever penetrated before; where order was an accidental relation obnoxious to nature; artificial compulsion imposed on motion; against which every free energy of the universe revolted; and which, being merely occasional, resolved itself back into anarchy at last. He could not deny that the law of the new multiverse explained much that had been most obscure, especially the persistently fiendish treatment of man by man; the perpetual effort of society to establish law, and the perpetual revolt of society against the law it had established; the perpetual building up of authority by force, and the perpetual appeal to force to overthrow it; the perpetual symbolism of a higher law, and the perpetual relapse to a lower one; the perpetual victory of the principles of freedom, and their perpetual conversion into principles of power; but the staggering problem was the outlook ahead into the despotism of artificial order which nature abhorred. The physicists had a phrase for it, unintelligible to the vulgar: "All that we win is a battle—lost in advance—with the irreversible phenomena in the background of nature."[19]

The problem for Adams was not simply that the constellation of physical energies had changed, or that a new grammar of motives had been introduced; the real rupture had occurred in the idiom of experience itself and the kinds of moral and spiritual calculus required to measure its consequences. In scientific parlance, this amounted to a paradigm change or, in critical terms, a revolution in metaphor. For Adams the

different traditions, such as Eric J. Sundquist's "The Country of the Blue," in *American Realism*, ed. Eric J. Sundquist (Baltimore: Johns Hopkins University Press, 1982), 3–24.
[19]Adams, *The Education*, 457–58.

question of what to call it was less disturbing than the issue of what to make of it. The only analogue he could imagine to the cataclysmic changes foreshadowed in 1900 was the year 310, when Emperor Constantine began to establish Christianity as the official religion of the Roman Empire. For Adams, then, all the intellectual and ethical coordinates were rendered impotent after 1900, and Alfred Kazin has argued that much of American writing since has been an attempt to register the experiential meanings of this change Adams was the first to describe and to devise strategies for coming to terms with it.[20]

Theodore Dreiser provides one of the most powerful representations of this newly reconfigured world in his sympathetic portrayal of Clyde Griffiths as a "wisp in the wind of social forces" in *An American Tragedy*; F. Scott Fitzgerald offers another in his depiction of the pulverization of James Gatz at the hands of Tom Buchanan's brutal power and Daisy Fay's cruel indifference in *The Great Gatsby*. Force, power, and energy are also the essential metaphors of Ernest Hemingway's experiments with the short story in *In Our Time*, and they figure as elements only intermittently suppressible—and then often with disastrous and not fully comprehended consequences—in Willa Cather's novels of the Nebraska prairies. Power becomes the explosive feature that must be prevented from turning suicidal, or at least self-hating, in confessional poets such as Robert Lowell, Sylvia Plath, and Anne Sexton; in the writings of African Americans like Ralph Ellison and James Baldwin and of women generally, power constitutes the factor whose social and political transvaluation is the only antidote to its racist and sexist misuse; and it is synonymous with the component that is running down in Thomas Pynchon's fantasies of entelechy.

A world so completely organized around and dominated by power, by sheer potency, is a world no longer susceptible to understanding in terms of such Enlightenment values as modulation, balance, common sense, reasonableness, freedom, skepticism, happiness, autonomy, and optimism. It is a world comprehensible only in terms of religious myths of catastrophe, of metaphysical narratives of rupture, division, and disinheritance. As a consequence, the Enlightenment has become the absent, or at least the forgotten, integer in the American equation of the relationship between faith and knowledge. For example, there is no chapter either on the Enlightenment or on the legacy of Enlightenment thinking

[20]Alfred Kazin, *American Procession* (New York: Knopf, 1984).

and feeling in the new *Columbia Literary History of the United States.* There is not even a single entry on the Enlightenment in any of the five editions of the *Oxford Companion to American Literature.* In comparison with the astonishing number of major monographs that explore the religious dimensions of nineteenth- and twentieth-century American literature, one is pressed to come up with a single text, other than fugitive remarks sprinkled through Howard Mumford Jones's *O Strange New World* and his *Belief and Disbelief in American Literature,* that does the same thing for the Enlightenment and American writing.[21]

The one recent exception, surely, is the criticism of Lewis Simpson, and particularly his *Brazen Face of History,* where it is argued that American literature has been obsessed (as William Ellery Channing predicted it would be in his 1831 "Remarks on a National Literature") with "the perfectibility of mind in America," though in a decidedly negative way; "Its force (as [John] Adams may be said to have forecast) is to be estimated in terms of the ironic challenging of it in our letters rather than its literary affirmation."[22] Thus the characters who have their origination in the mind but then experience the mind's inability to gain dominion over nature and history—the list begins, according to Simpson, with Cooper's Leatherstocking and passes on to Poe's Roderick Usher, Hawthorne's Robin Molineux, Melville's Ishmael, Mark Twain's Huckleberry Finn, Hemingway's Jake Barnes, Fitzgerald's Jay Gatsby, Faulkner's Quentin Compson III, and Robert Penn Warren's Jack Bur-

[21]Emory Elliot, ed. *Columbia Literary History of the United States,* (New York: Columbia University Press, 1988); James David Hart, ed. *Oxford Companion to American Literature* (New York: Oxford University Press, 1965; rev. and enl. 1983); Howard Mumford Jones, *O Strange New World: American Culture, The Formative Years* (New York: Viking Press, 1964; and Westport, Conn.: Greenwood Press, 1982); and idem, *Belief and Disbelief in American Literature* (Chicago: University of Chicago Press, 1967). Some of the most obvious examples of books in the postwar period discussing the religious aspects of American literature would include F. O. Matthiessen, *American Renaissance*; Charles Feidelson, *Symbolism and American Literature* (Chicago: University of Chicago Press, 1953); Chase, *The American Novel and Its Tradition*; R.W.B. Lewis, *The American Adam: Innocence, Tragedy, and Tradition in the Nineteenth Century* (Chicago: University of Chicago Press, 1955); Roy Harvey Pearce, *The Continuity of American Poetry* (Princeton: Princeton University Press, 1962); Leslie Fiedler, *Love and Death in the American Novel* (New York: Dell, 1960); John F. Lynen, *The Design of the Present* (Princeton: Princeton University Press, 1969); Sacvan Bercovitch, *The American Jeremiad* (Madison: University of Wisconsin Press, 1979); David S. Reynolds, *Beneath the American Renaissance: The Subversive Imagination in the Age of Emerson and Melville* (New York: Knopf, 1988); and, most recently, the last chapter of Andrew Delbanco's *The Puritan Ordeal.*

[22]Lewis Simpson, *The Brazen Face of History: Studies in the Literary Consciousness in America* (Baton Rouge: Louisiana State University Press, 1980), 55.

den—all attest to the literary questioning of the Enlightenment para-
digm. Otherwise Puritanism, or at least Calvinism, has carried the day,
managing to be connected by historians and critics to an enormous com-
pany of American writers that include Franklin, Emerson, Thoreau,
Theodore Parker, Francis Parkman, Frederick Douglass, Hawthorne,
Melville, Emily Dickinson, Jones Very, the later Mark Twain, Henry
James, Henry Adams, Edwin Arlington Robinson, Wendell Phillips,
Vachel Lindsay, Paul Elmer More, Irving Babbitt, Robert Frost, Ernest
Hemingway, T. S. Eliot, Marianne Moore, Wallace Stevens, William
Faulkner, Katherine Anne Porter, Robert Penn Warren, James Baldwin,
Robert Lowell, James Agee, Flannery O'Connor, and various others.

THE TRADITIONAL MALE NARRATIVE

Thus it should be hardly surprising that the traditional modern way of
telling the story about post-Enlightenment American literature is to leave
the Enlightenment pretty well out of it and to treat religion as an attribute of the imagination and an aspect of form. Religion becomes associated with a quality of mind obsessed with moral oppositions and
suspicious of thematic closure, indeed, skeptical of all metanarratives—
a mind that characteristically tends to explore extreme ranges of experience and to rest in dichotomous, even conflicting or contradictory,
frames of thought. Far from seeking through Christian strategies of redemptive catharsis to reconcile division and dissonance, the American
literary imagination, male and female, so this narrative goes, has concentrated its most important energies on exploring the aesthetic and even
religious possibility of forms of alienation and disorder, often in morally
equivocal ways.[23] Hence even in a standard work like *The Scarlet Letter*,
where transgression and repentance, autonomy and submission, and
freedom and servitude constitute the principal poles between which
much of the action oscillates, the novel resists all impulses toward intellectual or spiritual resolution by terminating, finally, in an image of
tragic separation. Hester and Dimmesdale both remain true, but their
fidelity merely succeeds in condemning them to opposite or, at the very
least, to apposite ways of being.

  The customary way of reading the religious meaning of nineteenth-
and twentieth-century literature has consequently gone something like

[23]Chase, *The American Novel and Its Tradition*, 11.

this. If the representative American literary imagination displays characteristics that are undeniably Manichaean, these internal divisions have not resulted from its absorption with the predicament of human iniquity and its transcendence, or with the problem of sexual domination and its displacement. They have derived instead from writers' preoccupation with the problem of human freedom and the impediments to its realization. When this preoccupation has taken narrative form, it has typically produced narratives that diverge sharply from the traditional pattern of the Protestant story about repentance and possible regeneration through faith, even when they use many of its presiding symbols, for the sake of telling a tale about the limitations of selfhood and their heuristic value. This is a narrative, then, that turns on a dialectic that makes only the faintest bow backward in the direction of the Enlightenment's ideology of mediated freedom before attempting to reconcile a later romantic quest for unmediated being with the residue of an earlier Puritan, or at any rate Protestant, sense of human impotence and the need for self-abasement.

Tony Tanner captured the religious essence of this story about as well as anyone else by noting that it is predicated on "an abiding dream . . . that an unpatterned, unconditioned life is possible in which your moments of stillness, choices and repudiations are all your own."[24] This is what, for example, Isabel Archer seems to express when in *The Portrait of a Lady* she confesses that "nothing that belongs to me is any measure of me, everything, on the contrary, is a limit and a perfectly arbitrary one."[25] It is the same conviction that in Faulkner's *Absalom, Absalom!* solidifies Thomas Sutpen's desire to wrest a house and a dynasty from a hundred square miles of Mississippi wilderness, as though, like the central figures in *The Great Gatsby* or "Song of Myself," he was born of some Platonic conception in his own mind. It is the dream of an individual who, like Captain Ahab in *Moby-Dick*, would be "free as the air" but discovers that "he is down in all the world's books."[26]

The corollary to this romantic dream amounts to a correspondent and not un-Calvinist dread, to quote Tanner again, "that someone else is patterning your life, that there are all sorts of invisible plots afoot to rob you of your autonomy of thought and action, that conditioning is ubiq-

[24]Tony Tanner, *City of Words* (New York: Harper and Row, 1971), 15.
[25]Henry James, *The Portrait of a Lady*, ed. Robert D. Bamburg (New York: Norton, 1975), 175.
[26]Herman Melville, *Moby-Dick*, 392.

uitous."[27] Thus Hawthorne again, in Chillingworth's self-excusing confession to Hester: "My old faith, long forgotten, comes back to me, and explains all that we do and all that we suffer. By thy first step awry, thou didst plant the germ of evil; but, since that moment, it has all been a dark necessity."[28] Or the narrator in Faulkner's *Light in August*, who tends to view Joe Christmas and Percy Grimm as pawns on a chessboard drawn ever closer to their fated confrontation by an invisible Player.

The traditional American strategy for dealing with this situation and narratively encompassing it is to submit the dreamer to the dread to determine what, if anything, he or she can learn from the experience. But because this experiment in what might be called liberal self-revisioning usually takes place in idyllic natural surroundings set at some distance from the world of women and children, and in the company of social others whose moral and spiritual attributes simply mirror the values their protagonists long to acquire even when they can nowhere be seriously applied, it has been criticized as dangerously antinomian and imperialistic by some critics and characterized as a "melodrama of beset manhood" by others.[29]

THE FEMINIST COUNTERNARRATIVE

In any event, we now know that this way of constructing and reading the story of nineteenth- and twentieth-century American literature and its relation to religion, and particularly to Protestant Christianity, is not quite accurate, or at least does not comprise the whole story. Owing largely to the work of feminist critics, we know, for example, that Protestant orthodoxy of a certain kind has played a much more active role in the formation of some post-Enlightenment literature than was formerly acknowledged, and that within this literature it has proved as vital a force for cultural criticism and renewal as the revisionary liberalism associated with many of the writers of the so-called male canon. Interestingly enough, the reinstatement of Protestant religious orthodoxy in this feminist counternarrative to the canonical story has been secured

---

[27]Tanner, *City of Words*, 15.
[28]Nathaniel Hawthorne, *The Scarlet Letter*.
[29]For an example of the first characterization, see Quentin Anderson, *The Imperial Self* (New York: Knopf, 1971); for an example of the second, see Nina Baym, "Melodramas of Beset Manhood: How Theories of American Fiction Exclude Women Authors," in *The New Feminist Criticism*, ed. Elaine Showalter (New York: Pantheon, 1985), 63–80.

only at the expense of more or less completely discrediting the Enlightenment altogether.

The feminist counternarrative construes the Enlightenment—especially its stereotypical attitudes toward reason, nature, gender, liberty, and the realm of the personal and the intimate—as expressions of a patriarchal structure characteristic of much revolutionary and post-revolutionary society that had to be challenged, and in considerable measure displaced, if women were to be empowered to assume something like a position of equality within the economy of human affairs. The instrument of their empowerment in this counternarrative turns out to be the religion of early nineteenth-century Protestantism, once its redemptive energies were released in the evangelical enthusiasm of the Second Great Awakening. These energies helped legitimate a new sentimentalization of American piety that resituated the institutions of the family at the center of American society and redefined motherhood and the rituals of homemaking and child-rearing as central mysteries in a new feminist, almost Eleusinian, cult of domesticity.

A story told most vividly in the writings of critics like Jane Tompkins and Cathy N. Davidson, it finds abundant exemplification in the antebellum soteriology of sentimental novels ranging from Susanna Rowson's *Charlotte Temple*, Hannah Foster's *The Coquette*, and Catherine Sedgwick's *Hope Leslie* to Susan Warner's *The Wide, Wide World*, and it achieves a kind of consummation in Harriet Beecher Stowe's *Uncle Tom's Cabin*.[30] Here Christian self-sacrifice—Little Eva's no less than Uncle Tom's—performs, at least for women, an invaluable kind of cultural work whose subtly dialectical patterns of critique and recovery, of repudiation and resurrection, can be traced even more easily in such later works as Elizabeth Stoddard's *The Morgesons*, Kate Chopin's *The Awakening*, and Sarah Orne Jewett's *The Country of the Pointed Firs*. As feminists point out, this is a literature that explicitly in some cases, implicitly in others, questions the prevailing image of culture as dominated by upper-class white males who use the instruments of rationality, moderation, common sense, and civic virtue to consolidate their power

---

[30]Jane Tompkins, *Sensational Designs* (New York: Oxford University Press, 1985), and Cathy N. Davidson, *Revolution and the Word* (New York: Oxford University Press, 1986). A related but somewhat different narrative emerges from the study Tania Modleski has made of models of feminist self-description and ideological resistance offered by popular art forms such as gothic novels, Harlequin romances, and daytime soap operas in *Loving with a Vengeance: Mass-produced Fantasies for Women* (New York: Methuen, 1982).

over women. This literature seeks to replace it with a more sentimental, or at least less agentic, image of culture as a kind of family held together by the sacrificial action of females whose heroic submission to the pro- creative and nurturing responsibilities of the household can, and should, be interpreted as a symbol of strength rather than of weakness—a sym- bol with the power to transform the family into a source of moral and spiritual rebirth for society as a whole.

According to some feminists, however, this feminist counternarrative never quite manages to escape the pull of the masculine, and thus En- lightenment, values that it would repudiate. Even if the piety of a Little Eva eludes Ann Douglass's charge that Christianity in *Uncle Tom's Cabin*, like religion in the sentimental novel generally, runs the risk of functioning for its readers as "camp," as a form of narcissistic nostalgia, the counternarrative itself never succeeds, as Elizabeth Fox-Genovese has recently pointed out, in freeing women from the culture of men. By politicizing the culture of sentimentality, the feminist counternarrative, like the fiction that illustrates it, merely reinscribes the values of white, male, elite individuality, and the ideology of dominance it supports, in the religious sensibility of women.

This becomes clear, Fox-Genovese maintains, when one compares the writings of women in the Northeast with those from the South. As it turns out, in the South many female writers, both African American and white, were made as uncomfortable by prevailing models of woman- hood—particularly if those models sought to resegregate women in a gendered ghetto of religious sensibility isolated from the world of men— as they were by the images that men were trying to impose on them. No less assiduous than their Northern counterparts in exploring their own identity and independence, these Southern writers nonetheless were just as emphatically opposed to "the northeastern model of individual- ism"—Augusta Jane Evans's spectacularly popular *Beulah* is the exam- ple Fox-Genovese invokes—"and celebrated woman's acceptance of her proper role within marriage and, above all, her willing subordination to God who guaranteed any worthy social order."[31] Thus if empowerment is what many Southern women sought, they did not find it either by dissociating themselves from the world of men or by repudiating the dominant culture men had created to maintain, through religious and

---

[31]Elizabeth Fox-Genovese, "American Culture and New Literary Studies," *American Quarterly* 42 (March 1990): 21.

secular values, their control over women. Rather, they achieved it by using that cultural world for their own purposes:

> Women and African-Americans, including African-American women, have developed their own ways of criticizing the attitudes and institutions that hedged them in. Confronted with rigidly class-, race-, and gender-specific models of acceptability, they have manipulated the language to speak in a double tongue, simultaneously associating themselves with and distancing themselves from the dominant models of respectability. Their continuous negotiation with the possibilities that the culture has afforded them has had nothing to do with a mindless acceptance of themselves as lesser. It has had everything to do with their determination to translate the traditions and values of their own communities into a language that would make them visible to others—and with their own determination to participate in American culture.[32]

I contend that one of the reasons why women of all colors, north and south (to say nothing of many men), may have been unable to find, in either the feminist narratives of the Northeast and the South or the traditional male narrative, a language into which "to translate the traditions and values of their own communities" so that they might become "visible to others" is because both of those narratives, at least as they have been historically reconstructed, may have misconstrued the literary relations between colonial American religion and the American Enlightenment. More particularly, the narratives may have misconceived or underestimated what was achieved as a consequence. This is a large claim that I cannot hope to support with sufficient detail here; all I can do for the present is sketch some of its main elements and hope that its further refinements and necessary extensions can be inferred by the discerning reader.

REINSCRIBING ASPECTS OF THE ENLIGHTENMENT

In this revisionist narrative, which is in truth less interested in countering its feminist and male canonical competitors than in complementing them, the Enlightenment is accorded an importance rather different from contemporary estimates. The contemporary estimate is the one furnished by Henry F. May, which assumes that the Enlightenment's largest impact on the formation of post-Enlightenment literary and intellectual culture in the United States derived from those traditions that emphasized moderation and common sense, what May calls the rational and

[32]Ibid., 22.

didactic Enlightenments, and exercised the slightest influence through those traditions that were utopian and critical, namely, the revolutionary and especially the skeptical Enlightenments. Indeed, May is convinced that the tradition of the village atheist, which descends from Voltaire and Diderot and runs in America from Abner Kneeland to Clarence Darrow, has never led more than a minor and distinctly paradoxical existence in this country, because religious iconoclasm here has rarely amounted to a questioning of all moral values, and the deeper skepticism associated with Hume that is prepared to doubt the operations of all minds "and the validity of all general principles" found, until recently, no fertile soil in America.[33]

In the narrative I propose, the relative contribution of these several strains needs to be reversed almost exactly. The Enlightenments that seem to have played the most influential role in shaping American literature in the modern age were the revolutionary and, particularly, the skeptical Enlightenments, and they did so often by combining forces to challenge, and eventually to undermine, the very foundations of Protestant thinking in much nineteenth-century literature. Thus skepticism of the Human variety, which puts all mental operations in doubt, has erupted intermittently but recurrently throughout nineteenth- and twentieth-century American writing and can be found in works ranging from *The Narrative of Arthur Gordon Pym* and *Pierre* to Quentin Compson's anguished meditations in *Absalom, Absalom!* and the torments of many of John Berryman's Henry poems. The trope of the village atheist was given a new cynical twist in the nineteenth-century emergence of the figure of the confidence man, a figure first anticipated by some of the stratagems Benjamin Franklin reports adopting as a young man in his *Autobiography*; then memorialized in Melville's novel by that title; later given feminine coloration in some of Emily Dickinson's poems on God's duplicity; carried forward in that admonitory strain of Robert Frost's poetry that includes "Design," "Fire and Ice," and "Provide, Provide"; rendered comical, corrosive, or both in Wallace Stevens's "Emperor of Ice-Cream" and "A Hightoned Old Christian Woman"; and eventually pushed to brilliant extreme in Ralph Ellison's portrait of Rinehart the Runner in *Invisible Man*. Furthermore, these currents of religious skepticism, as David S. Reynolds has shown in reference to the writers of the American Renaissance, have always been fed

[33]May, *The Enlightenment in America*, 360.

by a vast underground literature that is by turns witty, derisive, caustic, iconoclastic, subversive, and parodistic.[34]

Another way of saying this would be to suggest that some of the most important work of the skeptical or critical Enlightenment in France and England, if not the revolutionary Enlightenment as well, was not accomplished in the eighteenth century but, rather, in the nineteenth, and not on the European side of the Atlantic but on the American side. That work proceeded, at least from a literary perspective, toward the dismantling of virtually all of the religious assumptions on which American literary culture was then based. At the beginning of the century it was assumed that the chief representational function of literary art was to legitimate a world centered on God and illustrative of his purposes particularly as they were revealed in the orderly processes of Nature and as they were worked out in the unfolding salvific pattern of History. This theory of representation is perfectly exemplified in the "prospect" or "rising glory" poems of the misnamed Connecticut Wits, where in texts like *The Rising Glory of America, The Conquest of Canaan, Greenfield Hill,* and *The Columbiad,* poets such as Philip Freneau, Timothy Dwight, and Joel Barlow envisaged a redemptive future for the United States whose symbolic outlines were to become even more familiar much later in such concepts as the Monroe Doctrine and manifest destiny.[35] By the end of the century, it would be fair to say that in critical terms the only residue of this theory was a belief in the importance of representation itself and in the perceptual instrumentalities that made it possible. Those instrumentalities amounted to what was variously meant by the term *consciousness,* now understood as meaning not an entity so much as a function, and in turn held to be accountable for representing little more than the processes and perspectives that made it up.

FORESHADOWING THE PRAGMATIST TURN

This story is one version of what I have been calling the pragmatist narrative, and virtually the whole of it is proleptically present in what is generally conceded to be America's greatest epic, Herman Melville's *Moby-Dick.* Often interpreted as a representation of the nineteenth cen-

---

[34]Reynolds, *Beneath the American Renaissance.*
[35]An excellent discussion of the cultural metaphysics of this tradition can be found in John McWilliams, "Poetry in the Early Republic," in Elliott et al., *Columbia Literary History of the United States,* 156–67.

tury's absorption with the issue of deicide, *Moby-Dick* has too rarely been read as also a prefiguration of the kind of pragmatic consciousness that was, in the later nineteenth and subsequently the twentieth century, to take its place. Moreover, *Moby-Dick* is a work whose rootage, through much of the text devoted to Ahab's concerns, in the theological world of seventeenth-century Puritan metaphysics is nicely balanced by its structural reliance, during many of the stretches when Ishmael's voice becomes ascendant, on the literary form that was so often reappropriated in the intellectualized, ironic, satiric world of the eighteenth century, the form known as the anatomy.[36]

From a pragmatist's point of view, the problems that afflict Ahab are those of a latter-day Puritan who inherits a system of belief that can no longer answer or evade the questions he puts to it but who cannot escape the tyranny of the system itself. Ahab is the last, fullest, and most perverse flowering of the high Calvinist tradition in America, a tradition that now, in its death throes and in the name of Christian values that Ahab himself constantly transgresses, turns against itself by calling God himself to account. When God fails to listen, or from the text's perspective seems indifferent, the tradition then destroys itself in a maddened act of self-immolation.

This is not, of course, how Ahab experiences his own predicament. Ahab's experience is defined by his desire to determine what lies behind the pasteboard mask of appearance that has been shoved so brutally in his face. This desire is endlessly frustrated, for the mask turns out to be impenetrable, and its nearness only compounds the outrage. "That inscrutable thing is chiefly what I hate," says Ahab, indicating, Charles Feidelson long ago remarked, "the ambiguity of the meanings that lure him on and the resistance that objects present to the inquiring mind."[37] The only way Ahab can end his torture is by terminating his voyage in quest of truth, and so he settles for only one definition, or set of definitions, of the pasteboard mask and then hurls himself, all mutilated and mutilating, against it.

Ishmael's predicament seems to be the very opposite of Ahab's, or eventually becomes so. Initially daunted by the indefiniteness of the novel's quest for the mystery that lies behind the pasteboard mask—an indefiniteness Ishmael recurrently experiences in the earlier parts of the

---

[36]See Giles Gunn, *The Interpretation of Otherness: Literature, Religion and the American Imagination* (New York: Oxford University Press, 1979), 161–74.
[37]Melville, *Moby-Dick*, 144, and Feidelson, *Symbolism and American Literature*, 34.

book as the ultimate horror of a world that constantly blurs all distinctions in an insubstantial medium that seems, as he notes in "The Whiteness of the Whale," purposefully deceptive—Ishmael gradually becomes himself the vehicle through which we discover a world whose insubstantiality is but the reverse side of its fluidity and procreativity and diversity. Such a world can be comprehended only by a frame of mind that is the opposite of Ahab's. If Ahab's mind, outraged by a world that defies its quest for certainty, traffics in signs, equivalences, and linked analogies that are supposed to represent the things that they are, Ishmael's mind, undismayed as it finally becomes by the multitudinous expressivity of the world's plurality, trades in images, metaphors, and symbols that acknowledge the surplus of meanings that language carries within itself when it is used tropologically rather than allegorically.

The book's major movement is the transition from Ahab's mind to Ishmael's, from the "old consciousness," in D. H. Lawrence's terminology, that Ishmael initially shares with Ahab and that must be sloughed off, to the "new consciousness" that is forming underneath. The outmoded consciousness that we identify with Ahab and that Ishmael shares with him at the beginning is a theocentric, monologistic, and moralistic consciousness predicated on the possibility of dividing up the principalities and powers that comprise experience into opposing elements of divine and demonic, good and evil, love and hate, life and death, male and female. The new consciousness that begins to emerge underneath in the polyphonous, polymorphous discourse of Ishmael's narrative views these traditional oppositions as "interweavingly" intermixed in experience and responds by adopting an attitude that is tentative, experimental, provisional, improvisatory, eclectic, synoptic, changeable, and even contradictory.[38]

This consciousness is in many parts of the book no more than a matter of style, of an idiom as various and fluid as the circumstances of experience itself, but it is not too much to say that its creation and elaboration eventually becomes, as Daniel Hoffman was among the first to realize, the book's real spiritual destination.[39] That consciousness is identical with the style of Ishmael's buoyant, metaphoric voice as he records his "doubts of all things earthly" and his "intuitions of some things

[38]Much of my own interpretation of the book is indebted to Tony Tanner's introduction to *Moby-Dick* (Oxford: Oxford University Press, 1988), vii–xxviii.
[39]Daniel Hoffman, *Form and Fable in American Fiction* (New York: Oxford University Press, 1965), 233–78.

heavenly," while at the same time "knowing this combination makes neither believer nor infidel," but a person "who regards them both with equal eye."[40] This is the idiom of a consciousness that is far less interested in preaching a message or developing a philosophy than in exploring another way to be. This way of being could easily be called comic if it were not so close to the tragic. Founded on similar perceptions of life's cross-purposes, it simply recommends that we take a different attitude toward them. While tragedy says that there is no help for the misfortune it brings us save in that recognition itself, a recognition that ennobles those who are capable of it even as it seals their doom, comedy in the Melvillian mode replies that we dare not dwell on these facts in outworn terms of thought. In other words, we need some possibility for corrective discounting. Ahab's story shows what happens when, through the atrophy of consciousness, we lack this option; Ishmael's shows us how, through the adaptations of consciousness, we can stylistically create one: "In its vast assimilations, its seemingly opportunistic eclecticism, its pragmatic and improvisatory nonchalance, its capacious grandiloquence and demotic humour it is indeed a style for America—the style of America."[41]

THE PRAGMATIST REGRAFTING OF RELATIONS BETWEEN RELIGION AND THE ENLIGHTENMENT

So defined, consciousness in its late nineteenth-century variants was either what the Enlightenment had omitted from conception of the mind altogether or had too often truncated in that view; consciousness was also what a certain group of American philosophers and other intellectuals could not resist transforming into a new subject of intellectual and aesthetic investigation. With help from useful adversaries like Josiah Royce and important precursors such as Charles Sanders Peirce, William James, along with other pragmatists, was able to show how the Enlightenment's confidence in the work of the mind might yet yield additional discoveries into what had once been thought to be the sole property of American religion. It all depended on developing a method of intellectual inquiry that would permit consciousness to explore what remained still ineffable and undecidable but also still irrepressible on its own borders. James spoke of this as "the re-instatement of the vague to its proper

[40]Melville, *Moby-Dick*, ed. Harrison Hayford, 314.
[41]Tanner, introduction to *Moby-Dick*, xxvii.

place in our mental life."[42] What he meant by the "vague" was that whole mysterious shadow world of feeling, intuition, relations, and transitions that undergirds cognition and motivates action, but that continues to remain invisible or discredited in so many late nineteenth- and early twentieth-century versions of experience.

James's turn toward consciousness was thus a turn toward a new theory of representation, but a theory that now supposed that the reality in need of representation was not "substantive," to use James's words again, but "transitive." What awaited full exploration and expression was the whole realm of affect that the Enlightenment, with its more restricted understanding of mentality, had tended to discount, and that religion, with its more urgent requirements for certainty, often tended to engulf. Nor was pragmatism's affinity with both religion and the Enlightenment in this case any accident. For if some of the roots of the pragmatist impulse lay in the strongly experiential tenor of seventeenth- and eighteenth-century American religion, no less than in the anti-Calvinistic metaphysics of William James's father, much of its intellectual effectuality derived from a concentration on the practical, the immediate, and the particular that goes back directly to the anti-metaphysical bias of some of the most radical Enlightenment philosophes.[43]

According to this narrative, then, American philosophical pragmatism, at least as it began to work itself out in literary terms, was by implication, if not exactly by intention, a theory of representation that attempted to reconcile what was still epistemologically viable about the Enlightenment's quest for a sense of reality as personal, palpable, public, and practicable with what was still culturally exigent about American religion's imagination of an otherness that cannot be dismissed. As a theory of representation, then, American pragmatism was also a theory of belief. It was a theory about the nature of the real which postulated that if the real lies neither wholly beyond the self, in some hypostatizable world set against it, nor wholly within the self, in some unitary core of spiritual being or deposit of biological essence independent of the occasions of its actualizations, then the real can still be found in the experience of those processes, events, and actions by which the self and the world interact. These are processes which, when understood in re-

---

[42]William James, *The Writings of William James*, ed. John J. McDermott (Chicago: University of Chicago Press, 1977), 45.
[43]May, *The Enlightenment in America*, 109.

lation to the human agency that motivates them, are defined by the term *imagination*, and when understood in relation to the forms in which this agency realizes itself are called style.

At the risk of oversimplification, I would be prepared to suggest that this is the theory of reality variously put to the test in that kind of twentieth-century American literature we traditionally refer to as modern. The test itself ultimately turned on the question of how imagination and style are to be represented when their function is redefined as a symbolization of the concourse between a self that is no longer singular but plural, or at least diffuse, and a world that is no longer fixed but changing, or at least unstable. This was a test that obviously took a variety of forms, ranging from Hemingway's attempts to convey "what really happened in action; what the actual things were which produced the emotion you experienced," to Faulkner's efforts to recover what was present about the past in fictions whose elaborate methods of technique—unreliable narration, stream-of-consciousness writing, mythic parallels, chronological disorientation, historical flashbacks, montage effects, philosophical brooding, and structures of detection—were intended to historicize the readers' sense of the present.[44] In some cases, the test involved parsing something as indefinable as what Stevens meant by his reference in "The Snow Man" to the "Nothing that is not there and the nothingness that is." In others, it amounted to determining what happens when, as Eliot wrote in "Burnt Norton," "Words strain, / Crack and sometimes break, under the burden, / Under the tension, slip, slide, perish, / Decay with imprecision, will not stay in place, / Will not stay still."

As a theory of representation, however, this pragmatist belief about reality could still survive such tests—even in such desperate gestures of self-definition as Adrienne Rich's "Diving into the Wreck" or such self-doubting acts of social investigation as James Agee's *Let Us Now Praise Famous Men*—so long as the spirit of an increasing late modernist skepticism could be prevented from rebelling against consciousness itself by calling into question its belief that imagination or style represent not, as Robert Frost put it in "The Most of It," their "own love back in copy speech, / But counter-love, original response." Yet when the spirit of a more radicalized criticism began to invade the precincts of consciousness itself, its contents no less than its creations were quickly reduced to a

---

[44]Ernest Hemingway, *Death in the Afternoon* (New York: Charles Scribner's Sons, 1932), 2.

series of clichés, as in the stories of Donald Barthelme, what he calls the "dreck" of contemporary society, or to mere critical and aesthetic "junk," what John Barth portrays in *The Sot-Weed Factor* as the "refuse" of literary history.

Such postmodern works as these tend to presume that consciousness is no more than a construct comprised of "used" components that, like the trash left behind in secondhand cars when they are traded in, symbolize only, as Thomas Pynchon suggests in *The Crying of Lot 49*, the pathos of their own enervated disposability. In a world composed of little more than trash, or what Pynchon wittily refers to as "W.A.S.T.E.," the objects that consciousness was once held to represent—feelings, relations, transitions, intuitions, interruptions, aporias—dissolve into thin air, to be replaced by gestures, signs, marks as innocently empty of significance and as infinitely replicable and replaceable as the mind of Chance, the gardener in Jerzy Kosinski's *Being There*, or as indeterminate and sometimes unreadable as the "art of distilling / Weird fragrances out of nothing" that constitutes the subject of John Ashbery's *Self-Portrait in a Convex Mirror* and other poems.

RELATIONS BETWEEN RELIGION AND THE ENLIGHTENMENT IN THE POSTMODERN ERA

If this proposal suggests the emergence of a new postmodern literary culture that is now bent on confounding what I have called the pragmatist project—the project of regrafting those parts of the liberal, if not rationalist, heritage that survived the seductions of essentialism to those elements of the religious heritage that resisted the soporifics of certainty—it may still be a culture that, for all of its alienation from the religious enthusiasm surrounding it, has not seen the last of the Enlightenment. In late modernist and postmodernist American literature—or, better, in our present academicized understanding of it—the critical or skeptical Enlightenment is, in one of its forms, clearly in the process of seeking to avenge itself against its own earlier principal achievement. That achievement was the creation of the philosophical subject known as "Man" that in former eras underwrote such serious projects as democratic politics, Freudian psychology, and the humanistic tradition (and is still recognizable in James's notion of the pluralistic self) but in ours tends to be viewed as just another corrupt technique by which human beings have reinvented themselves as privileged objects of study.

This act of critical self-consumption has, to be sure, cleared the intellectual and cultural field of much of the metaphysical and moral debris that had accumulated there over the last several centuries, but it has at the same time left the field morally and spiritually eviscerated. To some intellectuals, this may merely signify America's return to the state of moral and spiritual poverty that has, on their reading, always been its natural condition, or that, according to some interpretations, has always been the condition most propitious for its creative development. Stanley Cavell has turned this double conviction into what is probably the most powerful defense ever mounted of an American philosophical tradition that originated with Emerson and was expanded by Thoreau, a tradition that is to some degree epitomized by the arresting image of the philosopher as the "hobo of thought" in search of what Cavell calls, after Emerson, "this new yet unapproachable America."[45]

Cavell's argument centers around the question of why America is "unapproachable." It is unapproachable in a negative sense because its official culture is conformist, which is the same thing as saying that for Emerson it is unoriginal. Being unoriginal, American culture does not, at least in its "official" formations, know what it might or could originate, does not even have a language to speak of such things. In this sense, America is unapproachable because it is undiscussable, and it is undiscussable because it offers no terms of approach to what it has not yet begun to be, to the experience, as Cavell says another way, that it has not had of what it has yet to experience. This may be as simple a matter as saying that America has—or, at least until Emerson's time, had—no language of its own, but Cavell questions whether, according to this logic, this claim can be supported. Cavell's way out of this dilemma is to turn back to the project of Emerson himself for what amounts to a description of his own philosophical practice in America's continuing economy of cultural scarcity:

The classical British Empiricists had interpreted what we call experience as made up of impressions and the ideas derived from impressions. What Emerson wishes to show, in these terms, is that, for all our empiricism, nothing (now) makes an impression on us, that we accordingly have no experience (of our own), that we

[45]Stanley Cavell, *This New yet Unapproachable America* (Albuquerque, New Mex.: Living Batch Press, 1989), 116.

are inexperienced. Hence Emerson's writing is meant as the provision of experience for these shores, of our trials, perils, essays.[46]

Making a virtue of necessity is Cavell's way, like Emerson's perhaps, of rendering unapproachability approachable. But even if one is persuaded (as I sometimes am) by this sanguine assumption that America's cultural opportunities are to be found in the discovery of its comparative cultural deprivation, there is no gainsaying that now, to use Stevens's metaphor, "the theatre has changed" and with it the kind of play that can be staged there. The scene may still pit religion against the Enlightenment, setting something like a religiously residual sense of solidarity with all those people that official cultures tend to marginalize against the ministrations of a "later Reason" that has at heart only its own self-redescriptions. Intellectuals like Richard Rorty, who think this way, are now convinced that these traditions have little or nothing to say to one another and, in fact, may never have had. As resources for helping us cultivate the kind of ironic perspective that will provide the greatest scope for personal self-creation or the greatest inducement to notice the pain and suffering of others, both the American Enlightenment and the American religious tradition have, by Rorty's lights, pretty well spent themselves. By this Rorty does not mean to imply that we have derived no moral benefit from Christianity and the Enlightenment. All he intends to maintain (although for him, as for many others like him, it is everything) is that those benefits—an increased sensitivity to the suffering of others in the one case, an enhanced appreciation of the need and importance of personal freedom on the other—are no longer tied to the worldviews that were initially developed to express them and are of little further help to us so long as they continue to obscure or repress the contingency of their own origins. Our need to relate ourselves to something larger than the self may be no less urgent than our need for better models of self-description, but these two needs now possess only attenuated connections with traditions once vital in the past and can in no sense, despite centuries of philosophical and theological effort, now be integrated with each other. This as much as suggests that the old contest between religion and the Enlightenment is essentially over, not because either side won, but only because most intellectuals and artists no longer see themselves as actors in that drama. The old problematics of their

[46]Ibid., 92.

relationship have not so much been solved as dissolved. And so the story ends, the poet said, not with a bang but with a whimper.

RELIGION, THE ENLIGHTENMENT, AND THE FUTURE OF THE PRAGMATIST NARRATIVE

But the story for pragmatism, and particularly for pragmatism as one way of resolving the relations between religion and the Enlightenment in American letters, has no ending; that, it could be said, is one of its main points. The object of the pragmatist narrative is less to reach closure than to suspend its achievement indefinitely for the sake of keeping the narrative from ending before all the voices implicated in it, all the parties with a vested interest in its outcome, get to be heard. This is a world, so pragmatism maintains, all of whose evidence is not in yet and never will be so long as anyone with a claim on its meaning has not yet had a chance to be understood. This in effect is to say that the Enlightenment still lives, at least so long as we continue to believe that a republic of opinions, no matter how various and even fractious, is to be preferred to the despotism of dogma, whether coherent or benign. By the same token, this is not to say that religion is dead, unless we are prepared to concede that all experience is subsumable within some biological, graphological, or ideological template. Religion and the Enlightenment continue to survive just insofar as we continue to have experiences capable of being shared, of being communicated, that exceed our rational grasp precisely at the point where we need to explain what makes them, at least to and for us, so singular and salient, so distinctive and decisive.

Another way of putting this would be to say that the pragmatic tradition in American writing has conceived for itself a different kind of consummation altogether, one that Stanley Cavell has tried to imagine for the relations between religion and the Enlightenment through his efforts to recover "the uncanniness of the ordinary" and that Richard Poirier has invoked through his suggestive notion of "writing off the self."[47] Fantasies of self-annihilation are, as Poirier well knows, hardly novel in Western literary history, just as he also knows that until the recent past they have most often been associated with dreams of redemption. But Poirier is interested in the project of self-evacuation and

---

[47]For Cavell, see his *In Quest of the Ordinary: Lines of Skepticism and Romanticism* (Chicago: University of Chicago Press, 1988); for Poirier, see his *The Renewal of Literature: Emersonian Reflections* (New York: Random House, 1987).

renewal neither as, in Christian understanding, a propaedeutic to salvation nor as, in Nietzsche and Michel Foucault, the inevitable outcome of the bankruptcy of those organizations or forms of life that have enabled human beings to reinvent themselves as privileged objects of study. In opposition both to the Christian and to the modern view of self-erasure, Poirier intends to define an American tradition that discovers the vitality of human presence in forms so alien to its traditional interests and sites of valorization as almost to link the human with energies that deny it.

As figured (for Poirier) in a group of writers that begins in America with Emerson and includes Thoreau and Whitman but also extends through William James and his father, Henry, to such moderns as Frost and Stevens from one generation, Ashbery and O'Hara from another (although it might just as well be said to begin with Anne Hutchinson and encompass such female writers as Anne Bradstreet, Emily Dickinson, and Elizabeth Bishop), the possibility of self-evacuation from those inherited descriptions that define human beings at present is precipitated by, and only leads to, moments whose transformative power have little to do with narratives of fulfillment and cannot be made available to ideology. In writers such as these Americans—whose association with the intellectual habits and assumptions of American pragmatism is evident in everything from their faith in the materials of ordinary experience and their distrust of absolutes to their delight in process, activity, and mutability and their conviction that truth is made rather than found, fabricated not given—such moments are preceded neither by catastrophe nor by collapse. Instead they are produced by the metaphorical capacities of language itself, when those capacities that enable language to swerve away from its own inherited meanings, to resist tropologically the technology of its own traditional usages, are seen as a source of empowerment that needs no sanctions, religious or otherwise, for the sense of personal enhancement that accompanies it. In the moment when punning, joking, and troping break the grip of institutionalized terminologies, self-emancipation is effected merely by the way the writing calls attention to the performative presence of the self even in gestures of its own dissolution or effacement.

The idea that human presence can be revealed in those very processes and prospects that apparently deny it has long been entertained by works of literature and just as assiduously avoided in works of criticism. Poirier attributes this avoidance to our seduction by a simple "either/or": either the Judeo-Christian self whose creaturely identity as a substantial entity is guaranteed by the metaphorical appellation "child of God," or the view Emerson enunciates in "Circles" where, by seeing every fact as the beginning of another series for which there is no necessary circumference, the self seeking realization in language is always dissolving, "since language has no fixed or ultimately rationalizing terms."[48] The seduction, in other words, has been to the view that religion and the Enlightenment are unalterably opposed in America. The alternative possibility that American literature, or at least one strain of it, so often invites us to explore, even though so few readers ever do, involves "discovering a form of the human which emerges from the very *denial* of its will to become articulate, or of looking at a landscape from which the familiar human presence has been banished and of enjoying this vista without thinking of deprivation."[49] These are occasions when the ordinary becomes exceptional, uncanny, "other," without being formulated as such. As in Whitman's "As I Ebb'd with the Ocean of Life," or Stevens's "The River of Rivers in Connecticut," or Bishop's "At the Fishhouses," we become aware of how "it is possible to confer value on moments of transformation or dissolution without looking ahead toward a narrative of fulfillment. The moment is endowed with something as vague as wonder or beauty, empty of the desire to translate these into knowledge."[50]

The pragmatic narrative thus transmutes the dialectic between religion and the Enlightenment not into another myth of eternal return such as the one Eliot envisioned at the end of "Little Gidding," where the end of our exploration is to arrive "where we started / And know the place for the first time," but into a new access to otherness. If this does not quite convert the philosopher into what Cavell touchingly calls "the hobo of thought," it transforms the thinker into what Thoreau described as a perpetual "saunterer"—a person with no vocation more compelling or fateful than to try to walk far out beyond the conventional oppositions of thought in search of a "somewhere" where we may "witness our own limits transgressed, and some life pasturing freely where we never wander."[51]

Is this how, as Cavell thinks, philosophy is successful or how philosophy is transcended? It scarcely seems to matter. The key to being is

[48]Poirier, *The Renewal of Literature*, 203.
[49]Ibid., 202.
[50]Ibid., 203.
[51]Cavell, *This New yet Unapproachable America*, 116.

still, as he, Poirier, Melville, and Whitman would all agree, the open road of experience—a road whose journeying can become edifying, enhancing, both personally and socially, only as we learn how to respond to moments when the ordinary becomes uncanny, when the familiar becomes strange, when the habitual becomes again "other," because it "is imagined," as Poirier states, "as if it were not less but, because extemporized within and also against existent forms, immeasurably more than the result of some 'arrangements of knowledge.' "[52]

[52]Poirier, *The Renewal of Literature*, 116, 202.

3

The rise and long life of the Protestant Enlightenment in America

MARK A. NOLL

At the end of the twentieth century the American Enlightenment, though not without its doughty defenders, is in trouble. That Enlightenment had taken root among America's leading thinkers during the second half of the eighteenth century and had survived until fairly recently as a dominant presence in American intellectual life. From the Revolution to roughly World War I it was overwhelmingly the prevailing framework for American thought. The most perceptive authorities, though differing in details, agree on the convictions that the generation of the founding fathers shared with guiding spirits of the European Enlightenment: first, that the material world, the world that could be known "experimentally" through the senses, was the surest foundation of all reality; second, that detached, rational, scientific inquiry was the ultimate arbiter of genuine knowledge; and, third, that by pursuing a more disciplined inquiry into the experience opened by the senses, humanity would progress to new heights of glory.[1] At the end of the twentieth century only the first

[1]See especially the definitions in Henry F. May, *The Enlightenment in America* (New York: Oxford University Press, 1976), xiv—"Let us say that the Enlightenment consists of all those who believe two propositions: first, that the present age is more enlightened than the past; and second, that we understand nature and man best through the use of our natural faculties."—D. H. Meyer, *The Democratic Enlightenment* (New York: G. P. Putnam's Sons, 1976), xii–xiv—"At its very center the Enlightenment represents the philosophical assimilation of the scientific revolution of the sixteenth and seventeenth centuries . . . there was, above all, a new faith in science . . . a heightened interest in the natural world, including, significantly, human nature . . . a growing impatience with mystery and 'metaphysics' [and] new hope for man."—and Henry Steele Commager, *The Empire of Reason: How Europe Imagined and America Realized the Enlightenment* (Garden City, N.Y.: Anchor Doubleday, 1977), xi–xii—"Alike in the Old World and the New, [the Enlightenment] had its roots in the same intellectual soil, and produced a common harvest of ideas, attitudes, and even of programs: recognition of a cosmic system

of these Enlightenment convictions—that material reality is the most basic reality—enjoys widespread acceptance, and even that view is challenged. Enlightenment optimism, by contrast, now seems childishly dated. The idea of scientifically pristine, rationally self-authenticating authority reels from so many blows—canon criticism and deconstruction, Geertzian anthropology and a philosophic turn to pragmatism, Critical Legal Studies and Continental critical theory, and above all the demythologizing of scientific detachment in the wake of Thomas Kuhn's *Structure of Scientific Revolutions*—that it is becoming difficult to credit the once universal aspiration to "turn the Newtonian trick."[2] If, as stated by Peter Gay, "the Enlightenment may be summed up in two words: criticism and power," then clearly in late twentieth-century America, criticism has triumphed over power, and the Enlightenment is no more.[3]

The contemporary situation may be explained in several different ways, as (to cite only a few of many possible examples) a long overdue retreat from philosophical overreaching, fallout from the clash between "scientific naturalism" and the absolutist ideology of American democracy, or the absence of integration among aspects of the modern identity.[4] Cultural pessimists with a grander vision may find Goethe's aphorism compelling: "All eras in a state of decline and dissolution are subjective; on the other hand, all progressive eras have an objective tendency."[5] Whether or not subjectivity is a sure indicator of decline, subjectivity in many forms has disconcerted the once proud certainties of

governed by the laws of Nature and Nature's God; faith in Reason as competent to penetrate to the meaning of those laws and to induce conformity to them among societies in many ways irrational; commitment to what Jefferson called 'the illimitable freedom of the human mind,' to the doctrine of progress, and—with some reservations—to the concept of the perfectibility of Man; an ardent humanitarianism that attacked torture, slavery, war, poverty, and disease; and confidence that Providence and Nature had decreed happiness for mankind."

[2] For the phrase "the Newtonian trick," see Charles A. Beard, "Written History as an Act of Faith," *American Historical Review* 39 (1934): 223. For an excellent description of recent assaults on the ideal of scientific objectivity, see Peter Novick, *That Noble Dream: The "Objectivity Question" and the American Historical Profession* (Cambridge: Cambridge University Press, 1988), 522–72.

[3] Peter Gay, *The Enlightenment: An Interpretation—The Rise of Modern Paganism* (New York: Knopf, 1966), xi.

[4] Richard Rorty, *Philosophy and the Mirror of Nature* (Princeton: Princeton University Press, 1979); Edward A. Purcell, Jr., *The Crisis of Democratic Theory: Scientific Naturalism and the Problem of Value* (Lexington: University Press of Kentucky, 1973); Charles Taylor, *Sources of the Self: The Making of the Modern Identity* (Cambridge, Mass.: Harvard University Press, 1989).

[5] *Conversations of Goethe with Eckermann*, trans. J. Oxenford (London: J. M. Dent & Sons, 1930), 126.

the Enlightenment. There is no longer an intellectual king in the New American Israel; all do that which seems right in their own eyes.[6]

In the midst of this "epistemological crisis," a singular curiosity attends the responses of the churches.[7] Catholics, though relatively late participants in the arena of American public discourse, have produced several proposals tackling the situation head on. Protestants, though present at the center of American civilization from the beginning, have uttered hardly a word about the crisis. Catholic neo-Thomists have proposed since the 1930s a series of alternatives to modern epistemological fashions. More recently Alasdair MacIntyre has produced a comprehensive indictment of the moral and epistemological reasoning of the Enlightenment, and has, along with ecclesiastical conservatives who make the case in other ways, suggested that traditional Catholic notions of authority could be reformulated for contemporary circumstances. A variety of other Catholics—for example, Bernard Lonergan and David Tracy—have also attempted thoroughgoing responses to the modern problems of method. The point here is not which of these proposals offers a better solution, but simply that for half a century or more there have been far-reaching suggestions from Catholics addressing first the pretensions and then the discontents of Enlightenment rationality.

By contrast, Protestantism in its many American manifestations has been largely mute on the specifically epistemological issues arising from the collapse of Enlightenment ideals.[8] Some representatives of the Protestant center do worry about such matters, but moderates of the old establishment seem preoccupied with the tasks of survival. Long before there was a widely perceived crisis, such ones became extraordinarily cautious about the possibility of a distinctly Christian framework of general knowledge as opposed to, say, a place for Christian social ethics or Christian political principles.[9] Evangelical moderates who have been aspiring for a place in the sun of respectability since World War II are

---

[6]The metaphor comes from the Book of Judges via the title of the last chapter of Novick, *That Noble Dream.*
[7]For the phrase "epistemological crisis," see Novick, *That Noble Dream,* 573, and Joyce Appleby, "One Good Turn Deserves Another: Moving beyond the Linguistic, a Response to David Harlan," *American Historical Review* 94 (1989): 1326, 1328.
[8]There are, of course, significant exceptions, some of which are mentioned later.
[9]See Dorothy C. Bass, "Ministry on the Margin: Protestants and Education," in *Between the Times: The Travail of the Protestant Establishment in America, 1900–1960,* ed. William R. Hutchison (New York: Cambridge University Press, 1989), 48–71, and for a sensitive contemporary discussion, Richard G. Hutcheson, Jr., "Are Church-related Colleges Also Christian?" *Christian Century* 105 (28 September 1988): 838–41.

more assertive than their counterparts in the mainstream churches about the possibility of distinctly Christian worldviews. But their energies, in keeping with evangelical tradition, regularly drift away from intellectual struggles to populist promotion.[10] Besides, a careful attention to the norms of Enlightenment objectivity has provided a way for evangelicals to work themselves back into the larger arenas of scholarship. To address directly the adequacy of those norms could threaten their return to respectability.[11]

From the Protestant Right and Left extremes there is, strictly speaking, no contemporary Christian voice on questions arising from the dissipation of Enlightenment certainties. The fundamentalist Right is so fully committed to formulations of rationality from the early American Enlightenment—as illustrated by the positivism of its creation science and its filiopietistic defense of the United States as a Christian nation—that the collapse of these formulations would bring on speechlessness. The modernist Left, by contrast, has for so long been committed to the shifting norms of university discourse as to have nothing specifically Christian, except emotion, to contribute to academic debate. This was true already in the 1930s for those who felt with sociologist Hornell Hart that, in R. Laurence Moore's summary, "scientists and other moderns would make room for religion when it no longer flew in the face of scientific certainties."[12] It has become painfully evident among a small class of the Protestant avant-garde in recent years who have been desperately eager to baptize the latest in secular trends.

If I exaggerate the recent silence of Protestants on troubling epistemological concerns, we are still left with the question of why, in relative terms, Catholicism, the junior partner in American church life, has had more to say about the epistemological dimensions of the American Enlightenment than Protestantism, the senior partner. The answer, I think, is to be found in the circumstances surrounding the wholehearted embrace by Protestants of a distinctly American form of the Enlighten-

---

[10]See Nathan O. Hatch, "Evangelicalism as a Democratic Movement," in *Evangelicalism and Modern America*, ed. George Marsden (Grand Rapids, Mich.: Eerdmans, 1984), 71–82, and idem, "Epilogue: The Recurring Populist Impulse in American Christianity," in *The Democratization of American Christianity* (New Haven: Yale University Press, 1989), 210–19.

[11]This strategy has been especially effective for biblical scholarship; see Mark A. Noll, *Between Faith and Criticism: Evangelicals, Scholarship, and the Bible in America* (San Francisco: Harper and Row, 1986), 97–99, 122–41.

[12]R. Laurence Moore, "Secularization: Religion and the Social Sciences," in Hutchison, *Between the Times*, 247.

ment during the revolutionary period and the decades immediately following. Historical investigation of those circumstances helps us address three important questions: First, how did American Protestants become so tightly bound to Enlightenment procedures and assumptions? Second, why did the rising tide of romanticism in the mid nineteenth century not dislodge Protestants from the Enlightenment? Third, why did the intellectual crises from the Civil War to the Depression not precipitate a reconsideration of Protestant commitment to Enlightenment standards?[13]

If in the following discussion I spend much more time on the first question and then treat the next two mostly as extended footnotes, it is because an understanding of the passionate wedding of Protestantism and the Enlightenment goes far toward explaining why divorce became unthinkable.[14]

Historians are rarely well equipped for moving from description to prescription. But the nature of these historical issues mandates that, at the risk of mocking the complexity of current questions, I offer in conclusion a brief suggestion—from the perspective of a Protestant rather than a historian of Protestantism—as to what now should be done.

THE ENLIGHTENMENT TO THE RESCUE OF PROTESTANTISM, 1776–1860

Christopher Hill once called the effort to define Puritanism "that dragon in the path of every student of that period."[15] The dragon is even more ferocious for the Enlightenment in America. For want of a definition faithful to actual historical circumstances, otherwise helpful stud-

---

[13]A fourth important question concerns Protestantism and science in the twentieth century, an issue that was the subject of careful attention at an earlier Woodrow Wilson Center symposium; see, among others, George M. Marsden, "Evangelicals and the Scientific Culture: An Overview"; Bruce Kuklick, "John Dewey, American Theology, and Scientific Politics"; David A. Hollinger, "Justification by Verification: The Scientific Challenge to the Moral Authority of Christianity in Modern America"; and Murray G. Murphey, "On the Scientific Study of Religion in the United States, 1870–1980," all in *Religion and Twentieth-Century American Intellectual Life*, ed. Michael J. Lacey (Cambridge: Cambridge University Press, 1989).

[14]The discussion that follows draws inevitably on earlier attempts I have made to chart other dimensions of this subject, especially "Who Sets the Stage for Understanding Scripture? Philosophies of Science Often Provide the Logic for Our Hermeneutics," *Christianity Today*, 23 May 1980, 14–18; "The Irony of the Enlightenment for Presbyterians in the Early Republic," *Journal of the Early Republic* 5 (Summer 1985): 149–75; and *Princeton and the Republic, 1768–1822: The Search for a Christian Enlightenment in the Era of Samuel Stanhope Smith* (Princeton: Princeton University Press, 1989).

[15]Christopher Hill, *Economic Problems of the Church, from Archbishop Whitgift to the Long Parliament* (Oxford: Clarendon Press, 1956), xii.

ies have obscured rather than illuminated the relation between Protestantism and the American Enlightenment. Some commentators, such as Henry Steele Commager and Adrienne Koch, have taken it for granted that America's Enlightenment can simply be equated with the constitutional achievements of the political founding fathers. Others, like Peter Gay, have not been able to see the tight bond between Protestantism and the Enlightenment in America because they assume that the Continental pattern, in which votaries of Enlightenment scorned traditional Christianity, supplies a universally valid picture fitting the circumstances in John Witherspoon's Princeton as well as Voltaire's Geneva.[16]

Henry F. May has provided a better way. The key to May's argument is the realization that eighteenth-century Americans perceived several Enlightenments, rather than just one.[17] His fourfold categorization makes it possible to see how American Protestants, though they repudiated principles and personalities often assumed to embody *the* Enlightenment, nonetheless themselves also fully embraced a form of the Enlightenment. In chronological and geographical terms, American Protestants responded warmly to forms of the Enlightenment from late seventeenth-century England and eighteenth-century Scotland, but proceeded from an attitude of ambiguity toward one of disgust for the Enlightenment as defined by continental Europeans of the eighteenth century and English radicals late in that same century. If we observe these discriminations, then we are in a position to grasp the complexities of Protestant engagement with the Enlightenment.

Americans in general held in high regard, but from afar, what May calls the moderate Enlightenment, exemplified by Isaac Newton and John Locke. By contrast, Protestants in America came to repudiate two

[16]Overconcentration on the political characterizes Commager, *The Empire of Reason*, and also Adrienne Koch, ed., *The American Enlightenment: The Shaping of the American Experiment and a Free Society* (New York: Braziller, 1965), a fine anthology but limited to the works of only five statesmen: Franklin, John Adams, Jefferson, Madison, and Hamilton. Peter Gay's seminal studies of the Enlightenment in Europe did not help him when he turned to American subjects, as in *A Loss of Mastery: Puritan Historians in Colonial America* (Berkeley: University of California Press, 1966), where he can say (92) that "the nineteen years" between 1739 and 1758 witnessed "the rebellion of the Enlightenment against Christianity," at the very time when the pupils of Edwards were beginning their lifelong task of showing how well Edwards's Calvinism could merge with selected principles of the Enlightenment.

[17]May, *The Enlightenment in America*. Similarly discriminating are Meyer, *The Democratic Enlightenment*, and J. R. Pole, "Enlightenment and the Politics of American Nature," in *The Enlightenment in National Context*, ed. R. Porter and M. Teich (Cambridge: Cambridge University Press, 1981), 192–214.

other forms of European Enlightenment, the skeptical as defined by Voltaire and David Hume and the revolutionary as in the work of Rousseau, William Godwin, and (after 1780) Tom Paine.

Some of the leaders of the new United States, such as Thomas Jefferson and Benjamin Franklin, found certain aspects of the skeptical and revolutionary views worthy of guarded attention.[18] Increasingly in the early years of the new nation, however, the sentiments of Protestants turned the other way. Elias Boudinot—sometime president of the Continental Congress, longtime director of the United States Mint, and an active Presbyterian layman—spoke for that growing body of opinion as he put the matter to a group of young men in 1807:

> The clumsy sophistry of Godwin; the pernicious subtilties of Hume, and the coarse vulgarities of Paine . . . these unhingers of human happiness, these presumptuous undoers of the labours of Antiquity . . . shall be discovered originating in the wantonness & pride of human intellect, making their progress by desolation & infamy; sapping all foundations of Society, & levelling all the props of morality; aiming, in a word, at the perfection of Man by extinguishing every Sentiment which raises him above the Brute.[19]

A fourth variety of Enlightenment, however, received a very different reception in Protestant America. This didactic Enlightenment, which has recently been the subject of fresh scholarly attention, was largely a product of Scotland. There three generations of philosophers and moralists— among whom Francis Hutcheson, Thomas Reid, Adam Smith, and Dugald Stewart were the leaders—struggled to restore intellectual confidence and social cohesion to the Enlightenment ideal. In the United States this form of Enlightenment came to dominate intellectual life for more than the first half-century of its existence.[20]

---

[18]Jefferson while president assisted Paine, for which he earned the opprobrium of many Protestants, but even Jefferson cooled somewhat toward Paine after the latter's publication of *The Age of Reason*, though perhaps from motives not directly related to religion; see Dumas Malone, *Jefferson the President: First Term, 1801–1805* (Boston: Little, Brown, 1970), 192–200.

[19]Elias Boudinot, "Young Gentlemen of the College," as printed in Mark A. Noll, "The Response of Elias Boudinot to the Student Rebellion of 1807: Visions of Honor, Order, and Morality," *Princeton University Library Chronicle* 43 (1981): 20.

[20]Among the most helpful of many recent books are S. A. Grave, *The Scottish Philosophy of Common Sense* (Oxford: Clarendon Press, 1960); Richard B. Sher, *Church and University in the Scottish Enlightenment: The Moderate Literati of Edinburgh* (Princeton: Princeton University Press, 1985); Istvan Hont and Michael Ignatieff, eds., *Wealth and Virtue: The Shaping of Political Economy in the Scottish Enlightenment* (New York: Cambridge University Press, 1983); and, for showing differences among the Scottish thinkers, Richard B. Sher and Jeffrey R. Smitten, eds., *Scotland and America in the Age of Enlightenment* (Princeton: Princeton University Press, 1990).

The influence of this didactic Enlightenment stretched broadly in the population at large, from Jefferson and Madison in the White House to the first professional scientists in the United States as well as to the literary pioneers of the new nation.[21] But the most articulate spokesmen for the Common Sense principles of the American Enlightenment were Protestant educators and ministers. These principles provided the basis for collegiate instruction at Unitarian Harvard, Baptist Brown, Congregationalist Yale, Presbyterian Princeton, and the rest of the nation's rapidly growing network of colleges, still at this stage almost exclusively the institutions of the churches. They defined mental habits for Protestants North and South, for dignified urban ministers and enterprising preachers on the frontier, for sober doctrinal conservatives and populist democratic polemicists.[22]

A wealth of outstanding writing has recently made the presence of this Protestant Enlightenment a historical commonplace. Still, there is something of a mystery about it. How did a Protestant tradition rooted in the Reformation and recently renewed by the New Light revivalism of John Wesley, George Whitefield, and Jonathan Edwards—in both instances movements stressing human disability as much as human capability, noetic deficiency as much as epistemic capacity, historical realism

---

[21]Garry Wills, *Inventing America: Jefferson's Declaration of Independence* (Garden City, N.Y.: Doubleday, 1978); Ronald Hamowy, "Jefferson and the Scottish Enlightenment: A Critique of Garry Wills's *Inventing America*," *William and Mary Quarterly* 36 (1979): 503–23; Roy Branson, "James Madison and the Scottish Enlightenment," *Journal of the History of Ideas* 40 (1979): 235–50; Herbert Hovenkamp, *Science and Religion in America, 1800–1860* (Philadelphia: University of Pennsylvania Press, 1978); John C. Greene, *American Science in the Age of Jefferson* (Ames: Iowa State University Press, 1984), 12–36, 411–12; and Terrence Martin, *The Instructed Vision: Scottish Common Sense Philosophy and the Origins of American Fiction* (Bloomington: University of Indiana Press, 1961).

[22]The two most helpful general studies are Sydney E. Ahlstrom, "The Scottish Philosophy and American Theology," *Church History* 24 (1955): 257–72, and Theodore Dwight Bozeman, *Protestants in an Age of Science: The Baconian Ideal and Antebellum American Religious Thought* (Chapel Hill: University of North Carolina Press, 1977). For the colleges, see Daniel Walker Howe, *The Unitarian Conscience: Harvard Moral Philosophy, 1805–1861* (Cambridge, Mass.: Harvard University Press, 1970); Francis Wayland (president of Brown University), *The Elements of Moral Science* (1837), ed. Joseph L. Blau (Cambridge, Mass.: Harvard University Press, 1963); John R. Fitzmier, "The Godly Federalism of Timothy Dwight, 1752–1817," Ph.D. dissertation, Princeton University, 1986, 159–211; Noll, *Princeton and the Republic*, 36–43, 117–23, 188–91, 284–86; and for collegiate instruction generally, D. H. Meyer, *The Instructed Conscience: The Shaping of the American National Ethic* (Philadelphia: University of Pennsylvania Press, 1972). For the Scottish Enlightenment among Southern Protestants, see E. Brooks Holifield, *The Gentlemen Theologians: American Theology in Southern Culture, 1795–1860* (Durham, N.C.: Duke University Press, 1978), 96–54, and Fred J. Hood, *Reformed America: The Middle and Southern States, 1783–1837* (Tuscaloosa: University of Alabama Press, 1980), 1–67, 88–112.

as much as social optimism—come to express itself so thoroughly in the language of the Enlightenment?

If the earliest Protestants had not been quite as eager as Tertullian to pose an antithesis between Athens and Jerusalem, they were nonetheless definite about proper intellectual procedure. Luther and Calvin were themselves able casuists, but they also consistently bemoaned the damage wrought by unchecked reason or the presumption that merely human learning could dictate to revelation. Luther, when he called reason "the devil's whore," was characteristically more flamboyant. Calvin could be no less direct: for "knowing God" and "knowing his fatherly favor in our behalf . . . the greatest geniuses are blinder than moles."[23] This earliest Protestant conception of intellectual life came much closer to medieval postures—*credo ut intelligam* (I believe so that I may understand), *fides quaerens intellectum* (faith seeking understanding)— than to eighteenth-century confidence in human reason. These early Protestants were, in addition, aggressively Augustinian. In their minds a sharp divide separated the elect from the lost, with implications, however imprecisely detailed, for ethics, epistemology, and metaphysics, as well as soteriology.[24]

Puritans were heirs of this Augustinian Reformation; their stance, though never without rivals, dominated religious thought in colonial British America. Like the earliest Protestants, the Puritans also campaigned against human self-sufficiency in epistemology and ethics. With them they expected a divine revelation to provide the starting place for thought in all areas of life. As John Cotton cited with approval the views of William Perkins, who was the leading Puritan of the generation that trained New England's founders, "the word, and scriptures of God doe conteyne a . . . platforme, not onely of theology, but also of . . . ethicks, economicks, politiks, church-government, prophecy, [and] academy."[25] For Puritans the symbol of arrogantly self-sufficient rationality was Aristotle, as it had been also for Luther and Calvin. How could a pagan philosopher of nature, they wondered, properly understand that truly

---

[23]See the good discussions in Paul Althaus, *The Theology of Martin Luther*, trans. R. C. Schultz (Philadelphia: Fortress Press, 1966), 64–71, and John Calvin, "The Limits of Our Understanding," II.ii.18, in *Institutes of the Christian Religion*, ed. J. T. McNeill, trans. F. L. Battles, 2 vols. (Philadelphia: Westminster Press, 1960), 1:277.

[24]See especially E. Harris Harbison, *The Christian Scholar in the Age of the Reformation* (New York: Charles Scribner's Sons, 1956), 103–72.

[25]John Cotton, "Copy of a Letter from Mr. Cotton to Lord Say and Seal in the Year 1636," in *Puritan Political Ideas, 1558–1794*, ed. Edmund S. Morgan (Indianapolis: Bobbs-Merrill, 1965), 168.

virtuous action flows only from a heart renewed by God's grace? William Ames (1576–1633), among the early Puritan intellects, posed the dilemma most sharply, but Cotton Mather (1663–1728) in America, nearly a century after Ames, still expressed the same distrust of natural or Aristotelian moral philosophy, which he called "a *Sham*" that "pretends to give you a Religion without a CHRIST, and a *Life* of PIETY without a *Living Principle*; a *Good Life* with no other than Dead Works filling of it . . . Study no other *Ethics*, but what is in the *Bible*."[26]

The Puritan distrust of autonomous reason survived with vigor into eighteenth-century America. Even as new varieties of confidence in human self-sufficiency replaced the old—as, that is, the rational and intellectualist ethics of Aristotle gave way to the affectional and volitional "new moral philosophy" of Lord Shaftesbury and Francis Hutcheson—the heirs of the Puritans firmly defended the priority of revelation over reason, of grace over self-assertion, of conversion over good taste.

At the middle of the eighteenth century America's two most important philosophers, Jonathan Edwards and Samuel Johnson, had become familiar with the new Enlightenment notions, but neither was pleased with them. Samuel Johnson (1696–1772), the most widely respected Anglican clergyman of his generation in America, was a proponent of revelation over reason, of John Hutchinson's biblically based science over the gravitational mechanics of Newton, and of Berkeleyan idealism over various forms of realism. He advocated philosophical idealism for a number of different reasons, but primarily because he believed that a slavish following of Bacon, Newton, and Locke would result in deism and the practical denial of God's activity in the world.[27]

Jonathan Edwards, who differed from Johnson on most strictly theological questions, joined him in swimming against the Enlightenment tide. Edwards's books on free will and original sin, and especially his

---

[26]Cotton Mather, *Manductio ad Ministerium* (1726), as quoted in Norman Fiering, *Moral Philosophy at Seventeenth-Century Harvard: A Discipline in Transition* (Chapel Hill: University of North Carolina Press, 1981), 40. On the pietistic character of Puritan epistemology, see also John Morgan, *Godly Learning: Puritan Attitudes towards Reason, Learning and Education, 1560–1640* (Cambridge: Cambridge University Press, 1986), 18–35, and Theodore Dwight Bozeman, "The Protestant Epistemology," in *To Live Ancient Lives: The Primitivist Dimension in Puritanism* (Chapel Hill: University of North Carolina Press, 1988), 51–80.

[27]See Joseph J. Ellis, *The New England Mind in Transition: Samuel Johnson of Connecticut* (New Haven: Yale University Press, 1973); Elizabeth Flower and Murray G. Murphey, *A History of Philosophy in America*, 2 Vols. (New York: Capricorn, 1977), 1:81–99; and Norman S. Fiering, "President Samuel Johnson and the Circle of Knowledge," *William and Mary Quarterly* 28 (1971): 191–236.

work *The Nature of True Virtue*, called into question the natural moral capacities that had become so important to the ethics of the Enlightenment and especially of Scottish moral philosophy. Edwards also repudiated the metaphysical dualism that Newton took for granted, that stood at the heart of Locke's epistemology, and that grounded the thinking of the Scots. According to Edwards, "that which truly is the substance of all bodies is the infinitely exact and precise and perfectly stable idea in God's mind, together with his stable will that the same shall gradually be communicated to us, and to other minds, according to certain fixed and exact established methods and laws."[28] In opposition to Common Sense philosophy, Edwards held that Newtonian physics required an idealistic metaphysics everywhere dependent on God, and he believed that true virtue arose not from a natural moral sense but from the supernatural grace of God.

In addition, Edwards and other Protestants at mid-century defended the Reformation conception of human nature that repudiated the high view of natural moral capacities underlying the ethics of the Scottish philosophy.[29] In particular, their view of ethics was conversionist; it divided sharply the whole of humanity between the redeemed, in whom God had implanted a "new sense of the heart" to know and love the ultimately virtuous, and the rest of humankind, which had to be content with self-centered or self-serving imitations of true virtue. This Augustinian picture of human nature was much more than the intellectual plaything of pedants, for it had provided the theology for the colonial Great Awakening of the 1740s, which some historians now regard as the single most influential event in prerevolutionary America.[30]

Finally, it is also pertinent to note that in Scotland the philosophy of Common Sense was linked to a Moderate Party in the kirk that self-

---

[28]Jonathan Edwards, " 'The Mind' and Related Papers," in *The Works of Jonathan Edwards: Scientific and Philosophical Writings*, ed. Wallace E. Anderson (New Haven: Yale University Press, 1980), 344.

[29]The argument on this repudiation in Norman Fiering, *Jonathan Edwards's Moral Thought and Its British Context* (Chapel Hill: University of North Carolina Press, 1981), has been modified slightly by Paul Ramsay's introduction to *Ethical Writings*, vol. 8 of *The Works of Jonathan Edwards* (New Haven: Yale University Press, 1989), 6–7 n. 5, 18 n. 3, 29 nn. 5–6, to suggest that Edwards was not as directly addressing the Scottish moral philosophy of Francis Hutcheson as Fiering contended.

[30]On the cultural importance of the Great Awakening, see Alan E. Heimert, *Religion and the American Mind from the Great Awakening to the Revolution* (Cambridge, Mass.: Harvard University Press, 1966); Gary Nash, *The Urban Crucible* (Cambridge, Mass.: Harvard University Press, 1979), 188–232; and Rhys Isaac, *The Transformation of Virginia, 1740–1790* (Chapel Hill: University of North Carolina Press, 1982), 143–80.

styled "evangelicals" resisted and even ridiculed. Moderate thought, one of the evangelicals spoofed, "has been . . . well licked into form and method by the late immortal Mr. Hutcheson."[31] The author of that sally was John Witherspoon, who migrated to America in 1768 to become president of Princeton. One might be forgiven for thinking that Witherspoon's rapid rise in the esteem of his fellow Americans would have inhibited the spread here of the Scottish Enlightenment that was so organically linked to his Moderate opponents in Scotland.

A problem, therefore, exists in explaining why American Protestants came so rapidly and so thoroughly to embrace the Enlightenment in its Scottish form.[32] The Reformation in which American Protestantism was rooted, the Puritan tradition that provided Americans their most articulate theological heritage, the Great Awakening through the writings of its leading exponents, and the newer influence of immigrant Scots who had opposed the Moderate Party—all make it harder rather than easier to see why American Protestants by 1800 would everywhere champion the naturalism, the optimism, and the scientific rationality that, albeit "pressed . . . into the service of traditional values,"[33] nonetheless still characterized their Enlightenment.

Several general circumstances contributed to the ease with which American Protestants accepted the Enlightenment in its Scottish form. Despite the warnings of Luther and Calvin, and the hope of the English Puritans that Peter Ramus could be substituted for Aristotle, Aristotelian reasoning quickly assumed the same place in Protestant university life that it had enjoyed before the Reformation. The Aristotelianism of Prot-

---

[31]John Witherspoon, "Ecclesiastical Characteristics" (1753), in *The Works of the Rev. John Witherspoon*, 4 vols. (Philadelphia: William W. Woodward, 1802), 3:229.

[32]Historians have shied away from causal explanations for the rise of the Scottish philosophy in America. Perry Miller seems to link it to the spread of revival (*The Life of the Mind in America from the Revolution to the Civil War* [New York: Harcourt, Brace, and World, 1965], 3–95); Lewis Perry simply notes that it was appealing because of "its avoidance of abstract dogma" (*Intellectual Life in America: A History* [New York: Franklin Watts, 1984], 199). Lawrence Cremin sees its appearance as part of a deliberate effort by the nation's intellectual leaders to create a republican, scientific, and evangelical culture (*American Education: The National Experience, 1783–1876* [New York: Harper and Row, 1980], 2–4). Flower and Murphey provide an excellent account of the philosophy itself but do not speculate on the larger background against which it appeared (*History of Philosophy in America*, 1:203–361). Early in this century, I. Woodbridge Riley helpfully explored both "intrinsic" and "extrinsic" explanations for the rise of the Scottish philosophy, but his extrinsic reasons concerned mostly the intellectual usefulness of Common Sense realism for "educational and ecclesiastical orthodoxy" (*American Philosophy: The Early Schools* [New York: Russell and Russell, 1907], 475–79).

[33]Meyer, *The Democratic Enlightenment*, xxvi.

estant scholastics thus kept alive the sort of universalistic rational inquiry that, in altered form, the Enlightenment would also promote.[34] Protestant pietism, for all of its commitment to heart religion, also anticipated certain aspects of the Enlightenment. Especially was this true for the pietist insistence on "experimental religion" that fit nicely into Enlightenment emphases on the privileged status of experiential knowledge.[35] In addition, the simple weight of European fashion bore down heavily on colonials in the American outback.[36] As in Scotland, existence on the margin of the British Empire could inspire resentment at the cultural imperialism of London, Oxford, and Cambridge. But there was no other way to go. A provincial who wanted to take part in that larger intellectual world had little choice but to accept its conventions which, by the mid eighteenth century, included the deification of Newton, engagement with Lockean epistemology, and growing confidence in an apparently limitless expansion of British power, wealth, and influence.

Yet in the end it was not general developments in theology, philosophy, or the zeitgeist that converted Americans from the idealism, Augustinianism, and conversionist ethics of Puritanism to the realism, optimism, and universalistic ethics of the Scottish Enlightenment. It was rather that the Scottish Enlightenment offered Americans exactly what they seemed to require to master the tumults of the revolutionary era. In the midst of what Nathan Hatch has called a "cultural ferment over the meaning of freedom," the intuitive, sensationalist ethics provided by the Scots offered an intellectually respectable way to establish public virtue in a society that was busily repudiating the props on which virtue had traditionally rested—tradition itself, divine revelation, history, social hierarchy, an inherited government, and the authority of religious denominations.[37] As Norman Fiering has put it, the "moral philosophy" of the eighteenth-century Scottish Enlightenment "was uniquely suited to the needs of an era still strongly committed to traditional religious

---

[34]Fiering, *Moral Philosophy at Seventeenth-Century Harvard*, 13–14, and, for a contextual defense of the Protestant recourse to Aristotle, Richard A. Muller, *Post-Reformation Dogmatics*, vol. 1 (Grand Rapids, Mich.: Baker, 1987).

[35]On connections between pious evangelicalism and the Enlightenment, see especially D. W. Bebbington, *Evangelicalism in Modern Britain: A History from the 1730s to the 1980s* (London: Unwin Hyman, 1989), 5–74. Fiering also shows how certain themes of the Cambridge Platonists that anticipated Enlightenment emphases also paralleled pietistic concerns (*Moral Philosophy at Seventeenth-Century Harvard*, 247).

[36]See especially John Clive and Bernard Bailyn, "England's Cultural Provinces: Scotland and America," *William and Mary Quarterly* 11 (1954): 200–213.

[37]Hatch, *Democratization of American Christianity*, 6.

values and yet searching for alternative modes of justification for those values."[38] For Protestants who wanted to preserve traditional forms of Christianity without having to appeal to traditional religious authorities, the commonsense reasoning of the Scottish Enlightenment was the answer.

Ironically, the colonial Great Awakening, which was conservative in its doctrine, had helped create the social conditions in which a didactic Enlightenment could flourish. The revival compromised the traditional importance of inherited structures by placing more emphasis on the individual's reception of God's grace than on the individual's place in a particular denomination or local congregation. Its ideal of the pure church hastened a sectarian fragmentation of the traditionally inclusive denominations. Its fervent millennialism encouraged a negative opinion of the theological past, and its extemporaneous mode of address undercut traditional reliance on classical patterns of public speech. In each of these ways, the Awakening loosened the bonds of tradition that had survived the migration from Old World to New.[39]

The Awakening also contributed to the general breakup of community and family cohesion that increasingly characterized eighteenth-century colonial life.[40] Land shortages in settled communities, the enticement of unsettled terrain in the regions beyond the mountains, and increasing opportunities for social advancement all militated against the authority of hereditary traditions. Eighteenth-century American society was not anarchical, but it was a place where ingenuity in meeting present needs paid greater rewards than simple deference to the past. In this New World environment, traditional or external authorities were increasingly on the defensive.

The imperial crisis after mid-century, which was experienced as both a political and a social challenge, sealed the fate of the Puritan worldview

---

[38]Fiering, *Moral Philosophy at Seventeenth-Century Harvard*, 300.

[39]Clarence C. Goen, *Revivalism and Separatism in New England, 1740–1800* (New Haven: Yale University Press, 1962); Jonathan Edwards, *Apocalyptic Writings*, ed. Stephen J. Stein, vol. 5 of *The Works of Jonathan Edwards* (New Haven: Yale University Press, 1977); Nathan O. Hatch, *The Sacred Cause of Liberty: Republican Thought and the Millennium in Revolutionary New England* (New Haven: Yale University Press, 1977), 55–96; and Harry S. Stout, "Part IV: Delivery, 1731–1763," in *The New England Soul: Preaching and Religious Culture in Colonial New England* (New York: Oxford University Press, 1986), 185–258.

[40]On those unsettling conditions, see Richard L. Bushman, *From Puritan to Yankee: Character and the Social Order in Connecticut* (Cambridge, Mass.: Harvard University Press, 1967), and James A. Henretta and Gregory H. Nobles, *Evolution and Revolution: American Society, 1600–1820* (Lexington, Mass.: D. C. Heath, 1987), 103–24.

and opened the door for a Protestant Enlightenment. Two great political tasks confronted the patriot leaders, and a third equally great difficulty faced the Protestants who joined the revolutionary cause. The first was to justify the break with Great Britain, that is, to define an ideology for revolution strong enough to overcome the weight of legal precedent, venerated traditions of British constitutionalism, and the sacred aura of British liberty that had enraptured the colonists only short years before during war with France. The second was to establish principles of social order for a new nation that was repudiating autocratic government, hierarchial political assumptions, and automatic deference to tradition. For Protestant leaders a third task was to preserve the hereditary position of Christianity in a culture that denied absolute sovereignty to any authority and that was turning against the structures of traditional religion (like the political episcopate or the establishment of Congregational churches in New England) as actively as it was turning against other inherited authorities.[41] Moreover, patriots needed not merely moral and intellectual justifications, but justifications untainted by Old World traditions associated with the corrupting forces of "tyranny."

For each of these tasks the reasoning of the Scottish Enlightenment proved irresistibly appealing. The fit between Scottish arguments and American requirements can be seen most easily by examining briefly the moral philosophy of Francis Hutcheson (1694–1746), the first great thinker of Scotland's Enlightenment. This brief discussion is not meant to suggest that Protestants in revolutionary America necessarily relied on Hutcheson for the details of their positions (although some important Protestant leaders did so) any more than it is to suggest that the standard college textbooks on moral philosophy of the antebellum period were slavish imitations of Thomas Reid (1710–96), the most widely plagiarized spokesman of the later Scottish Enlightenment.[42] Rather it is meant to show that Hutcheson's general ethical positions met several urgent needs in America. Church leaders especially, even if they did not know Hutcheson by name, nonetheless adopted his general approach to meet

---

[41]On the turn against establishments, see Thomas J. Curry, *The The First Freedoms: Church and State in America to the Passage of the First Amendment* (New York: Oxford University Press, 1986), 134–222.

[42]Or as Henry May once put it, "Hutcheson and [Samuel] Clarke [British apologist ca. 1720] early, Reid and [Dugald] Stewart [popularizer of Reid's views] late, seemed to answer the questions Americans wanted to ask" ("The Problem of the American Enlightenment," in *Ideas, Faiths and Feelings: Essays on American Intellectual and Religious History, 1952–1982* [New York: Oxford University Press, 1983], 19).

the cultural crises of their age.[43] Specifically, Hutcheson had developed a scientific, universal, and optimistic ethical theory that did not require the sanction of tradition. In addition, he had shown how such a perspective could justify colonial resistance to an unjust mother country, and he had provided up-to-date arguments that traditional Protestants could use to defend Christian faith. Hutcheson, in other words, illuminated the path that American Protestants trod to the Enlightenment.

First, Hutcheson sought the scientific credibility for his ethics that the Age of Newton required by drawing an analogy between the "moral sense" and the external senses that grounded Locke's psychology and Newton's physics. The "moral sense," according to Hutcheson, was as much a part of the "frame of our nature" as the physical senses.[44] Just as the physical senses made possible knowledge of the laws of physical nature, so the moral sense made it possible to know the natural laws of virtue. Second, Hutcheson's ethical theory was universalistic. It did not depend on an Augustinian or Puritan view of virtue, in which the action of God's grace was restricted to the elect. "Each one," as Hutcheson defined the moral sense in his *System of Moral Philosophy*, may recognize that there is "a natural and immediate determination to approve certain affections, and actions consequent upon them."[45] Third, reliance on the moral sense provided a way to escape the anarchy that Robert Filmer and Thomas Hobbes had predicated for nonauthoritarian societies. Moral perceptions of virtue and vice, honor and shame, were fully capable of leading to personal goodness and social harmony.[46] Finally, Hutcheson argued that people may rely on the communications of the moral sense without needing to trust the discursive arguments of others or the hoary dictates of the past. Hutcheson's ethics, like those of the Puritans or Edwards, were affectional. Unlike the early systems, however, Hutcheson required no special place for a revelation from beyond the individual, or even for authoritative direction from other human

---

[43]This brief overview of Hutcheson draws from Jane Rendall, ed., *The Origins of the Scottish Enlightenment* (New York: St. Martin's Press, 1978); Flower and Murphey, *History of Philosophy in America*, 1:224–81; Mark Valeri, "Francis Hutcheson," in *American Colonial Writers, 1735–1781*, ed. Emory Elliott (Detroit: Gale, 1984), 310–17; and Fiering, *Moral Philosophy at Seventeenth-Century Harvard* and *Jonathan Edwards's Moral Thought*.

[44]Frances Hutcheson, *Essays on the Passions* (3d ed., 1742), as quoted in Fiering, *Moral Philosophy at Seventeenth-Century Harvard*, 201.

[45]Frances Hutcheson, *System of Moral Philosophy* (1755), in Rendall, *Origins of the Scottish Enlightenment*, 80.

[46]See the discussion in Fiering, *Moral Philosophy at Seventeenth-Century Harvard*, 200–205.

sources. Humans knew ethical maxims simply by nature and could simply by nature do the good that harmonious human existence required.

Reasoning like Hutcheson's contributed only one strand to the "real Whig" tradition that undergirded the drive for American independence. But that drive was thoroughly of a piece with the general spirit of the Enlightenment. Whatever Puritan or explicitly biblical elements may have contributed to the ideology of the American Revolution, this ideology shared fully the assumptions of the moderate Enlightenment.[47] "Real Whig" thought was predicated on a defense of natural rights, in America it sustained a continual optimism concerning capacities to create the world anew, and it staked its future on an ability to discover natural resources for pressing social needs.[48] Political realists like James Madison, Alexander Hamilton, and John Adams might in different ways temper Enlightenment optimism concerning the new order, but they never doubted that the secret of the Revolution's success lay in discovering the moral laws of human behavior through "the science of politics" and putting them to use in creating a new age, a process historian Gordon Wood has called the "consuming passion of the Enlightenment."[49]

The general influence of the Revolution on American thought was such that the form of reasoning by which patriots justified their rebellion against the Crown instinctively became also the form of reasoning by which political and religious leaders sought a stable social order for the new nation and by which Protestant spokesmen defended the place of traditional faith in a traditionless society.

The particularly Enlightenment character of this reasoning was its trust in objectivity, its devotion to a principle of privileged scientific inquiry. Protestant commitment to this form of the Enlightenment was thoroughgoing because it seemed to work so well—it did justify the rebellion, it did establish social order (politically in a constitution infused with the principles of moral philosophy, intellectually through a colle-

---

[47]See Commager, *The Empire of Reason*; Bernard Bailyn, *The Ideological Origins of the American Revolution* (Cambridge, Mass.: Harvard University Press, 1967), 26–30; May, *The Enlightenment in America*, 278–304; Morton White, *The Philosophy of the American Revolution* (New York: Oxford University Press, 1978); and especially Gordon S. Wood, "Conspiracy and the Paranoid Style: Causality and Deceit in the Eighteenth Century," *William and Mary Quarterly* 39 (1982): 401–41.

[48]Bailyn, *Ideological Origins*, 184–89; Gordon S. Wood, *The Creation of the American Republic, 1776–1787* (Chapel Hill: University of North Carolina Press, 1969), 44, and Douglass Adair, " 'That Politics May Be Reduced to a Science': David Hume, James Madison, and the Tenth Federalist," in *Fame and the Founding Fathers*, ed. Trevor Colburn (New York: Norton, 1974).

[49]Wood, "Conspiracy and the Paranoid Style," 414.

giate curriculum devoted to the teaching of moral philosophy), and it did make way for nearly a century's triumphant vindication of traditional Protestantism. Protestant commitment to this form of the Enlightenment became deeply ingrained, not only because it was so successful, but also because it was so intuitive, so instinctive, so much a part of second nature. For much of the history of the United States, Protestants denied that they had a philosophy; they were merely pursuing common sense.

The utility of this kind of Enlightenment reasoning was apparent. It was, most obviously, a mainstay of political argument. What weight could the traditional authority of the king in Parliament carry against the "self-evident truths," the "unalienable rights," or "the laws of nature" proclaimed by the Declaration of Independence? What need was there for a careful rebuttal of authorities, or even a careful perusal of Scripture, to justify rebellion, if it was transparent to the moral sense that such a rebellion was necessary?[50]

For Protestants, Enlightenment patterns of thought had even more uses than they did for the statesmen. Some were social. Guardians of American public virtue could now rely on the "moral sense" to restate traditional morality in a scientific form without having recourse to the traditional props for ethics, including even the special revelation of the Bible. Witherspoon, who as professor of moral philosophy at Princeton turned to the work of his former bête noire, Francis Hutcheson, for the content of his lectures, claimed that when we study our own minds, we end up with the proper principles for a just and stable society. He hoped that "a time may come when men, treating moral philosophy as Newton and his successors have done natural [philosophy], may arrive at greater precision" on ethical matters.[51]

Witherspoon's successor as president of Princeton, Samuel Stanhope Smith, was the most capable early systematizer of the American Enlightenment. In a work from 1787 defending the unity of humanity, Smith left no doubts about his belief in the harmony of the new science and the old religion: "I am happy to observe, on this subject, that the most

[50]For a fine discussion of the intellectual background of the political founders, see Daniel Walker Howe, "The Political Psychology of *The Federalist*," *William and Mary Quarterly* 44 (1987): 485–509.
[51]Witherspoon, "Lectures on Moral Philosophy," in *Works*, 3:369, 470. For Witherspoon's use of Hutcheson, see Jack Scott, ed., *An Annotated Edition of Lectures on Moral Philosophy by John Witherspoon* (Newark: University of Delaware Press, 1982), esp. 26–28.

accurate investigations into the power of nature ever serve to confirm
the facts vouched by the authority of revelation. A just philosophy will
always be found to be coincident with the true theology." He also left
no doubts about his faith in the power of the new moral philosophy to
move from an examination of one's own heart to universally valid principles of social order, a power that would be destroyed if humanity did
not constitute a unified species.

> The science of morals would be absurd; the law of nature and nations would
> be annihilated; no general principles of human conduct, of religion, or of policy
> could be framed; for, human nature . . . could not be comprehended in any sys-
> tem. The rules which would result from the study of our own nature, would not
> apply to the natives of other countries who would be of different spe-
> cies. . . . Such principles tend to confound all science, as well as piety; and leave
> us in the world uncertain whom to trust, or what opinions to frame of others.
> The doctrine of one race, removes this uncertainty, renders human nature sus-
> ceptible of system, illustrates the powers of physical causes, and opens a rich
> and extensive field for moral science.[52]

The paths marked out by Witherspoon and Smith were followed by
most of the country's major educators in the years before the Civil
War.[53] Exceptionally able books by Wilson Smith, Daniel Walker Howe,
and D. H. Meyer have shown how deeply ingrained this trust in Enlightenment procedure became.[54] Explicit in the lectures and textbooks of the
nation's academic leaders was the Enlightenment belief that Americans
could find within themselves resources, compatible with Christianity, to
bring social order out of the rootlessness and confusion of the new nation.[55]

[52]Samuel Stanhope Smith, *An Essay on the Causes of the Variety of Complexion and
Figure in the Human Species* (Philadelphia: Robert Aitkin, 1787), 109–10.

[53]See Hood, *Reformed America*, 10–46, on the specific influence of Witherspoon and Smith
in the South, and Robert M. Calhoon, *Evangelicals and Conservatives in the Early South,
1740–1861* (Columbia: University of South Carolina Press, 1988), 85: Witherspoon fashioned "a kind of secularized Calvinism that filled a real need in early national political
culture."

[54]Wilson Smith, *Professors and Public Ethics: Studies of Northern Moral Philosophers
before the Civil War* (Ithaca: Cornell University Press, 1956); Howe, *Unitarian Conscience*; and Meyer, *The Instructed Conscience*.

[55]On that confusion, see John M. Murrin, "The Great Inversion; or, Court versus Country:
A Comparison of the Revolution Settlements in England (1688–1721) and America
(1776–1816)," in *Three British Revolutions: 1641, 1688, 1776*, ed. J. G. A. Pocock
(Princeton: Princeton University Press, 1980), 376; David Hackett Fischer, *Growing Old
in America*, expanded ed. (New York: Oxford University Press, 1973), 112; and Gordon
S. Wood, "Evangelical America and Early Mormonism," *New York History* 61 (1980):
361.

The extent of Protestant incorporation of the Enlightenment, however, went much further than merely its utility for the moral direction of society. In fact, the Enlightenment entered deep into the fabric of Protestant life and thought—not replacing inherited Christian content as it did for Comptean positivists, but everywhere molding that content to meet the exigencies of the moment—and so established an enduring bond between Protestantism and the Enlightenment.[56] Every major feature of what came to be most distinctive about American Protestantism of the nineteenth century bore the indelible impress of the didactic Enlightenment. At the levels of high culture it was true for apologetics and theology.[57] For all major Protestant groups it influenced expectations concerning revival.[58] Among both common people and the elite it provided the framework for appropriating Scripture.[59]

In summary, with most forms of authority under attack in revolutionary America, the intuitive, universalistic appeal of the Scottish Enlightenment saved the day. The strength or weakness of the Scottish perspective as a narrowly intellectual system was never at issue in revolutionary America. The establishment of Scottish Common Sense philosophy as the dominant conceptual language for Protestant discourse was thus a by-product of a larger cultural transition. In revolutionary America there was no room for the philosophical idealism of Samuel Johnson or Jonathan Edwards, since the cry everywhere was for inde-

[56]On the unexpectedly important role of Comptean ideas, at least as perceived threat, see Charles D. Cashdollar, *The Transformation of Theology, 1830–1890: Positivism and Protestant Thought in Britain and America* (Princeton: Princeton University Press, 1989).

[57]See, for example, Bozeman, *Protestants in an Age of Science*; Holifield, *The Gentlemen Theologians*; Howe, *Unitarian Conscience*; Wilson Smith, "William Paley's Theological Utilitarianism in America," *William and Mary Quarterly* 11 (1954): 402–24; Frank Hugh Foster, *A Genetic History of the New England Theology* (Chicago: University of Chicago Press, 1907); Mark A. Noll, ed., *The Princeton Theology, 1812–1921* (Grand Rapids, Mich.: Baker, 1983); Edward H. Madden and James E. Hamilton, *Freedom and Grace: The Life of Asa Mahan* (Methuen, N.J.: Scarecrow Press, 1982); Richard T. Hughes and C. Leonard Allen, *Illusions of Innocence: Protestant Primitivism in America, 1630–1875* (Chicago: University of Chicago Press, 1988); and Patrick W. Carey, ed., *American Catholic Religious Thought: The Shaping of a Theological and Social Tradition* (New York: Paulist Press, 1987), 5–15, 73–83.

[58]See especially Charles G. Finney, *Lectures on Revivals of Religion* (1835), ed. William G. McLoughlin (Cambridge, Mass.: Harvard University Press, 1960).

[59]See, as a start, Nathan O. Hatch, "*Sola Scriptura* and *Novus Ordo Seclorum*," and George M. Marsden, "Everyone One's Own Interpreter? The Bible, Science, and Authority in Mid-Nineteenth-Century America," both in *The Bible in America*, ed. Nathan O. Hatch and Mark A. Noll (New York: Oxford University Press, 1982), 59–78, 79–100; and John H. Giltner, *Moses Stuart: The Father of Biblical Science in America* (Atlanta: Scholars Press, 1988).

pendence, practicality, and self-sufficiency.[60] There was also little room for the Augustinian, conversionist ethics of Edwards, because Americans required moral and political guidelines that were available equally and reliably to all.

One final feature of early natural affinities came powerfully into play as American Protestants embraced the didactic Enlightenment. In ways that have been probed extensively by a wealth of historical works, the process that witnessed Protestant alignment with the Enlightenment witnessed also Protestant alignment with the United States.[61] The contrast with revolutionary France could not have been greater: In France, liberty, the people, the Enlightenment, and the new sense of French national destiny stood against the church; in the United States, Protestantism identified itself with the people, the Enlightenment, democracy, republicanism, economic liberalism, and the sense of American manifest destiny.[62] This identification had profound intellectual effects. Protestant identity in America could be separated no more from its commitment to Enlightenment rationalism than from its belief in the divine character of the country and in God's ordination of democratic liberalism. All of the elements that went into the making of an American Protestant Enlightenment were melted together indistinguishably in the crucible from which also emerged the American nation.

[60]This judgment contradicts the conclusion of James Ward Smith that the reason why neither Edwards's nor Johnson's views "had any significant effect on the American mind of the later eighteenth century" was "primarily religious" (Smith, "Religion and Science in American Philosophy," in *The Shaping of American Religion*, ed. James Ward Smith and A. Leland Jamison [Princeton: Princeton University Press, 1961], 417). While Smith is no doubt correct in the wider sense of the term *religious*, it was the particular political and social situation of revolutionary America that provided the questions that religion was called upon to answer.

[61]See Hatch, *The Sacred Cause of Liberty*; John F. Berens, "The Sanctification of American Nationalism," in *Providence and Patriotism in Early America, 1640–1815* (Charlottesville: University Press of Virginia, 1978), 112–28; Ruth Bloch, *Visionary Republic: Millennial Themes in American Thought, 1756–1800* (New York: Cambridge University Press, 1985); and Mark A. Noll, George M. Marsden, and Nathan O. Hatch, *The Search for Christian America*, expanded ed. (Colorado Springs: Helmers and Howard, 1989).

[62]For a trenchant expression of those differences, see Alexis de Tocqueville, *L'ancien régime et la Révolution* (1967 ed.), 252–53, as translated and quoted in Thomas L. Pangle, *The Spirit of Modern Republicanism: The Moral Vision of the American Founders and the Philosophy of Locke* (Chicago: University of Chicago Press, 1988), 284 n. 8: "There is no country in the world where the boldest doctrines of the *philosophes* of the eighteenth century, in matters of politics, were more fully applied than in America; it was only the anti-religious doctrines that never were able to make headway." The connection between republican and Protestant themes in revolutionary America has received surprisingly little attention; for an exception, see James T. Kloppenberg, "The Virtue of Liberalism: Christianity, Republicanism, and Ethics in Early American Political Discourse," *Journal of American History* 74 (1987): 9–33.

THE EPISTEMOLOGICAL UNDERDETERMINATION
OF ROMANTICISM

A definite romantic strain was evident early in the development of Protestantism in the United States. To the extent that revivalism has an intrinsic romantic tendency, that strain was present from the earliest decades of Protestant settlement. In the nineteenth century, however, the romantic impulses multiplied. From one perspective, romanticism opposed the detached rationalism characteristic of the Enlightenment. A fine recent history describes the romantic strain in British evangelicalism as "the movement of taste that stressed, against the mechanism and classicism of the Enlightenment, the place of feeling and intuition in human perception, the importance of nature and history for human experience."[63] Hence romanticism may be regarded as an alternative to Enlightenment rationalism.

From the perspective of epistemology, however, romantic trends in American Protestantism brought far less change than first impressions might suggest. The spread of romantic tendencies in the nineteenth century should not be slighted. Their importance is suggested by noting the source of the following assertions: "With regard to moral subjects . . . the feelings destroyed by metaphysical investigation are the very objects to be investigated. . . . If this be weakened or destroyed, there is nothing left; and a man in this state is no more qualified to speak on these subjects than the deaf to discourse on music." Again, "so legitimate and powerful is this inward teaching of the Spirit that it is no uncommon thing to find men having two theologies—one of the intellect, and another of the heart."[64] These words are not from Horace Bushnell but from his longtime and often bitter enemy the Presbyterian confessionalist Charles Hodge.[65]

Bushnell's romanticism was central to his theological orientation, rather than, like Hodge's, an indifferently integrated part of a more scientific whole. Forceful essays published just before 1850 made Bushnell's far-reaching case for the subjective character of religious knowledge. In "Dogma and Spirit" (1848) Bushnell acknowledged that "opinion, science, systematic theology, or even dogma in the best possible sense of

[63]Bebbington, Evangelicalism in Modern Britain, 81.
[64]Charles Hodge, "Lecture to Theological Students" (1829), in Noll, The Princeton Theology, 112–13, and idem, Systematic Theology (1872–73), 3 vols. (Grand Rapids, Mich.: Eerdmans, n.d.), 1:16.
[65]On this underappreciated side of Hodge's thought, see also W. Andrew Hoffecker, Piety and the Princeton Theologians (Grand Rapids, Mich.: Baker, 1981), 44–94.

the term" were not irrelevant for Christians. They had "their proper place"—aiding education of the young, raising a testimony against unbelief, and initiating contacts with other forms of knowledge. For religious purposes, however, scientific learning of whatever source paled beside "a knowledge of God and Christian truth which is of the heart." The latter kind of knowledge was superior beyond question:

What is loftiest and most transcendent in the character of God, his purity, goodness, beauty, and gentleness, can never be sufficiently apprehended by mere intellect, or by any other power than a heart configured by these divine qualities. . . . Indeed, the gospel is, in one view, a magnificent work of art, a manifestation of God which is to find the world, and move it, and change it, through the medium of expression. Hence it requires for an inlet, not reason or logic or a scientific power so much as a right sensibility.[66]

The next year Bushnell expanded these notions in probably the most influential essay in the history of American theology, the "Preliminary Dissertation on the Nature of Language as Related to Thought and Spirit," preface to his work *God in Christ*. In it he directly attacked the penchant of Enlightenment Protestants to systematize morality and theology; he proclaimed "the very great difficulty, if not impossibility, of mental science and religious dogmatism." By contrast, Bushnell pointed to higher forms of knowledge:

The teachings of Christ are mere utterances of truth, not argumentations over it. He gives it forth in living symbols, without definition, without *proving* it, ever, as the logicians speak, well understanding that truth is that which shines in its own evidence, that which *finds* us, to use an admirable expression of Coleridge, and thus enters into us.[67]

With Bushnell we have a definite proposal for an alternative to the scientific rationalism of the American Protestant Enlightenment.

H. Shelton Smith and Conrad Cherry are correct in linking Bushnell's sensibility with the affectional theology of Jonathan Edwards.[68] But only to a point. The difference accounts for the reason why Bushnell's type of romantic alternative to the Protestant Enlightenment underdetermined epistemological issues. Whereas Edwards's affectional theology was a

[66]Horace Bushnell, "Dogma and Spirit" (published 1849), in *Horace Bushnell*, ed. H. Shelton Smith (New York: Oxford University Press, 1965), 63, 59.
[67]Bushnell, "Preliminary Dissertation on the Nature of Language as Related to Thought and Spirit," in ibid., 97, 98.
[68]Smith, ibid., 45, and Conrad C. Cherry, *Nature and Religious Imagination from Edwards to Bushnell* (Philadelphia: Fortress Press, 1980).

well-integrated part of a general worldview—with a highly regarded place for scientific knowledge in addition to a well-articulated cosmology to explain the relation between affective knowledge and scientific knowledge (as different ways of apprehending the mind of God)—Bushnell proposed his romantic view of God and the self as an alternative standing alongside, or opposed to, scientific knowledge. Bushnell's views thus resembled those that Samuel Taylor Coleridge developed in *Aids to Reflection*, in postulating two contrasting kinds of knowledge—"understanding" for dealing with the ordinary tasks of life and "reason" for intuiting God and the higher realities—that were also not related in an obvious way.[69]

Other nineteenth-century theologians, like Hodge, Edwards A. Park, and Henry Boynton Smith, labored mightily to show how affective and objective knowledge could be integrated within one coherent system. Hodge's and Park's accounts have not carried the weight of Bushnell's because they too easily (though in contrasting ways) translated the affective back into the objective.[70] Henry Boynton Smith was more effective in integrating the two, but he did so with a Germanic Christocentrism that had little impact on pragmatic and realistic America.[71] Only Bushnell among his peers succeeded in providing a convincing case for the foundational character of affectional knowledge. But if Hodge and Park failed to give such knowledge its due, Bushnell failed to show how it related to the objective sort of knowledge that had enjoyed a privileged position in American reflection since the Revolution. Unlike Edwards, who by his idealism found a place for science within the same cosmology that undergirded his affectional soteriology, Bushnell remained content with the procedures and assumptions of Enlightenment rationality when he turned to questions of the physical world.

Bushnell's reason for rejecting Charles Darwin is telling at this point. With most other learned Americans, both scientists and theologians, in the first twenty years after the publication of *On the Origin of Species* in 1859, Bushnell felt free to dismiss Darwin as simply unscientific. Bushnell expressed his opposition to evolution with flair: "If there is no sta-

[69]Smith, introduction to *Horace Bushnell*, 27–28.
[70]The significant exchange of seven essays between Park and Hodge began with Park, "The Theology of the Intellect and That of the Feelings," *Bibliotheca Sacra* 7 (July 1850): 533–69, and Hodge, "The Theology of the Intellect and That of the Feelings," *Biblical Repertory and Princeton Review* 22 (October 1850): 642–74.
[71]See Richard A. Muller, "Henry Boynton Smith: Christocentric Theologian," *Journal of Presbyterian History* 61 (1983): 429–44.

bility or fixity in species, then, for aught that appears, even science itself may be transmuted into successions of music, and moonshine, and auroral fires. If a single kind is all kinds, then all are one, and since that is the same as none, there is knowledge no longer."[72] Strikingly enough, Bushnell's attack on Darwin's science sounded very much like the supernatural rationalists' attack on Bushnell's affectional theology. Charles Hodge, for example, thought that Bushnell's "Preliminary Dissertation on the Nature of Language" came from a "vague ecstacy of feeling, or spiritual inebriation"; it was "a splendid work of art" by "a poet," but provided no substantive theological knowledge.[73] For Bushnell to have made a comprehensive contribution to epistemology he needed affectional reasons, or at least an affectional cosmology, for rejecting evolution.

Bushnell viewed religious knowledge as an addition to scientific knowledge. Thus his views carved out a breathing space for the human spirit over scientific rationalism. But Bushnell does not seem to have taken up the project of saying how the two should relate. He did not call into question widespread assumptions about the privileged place of scientific rationalism, only its hegemony. The Enlightenment, though now with a rival, still lived.

For American intellectual life as a whole, it turned out to be a pretty puny rival. Hodge's and Bushnell's other critics contended that by stressing so heavily the mystical side of faith, Bushnell had reduced its ability to count as *real* knowledge. Only a few decades later the arbiters of America's new universities would make the same implicit judgment, only now with a conception of *real* scientific knowledge that had evolved beyond Hodge's meaning of the term. Although theological study had been the dominant form of postbaccalaureate higher education for the first ninety years of the United States, it quickly lost its place in the transformation of higher education after the Civil War. In the new university, theology could be elbowed aside easily—Hodge's type because it was poor science, Bushnell's type because it did not claim to be science

---

[72]Horace Bushnell, "Science and Religion," *Putnam's Monthly Magazine of Literature, Science, Art, and National Interests* (1868), 271, as quoted in Jon H. Roberts, *Darwinism and the Divine in America: Protestant Intellectuals and Organic Evolution, 1859–1900* (Madison: University of Wisconsin Press, 1988), 44. See also Thomas Paul Thigpen, "On the Origin of Theses: An Exploration of Horace Bushnell's Rejection of Darwinism," *Church History* 57 (December 1988): 499–513.

[73]Charles Hodge, "Bushnell's Discourses," *Biblical Repertory and Princeton Review* 21 (1849): 274, 296, 298.

at all. Enlightenment standards, which Bushnell had called into question, brooked no rival.[74]

THE ENLIGHTENMENT AND
THE DIVISION OF PROTESTANT THOUGHT, 1865–1929

If the antebellum bond between the Enlightenment and Protestantism was as secure as I have suggested, the intellectual situation in 1900 looks like a puzzle. By that time a different kind of science had replaced the earlier doxological Baconianism, and the academy had grown inhospitable to the earlier cultural alliance between science and Protestantism. In this situation there was an unprecedented intellectual division among Protestants, caused in large part by contrasting opinions on the merits of the new science. Through a complicated set of maneuvers in which the role of the churches has never been adequately studied, intellectual life in the academy was encouraging new forms of science at the same time as it was replacing the traditional religious framework for a more secular one. Nothing less than an intellectual revolution was under way. Nonetheless, the postbellum transformation of formal intellectual life resembled the antebellum rise of romanticism in one important respect. Where both challenged substantially the content of the original American Enlightenment, neither called into final question its ideals of privileged scientific inquiry and confidently expectant progress.

Several possible reasons may be given for the rapid shift in American intellectual life after the Civil War. Some deal with new kinds of scholars, others with new influences from Europe, new configurations in the American economy, or new social expectations for mass culture.[75] Yet it is also possible to see the eclipse of America's Protestant Enlightenment as a delayed reaction to the creation of America's Protestant Enlight-

[74]My understanding of the debates surrounding Bushnell owes a great deal to D. G. Hart, "Divided between Heart and Mind: The Critical Period for Protestant Thought in America," *Journal of Ecclesiastical History* 38 (1987): 254–70, and idem, "Poems, Propositions, and Dogma: The Controversy over Religious Language and the Demise of Theology in American Learning," *Church History* 57 (1988): 310–21.

[75]On this massive subject, the following offer expert orientation and important arguments: Laurence R. Veysey, *The Emergence of the American University* (Chicago: University of Chicago Press, 1965); Burton J. Bledstein, *The Culture of Professionalism: The Middle Class and the Development of Higher Education in America* (New York: Norton, 1976); Bruce Kuklick, *The Rise of American Philosophy: Cambridge, Massachusetts, 1860–1930* (New Haven: Yale University Press, 1977); and Alexandra Oleson and John Voss, eds., *The Organization of Knowledge in Modern America, 1860–1920* (Baltimore: Johns Hopkins University Press, 1979).

enment. In these terms, what was gained by joining the faith so securely to the intellectual fashions and the national needs of 1800 was lost when the fashions and the needs changed after the Civil War. Or at least this is the persuasive case made recently by historian James Turner. Modern unbelief, he concludes, "resulted from the decisions that influential church leaders—lay writers, theologians, ministers—made about how to confront the modern pressures upon religious belief. [Their] choices, taken together, boiled down to a decision to deal with modernity by embracing it—to defuse modern threats to the traditional bases of belief by bringing God into line with modernity."[76]

When they made these decisions, however, American Protestants paved the way for modern unbelief. Faced with the prestige of Newtonian science, Protestants chose to invest the Argument from Design with all-encompassing force as an apologetic for Christianity. Faced with increasing reliance on rationalized technique, Protestants chose to defend God as the quintessence of modern rationality. Faced with the prevailing moralism of the Enlightenment, Protestants chose to defend God as a Cosmic Person supremely devoted to the well-being of humanity as that well-being was defined in the modern age. Each of these choices enabled Christians to maintain traditional faith and yet also to win the approval of the world. Each allowed Protestants to participate in modern life without sacrificing the faith.

The domestication of God to which these choices led troubled few Protestants until it was too late. As modern standards in science, reason, and morality continued to evolve, however, there came a day when the effort to justify God by these canons of modernity seemed, to an elite body of intellectuals, hardly worth the effort. They found God a superfluous hypothesis. Thus, after Darwin, the Argument from Design became an object of faith rather than a prop for belief. After the crises of industrialization and urbanization, God seemed an irrelevancy for solving the moral dilemmas of the day. The effort to keep God in step with the modern world eventually led some people to conclude that the world was getting along just as well without him. From that thin edge of unbelief in the second half of the nineteenth century has emerged the great intellectual institutions of the twentieth century in which the conventions of traditional Western discourse are thoroughly reversed. Where once it

---

[76]James Turner, *Without God, without Creed: The Origins of Unbelief in America* (Baltimore: Johns Hopkins University Press, 1985), 266.

had been unthinkable not to believe in God, it has now become nearly unthinkable to treat God as a necessary foundation for any serious reflection, intellectual or moral.

Whatever the exact role of Protestants in bringing about the altered state of affairs may have been, it is abundantly clear that a new intellectual world had dawned. Views of science were changing from static and mechanistic to developmental and organic, attitudes toward academic work from teleological and doxological to progressive and functional, perspectives on religion from particularistic and theistic to universalistic and agnostic.

If the Scottish Common Sense form of the American Enlightenment had passed away, however, surprisingly little change had taken place in the epistemological attitudes inherited from that earlier Enlightenment. Things had taken a turn that created problems for the hereditary bond between Protestants and the Enlightenment, but earlier attitudes toward truth still prevailed, perhaps with more vigor than ever.

Denizens of the new university grew out of the restraints Protestantism once exercised on Enlightenment rationality. Now that science was liberated from the control of the theologians, it had a thing or two to show its former guardians. Or at least educators like Andrew Dickinson White thought so, as in the historian's role he cheered on the forces of modernity in his *History of the Warfare of Science with Theology.* As the first president of Cornell University, White promised that his school would "afford an asylum for Science—where truth shall be sought for truth's sake, where it shall not be the main purpose of the Faculty to stretch or cut sciences exactly to fit 'Revealed Religion.' "[77] But liberated educators like White did not outgrow the attitudes toward inquiry that their now despised clerical predecessors had themselves promoted when they enlisted objective, value-neutral reason for God and America. Faith in progress achieved through scientific means was everywhere rampant at the turn of the century. If the eighteenth-century "Age of Enlightenment," as Peter Gay once said, "was filled with biologists, mathematicians, psychologists, aspiring to become the Newton of their discipline," now the name had changed but the game remained the same.[78] In 1894

---

[77]Quoted in Henry Warner Bowden, *Church History in the Age of Science: Historiographical Patterns in the United States, 1876–1918* (Chapel Hill: University of North Carolina Press, 1971), 7.
[78]Peter Gay, *The Enlightenment: A Comprehensive Anthology* (New York: Simon and Schuster, 1973), 64.

Henry Adams wrote his fellow members of the American Historical Association urging them on to what can only be called the Darwinian trick: "No teacher with a spark of imagination or with an idea of scientific method can have helped dreaming of the immortality that would be achieved by the man who should successfully apply Darwin's methods to the facts of human history."[79] The other great minds of the age shared Adams's enthusiasm, as Bruce Kuklick aptly summarizes:

> Dewey, Royce, Charles Peirce, and others . . . urged that loyalty to science would enable human beings to achieve existential integration most adequately. Mankind would make its greatest advance when the scientific method was applied to questions of ethics. Control would grow ever more rich and complex. The quality of human experience would change for the better and, consequently, human selves also.[80]

Again it is necessary to change only one word to bring a conclusion of Peter Gay's concerning Enlightenment Europe up to date for late nineteenth-century America: "What united the philosophes [read, America's leading men of letters] above all else was confidence in the critical method."[81]

Within the academy, the combination of continued Enlightenment confidence in scientific rationality and the break from Protestantism was not propitious for theology. George Burton Adams took his cue from Horace Bushnell when he addressed the American Historical Association as its president in 1908, but his conclusion was a devastating reversal of Bushnell's. The job of historians, Adams urged, was "to ascertain as nearly as possible and to record exactly what happened." Questions concerning "the philosophy of history" are wisely left to "poets, philosophers and theologians." Historians know that "at the very beginning of all conquest of the unknown lies the fact, established and classified to the fullest extent possible." Others, presumably the poets, philosophers, and theologians, may yield to "the allurements of speculation," but "the field of the historian is, and must long remain, the discovery and recording of what actually happened."[82]

---

[79]Henry Adams, "The Tendency of History," *Annual Report of the American Historical Association for 1894*, 18–19, as quoted in W. Stull Holt, "The Idea of Scientific History in America," *Journal of the History of Ideas* 1 (1940): 356–57.
[80]Bruce Kuklick, *Churchmen and Philosophers: From Jonathan Edwards to John Dewey* (New Haven: Yale University Press, 1985), 202.
[81]Gay, *The Enlightenment: A Comprehensive Anthology*, 17.
[82]George Burton Adams, "History and the Philosophy of History," *American Historical Review* 14 (1909): 223, 236.

Where did the triumph of these attitudes leave Protestants? Painful decisions faced the heirs of those who before mid-century had operated from a base of Christian faith and scientific rationality in restful harmony. A threefold division of nineteenth-century Protestantism came about in response to the new challenge. Some, who would be called modernists, moved with the times, conceded the hegemony of the new science, and sought (usually through Bushnell's proposal) to preserve in a new form the old harmonies of the American Protestant Enlightenment.[83] For them irrelevancy threatened as dictated by the place of poetry, philosophy, and theology in the new intellectual economy.

Others, the later fundamentalists, made a more complicated response.[84] They moved both with and against the times—with, by adopting the new applied technologies of mass media and public marketing,[85] against, by resisting the evolution of the old science into the new. They too attempted to preserve the American Protestant Enlightenment, but with its old content as well as its old form. For them loomed *Kulturkampf*, or at least the frustrations of those who defend a paradigm after the authorities on normal science have decreed it lapsed.

By far the majority of Protestants vacillated in the middle, nostalgic for the old intellectual harmonies, unsettled by the tendency of the new science to dismiss traditional Christian convictions, but unwilling to decide decisively for either the old paradigm with its tethered science and commandeering faith or the new with its liberated science and second-class faith.[86]

Almost no Protestant seems to have been aware that there might have been a fourth option—to repudiate the Enlightenment, old style and new style, in order to call into question the two fundamental axioms that had determined Protestant intellectual life in the United States since the

---

[83]William R. Hutchison, *The Modernist Impulse in American Protestantism* (Cambridge, Mass.: Harvard University Press, 1976), esp. 87–94 on accommodations with the new science.

[84]George M. Marsden, *Fundamentalism and American Culture: The Shaping of Twentieth-Century Evangelicalism, 1870–1925* (New York: Oxford University Press, 1980), esp. 55–62 and 212–21 on the scientism of fundamentalists.

[85]On the psychological and technological modernity of fundamentalism, see Douglas Frank, *Less than Conquerors: How Evangelicals Entered the Twentieth Century* (Grand Rapids, Mich.: Eerdmans, 1986), and Martin E. Marty, *Modern American Religion: Volume I, The Irony of It All, 1893–1919* (Chicago: University of Chicago Press, 1986), 208–47.

[86]A good account of this middle group is found in Grant A. Wacker, "The Holy Spirit and the Spirit of the Age in American Protestantism, 1880–1910," *Journal of American History* 72 (1985): 45–62.

Revolution—that there was such an irreplaceable thing as detached, authoritative, value-neutral inquiry, and that Protestantism would be lost if it did not exercise a patrimonial custody over American civilization. Despite its logical possibility, this option was almost impossible to conceive, given the era's apotheosis of systematic scientific method and the celebrated history of Protestant centrality in American civilization.

As it happened, the Protestant-Enlightenment synthesis, though battered, did survive. The new American university threw up major problems of fact to Protestants, but it did not overthrow hereditary Protestant trust in the conventions of Enlightenment method.

BEYOND THE ENLIGHTENMENT?

The historical account, which is now over, should help to answer at least one question. Why have Protestants contributed so relatively little in response to the modern crisis of the Enlightenment? The answer: because they contributed so much to securing the Enlightenment in America.

Now we have a different situation. However defined—a revolt against formalism, the arrival of the postmodern, a collapse of the positivist paradigm—the certainties of the American Enlightenment no longer hold sway. American Protestants, who have lived for two hundred years with those certainties, find themselves in a new world. Lingering dreams of Christian America notwithstanding, Protestants are no longer the privileged custodians of American civilization. Nor are the Enlightenment verities they once embraced any longer axiomatic in the wider culture. A murderous cross fire assaults the ideal of scientific rationality. Optimism has vanished with cracks in the mirror of nature and the closing of the American mind. Hope in permanent solutions arising from concentrated attention to nature, material or human, lies buried under nihilistic rubble.

That hope, and indeed the whole magnificent edifice of the Enlightenment, has also been assaulted recently from a different quarter. Words from the president of Czechoslovakia—the strangest (to modern ears) of all imaginable words coming from the strangest of all possible places— would render irrelevant both Enlightenment hubris and post-Enlightenment despair:

The most dangerous enemy today is no longer the dark forces of totalitarianism, the various hostile and plotting mafias, but our own bad qualities. My presidential program is, therefore, to bring spirituality, moral responsibility, humaneness, and humility into politics and, in that respect, to make clear that there is something higher above us, that our deeds do not disappear into the black hole of time but are recorded somewhere and judged, that we have neither the right nor a reason to think that we understand everything and that we can do everything.[87]

In this situation, which is so different from the world in which they have lived for two hundred years, do Protestants have anything to say? Almost certainly Protestants do have something to say, but being able to say it requires a certain distancing from the Enlightenment tradition with which they have been linked for such a long time. Protestant voices that are responding freshly to the current epistemological situation, for example, are more or less accented. They arise from Protestants who are neither members of the traditional American elites nor long habituated to Enlightenment assumptions. Thus, liberation theologians are advancing insights from Latin America and the black ghetto as a corrective to America's Protestant mainstream.[88] The Lutheran two-kingdom epistemology of the Yale school is attempting to reassert in postmodern terms the self-authenticating character of Christian language.[89] The uncompromising Mennonite radicalism of John Howard Yoder and (if a Texas Methodist can be called an Anabaptist) Stanley Hauerwas is promoting a view of the church in opposition to the world.[90] The Dutch Reformed antifoundationalism of Alvin Plantinga and Nicholas Wolterstorff is defending the epistemic rights of those who find Jesus Christ their only comfort in life and in death.[91] These are, without doubt, Protestant

[87]Václav Havel, "The Future of Central Europe," *New York Review of Books*, 29 March 1990, 19.

[88]For example, Alfred T. Hennelly, ed., *Liberation Theology: A Documentary History* (Maryknoll, N.Y.: Orbis, 1990), and Cornel West, *Prophesy Deliverance! An Afro-American Revolutionary Christianity* (Louisville, Ky.: Westminster Press/John Knox, 1982).

[89]For example, Hans W. Frei, *The Eclipse of Biblical Narrative: A Study in Eighteenth and Nineteenth Century Hermeneutics* (New Haven: Yale University Press, 1974), and George A. Lindbeck, *The Nature of Doctrine: Religion and Theology in a Postliberal Age* (Philadelphia: Westminster Press, 1984).

[90]For example, John Howard Yoder, *The Politics of Jesus* (Grand Rapids, Mich.: Eerdmans, 1972), and Stanley Hauerwas, *A Community of Character: Toward a Constructive Christian Social Ethics* (Notre Dame, Ind.: Notre Dame University Press, 1981).

[91]For example, Nicholas Wolterstorff, *Reason within the Bounds of Religion*, 2d ed. (Grand Rapids, Mich.: Eerdmans, 1984); Alvin Plantinga, "Justification and Theism," *Faith and Philosophy* 4 (1987): 403–26; and Alvin Plantinga, "Positive Epistemic Status and Proper Functions," in *Philosophical Perspectives* 2, *Epistemology*, ed. James E. Tomberlin (1988), 1–50.

words for post-Enlightenment Americans, but they come from branches of Protestantism that sprang up relatively late in the United States.

The search for resources within America's historic Protestant traditions that could be helpful at this moment must go back a considerable distance to a time before Protestants made the strategic moves that James Turner rightly characterizes as losing the soul by trying to gain the world. "Church leaders," he concludes,

> too often forgot the transcendence essential to any worthwhile God. They committed religion *functionally* to making the world better in human terms and *intellectually* to modes of knowing God fitted only for understanding this world. They did this because trying to meet the challenge of modernity, they virtually surrendered to it. . . . They did not grasp firmly enough that [belief] did not simply have to jump to the new, that belief could modify secular wisdom in the very process of adapting to it.[92]

If Turner has rightly described the deficiencies of the Protestant Enlightenment heritage for current epistemological purposes, however glorious its heritage in other areas, could we find a resource for today if we went back in time before American Protestants became American Enlightenment Protestants? In other words, we may finally be ready for Jonathan Edwards—not, that is, the details of Edwards's specific positions, but the cast of his thought in tension with the Enlightenment.[93] If there is to be a Protestantism able to exploit the wisdom of the Enlightenment, while liberated from the limits of the Enlightenment, it may well be a Protestantism that looks like Edwards's. His faith exemplified the full-blown theism that was also visible in Augustine, the Catholic mystics, the Protestant reformers, and, among Edwards's near contemporaries, Nicholas Malebranche and George Berkeley. This sort of Christianity affirms not just that God is the creator and passive sustainer of the world but also that his energy is the source of the world's energy and his will the foundation of its existence. It affirms that these principles are the basis for reasoned discourse rather than what first needs to be

---

[92]Turner, *Without God, without Creed*, 267. Charles Cashdollar's careful study of positivism leads him to see less irony and less destructive accommodation in the Protestant adjustment to Enlightenment standards of rationalism and ethics; Cashdollar, *The Transformation of Theology*, 448.

[93]An appeal to "recover" Edwards might mean for Protestants something like the twentieth-century "recovery" by Roman Catholic theologians of Thomas Aquinas, whose example in addressing the Aristotelian "Enlightenment" of his day has inspired many different forms of retrieval. A forceful statement of Edwards's contemporary relevance, cast in these terms, is Robert W. Jenson, *America's Theologian: A Recommendation of Jonathan Edwards* (New York: Oxford University Press, 1988).

demonstrated by reasoned discourse. This kind of theism stresses the world's radical dependence on God, the human mind's derivative relation to the divine mind, and the benevolent intention of God to share with humans an understanding of the reality he sustains.

Such views oppose the deistical notion that God made the world, established its laws, created humans with certain mental capabilities to understand the world, and then stepped back to see what would happen. Since the mid eighteenth century, Christians, no less than nonbelievers, have been enamored of this Enlightenment view of God. It is a view that fueled the search for Arguments from Design to demonstrate the existence of God, that led to increasingly frenzied efforts at demonstrating the benevolence of God in the face of supposedly autonomous standards of justice, that heightened concern for the apologetic value of miracles as events where God *intervenes* in a world proceeding normally under its own inner compulsion, and that placed a great burden on believers to justify their faith rationally with the procedures that the great scientists used to reason about nature. Against these Enlightenment conceptions of God, Christians like Malebranche, Berkeley, and Edwards postulated a deity who filled the universe he had created, who activated the minds he had made in his own image, who brooded over the world with constant love as well as distant power.

Edwards's specifically intellectual stance did not receive its due in its own day, because it was swimming against an overwhelming tide.[94] Thought about the world, so the new orthodoxy of the eighteenth century ran, must begin with the world; thought about God must begin with human nature; thought about revelation must rest on a natural foundation. Edwards's protests, however skillful, were in vain. His plaintive comments on eighteenth-century embarrassment with revelation expressed his perspective well:

[94]In this section I draw on Fiering, *Jonathan Edwards's Moral Thought*; Anderson, *Works of Edwards: Scientific and Philosophical Writings*; Ramsay, *Works of Edwards: Ethical Writings*; Harold Simson, *Jonathan Edwards: Theologian of the Heart* (Grand Rapids, Mich.: Eerdmans, 1974); many of the essays in Nathan O. Hatch and Harry S. Stout, eds., *Jonathan Edwards and the American Experience* (New York: Oxford University Press, 1988); and, still for inspiration if not for details, Perry Miller, *Jonathan Edwards* (New York: William Sloane, 1949). On this topic I have written at greater length in a review of Fiering's two books in *Reformed Journal*, February 1983, pp. 22–28, and in two essays, "The Contested legacy of Jonathan Edwards in Antebellum Calvinism: Theological Conflict and the Evolution of Thought in America," *Canadian Review of American Studies* 19 (1988): 149–64, and "Jonathan Edwards and Nineteenth-Century Theology," in Hatch and Stout, *Jonathan Edwards and the American Experience*, 260–87.

No great reason can be given why men should have such an inward disposition to deny any immediate communication between God and the creature, or to make as little of it as possible. . . . And therefore these doctrines are so much ridiculed that ascribe much to the immediate influence of the Spirit, and called enthusiasm, fanaticism, whimsy, and distraction; but no mortal call tell for what.[95]

Edwards's greatest contribution may be the example he set for discriminating analysis of the intellectual discoveries and assumptions of his day. Edwards not only possessed a strong belief in Antithesis—denying to human nature what belonged to God's particular activity alone—but he also possessed a strong belief in Common Grace—granting to human nature what God in his mercy had shed abroad in the world. Common Grace showed Edwards, for example, how much he could learn from Newton's science and the new moral philosophy. Edwards did not make a great deal of his commitment to the idea of Common Grace, because as Norman Fiering surmises, "Edwards assumed . . . that in a world already obsessed with the secular pursuit of conventional virtue and moral respectability, religion had to play a different and higher role than that of strengthener of public morals." Yet "Edwards . . . contributed significantly to . . . the belief that the elements of Judaeo-Christian morality have fixed, natural foundations rooted in the rational structure of the world."[96] To a limited but genuine extent, therefore, Edwards could agree that "Christian truth" was accessible to all people, especially those who distinguished themselves as the great intellects of the age. Only after thoroughly digesting what such ones had said was it appropriate to draw lines between nature and grace.

For Edwards, unlike Bushnell, the intellectual issue was much more complicated than simply finding room alongside scientific rationality for a God-oriented concept of religion. He was not worried, as modern fundamentalists seem to be, that nature (in his terms, the "new moral philosophy") would devour grace (the Puritan pietism). Along with his contemporaries Malebranche and Berkeley, Edwards knew that researchers could have confidence in the independent reality of events beyond themselves, and in the mind's ability to follow the course of external developments, because God moment by moment sustained the world. These Christians affirmed comprehensive theism in part because

[95]Jonathan Edwards, *Treatise on Grace*, as quoted in Fiering, *Jonathan Edwards's Moral Thought*, 127–28 n. 51.
[96]Fiering, ibid., 355.

they felt that only such a theism could undergird the unusually productive potential of science. Theirs was a Christian idealism with a large place for study of the natural world.

Yet Edwards also held that, however dignified and worthy of study the realm of nature was, it was always positioned within the realm of grace. Most other American Protestant thinkers in the eighteenth century sounded as if they wanted the reverse—to give grace its due, but always within the framework of nature. This latter stance overwhelmed Edwards's position and contributed, along the lines James Turner outlines, to the secularization of the West. Yet as Edwards himself affirmed, neither the new science nor the new moral philosophy was to be scorned, since both really did illuminate a part of the natural world that God created every moment anew. Edwards's power lay in his careful discrimination between nature and grace, his ability to treat natural capacities and discoveries as gifts of God's Common Grace, and his ultimate resolution to see every discovery about nature (from whomever it might come) as a gracious bestowal from God.

Approaching the realms of nature and grace in this way, however, Edwards is nearly isolated in American Christian history. As James Ward Smith once put it in a fine essay on religion and science, Edwards alone of his American contemporaries heralded the "Newtonian corpus" while rebuking the "deeper spirit" of the Enlightenment.[97] In the eighteenth century, that is, Edwards was nearly unique in saying "No, but . . ." to the Enlightenment. For him, the Enlightenment led to great errors and the dethroning of God, but it still provided significant truths about the world that God sustains. The rationalists of his day and modernists since have said simply "Yes" to the Enlightenment. Matter in motion and the natural endowments of the mind can indeed ground ultimate reality. Moderates and evangelicals in Edwards's day and since have said "Yes, but . . ." to the Enlightenment. They have agreed with the intellectual world at large in resting the Bible on natural proofs, in defending the supernatural by the material, and in grounding benevolence on a utilitarian sense of what God can do for the righteous. The controversy between evangelicals and moderates arises not from the framework of their thought, but from differences on how best to maintain a supernatural faith within this natural framework. Sectarians in Edwards's day and fundamentalists in the twentieth century have seemed to say

[97]Smith, "Religion and Science in American Philosophy," 413–14.

"No" to the Enlightenment, but in fact have been saying "Yes, but . . ." with the evangelicals.[98] They pretend to take nothing from nature, and so do not see how thoroughly their understanding of Scripture, conversion, and the Christian life rests on the assumptions of the Enlightenment.

In the late twentieth century Protestants who took to heart the example of Edwards could not simply repeat his arguments. Times *have* changed. Discussions in epistemology, metaphysics, and ethics, not to speak of biblical study and theology, have posed new challenges. But the Edwardsean stance may still provide a way for showing Protestants how to welcome, with wide-open arms, the gifts of God in both nature and grace; and it may show them how to tell the difference.

The one jarring note with this recommendation is that we cannot have Edwards the metaphysician and Edwards the ethicist without also Edwards the evangelist. The God who ordered nature and morality for Edwards was also the God who drew the sinner to Christ. To benefit from Edwards's perspective, which makes possible a modest but genuine knowledge of both physical and moral nature, one needs to know the God who confronts humanity in judgment and grace. An Edwardsean call to conversion, however, flies directly in the face of the Enlightenment ethos of toleration that lingers powerfully after the evacuation of the Enlightenment mind. But such an offense to Enlightenment good taste may be what it takes not only for better discussion of the public good and more responsible promotion of intellectual life but also for the liberation of spirit and mind that the very word "Enlightenment" once evoked in earlier, less ironic times.

[98]For much the same reading of Protestant sectarianism and the Enlightenment, see Marsden, "Evangelicals and the Scientific Culture," in Lacey, *Religion and Twentieth-Century Intellectual Life*, 26–33.

4

American Catholicism and
the Enlightenment ethos

PATRICK W. CAREY

Currently, American Catholicism is marked by two apparently contradictory phenomena. On the one hand, as some sociologists tell us, American Catholics are in the midst of a major religious revival.[1] On the other hand, as the news media have revealed since the late 1960s, American Catholicism is in a period of unprecedented internal revolution, discontent, and conflict over a variety of religious and moral issues that created a large decline in active church membership. *Newsweek* was so impressed by the statistics of decline of allegiance that its 4 October 1971 cover asked, "Has the Church Lost Its Soul?"[2] The reports of a contemporary revival and the simultaneous impressions of decline and conflict, although both are perhaps exaggerated, have enough truth in them to demand some kind of explanation about the staying power of religion, and in this case of Catholicism, in the face of conflict.

Some observers would say that both the conflicts and the revival are continuing effects of the two revolutions of the 1960s: the American cultural and social protest movements and the Second Vatican Council, which brought about a fundamental shift in Catholic consciousness to one more sympathetic to modernity. No doubt, the two revolutions, combined as they were in the American Catholic community, created an upheaval of earthquake proportions that continues to produce tremors. But these events in themselves do not adequately explain the internal

[1]George Gallup, Jr., and Jim Castelli, *The American Catholic People: Their Beliefs, Practices, and Values* (New York: Doubleday, 1987), 42.
[2]For analysis of survey data, see *Newsweek*, 4 October 1971, 80–89; see also the cover story "U. S. Catholicism: A Church Divided," *Time*, 24 May 1976, 46–59.

conflicts and simultaneous continuity of religious life that sustains a Catholic sense of transcendence and community.

The revival would be easy enough to explain on the basis of a recurring pattern of religious revivalism in American history. The conflicts of the present, though, are qualitatively different from past dissensions in American Catholicism because they involve fundamental disagreements over particular aspects of official church teaching or discipline. The internal controversies are so intense not only because of a more sympathetic approach to modernity but also because that sympathy for modernity is cautious and, at least in the case of those who remain within the church, critical. Those who are in conflict and continue to remain in the church do so, I suppose, because they continue to find in the larger Catholic tradition religious sensibilities and a way of life that are and have been opposed to significant elements of an Enlightenment ethos at the heart of modernity.

This essay outlines briefly the larger historical American Catholic encounter with an Enlightenment ethos that many European as well as American Catholics perceived as the intellectual, social, and political roots of modern society. From the late eighteenth century to the present, the conversation and controversy between the Catholic tradition and Enlightenment values have shaped Catholic sensibilities and mentality. The term *Enlightenment ethos* is used in this chapter to describe a sometimes contradictory configuration of ideas, values, and sensitivities that Catholics perceived as both promise and threat and that were generally associated with a modern mentality, even when they did not always trace this mentality to the eighteenth-century Enlightenment. The Enlightenment ethos could and did mean the reassertion of the dignity of human reason and freedom, the humanization of law, the struggle against superstition, the fostering of a legitimate subjectivity and historicity, the spread of popular education, and the rise of religious liberty. For the most part, however, Catholics came out of a tradition that has found it much easier to criticize the limits of the Enlightenment project than to evaluate its benefits. Thus the Enlightenment ethos has been interpreted primarily as religious indifferentism, rationalism, agnosticism, naturalism, and materialism.

From the late eighteenth to the mid twentieth century, American as well as European Catholics frequently criticized an autonomous rationalism as the core of the modern intellectual, social, and political life.[3]

---

[3]For a general bibliography of the European Catholic reactions to the Enlightenment, see Wolfgang Muller et al., *The Church in the Age of Absolutism and Enlightenment*, vol. 6

The rise of the Enlightenment's autonomous reason, having its remote historical or religious source in the Protestant principle of the private interpretation of the Scriptures, led to a subjectivism and individualism in political and economic life as well as in religion. The Enlightenment ethos destroyed the natural and spiritual bonds of community by making family, church, and state matters of autonomous choice divorced from any dependence on created nature and divine revelation. The modern development of individual autonomy ultimately led to an anthropocentric liberty that displaced the authority of God, revelation, and the church.

The negative perception of modern developments reflected the hostile effects of the French Revolution on the European Catholic Church, which lost its hegemony and influence over European political and social life. Although Catholics never had any hegemony or much influence in American society, they experienced a hostile environment from nativism and the hegemony of a Protestant culture that served almost the same function in the American Catholic mind as did the French Revolution in the Roman Catholic mind.

In response to this perception of a hostile environment—which reinforced the internal bonds of unity and community—the nineteenth- and twentieth-century Catholic project attempted to develop a Catholic understanding of the use of reason and will, to regain some of the church's spiritual influence in the realm of political and economic life, and to restore a sense of divine transcendence and its corollary human dependence and interdependence, which Catholics believed to have been diminished or lost in the modern world. Gradually, in response to the Enlightenment ethos, Catholics articulated their own understanding of reason, the individual, community, church, state, freedom, authority, justice, the common good, and society in ways they perceived to be consistent with reason and revelation.

For most members of the church, Catholic sensibilities on these issues flowed not so much from papal statements, rational argumentation, or intellectual and theological defenses, as important as these were, but from their personal and communal involvement in the signs and symbols of public worship, the sacramental system, pious practices of prayer and

of *History of the Church*, ed. Hubert Jedin and John Dolan (New York: Crossroad, 1981), 586, 615–44, and Patrick W. Carey, *People, Priests, and Prelates: Ecclesiastical Democracy and the Tensions of Trusteeism* (Notre Dame, Ind.: University of Notre Dame Press, 1987), 298.

cult of the saints, catechetical training in the fundamentals of a creedal tradition, parish life, and their voluntary participation in building up a free institutional church in a free society. Their understandings of person, community, and justice were integral to their total religious way of life. Because of their social circumstances in American society and the exigencies called forth by them, American Catholic leadership concentrated almost exclusively on building ecclesiastical structures that would serve the religious, social, and educational needs of a Catholic population that was continually expanding, primarily because of immigration.

The focus on a practical religious life and the building of institutions left little time, energy, or resources for the development of a creative Catholic intellectual tradition in the United States. The Catholic opposition to the Enlightenment's emphasis on self-criticism, creativity, and novelty as the distinguishing fruits of the intellectual life also explains that failure. For many Catholics, moreover, a genuine intellectual life meant a transmission of a body of unchanging truths that needed penetration and exposition but little development, to say nothing of revision. What did develop in American Catholicism was an apologetical tradition and literature—the chief genre of American writing until the mid twentieth century, which this essay analyzes as a primary source for uncovering the American Catholic understanding of the limits and benefits of the Enlightenment ethos. This literature was the result of the post-Reformation polemical atmosphere in the West and of specific nativist charges that Catholicism and American ideals were incompatible in principle and in practice.

American and European Catholics countered the individualism and subjectivism they perceived in modern culture by centering their apologetical literature on the necessity of the church itself as a concrete historical religious community of faith that incarnated the divine in its sacramental celebrations and in its hierarchical structures. The church for them was not just another institution, but the medium of salvation and a divine response to a fundamentally human yearning for community and authority.

The Catholic emphasis on community and authority corresponded to the various ethnic Catholic cultural emphases on religion itself as concrete, emotional, communal, and traditional (in the sense that religion was something given and inherited), as opposed to an emphasis on religious faith and life as abstract, intellectual, individual, and voluntary.

In their attempts to explain the human necessity of the church as an alternative to excessive voluntaryism and individualism in American society, Catholics frequently used the categories, language, methodologies, and structures of modern thought that were current in their own era. Although they sometimes used modern methods of argumentation and modern forms of thought to communicate a traditional Catholic perspective, they often unwittingly and occasionally self-consciously tried to find a synthesis between their own emphasis on mediated grace, community, and authority and the modern emphasis on nature, the individual, and freedom.

Although Catholics fundamentally agreed among themselves in their understanding of the negative elements of the Enlightenment ethos in the modern world, they differed from one another periodically in their assessments of what in that ethos was valuable and beneficial for the human condition, and not only consistent with but inherently related to the Catholic tradition. The remainder of this essay focuses on these two themes: the united battle against Enlightenment autonomy and the intramural conflicts over a proper evaluation and appropriation of what was valuable in that ethos.

ENLIGHTENMENT CATHOLICISM

During the late eighteenth and early nineteenth centuries, American Catholics played an insignificant role in the development of the moderate American Enlightenment but were significantly influenced by it, and indeed their initial institutional formation took shape within its context.[4] American Catholics enthusiastically accepted the American republican form of government, the constitutional provisions for nonestablishment, and the free exercise of religion and, furthermore, saw their acceptance of these American political principles and practices as consistent with

[4]Little has been written on Catholic appropriations of, and reactions to, the American Enlightenment ethos. It is no surprise that Henry May made no mention of American Catholics in *The Enlightenment in America* (New York: Oxford University Press, 1976). They were a tiny minority during the late eighteenth and early nineteenth centuries and they made no original intellectual contribution to Enlightenment thought. For some recent historical descriptions and analyses of an Enlightenment Catholicism, see, e.g., Patrick W. Carey, ed., *American Catholic Religious Thought: The Shaping of a Theological and Social Tradition* (New York: Paulist Press, 1987), 3–15; Joseph Chinnici, "Politics and Theology: From Enlightenment Catholicism to the Condemnation of Americanism," unpublished paper, ser. 9, no. 3, Notre Dame Cushwa Center Working Papers Series, spring 1981; and Margaret Mary Reher, *Catholic Intellectual Life in America: A Historical Study of Persons and Movements* (New York: Macmillan, 1989), 1–28.

their own religious tradition. Even in their understanding of faith and religious life they were, like their Protestant neighbors of the didactic Enlightenment, moderately influenced by the Age of Reason.

Although the American Catholic view of the Age of Reason was in general derived from, and in agreement with, a European Catholic perspective, the latter view was modified in the United States by what most American Catholics perceived as the benign and actually beneficial social and political consequences of the American Enlightenment. The American Catholic acceptance of a constitutional state, religious liberty, and separation of church and state contrasted sharply with the nineteenth-century papal rejection of them. Joseph Komonchak has argued that the papacy throughout the nineteenth and early twentieth centuries consistently rejected the philosophical dimensions of the Enlightenment ethos primarily because of the social and political consequences.[5] This was not the case in the United States, where Catholics separated the philosophical from the political dimensions of the Enlightenment. From Bishop John Carroll in the 1780s to John Courtney Murray, S.J., in the 1950s and 1960s, most Catholic writers frequently and consistently distinguished the beneficial political effects of the American Enlightenment from the Jacobin political results of the French Enlightenment tradition.[6]

Because American Catholic leaders like John Carroll, the French émigré bishops, and Irish immigrant bishops like John England accepted religious liberty, separation of church and state, and voluntarism (which was part of the Anglo and Irish Catholic historical practice), they also helped to shape a new role for the church in a republican state. John England, bishop of Charleston, South Carolina (1820–42), clearly artic-

---

[5]The nineteenth- and early twentieth-century papal reactions to the Enlightenment ethos—culminating in the definitions of Vatican I, the institutional establishment of neo-Thomism as the philosophical and theological form of Catholic orthodoxy, and the condemnations of modernism—were, unlike the vacillation here and there in eighteenth- and nineteenth-century European Catholicism, almost exclusively negative. For a recent description of the papal position, see Joseph Komonchak, "The Enlightenment and the Construction of Roman Catholicism," in *CCICA Annual* (Notre Dame, Ind.: Catholic Commission on Intellectual and Cultural Affairs, 1985), 31–59.

[6]On this topic, see Elwyn A. Smith, "The Catholic Tradition," in *Religious Liberty in the United States: The Development of Church-State Thought since the Revolutionary Era* (Philadelphia: Fortress Press, 1972), 156–245, and Patrick W. Carey, "American Catholics and the First Amendment: 1776–1840," *The Pennsylvania Magazine of History and Biography* 113 (July 1989): 323–45, esp. 324 n. 1 for other studies. There were, of course, some exceptions to this general pattern of acceptance. John A. Ryan in the 1920s and Joseph Fenton in the 1950s, for example, saw the practical benefits of American religious liberty, but they perceived the union of church and state to be the ideal relationship between the two.

ulated that new role. The church's mission in American society, he argued, was primarily spiritual, a role that was consistent with the church's function in primitive Christianity. The church, however, had a respon- sibility for the well-being of society, which it could foster only by persuasively promoting among its people republican virtue, defined by England in common with other Americans as zeal for the public good over the private.[7] Catholicism's spiritual and moral role in American society was to persuade believers, on religious grounds, to be responsible citizens.

The influence of the Enlightenment is also reflected in American Catholic apologetics. Whether they battled with deists, Unitarians, or evangelical Protestants, apologists tried to establish the rational grounds for their beliefs and traditions. As a number of late eighteenth- and early nineteenth-century American Protestants relied heavily on Scottish Common Sense realism in their theology, so American Catholics followed the eighteenth-century Cartesian-influenced Gallican apologetic, which was developed to respond to charges raised by deists against revealed religion. Catholic apologetics, therefore, became increasingly characterized by the Cartesian turn to the subject and by its use of reason to provide grounds for the acceptance of supernatural faith.

The primary purpose of Catholic apologetics was to establish the credibility of Christian revelation and the infallible authority of the Catholic Church in reaction to deism and Protestantism, thus placing the burden of proof on reason's ability to discover evidences for faith. Ultimately the apologetical task was to provide a rational justification for faith itself. Such an approach was a radical departure from an older method of faith seeking understanding. Catholics accepted the new method primarily because the terms of the discussion had been set by those outside the older tradition, and if they were to make faith a matter of rational assent they had to accept the deist starting point of the denial of historical revelation, or the Protestant starting point of the denial of the church's authority. In both cases, the subject's reason came to serve as an arbiter for deciding the validity of rational and convincing evidence.

The Cartesian-influenced apologetics of reason prevailed in American Catholicism during the antebellum period and, modified after Vatican I (1870), it became almost an officially approved method of apologetics.

---

[7]Ignatius Reynolds, ed., *The Works of the Right Rev. John England*, 5 vols. (Baltimore: John Murphy, 1849), 4:228 (hereafter cited as England, *Works*).

That apologetic is reflected clearly in the works of John Carroll, Anthony Kohlmann, and John England, who argued, on the basis of historical evidence and the "fact of revelation," that it was reasonable to accept the Catholic Church's infallible authority in the interpretation of revelation because one could show the credible evidence for the establishment of this authority.[8]

The individual's reason had a definite, though admittedly limited, role in establishing grounds for belief and for submission to an infallible authority. According to Kohlmann, the biblical and historical evidences for the actual fact of revelation supplied only "motives of extrinsic [not intrinsic] credibility."[9] Reason could discover whether God had revealed, but, Kohlmann argued in opposition to Unitarianism, reason was incapable of examining the intrinsic nature of the mysteries revealed. Reason could not discover whether the Christian mysteries agreed with the "natural ideas of reason" or whether they were intelligible to reason. Once reason discovered the fact of an infallible revelation, it was bound to submit to the authority of the revealer or to the authority of those who infallibly proposed those propositions for belief.[10]

Apologists like Carroll taught that submission to the doctrines of the church was not slavish credulity. One's faith and obedience had to be rational, free, and follow from a conviction of conscience. That conviction, moreover, should be the result of the prevailing force of truth, after a free examination of its grounds and motives, and not merely the product of education.[11]

There was something in the Enlightenment's emphases on reason and freedom that was consistent with Christianity, but the Catholic understanding of reason differed radically from a view of reason as autono-

[8]For examples of this apologetic, see John Carroll, "An Address to the Roman Catholics of the United States of America by a Catholic Clergyman" (1784), in Thomas O'Brien Hanley, ed., *The John Carroll Papers*, 3 vols. (Notre Dame, Ind.: University of Notre Dame Press, 1976), 1:82–144 (hereafter cited as *JCP*); Anthony Kohlmann, *Unitarianism: Philosophically and Theologically Examined*, 2 vols. (Washington City: Henry Guegan, 1821; 1822); and John England, "Discourse before Congress" (1826), in England, *Works*, 4:172–90. Another representative work of the Catholic Enlightenment mentality, not considered here, is Felix Varela's *Letters to Elipidio*, 2 vols. (1835–38), in Felipe J. Esteves, ed., *Felix Varela: Letters to Elipidio* (New York: Paulist Press, 1989). Varela, a Cuban exile who was a pastor in New York City (1826–51), wrote against irreligion and superstition (which he saw as a partial cause of irreligion) and advocated a synthesis of Christianity and freedom in the new society created by the Enlightenment.
[9]Kohlmann, *Unitarianism*, 1:16.
[10]Ibid., 36.
[11]*JCP*, 1:84.

mous. For Carroll the leading feature of rational investigation was not an indifference or perfect neutrality to truth or falsity prior to inquiry, as some (such as Charles Henry Wharton, an ex-Jesuit and Carroll's cousin) had argued. Reason was not an autonomous agent, independent of family upbringing, communal attachments, and personal commitment; therefore, inquiry need not abandon principles or suspend belief in order to be rational and free. What was necessary was "a mind open to conviction, and a disposition to embrace the truth, on which side soever it shall appear, and to receive the evidence that shall arise in the course of the trial."[12]

Reason, however, was not the only mode of knowing, nor was it the highest. Although reason could discover rational grounds for faith, faith had an existential priority over reason and in fact informed and perfected it. Faith, as defined by John England, "is not folly, it is not abject slavery of the mind, it is not visionary fanaticism, it is not irrational assent to unintelligible propositions; but it is believing upon the testimony of God what human reason could not discover, but what a provident and wise Deity communicates for the information of our minds and the direction of our will."[13] Faith, though not contrary to reason, was above it and received the ultimate ground for its authority from a supernatural power outside of history.

Although apologists had a supreme confidence in reason in political thought and apologetics, they had little confidence in its capacities in the realms of piety and virtue. This is particularly clear in a number of John Carroll's sermons, which appear to be from the 1790s. Like some American Protestants, Carroll believed that an autonomous rationalism had seriously affected American views of the Christian life. Thomas Paine's *Age of Reason*, the preoccupation with the essentials of natural religion, and the French Revolution had produced what Carroll called an "age of infidelity." Unbounded confidence in reason and human capacity had created, Carroll feared, a climate of Pelagianism in America to which his Catholic congregations were not entirely impervious. Some Catholics, he told one of his congregations, were influenced by a "presumptive infidelity, which inspires a daring confidence in themselves, and a bold assurance that they need not other direction besides that which their own reason suggests to them."[14]

[12]Ibid., 85.
[13]England, *Works*, 4:175.
[14]*JCP*, 3:375.

Reason alone was unable to guide Christians not only to their eternal salvation but even to a clear discovery of the essential tenets of natural religion or the first principles of natural law. Carroll upheld the value of reason, but said it needed to be animated and enlightened by divine revelation to realize its full potential. Reason was so liable to be blinded by passion, warped by prejudices, bewildered by the subtleties and contradictions of even the most brilliant and well-educated human speculations that it could not by itself provide adequate evidence and motivation for moral and religious duties to God and to one's neighbors. Most human beings, moreover, had neither the time, education, opportunity, nor talent to investigate the foundations for the existence of God, their own duties, and most certainly could not discover the ultimate end of their creation. This historical experience proved to Carroll the necessity of a divine revelation. Divine enlightenment was a providential aid to endow all human beings with sufficient authority and motivation for virtue and was absolutely essential for disclosing the supernatural means and end of all virtue.[15]

Carroll, Kohlmann, England, and other Catholics, like those Protestants influenced by the Scottish Common Sense philosophy, embraced Enlightenment values, but on their own Christian terms. They did not perceive religious or political authority as the antithesis of reason, or simply as a means of supplying order at the price of reason. In the realms of apologetics and politics, they trusted human nature and the powers of rational persuasion. That this confidence was not always consistent with the deeper strains of their piety is, it seems to me, one of the intellectual aberrations of the age in which they lived. It also demonstrates, though, that for them there were inherent limits to their acceptance of the Enlightenment, regardless of how logically inconsistent it may have been. In this regard, their tradition had a fundamental priority over their accommodation to Enlightenment methodology. For them reason, although valid for discovering motives of credibility, was always in the service of faith, not its judge, arbiter, or autonomous critical agent.

In spite of their cautious accommodation to the Enlightenment, Catholic apologists did not perceive the inherent individualism in their approach, the Cartesian-like dualism, the extrinsic view of revelation, the reduction of faith to intellectual assent, the elitism inherent in the evidentiary approach to the grounds of faith, and the almost exclusive em-

[15]Ibid., 378.

phasis on the external authority of the church. They were, logically if not in fact, promoting by the apologetical methods they employed the very individualism, secularism, and rationalism they opposed. These weaknesses would be brought to light during the Catholic romantic movement of the middle 1840s.

ROMANTIC CATHOLICISM

A more fundamental critique of the Enlightenment ethos and of the Catholic attempt to adopt some of its measures arose within Catholicism in the middle 1840s and reflected to a considerable extent the kind of "religious revolution" that was taking place in other segments of American society.[16] The reaction came from those converts to Catholicism, like Orestes A. Brownson and Isaac Hecker, who had been influenced by transcendentalism and the American Oxford movement[17] and who became the primary leaders of an American Catholic romantic movement.[18]

Brownson, Hecker, and a host of others during the mid nineteenth century directly challenged the Enlightenment ethos and the political, social, and religious culture it had created. The eighteenth century—with its emphases on the autonomous individual, a cold and calculating rationalism, and a sense of independence from all external authority and tradition—had created a modern cultural monster Brownson blasted both before and after his conversion to Catholicism. The modern world and American culture, under the grip of the Age of Reason, had lost touch with essential human life and with the spiritual dynamism that

[16]Sydney E. Ahlstrom, "The Romantic Religious Revolution and the Dilemmas of Religious History," *Church History* 46 (June 1977): 149–70.
[17]By the "Oxford movement" I am referring to the theological movement within the American Protestant Episcopal Church during the late 1830s and early 1840s that was centered at New York City's General Theological Seminary, where some professors and students stressed a return to ritualism, sacramentalism, and the authority of tradition and the creeds in the church. It was a movement against the individualistic and revivalistic tendencies in American evangelical traditions. On this topic see Sydney E. Ahlstrom, *A Religious History of the American People* (New Haven: Yale University Press, 1972), 626–32, and Clarence W. Walworth, *The Oxford Movement in America* (New York: United States Catholic Historical Society, 1895).
[18]For literature on the romantic movement, see Patrick W. Carey, "American Catholic Romanticism, 1830–1888," *Catholic Historical Review* 74 (October 1988): 590–606; idem, *Orestes A. Brownson: Selected Writings* (New York: Paulist Press, 1989); John Farina, ed., *Isaac T. Hecker: The Diary: Romantic Religion in Ante-Bellum America* (New York: Paulist Press, 1988); and Reher, *Catholic Intellectual Life in America*, 28–61.

was at its heart. In politics, reason had made individuals little gods, destroying any sense of a common good or any sympathy for a political community and authority. In economic life, an incipient capitalism, the rabid pursuit of wealth, and the commercialization of society were gradually breaking the bonds of social solidarity and annihilating the economic equity that was the logical extension and promise of the democratic revolution. The nation's economic life was the cause as well as the result of an increasingly unreflective and spiritually dead American society. In religion, feelings, sensitivities, and intuition had been buried by the search for a reasonable and ultimately lifeless and mysteryless Christianity. Such a critique of mid nineteenth-century American society sent Brownson in quest of a more spiritual and therefore a more fully human vision and experience.

By 1840, while still within the Unitarian-transcendentalist fold, Brownson had accepted the Kantian critique of reason as the ground for the possibility of belief. His own intellectual search for some objective condition for the possibility of religious experience and knowledge led him to criticize the supernatural rationalism of Unitarianism on the one hand and what he perceived to be the subjective idealism of Ralph Waldo Emerson's and Theodore Parker's transcendentalism on the other. Brownson discovered, while reading the French Saint Simonian Pierre Leroux, what he called the doctrine of life by communion, which he saw as an intellectual solution to the problems in contemporary society and as an escape from the subject-object dichotomy that had prevailed in modern thought since the time of Descartes.

For Brownson, following Leroux, there was an ontological communion behind and supporting all the appearances of life, creating a fundamental organic unity in the whole of reality: a unity of humanity, nature, and God. There was a living communion behind the state and the political order, a fundamental constitution beyond choice and human creation. The state and the society it governed, therefore, were not just a voluntary compact or a collectivity of individuals whose choice determined what justice was or whose collective reason was the source of political authority. There was a spiritual communion behind reason and choice that was the ground of society and authority. Life in this communion, moreover, was not just an ahistorical or purely spiritual ideal, it was actualized concretely in history as a continuous inner life that tied together past, present, and future. Although universal in time and space, it was realized in created nature through signs and symbols and was thus available to all. It was a life that had the simultaneous force of authority and freedom and could be felt, imagined, and intuited, though could never be fully expressed with human reason or through human activity. It was this life that had been obscured during the Age of Reason; it was this life that was in need of recovery in the present age, and only those reforms that were truly spiritual would have any lasting effect on the human condition.

Following Leroux, Brownson asserted that all life as well as all thought was the result of the interaction (or communion) of subject and object. All life and thought, therefore, were simultaneously objective and subjective. The human subject could not exist, live, or grow without communion with some object outside of the self. All human life developed or progressed by communion with nature, other humans, and God, giving rise to three institutions as the media of that life: property, state or society, and religion or the church. Out of this doctrine of life by communion, Brownson eventually developed, in conjunction with his understanding of Providence (as the free intervention of God in history), arguments for the necessity of a church that was the historic and organic continuation of the Incarnate divine life. This was not merely an ideal church or a purely phenomenal institution, but a sacramental reality having an inner divine authority that Brownson perceived as the condition for the possibility of religious faith and social reform.

Hecker agreed with Brownson in acknowledging the absolute necessity of a visible universal church as the medium for personal and social regeneration. He told Brownson before his conversion

That all outward reforms presuppose an inward regeneration of the heart as their cause and foundation and no institution but the Church has the power to effect this nor has this aim [in] view. Therefore I would yield myself up wholly to the Church as the only means of Redeeming the Race from the innumerable evils under which we now suffer.[19]

By the early 1840s Brownson and Hecker had both become, as they repeatedly admitted, church men. For them this meant that they must labor for the union and universality of a visible church as the prerequisite for all other reform movements in society.

In 1844 both decided that the church they were seeking could be

---

[19]Hecker to Brownson, 15 March 1844, in Joseph F. Gower and Richard M. Leliaert, eds., *The Brownson-Hecker Correspondence* (Notre Dame, Ind.: University of Notre Dame Press, 1979), 86.

found only in Catholicism, where the inner individual quest and intuitive need for union and reform correlated synthetically with the visible revelations and sacramental communications of divine love and grace. Freedom and authority were not antagonistic in the life of communion; they were dialectically a part of one indivisible whole. The spiritual life was simultaneously deeply personal, not individual, and inherently communal. The self was by definition in communion—with God, nature, and other selves.

The doctrine of communion—modified somewhat in the 1850s by the ontologism, traditionalism, and Augustinian illuminationism of Vincenzo Gioberti[20]—emphasized in particular the role of intuition in knowing and grasping the divine existence and presence, the natural aspirations for God that corresponded to the external revelations of grace in the sacramental church, and the Incarnation itself as the culmination of the divine creative act in history. The doctrine was an attempt to overcome the dualism inherent in the older Catholic apologetic by making, as Brownson repeatedly said, nature and the supernatural as two distinct, though not separated, parts of one dialectical whole, which was made intelligible and available to human persons through intuition and tradition. Religious experience and faith, therefore, depended not on the external evidences of reason but on the primordial communion that was the result of the divine creative act and the providential gift of the Incarnate Word.

Brownson and Hecker saw the necessity of the church not only as a concrete medium of individual and social salvation but also as one of the constituent elements of society itself. The individual, with natural dignity and freedom, the state, with constitutional authority, and religion or the church, with a power independent of both and mediating between them, were the three essential elements of society—all of them bound together in communion, but each free in its own sphere and in

[20]Ontologism and traditionalism had a variety of different manifestations in Europe during the middle of the nineteenth century. Briefly, the ontologists believed that the unconditional noumenal reality of being, grasped through intuition, grounded the order of knowledge, reflection, and understanding. A modified form of traditionalism held that God's primitive revelation, transmitted to Adam by language, contained essential moral and religious truths, which Adam then passed on to succeeding generations by tradition to aid reflection and to provide certitude in understanding. On European Catholic forms of ontologism and traditionalism, see Gerald A. McCool, *Catholic Theology in the Nineteenth Century: The Quest for a Unitary Method* (New York: Seabury Press, 1977), 37–58, 67–81, 113–28, and Bernard M. G. Reardon, *Religion in the Age of Romanticism: Studies in Early Nineteenth Century Thought* (Cambridge: Cambridge University Press, 1985), 145–56.

accord with its own intrinsic nature. The church was necessary in society to preserve simultaneously individual freedom and government authority and to protect society itself from both anarchy and despotism.

The church was an essential element in the political as well as the social order. It upheld a view of society as a spiritual communion of human beings with their maker; hence the church saw people as free, related, and organically united. Brownson held up little hope that social and economic questions could be settled satisfactorily by a political economy or social reform schemes that were devoid of a Christian anthropology and communal view of society. In 1867, he complained:

> The last thing to be relied on for adjusting any social question, elevating any class to social or civil equality, or making freedmen really freemen, is political economy, which treats man not as a free moral agent, or as a social being, but simply as a producing, distributing, and consuming machine, placed in the same category with the steam-plough, patent reaper, spinning-jenny, and the power loom.[21]

Without the insight and power of charity, all reforms would fail. The church was needed in society to keep all philanthropic and reform movements under the influence of divine charity, as a theological virtue and not just a philanthropic option.

Brownson in particular believed that many members of American society, Catholics as well as others, had only the most extrinsic view of the relationship between religion and society. In this extrinsic view, religion or the church was purely an instrument or foreign auxiliary to promote the integrity and stability of society by providing motivation and ultimate grounds for being moral and public spirited, by elevating civic virtues to the rank of religious virtues. For Brownson, religion was integral to society, not merely an extrinsic support. Religion and the state "are in the same order, and inseparable though distinct parts of one and the same whole."[22] The church's real power in society was that of communicating and realizing love as the unifying force of all societies. The church's very presence in society was a visible and continual reminder of the essential spiritual communion of love at the base of society itself, making politics and economics, as well as all other areas of human endeavor, integrally related to one another and essentially governed by the divine power of love. From this perspective there could be no legitimate talk of the absolute in-

---

[21]Henry F. Brownson, ed., *The Works of Orestes A. Brownson*, 20 vols. (Detroit: Thorndike Norse, 1882–87), 14:446.
[22]Ibid., 18:69.

dependence or autonomy of any human activity. Everything human had a spiritual and a moral dimension to it. Although the church's power in society was essentially ontological, it was legitimately exercised only persuasively and morally, not juridically or coercively.

Just as grace did not destroy nature but left it free, so also religion or the church did not annihilate either individual freedom and dignity, governmental authority, the legitimate autonomy of the sciences, or the freedom of political and economic life. The church and religion, like grace itself, should uplift the natural and bring it to its final perfection. Thus the church and religion should have an interest in all natural human activities to remove the corruptions and to direct the natural to its supernatural core and destiny.

The antebellum Catholic romantic reaction to the Enlightenment ethos emphasized an integral dialectical harmony between nature and the supernatural, the organic and essentially incarnational dimensions of communal life, the role of intuition and tradition in knowing God, and communion with the divine as the a priori condition for faith, religious knowledge, and all human activity. Although the romantics tended to emphasize those elements in the Catholic tradition that their immediate predecessors failed to acknowledge, they too failed to see the weaknesses of their own position.

Their quasi-idealist and ahistorical view of the church as the spiritually organic and concrete continuation and actualization of the Incarnation made the church itself, though within history and composed of human beings, impervious to historical change and untouched by human sinfulness and corruption. Such a position made it difficult for romantic Catholics to respond to critical questions raised by historians and positivists in the late nineteenth century. The role of the cross and resurrection, to say nothing of Christ's earthly ministry, was also notably absent from this theological perspective. In addition, a tendency toward fideism, making all true knowledge ultimately depend on the divine creative act, characterized this position.

In the period immediately after the Civil War—as Americans became more conversant with Charles Darwin's thought, historical criticism, and positivism—Catholics saw a new issue arising. Brownson, Hecker, and their colleagues gradually concluded that the antebellum polemical battles with Protestantism were over[23] and that the problem of the necessity

---

[23]I do not want to overstate the case here. Protestant-Catholic polemics continued throughout the post–Civil War period and so did the apologetical efforts to defend the distinctive

of the church, important as it was, was no longer the most significant issue. A new age of unbelief had arrived,[24] and the possibility of unbelief was now more widespread in America than ever before. For Brownson in particular the radical issue was to demonstrate the validity of Christian theism against various political, scientific, and philosophical naturalisms. These naturalisms were attempts to "explain man and the universe, or the cosmos, without the recognition of God as its first or its final cause."[25] Brownson's post–Civil War vindications of Christian theism—found in *The American Republic* (1865), "An Essay in Refutation of Atheism" (1873–74), and "Philosophy of the Supernatural" (1876)[26]—were based on his own previous ontological and modified traditionalist arguments.[27]

Hecker's understanding of the post–Civil War problem was less philosophically inclined than Brownson's and more preoccupied with the relations between the church and the age, a theme that would continue to assert itself with increasing vigor during the Americanist crisis at the end of the century. For Hecker, the main question of the 1880s was, "How can religion be made compatible with a high degree of liberty and intelligence?"[28] More optimistic than Brownson, Hecker saw that the development of free civil institutions and the spread of enlightenment had created an atmosphere in the modern world that was conducive to "the progress of true supernatural life among men." He wrote *The Church and the Age* (1887) to show that modern liberty, so far as true,

elements of Catholic beliefs and practices, as is evidenced by the popularity of Cardinal James Gibbons's *The Faith of Our Fathers* (1876), which went through more than one hundred editions and sold more than 2 million copies between 1876 and the early twentieth century; see John Tracy Ellis, *The Life of James Cardinal Gibbons: Archbishop of Baltimore 1834–1921*, 2 vols. (Milwaukee: Bruce, 1952), 1:145–52.
[24]James Turner, *Without God, without Creed: The Origins of Unbelief in America* (Baltimore: Johns Hopkins University Press, 1985).
[25]Brownson, *Works*, 2:1–2.
[26]Ibid., 18:1–222, 2:1–100, 2:271–83.
[27]In the late 1860s and early 1870s a vigorous debate arose in American Catholicism over precisely what Rome had condemned in the ontologism and traditionalism of Vincenzo Gioberti and the Louvain school. A few clergy, especially John Lancaster Spalding, had been educated in the American School at Louvain, where a moderate traditionalism and ontologism prevailed until the late 1860s. The American School at Rome after the 1850s, moreover, apparently produced a few clergy who were sympathetic to Italian ontologism and critical of the Cartesian scholasticism they found within Catholicism. I say apparently because Catholic newspaper accounts of the late 1860s indicate that several Roman-trained priests took the side of the ontologists in the battles. There is no study of this phenomenon in American Catholicism; I am currently examining the debate and hope to publish an account of its significance in the near future.
[28]Isaac Hecker, *The Church and the Age: An Exposition of the Catholic Church in View of the Needs and Aspirations of the Present Age* (New York: Office of the Catholic World, 1887), 2.

and the increase of intelligence, so far as "guileless," were invaluable helps to the "spread of Catholicity and the deepening of that interior spirit which is the best result of true religion." He also argued, in accord with his antebellum synthetic view of life, that there was indeed a harmonious relationship between the interior action of the Holy Spirit in the individual's soul with its exterior action in the "public authority of the Church."[29]

AMERICANISM AND MODERNISM

From the middle 1880s until the early twentieth century, American Catholics split into two opposing camps, usually identified as liberal and conservative,[30] as they battled each other over how they should respond to the new issues Brownson and Hecker had identified. The old controversy between Catholics and Protestants, Bishop John Lancaster Spalding noted, had to a large extent lost its meaning. Much like Brownson, he argued that the new conflict was between the church and infidelity.[31] Even the optimist Archbishop John Ireland saw the new situation in a similar vein. In a speech on the roles of private and public schools in the United States, he told the National Education Association that he would welcome the opportunity to join forces with Protestantism in counteracting the "blast of unbelief" that was besetting American society. Unbelief, irreligion, materialism, and secularism were becoming the destroyers of "Christian life and of Christian civilization."[32] Protestant

---

[29]Ibid., 1–2.

[30]For a definition of what these terms meant at the time, see "Letter of William Kerby to Edward Kerby Concerning Liberals and Conservatives in the American Church," 11 April 1897, in Colman J. Barry, O.S.B., *The Catholic Church and German Americans* (Milwaukee: Bruce, 1952), 323–25. For historical accounts of the Americanist debates see Robert D. Cross, *The Emergence of Liberal Catholicism in America* (Cambridge, Mass.: Harvard University Press, 1958), and Thomas T. McAvoy, C.S.C., *The Great Crisis in American Catholic History, 1895–1900* (Chicago: Henry Regnery, 1957). The liberal or Americanist leaders were Archbishop John Ireland of St. Paul, James Cardinal Gibbons of Baltimore, Archbishop John Keane of Dubuque, Bishop Denis O'Connell of Richmond, at times Bishop John Lancaster Spalding of Peoria, and a few of the Paulists, Sulpicians, and diocesan clergy. The conservatives or anti-Americanists were Archbishop Michael Corrigan of New York, Bishop Bernard McQuaid of Rochester, Bishop Frederick Katzer of Milwaukee, and many of the Jesuit and German clergy.

[31]John Lancaster Spalding, *Essays and Reviews* (New York: Catholic Publication Society, 1877), 44; idem, *Religion, Agnosticism and Education* (Chicago: A. C. McClurg, 1902), 184; and idem, *Things of the Mind* (Chicago: A. C. McClurg, 1894), 190, 212, 214.

[32]John Ireland, *The Church and Modern Society* (New York: D. H. McBride, 1903), 221–22.

and Catholic attempts to win out over each other had played into the hands of secularists and unbelievers.

That the problem of unbelief was a significant context for the late nineteenth-century internal battles, generally known as Americanism and modernism, has rarely been commented on, but it is clear in a number of publications from the Americanizers as well as their opponents. One reason why this context of the debate has received so little attention is that the Americanizers saw unbelief as an accidental characteristic of contemporary culture while their opponents saw it as an essential one. The Americanizers, moreover, were caught up in the late nineteenth-century beliefs in evolution and development and saw their own intellectual and cultural programs as part of the progressive era. John Ireland, for example, frequently asserted that "progress is the law of God's creation."[33] John Lancaster Spalding was even more explicit: "The controlling idea of the nineteenth century in philosophy and science is that of organic unity, implying a world-wide process of development. Hence the point of view is that of history."[34]

According to the Americanizers, the church needed to accommodate itself to American culture and the new sciences so that it could influence both in the direction of faith and thereby counteract the influence of unbelief. The problem was cultural and social as well as intellectual and, therefore, a twofold response was needed. On one level, Catholicism had to demonstrate its compatibility with American social and cultural values. A few of the Catholic bishops and clergy called for the cultural Americanization of immigrants as a means of demonstrating the affinity of the church to American political and social values. Some of them also advocated cooperation with the public school system; supported the legitimate aspirations of the poor, workers, and labor unions; attended ecumenical gatherings and called for a public exchange of theological and ecclesiological perspectives; asserted the superiority, or at least the beneficial results, of American provisions for religious liberty and separation of church and state; and called on the laity to develop a religiously motivated public spirit for the transformation of society.

Catholics also had to meet the serious intellectual challenges raised by contemporary naturalism. But the primary problem for Catholics, according to John Lancaster Spalding, was that they had no institutions

[33]Ibid., 151, 152, 155, 165, 380, 408–9, 410, 411.
[34]John Lancaster Spalding, *Religion and Art and Other Essays* (Chicago: A. C. McClurg, 1905), 68.

of higher learning that could address the serious intellectual issues of the day. Therefore, Spalding pushed for the creation of a major Catholic university in the country, one that could develop the minds and hearts of a new generation of intellectuals who would not merely laugh or scoff at the naturalists but develop "a comprehensive philosophy, which, starting from a true theory of knowledge will embrace the whole range of science, and by correcting the false interpretations of its data, will educate men and lead them to see that a theory of the universe which excludes God is not only unintelligible, but destructive of the essential principles of reason."[35] Like Brownson, Spalding had been nurtured in Catholic ontologism and moderate traditionalism. Education was for him the sine qua non for the development of intuitive first principles that arose from the law of organic communion. Nothing could be gained on the intellectual front either by rejecting errors in detail or by showing that certain data of science are in accord with revealed truth. The problem was radical and the solution had to be the development of an inclusive epistemology. A Catholic university, moreover, had to be in the forefront of "scientific research."[36]

Although a number of other American bishops shared Spalding's enthusiasm for creating a Catholic university in the United States, few, if any, shared his vision of the role of higher education. Fellow enthusiasts like Ireland had a more utilitarian view of Catholic higher education. The church should take on the work of imparting secular knowledge because when secular knowledge was withdrawn from the influence of religion, it almost inevitably became injected with the "poison of unbelief or of indifference, and turned into positive peril for the faith." Catholic higher education would be a means of preserving the faith and imparting to Catholics a kind of religiously influenced secular knowledge that would enable them to have a significant impact on society.[37]

During the 1890s and the early 1900s a few leading thinkers at the Catholic University and some eastern seaboard seminaries called for an open dialogue between Catholic and modern patterns of thought. These quasi modernists, as they have been called, asserted that Catholic clerical

---

[35]Spalding, *Things of the Mind*, 217. In 1889, the American bishops established the Catholic University of America in Washington, D.C., and in the early twentieth century it set the pattern for the development of Catholic higher education.

[36]John Lancaster Spalding, *Education and the Higher Life* (Chicago: A. C. McClurg, 1890), 184.

[37]John Ireland, *The Church and Modern Society* (St. Paul, Minn.: Pioneer Press, 1904), 2: 292–93.

studies and theological education in general should develop and use the new sciences—particularly historical criticism, biblical criticism, sociology, and psychology—in theology. This quasi-modernist predilection for empirical studies was a movement away from both the objective idealism and intuitive epistemology of Brownson and Hecker, and the kind of scholasticism that prevailed in much of Catholic thought.

Within the context of this general call for accommodating Catholic studies to the new sciences, a few intellectuals began to show precisely how Catholic doctrines were compatible with the new developments in philosophy and science. John Zahm of the University of Notre Dame published a series of articles and a major book, *Evolution and Dogma* (1895), to show that a theistic view of evolution was consonant with a Catholic understanding of creation and history.[38] John Hogan, S.S., a priest and teacher at New Brighton Seminary outside of Boston and later professor at the Catholic University, called for more historical investigations in Catholic theology. The modern tendency, he wrote in 1898, "leads to the development of theology on the lines of history and philology, and its future as a living science is clearly in that direction."[39] A theological education based exclusively on metaphysical principles was clearly inadequate. Other professors, like William Kerby and John A. Ryan of the Catholic University, applied sociology and economics to theological discourse.

In biblical studies, professors such as Francis E. Gigot, S.S., of St. Joseph's Seminary at Dunwoodie, New York, called on Catholics to apply higher criticism. "The time is gone," he wrote in 1900, "when the questions involved in the higher criticism might be simply identified with rationalistic attacks upon the revealed word. Again, one can no longer afford to be ignorant of topics which, perhaps more than any other at present, engross the attention of the intellectual and religious world."[40] The *Catholic University Bulletin* and the *New York Review* became the primary organs for the dissemination of quasi-modernist ideas.

Those who opposed the Americanists' practical programs and the accommodationist approaches to the new sciences did not perceive that they shared many of their opponents' estimates of the secularization of

---

[38]On Zahm, see Ralph E. Weber, *Notre Dame's John Zahm: American Catholic Apologist and Educator* (Notre Dame, Ind.: University of Notre Dame Press, 1961).
[39]John Hogan, "Seminary and University Studies," *American Ecclesiastical Review* 19 (1898): 366 n. 1.
[40]Francis E. Gigot, "The Study of Sacred Scripture in Theological Seminaries," *American Ecclesiastical Review* 23 (September 1900): 234.

the age. For the conservatives, as for Pope Pius IX and the First Vatican Council whom they frequently quoted, the age was almost in essence one of rationalism, secularism, and naturalism. The church, the realm of the supernatural, could not be compromised with this age. They believed that the Americanist spirit of accommodation was essentially a disguise for cultural and theological capitulation to values that were contrary to the Catholic tradition. The Americanizing bishops, clergy, and their professorial cohorts were cultural chauvinists and theological minimizers. By using scientific methods, social sciences, and biblical criticism, the professors in particular tended to "limit and reduce the authority of the magisterium of the church as far as possible."[41]

The opponents had accepted the dominant post–Vatican I neoscholastic apologetic that reasserted the authority of reason and the church as a solution to the various fideisms, subjectivisms, and autonomous rationalisms of the age. Most American Jesuit colleges in the era after Vatican I used apologetical texts that reflected this perspective. Opposition to the Americanists and the incipient modernists was part of the larger post–Vatican I official Roman Catholic mentality. Where the Americanists saw an opportunity for giving a specific spiritual or Catholic direction to contemporary cultural and scientific currents by reconciling Catholic tradition with what was best in those currents, the opponents saw dangers to the preservation of a unique Catholic identity.

The controversies in American Catholicism soon made their way to Europe, where they became entangled with ecclesiastical politics in France and Italy over the proper relations between Catholicism and the modern state.[42] The European conflicts came to full public focus with

---

[41]Joseph Schroder, "Theological Minimizing and Its Latest Defender," *American Ecclesiastical Review* 5 (July 1891): 56.

[42]The Europeans, of course, perceived the issues to be theological as well as political. The English Catholic modernist George Tyrell was familiar with the discussions in the American church, and when he read John Lancaster Spalding's *Opportunity and Other Essays* (1900), he found it difficult to believe that it was authored by a Roman Catholic bishop, "so full as it is of palpitating sympathy with all that is best and most Catholic in modern thought" (quoted in David F. Sweeney, *The Life of John Lancaster Spalding* [New York: Herder and Herder, 1966], 283). The French modernist Alfred Loisy, on the other hand, was disappointed to learn in discussions with Ireland and Spalding that they had fixed ideas only on social and political matters: "On these points alone are they in opposition to the Roman curia, but as far as our questions are concerned, they know little" (quoted in ibid., 282). In 1901, the arch anti-Americanist in France, Charles Maignen, who in the late 1890s had been the foremost critic of Walter Elliott's biography of Hecker, censured Spalding's *Opportunity* as typical of the Americanist mentality. He charged that the "fundamental error of Americanism is found here in its extremity: confidence in one's self, exaltation of the human personality, the adaptation of the Church to the age,

the French translation of Walter Elliott's *The Life of Father Hecker* in 1897. In Hecker, the French liberals saw an exemplary model of the relationship between Catholicism and the modern world and the conservatives saw an example of theological capitulation. The issues came to a head in 1899, when Pope Leo XIII published *Testem Benevolentiae*, censuring what he perceived to be Pelagian tendencies inherent in the new opinions and attitudes regarding the church's adaptation to modern theories and methods. Although he did not in fact denounce the Americanists or hold them personally accountable for the charges he made, he sent them a clear warning. Pope Pius X reinforced Roman opposition to the accommodating spirit of the age in *Pascendi dominici gregis* (1907), which condemned modernism as the "synthesis of all heresies."

The Americanists and the incipient modernist professors were singed by the two papal firebrands but denied that they held any of the condemned positions, while their opponents welcomed the warnings and asserted that they were indeed timely correctives to current directions in American Catholic life and thought. The Catholic animus against the Enlightenment ethos was so generally shared, by the American Catholic liberals as well as the conservatives, that the condemnations could be equally accepted by all sides, whether they admitted the American existence of the condemned errors or not. Thus, for all practical purposes, the two encyclicals effectively and practically killed the incipient Americanist and modernist movements without much protest, brought to an end the overt battles in the American church, and reinforced and legitimated an antimodernist neo-Thomist mentality that would come to characterize a growing number of younger scholars by the 1920s.

NEO-THOMISM

In the wake of the papal condemnations of Americanism and modernism, younger American Catholic scholars in the early twentieth century began to take up neo-Thomism,[43] which had been officially promulgated

the worship of the future and contempt for the past" (see *La Verité française* [Paris], 1 August 1901, translated in *The Review* [St. Louis] 9 [May 1902]: 273–76).

[43]This section could be called neoscholasticism rather than neo-Thomism, because, as Maurice DeWulf noted years ago, neo-Thomism "labors under the obvious disadvantage that it likens the new philosophy too exclusively to the thought-system of some particular individual, whereas in reality this new philosophy is sufficiently large and comprehensive to pass beyond the doctrinal limitations of any individual thinker" (see his *Scholasticism Old and New: An Introduction to Scholastic Philosophy Medieval and Modern*, trans. P. Coffey [Dublin: M. H. Gill and Son, 1907], 159). I have preferred to use the term

by Pope Leo XIII's encyclical *Aeterni Patris* (1879) but which had had little extensive influence in the United States in the nineteenth century. Neither Ireland or Spalding nor many of the other nineteenth-century episcopal or clerical leaders had been educated explicitly in neo-Thomism.[44]

Nineteenth-century seminary education was extremely eclectic. Most American clergy, whether educated in the United States or in European seminaries and universities, were taught either the seventeenth-century Gallican theologies, a Cartesian-influenced Gallican apologetics, a manual textbook scholasticism, or some form of traditionalism and ontologism.[45] Some American Catholic intellectuals, like Brownson and the quasi-modernist theologians, in fact, were cautiously critical of the rising Roman neo-Thomism in the middle and late nineteenth century.

Although officially promulgated in 1879, neo-Thomism did not become institutionalized in American seminaries and colleges or become a self-conscious revival movement until the 1920s.[46] The revival continued into the 1950s, dominating much of American Catholic thought like no single system of thought had done in the nineteenth century. The neo-Thomists revived a certain cluster of ideas which included an Aristotelian metaphysics, a realist epistemology, and a teleological view of nature. They reaffirmed the capacity of reason to comprehend all reality (including the existence of God), the harmony and intelligibility of the world, the unity of truth, the transcendental moral order of the universe,

---

neo-Thomism here, however, because as a matter of fact Thomas Aquinas's work was the central focus of the new movement in philosophy and theology.

[44]Within nineteenth-century American Catholicism, of course, there were a few isolated neo-Thomists. In the 1870s some Jesuits, like the theologian Camillo Mazzella (1833–1900) at Woodstock Theological College in Maryland and the philosopher Walter H. Hill (1822–1907) at Saint Louis University, promoted what Gerald McCool has called a commentator's Thomism, but these men had no "real understanding of modern science and culture" and therefore were unable to show the relevance of Thomism to the modern world (see Gerald A. McCool, S.J., *Catholic Theology in the Nineteenth Century: The Quest for a Unitary Method* [New York: Seabury Press, 1977], 238, 243–44).

[45]See Charles A. Hart, "Neo-Scholastic Philosophy in American Catholic Culture," in Charles A. Hart, ed., *Aspects of the New Scholastic Philosophy* (New York: Benziger Brothers, 1932), 17.

[46]The best studies of the rise of neo-Thomism and the Catholic revival are Philip Gleason, "In Search of Unity: American Catholic Thought, 1920–1960," *Catholic Historical Review* 65 (April 1979): 185–205; William M. Halsey, *The Survival of American Innocence: Catholicism in an Era of Disillusionment 1920–1940* (Notre Dame, Ind.: University of Notre Dame Press, 1980); and Arnold J. Sparr, *To Promote, Defend, and Redeem: The Catholic Literary Revival and the Cultural Transformation of American Catholicism, 1920–1960* (New York: Greenwood Press, 1990). I am dependent on all three sources for much of this section.

the certitude of faith, and the authority of the hierarchy to foster uniformity of doctrine and discipline within the church. Many, too, saw in the movement a corrective to the modern world's excessive individualism, rationalism, empiricism, subjectivism, pragmatism, and relativism. In attacking these modern developments of subjectivity and historicity, the neo-Thomists became preoccupied with establishing and fostering a unity of Catholic thought.

The receptivity to neo-Thomism can be attributed to social circumstances within early twentieth-century American Catholicism as well as to the institutional mandate. The drive toward a unity of thought corresponded to the movements toward more social and ecclesiastical unity within American Catholicism. During the 1920s (after the immigrant restriction laws) the hierarchy in large urban dioceses began to stabilize and unify the various ethnic communities by building efficient and centralized esslesiastical bureaucracies. Neo-Thomism fit into this ecclesiastical development, serving social and institutional interests as well as intellectual ones. It is for some of these reasons that Philip Gleason has interpreted neo-Thomism as Catholic ideology.[47]

That the rise and spread of neo-Thomism corresponds to the rise of neo-orthodoxy in American Protestantism is also instructive about the role of the movement in American society. Both were in search of the fundamental roots of their respective religious traditions in an age that both perceived, with different degrees of intensity, as having lost its way. Both movements were critical of the evolutionary optimism, relativity, and anthropocentrism of the nineteenth century and both reasserted the central reality of the supernatural in human life. Both, moreover, incorporated some of the dynamics of the late nineteenth century: Neo-orthodoxy accepted the historical consciousness, biblical criticism, social awareness, and a guarded use of science in the theological enterprise, neo-Thomists placed supreme confidence in reason's ability to discover truth and, at least initially, called for a dialogue between neo-Thomism and the new empirical sciences and modern philosophies.

Although they shared some common general tendencies, the two movements were separated by fundamental and traditional Protestant-

---

[47]Philip Gleason, "Keeping the Faith in America," in *Keeping the Faith: American Catholicism Past and Present* (Notre Dame, Ind.: University of Notre Dame Press, 1987), 169. See also Gleason's "Neo-Scholasticism as Preconciliar Ideology," in *CCICA Annual* (Notre Dame, Ind.: Catholic Commission on Intellectual and Cultural Affairs, 1988), 15–25.

Catholic differences. The neo-orthodox, for example, relied on Scripture more than natural law as a source for theological reflection. The neo-Thomists had a more optimistic view of human nature and the capacities of human reason than did the neo-orthodox. Justification within the neo-Thomistic framework was more transformative than forensic, and therefore the neo-Thomists placed more emphasis on the human efforts of the redeemed person and community than did the neo-orthodox. The neo-orthodox were more skeptical and critical of the powers of church and state.

American Catholic neo-Thomism developed in three stages, each of which had a dominant characteristic. In its initial stage, between 1895 and the early 1920s, it focused on a dialogue between itself and the modern empirical sciences. From the early 1920s to the middle of the 1930s, the rising young neo-Thomists became extremely antimodernist in outlook and articulated a commonsense approach to the use of reason in philosophy. From the middle of the 1930s to the late 1950s, the neo-Thomists, following Jacques Maritain, developed a constructive theological as well as philosophical Catholic vision for the modern free and pluralist society which they accepted.

Originally in the 1880s, Leo XIII and especially Louvain's Désiré Mercier (1851–1926) envisioned the neo-Thomist revival not simply as the archaeological recovery of scholastic patterns of thought but as a philosophical movement in dialogue with modern philosophy and the new sciences—to purify them, to be sure, but nonetheless to engage them in genuine intellectual exchange. At Louvain, Mercier put this vision into practice. That may also have been the original intent of Father Edward Pace (1861–1938) at the Catholic University of America. Pace had received a doctorate of sacred theology (1886) from the Propaganda College in Rome, where he studied under the neo-Thomist Francesco Satolli, and a doctorate of philosophy (1891) from the University of Leipzig, where he studied under the empirical psychologist Wilhelm Wundt. In 1895, Pace helped to establish the School of Philosophy at the Catholic University in Washington, D.C., which became a center for the spread of neo-Thomist philosophy.

Pace and a number of other young professors at the Catholic University inaugurated an era of dialogue between neo-Thomist philosophy and the new social sciences. The antimodernist scare, however, prevented theologians and biblical scholars from engaging in a philosophical and scientific exchange; in the area of religious (or catechetical, not theological) education, though, Catholic University scholars like John M. Cooper (1881–1949) and Thomas E. Shields (1862–1921) applied modern scientific methods (e.g., from empirical psychology and anthropology) to the ways of communicating the faith even after *Pascendi*. But, for all practical purposes, Pace's Louvain-like neo-Thomist sympathies for relating empirical sciences and philosophy did not carry the day in American Catholicism.[48]

The antimodernist phase began to appear in the period from 1920 to 1935. The essence of modernism, in the English Catholic historian Christopher Dawson's estimate, was the antidogmatic principle. Inherent in modernism was a rationalistic skepticism about the supernatural as an object of certain knowledge, an individualism and subjectivism that was fatal to all religious authority and community, and a belief that science, using unaided reason, could produce unlimited progress. Neo-Thomism offered a way out of this closed worldview. Its institutionalization in a number of American seminaries and colleges, however, did not produce the dialogue with modern thought that was originally intended. Rather, it created a number of young neo-Thomists who, unlike Pace and a few others, neither engaged in genuine research of Aquinas's thought nor were conversant with modern philosophy.[49]

A few students, such as Virgil Michel, O.S.B., the pioneer of the American liturgical movement, protested against the rise of a kind of neo-Thomism that developed in isolation from contemporary patterns of thought. "If we refuse," Michel wrote in 1921, "to see the standpoint of others, or ignore their sincerity, we are not only shutting off all possibility of assisting them, but we are actually building a wall around ourselves and closing to them all avenues of approach."[50] American Catholic philosophers needed to demonstrate a competence in other philosophical traditions and to engage them in a genuine dialogue. The problems here, though, were manifold. Catholic higher education had not matured enough to produce the kind of dialogue Michel envisioned, there were no Catholic journals for the distribution of scholastic

[48]He shared these sympathies with the Louvain historian of scholasticism Maurice DeWulf, who taught at Harvard University during the early twentieth century. On DeWulf's views, see his *Scholasticism Old and New*.
[49]Examples of this mentality can be found in the early issues of *The Modern Schoolman* (1925–), the first American Catholic journal of neoscholasticism, and in the works of young Jesuits like Bakewell Morrison's *The Catholic Church and the Modern Mind* (Milwaukee: Bruce, 1933) and *Revelation and the Modern Mind* (Milwaukee: Bruce, 1936).
[50]Virgil Michel, "The Mission of Catholic Thought," *American Catholic Quarterly Review* 46 (1921): 662–63.

thought, and Catholics either refused to or simply did not take part in national and philosophical organizations where such thought could be discussed. This situation began to change by the middle 1920s.

The founding of the *Modern Schoolman* (1925), *Thought* (1926), *The New Scholasticism* (1927), and the American Catholic Philosophical Association (1926) signaled the beginning of a more widespread and systematic study of scholasticism and Thomism. Fulton J. Sheen's *God and Intelligence in Modern Philosophy* (1925) was an early representative of what he and others called a commonsense Thomistic philosophy, meaning that "the natural, spontaneous, primitive, infallible judgments of the human reason constitute common sense. These judgments are not reflective judgments; they are immediate."[51] Such judgments were common to all because they arose from human nature. Sheen's work reasserted the validity of a rational demonstration of God's existence and the necessity of perceiving the intellectual content of religious faith and experience.[52] The problem with modern—that is, Kantian and post-Kantian nonrational—approaches to God and religious experience was that their starting point was basically anthropocentric. Sheen, like other commonsense Thomists, wanted to restore a realist epistemology that made being the measure of the mind and a transcendent God the measure of religious experience.

By the end of the 1920s various forms of neo-Thomist thought were developing in new departments of philosophy at a number of Catholic universities and colleges. Saint Louis University, Marquette, Notre Dame, Fordham, Boston College, as well as Catholic University became centers of philosophical neo-Thomism, drawing their professors from the Medieval Institute at Toronto, the Institute of Thomistic Philosophy at Louvain, or from the Catholic University itself. By 1966, a survey indicates, 57.3 percent of the philosophers teaching in Catholic universities and colleges called themselves neo-Thomist.[53] Philosophy, not theology, moreover, was the primary integrating discipline within Catholic colleges and universities during the early twentieth century. Departments of systematic theology were not organized in many Catholic colleges until the 1950s.

From the mid-1930s to the late 1950s, the neo-Thomist revival took

---

[51]Fulton J. Sheen, *God and Intelligence in Modern Philosophy: A Critical Study in the Light of the Philosophy of Saint Thomas* (New York: Longmans, Green, 1925), 143.

[52]Sheen saw that ultimately this intellectual restoration would be "the condition of economic and political restoration" (ibid., 8). In the 1920s, however, he never addressed the economic and political issues.

[53]Halsey, *The Survival of American Innocence*, 139.

a new turn. Although the neo-Thomists remained antimodernist in outlook and continued to emphasize reason, they now began to create a vision of Catholic culture that thoroughly integrated life and thought, religion and culture. Many would take their cue for this new mission from Jacques Maritain's *True Humanism*, which was defined as the humanism of the Incarnation.[54] The neo-Thomist mission was to restore in the Catholic community a sense of supernatural and sacramental humanism.

Maritain's true humanism had been anticipated as early as the middle of the 1920s, when several movements with interlocking concerns about the transformation of society had arisen in American Catholicism. In 1924, Michael Williams established *Commonweal* magazine to raise the cultural and intellectual consciousness of the Catholic laity so that it could become a potent force for applying Catholic principles to larger issues in society. At about the same time, Virgil Michel, O.S.B., and several other scholars criticized the prevailing juridical ecclesiology and devotional piety in the American church and called for a revival of the sacramental sense that would lead to a restoration of a mystical body concept of the church and a liturgically centered piety. In the early 1930s, Dorothy Day and Peter Maurin initiated the Catholic Worker Movement, which not only incorporated the awareness of lay responsibility and the need for a renewal of the liturgical-sacramental dimension of Catholic culture but also applied the personalism of Emmanuel Mounier to their understanding of the individual's Christian call to serve those in need.

By the end of the 1930s, the biblical movement was under way and, like the liturgical and catechetical movements, of which it was initially a part, had called for a return to the sources of the Christian tradition. In 1940, American Catholic theologians began to publish *Theological Studies*, the first explicitly theological journal since the short-lived quasimodernist *New York Review*. Twenty years after the organization of American Catholic philosophers, the theologians organized themselves into the Catholic Theological Society of America (1946) to bring about a more concerted theological reflection and exchange than had happened in the past. After World War II, a host of lay movements arose as local cells of reflection and action in the areas of marriage, family, youth, and social justice.

This preoccupation with integrating religion and life is exemplified

[54]Jacques Maritain, *True Humanism* (New York: Charles Scribner's Sons, 1938), 65.

clearly in the thought of John Courtney Murray, S.J., professor of theology at Woodstock College in Maryland. In the 1940s, Murray declared that American Catholic positions on social justice would never be taken seriously in public debates by other Americans until Catholics systematically removed the old American suspicions that Catholicism—if not American Catholics themselves—was doctrinally opposed to religious liberty. Catholics, he argued, had to demonstrate systematically the principles on which they adhered to religious liberty. By doing so, he believed, they would not only remove the old suspicions about a Catholic desire to control the United States, but also enable American Catholics freely to engage other Americans in a much-needed discussion about issues of justice and peace in society.[55]

Murray combined the transtemporal principles of the neo-Thomist natural law tradition with a historical consciousness, which was not a part of that tradition, to create an understanding of the concrete human situation in which "religious pluralism is theologically the human condition." The political movements for religious liberty during the past two centuries, he argued, were expressions of the demands of "natural law in the present moment of history."[56] This evolving consciousness of human dignity and freedom was consistent, he asserted, with a similar development in official Catholic papal teachings. In a historical-critical examination of recent papal teachings on the state and social justice, Murray showed that the papacy had developed a view of the human person's dignity in modern society that could, without violence to Catholic teaching, be applied to the previous modern developments of religious liberty. The historical emergence of constitutional protections for religious liberty were in fact a legitimate development of the Catholic tradition itself, although the church had not yet made this application.

In the middle of the 1950s, Murray's views on religious liberty clashed with those of Francis J. Connell and Joseph Fenton, professors of theology at the Catholic University, his Roman religious superiors, and Cardinal Alfredo Ottaviani, head of the Congregation of the Holy Office in Rome. Such resistance to Murray's views represented one of the last Catholic efforts before the Second Vatican Council to reject one of the major political contributions of the Enlightenment era. Behind Murray's

---

[55]On Murray, see Donald E. Pelotte, S.S.S., *John Courtney Murray: Theologian in Conflict* (New York: Paulist Press, 1975).
[56]John Courtney Murray, *The Problem of Religious Freedom* (Westminster, Md.: Newman Press, 1965), 19, 109.

defense of religious liberty, however, was not an ambition to come to terms with an Enlightenment mentality. He had other objectives in mind: He wanted Catholics, from their own religious perspectives and from the tradition of reason and law, to engage their fellow Americans in a public conversation about the quality of the common life in a free and pluralist society.

The American Catholic pursuit of unity in the midst of cultural diversity during the first half of the twentieth century reflected the prevailing and dominant influence of neo-Thomist patterns of thought. Whether they located the precise center of Catholic unity in a Christian rationalism, as did the philosophers, or a sacramental sense, as did the liturgical movement, or a Christian personalism, as did the Catholic Worker Movement, the intellectuals were for the most part governed by a belief that there was a fundamental irreducible core that held the Catholic tradition together. This did not mean that American Catholic thinkers were in basic agreement on any particular issue. There were significant divisions and disagreements within the neo-Thomist philosophical movement,[57] to say nothing of the other movements. The search for unity did not in fact mean uniformity, but it did reflect fundamental aspirations and created a climate of opinion and expectations that at times placed undue philosophical and cultural burdens on the vision itself.[58]

Some participants in the movement overloaded the concept of unity and were singularly blinded to elements of diversity even within their own ranks. Within the quest for an integral Catholicism were seeds of its own destruction. The different movements in search of unity were held together by a common goal, a common opposition to what they perceived to be the intellectual disillusionment, individualism, materialism, and secularism of society, and by a common and well-organized ecclesiastical structure—all of which masked the difference that later became apparent once the goal was no longer shared and modern society was viewed more positively. The neo-Thomist philosophy, too, was not well integrated with or suited to the historical methods employed in biblical research and liturgical studies. The vision, however, held all

[57]Gerald A. McCool, *From Unity to Pluralism: The Internal Evolution of Thomism* (New York: Fordham University Press, 1989), had made the point that twentieth-century Thomism, although it aspired to unity of thought, actually developed an internal pluralism.
[58]This point has been made, correctly I believe, in Gleason, "In Search of Unity," 185–205.

these movements together until after the Second Vatican Council, when subjectivity, historicity, and diversity came to be valued with almost the same passion that characterized the neo-Thomists' enthusiasm for objectivity, permanence, and unity.

AFTER VATICAN II: MODERNITY AND PLURALISM

The Second Vatican Council's *Pastoral Constitution on the Church in the Modern World* (*Gaudium et Spes*) and *Declaration on Religious Freedom* (*Dignitatis Humanae*), as some critics interpret them, brought to an end the official Catholic battle with an Enlightenment ethos that valued subjectivity and historicity, and called for an authentic dialogue with contemporary thought patterns. These documents, however, grew out of theological debates that had developed in the preconciliar age. The Council meant to reopen rather than close the discussion of the relationship between Catholicism and modernity.

Throughout the preconciliar period American Catholics had accepted the modern constitutional state and the new role assigned to the church in a free and pluralist society. From this perspective, Vatican II had little effect on American Catholicism. In addition, preconciliar American Catholic apologists repeatedly refused to reduce religion, Christianity, or Catholic claims to the realm of the private. Whether influenced by the Enlightenment, romanticism, or neo-Thomism, the apologists, despite the narrow criticism of what they considered the inherent defects of an exclusive subjectivism and individualism in modern thought, periodically claimed that faith had communal, public, and universal dimensions that must be made intelligible to all. That they were largely unsuccessful in making it universally available did not destroy the aspiration.

Although American Catholics were not entirely unprepared by reflection and experience for the discussions at the council, they were largely unaware of the modern theological developments that had been taking place in the European Catholic community after World War II. At the council neo-Thomistic philosophical and theological presuppositions were rigorously scrutinized and challenged by European Catholic theologians who had either a historically or a biblically oriented theology, or who had transformed the Thomistic thought patterns by sympathetically incorporating those modern philosophies that emphasized subjectivity and existential experience.

Postconciliar American Catholic scholars, educated in a variety of schools, have given modern philosophical and theological movements a more sympathetic reading than did the older neo-Thomists. The variety of educations, the appropriations of different philosophical systems, and the use of diverse methodologies produced a pluralism in American Catholic perspectives that clearly departed from the theological and philosophical unity of the immediate past, where unity of thought and meaning was somewhat presupposed and where the greatest problem was discovering an authentic Catholic response to the secularity and pluralism outside of the Catholic community. The new development represented a breakup of the American Catholic intellectual synthesis that had been developing since the early 1920s and, in conjunction with a number of other changes, produced a variety of tensions and conflicts within the American Catholic community.

The intellectual diversity that developed in the postconciliar period corresponded to certain sociological changes that had been taking place in American Catholicism since World War II. American Catholics were becoming more socially and economically mobile, moving into the suburbs and becoming thereby more clearly identified with the cultural and social pluralism of American society. The council unleashed for many Catholics the implications of that social movement. Liturgical reforms, institutional restructuring, and a willingness to learn from intellectual and social developments outside the church created in visible ways a growing pluralism within the church. Pluralism that had been previously perceived an external fact was now an internal one, and the pluralism within was not just cultural (American Catholic ethnic communities had experienced cultural pluralism in the past) but intellectual.

Old questions arose with a new urgency in the midst of this developing pluralism within. How can the Catholic believer relate to the thought patterns and methodologies of the modern scientific and secular age and still remain faithful to the authentic tradition? How and what does the Catholic theologian communicate to and learn from those communities of meaning, values, and beliefs that he or she does not entirely share? Furthermore, in a situation of external and internal pluralism, is unity of Catholic thought still possible or desirable?

In the midst of these questions, too, was the continuing problem of evaluating the Enlightenment ethos and modernity. Among postconciliar Catholic intellectuals the Enlightenment ethos and modernity came to be appreciated and appropriated more than in the past, but still there were internal quarrels about the extent of legitimate appropriation. The postconciliar responses to this process of reevaluation have produced at least three different camps within American Catholicism, with a great variety both within and among them. Behind the three camps, however, are varying degrees of a continuing Catholic uneasiness and conflict with contemporary forms of the Enlightenment ethos.

The first group has concentrated its assault primarily on the modernity within contemporary American Catholicism. In this camp are those who believe that many American Catholics, particularly those in the liberal clerical and theological reform movements, have forsaken the commitment to the supernatural and have sold out to modernity. James Hitchcock, professor of history at Saint Louis University, has clearly articulated this perspective in several of his books, including *The Decline and Fall of Radical Catholicism* (1971), *The Recovery of the Sacred* (1974), and *Catholicism and Modernity: Confrontation or Capitulation?* (1979). In the popular ecclesiastical revival after Vatican II, Hitchcock charges, the word "supernatural" "has been rendered suspect." In fact, following the judgment of sociologist Peter Berger, Hitchcock asserts that "those who believe in the supernatural are now a 'cognitive minority' in the Western World." Many post–Vatican II Catholic reformers, he claims, have collapsed the distinction between the natural and the supernatural. Therefore, many of the popular manifestations of reform are really a "flight from the eternal," and a "flight from absolutes in ethics" to "a comfortably this-worldly religion."[59]

Hitchcock goes on to hold that, rather than maintain a sense of history and the traditional values of Catholicism, many reformers have "fully embraced a liberalized Christianity [that] cannot in fact tolerate a staunchly other-worldly Catholicism" despite their talk of a pluralistic church. The so-called pluralism within Catholicism, with talk of dissent and alternate theologies, is primarily a "media event." A religious group like the Catholic Church must be "interiorly cohesive, with strong leadership and firm beliefs" if it is ever to be effective or have an impact "within the overall pluralistic framework of society." The media have created the impression that Catholicism, because of contemporary internal dissensions, no longer has a cohesive center and authoritative teachings. Hence the liberals feel free to entertain theological and moral views at variance with the clearly articulated positions of the church. Hence also the liberals attempt to use the media to forge a new consensus

[59]James Hitchcock, *Catholicism and Modernity: Confrontation or Capitulation?* (New York: Seabury Press, 1979), 4, 9, 93.

within Catholicism. Thereby, they have created the "illusion of pluralism" within the church. The current need in Catholicism, therefore, is for reaffirmation and reassertion of traditional Catholic values and teachings in order to mount a cohesive Catholic program in a socially and culturally pluralistic world.[60]

Avery Dulles, S.J., professor of theology at the Catholic University, represents a moderately reformist-minded theological position, one that is aware of the historically and socially conditioned nature of theological conceptualization and is, therefore, open to a legitimate reform and pluralism within theology. He has been primarily concerned with inner church problems, which are in his estimate a reflection of the clash between culturally conditioned traditional patterns of thought and contemporary forms of conceptualization. The internal tensions in the church he interprets primarily as the result of those who can see only two options in the church, either a servile conformism to the past or a defiant rebellion against such conformism. Both of these options for him reflect the nonhistorical thinking that has been the result of the Enlightenment and certain forms of neo-Thomism.

Dulles has tried to demonstrate the necessity of the survival of dogma, but he conceives of dogma not as some kind of "intellectual strait jacket." For him the "Christian self-understanding and the structures of the Christian community must be overhauled in order to correspond with the presuppositions, concerns, thought-forms, patterns of life, communications systems, and technical possibilities offered by the contemporary world."[61]

Influenced considerably by Michael Polanyi, Bernard Lonergan, Karl Rahner, and a host of contemporary European theologians, Dulles has distinguished between learning, which is the acquisition of what has already been achieved by others in a particular scientific or religious community, and discovery, which is more original conquest of the mind. In a religious community, as in the scientific community, both learning and discovery, both authority and personal insight are necessary in the human quest for knowledge. For Dulles, therefore, in all human traditions, religious as well as scientific, the transmission of knowledge and skills involves a constant process of revision. Dulles's theological project has been an attempt to achieve a general vision of the "dialectical

[60]Ibid., 11, 85, 86, 88.
[61]Avery Dulles, *The Survival of Dogma* (New York: Doubleday, 1971), 12.

interpenetration between stability and change, fidelity and initiative" in his examination of the relationship between Christian faith and its historical forms.[62]

In 1971, Dulles described the development of the Catholic Church's magisterium from the nineteenth to the mid twentieth century as a progressive alienation from the modern world. "In proportion as the thinking of secular society became self-critical, relativist, concrete, and future-oriented, the magisterium became more authoritarian, absolutist, abstractionist, and backward-looking."[63] The task at hand, therefore, was to enter into dialogue with the modern patterns of thought, not just to copy them but to find a creative synthesis that would transcend the limits of both of the past approaches. The task of the modern church was dialogue, not a continuation of confrontation, which was really a failure to understand what was truly beneficial in the modern thought patterns.

Since 1975, the year of the "Hartford Appeal"[64] and publication of David Tracy's *Blessed Rage for Order*, Dulles has seen himself as a theologian mediating between ecclesiastical conservatives and liberals in his own evaluation of the church's relation to pluralism and the modern secular world:

Unlike many ecclesiastical conservatives, I hold that adaptation need not be a form of capitulation to the world, but that an adapting church should be able to herald the Christian message with greater power and impact. Unlike certain liberals, I am deeply concerned that the church, in its efforts at adaptation, should avoid imitating the fashions of the nonbelieving world and should have the courage to be different. Difference is not to be cultivated for its own sake but is to be fearlessly accepted when Christ and the Gospel so require.[65]

Dulles has become increasingly concerned since the mid-1970s that some contemporary theologians have uncritically accepted prevailing ideas, and he is afraid that such an accommodation could lead theologians to dissolve the distinctiveness of Catholic Christianity. Although he is open to pluralism within Catholicism (his use of a "models"

---

[62]Ibid., 13.

[63]Ibid., 114.

[64]"An Appeal for Theological Affirmation" (subscribed to by twenty-four prominent American Catholic and Protestant theologians, Avery Dulles among them) asserted, among other things, the need to recover "a sense of the transcendent" and charged that some contemporary theological themes were "false and debilitating to the church's life and work"; the appeal condemned thirteen current themes it so characterized. See Dulles's *The Resilient Church: The Necessity and Limits of Adaptation* (Garden City, N.Y.: Doubleday, 1977), 191–95.

[65]Dulles, *The Resilient Church*, 1, 5.

approach to theology reveals his catholic or inclusive approach), he does not believe that the theologian can explain Christianity to the modern pluralistic and secular world on the basis of publicly verifiable criteria or without an explicit religious commitment to Christianity. At this point in particular Dulles has become critical of theologians such as Tracy, who have, Dulles believes, appropriated the empirical model of the positive sciences in their theology.[66] Dulles disagrees especially with those who believe that at the level of fundamental theology—that is, the theology that attempts to explicate the universal significance of Christianity—a firm religious commitment is "unnecessary, even dangerous." He asserts that fundamental as well as dogmatic theology demands persons committed to Christianity if theology is to be "adequately practical." He maintains that the "fundamental theologian may legitimately draw upon the testimony of tradition," because fundamental theology is "inseparable from dogmatics."[67] Thus in the contemporary world an adequate fundamental theology presupposes commitment and denies the adequacy or possibility of a completely scientific objectivity.

David Tracy, professor of philosophical theology at the Divinity School of the University of Chicago, represents a third camp within American Catholicism. Tracy has been less directly concerned than Dulles about intraecclesial Catholic problems and more preoccupied with developing a role for the discipline of Christian theology in public conversations about truth and meaning in the common life. He calls his own theological position "revisionist" because it transcends the limits while appreciating the benefits of traditional and modern self-understanding. Like Dulles, he sees a number of valuable and permanent contributions to the modern world from the Enlightenment: the demand for emancipatory reason and freedom from the bonds of oppressive and mystifying traditions; the belief in critical reason and civilized discourse; the need for authentic tolerance of differences and real cultural, political, and civic pluralism.

Like the postmoderns Freud, Marx, and Nietzsche, and to a certain extent like the transcendental Thomists (such as Bernard Lonergan and Karl Rahner), Tracy sees that these benefits were accompanied by positions that make the Enlightenment tradition, like most intellectual

[66]Avery Dulles, "Authority and Criticism in Systematic Theology," *Theology Digest* 26 (winter 1978): 392.
[67]Avery Dulles, review of David Tracy's *Blessed Rage for Order*, in *Theological Studies* 37 (1975): 310–11.

traditions, ambiguous. His cataloging of problems in the Enlightenment ethos, too, though more perceptive, is consistent with many of the earlier American Catholic critiques: the reduction of reason in the contemporary world to mere instrumental rationalism; the creation of an autonomous subject whose judgments about truth and meaning have become a matter of an all-embracing subjective and ultimately consumerist taste; the conversion of all interpretation to pure rational technique; and the illusion that, if we are autonomously conscious and rational, we need fear no further illusions.[68]

Like John Courtney Murray, Tracy accepts the freedom and pluralism of the modern world and wants to create a genuine dialogue about the common public life between Christian theology and the plurality of contemporary voices who shared that interest. Tracy, however, perceives the limits of Murray's rational and natural law approach to civic discourse in a complex technological society and has tried to develop a comprehensive conversation that would affirm the validity of pluralism itself. His acceptance of pluralism as an internal and truly beneficial religious and cultural reality, therefore, is clearly distinguished from Murray's vision of pluralism as a reality external to the church and the self. Unlike Murray, moreover, Tracy accepts pluralism in theology and in modern patterns of thought as a "fundamental enrichment of the human condition" and as something that is inherent in that condition.[69] Accepting the condition of pluralism "allows each theologian to learn incomparably more about reality by disclosing really different ways of viewing both our common humanity and Christianity."[70] In his view this acceptance is not a capitulation to a consumerism mentality, that is, picking and choosing whatever theology or modern pattern of thought best fits one's current needs. Such a mentality would ultimately result in theological chaos and mental confusion. A responsible pluralism must include an affirmation of truth and public criteria for that affirmation.

Contemporary Christian theologians like Tracy, though, find themselves in a dilemma. They are simultaneously committed to the modern world and to the God of Jesus Christ, but "neither the traditional Chris-

---

[68]For a catalog of the benefits and limits of the Enlightenment ethos, see David Tracy, *The Analogical Imagination: Christian Theology and the Culture of Pluralism* (New York: Crossroad, 1981), 39, 67, 78, 346, 350.
[69]Ibid., xi.
[70]David Tracy, *Blessed Rage for Order: The New Pluralism in Theology* (New York: Seabury Press, 1975), 3.

tian self-understanding nor recent modern self-understanding nor any combination thereof will suffice to resolve that dilemma." Tracy's fundamental theology, therefore, is directed to a "basic revision of traditional Christianity and traditional modernity." By revising both traditions, Tracy tries to demonstrate "that the Christian faith is at heart none other than the most adequate articulation of the basic faith of secularity itself." Fundamental theology, if it is to be a science, must "use only publicly verifiable criteria" because the Christian truth claims themselves are universal and public, not private. Therefore, the fundamental theologian's task "is best understood as philosophical reflection upon the meanings present in common human experience and the meanings present in the Christian tradition.[71]

Tracy sees all theology, whether fundamental or systematic, as a legitimate and appropriate "public discourse" within the church, the university, and society—the three publics to which all theologians, whether they are aware of it or not, speak. A primary difference between the fundamental and the systematic theologian lies in the fact that the fundamental theologian critically analyzes the Christian truth claims "without any appeal to personal belief-warrants." The systematic theologian, on the other hand, "interprets the meaning and truth of a particular religious tradition from a personal faith stance of involvement in and commitment to the tradition itself."[72] Realizing that modern humanity has a profound sense of historical relativity, Tracy argues that the systematic theologian needs to reinterpret the classical events, persons, images, and texts of the religious tradition in a systematic, inherently coherent, and fully public way that is in accordance with the demands of one's own primary religious confessions. "I can never simply repeat," Tracy says, "the [Christian] classics to understand them. I must interpret them or their publicness will become private."[73]

Tracy, Dulles, and Hitchcock represent the diverse evaluations of an Enlightenment ethos both within and outside of Catholicism. But behind this contemporary pluralism of perspectives and methodologies there is something still at odds with a modernity that has been emancipated or separated from a personal and communal commitment to Christ and to

---

[71]Ibid., 4, 10, 27, 34, 45.
[72]David Tracy, "Theological Classics in Contemporary Theology," *Theology Digest* 25 (Winter 1977): 348.
[73]David Tracy, "The Public Character of Systematic Theology," *Theology Digest* 26 (Winter 1978): 401–2.

fundamental spiritual aspirations. The Catholic tradition—preserved, reformed, and/or revised—continues to provide critical and imaginative alternatives to a contemporary world that relies too exclusively on an instrumental rationality and a consumerist subjectivism. Behind fundamental disagreements over ecclesiastical and moral issues, too, lies a basic Catholic sensibility for transcendence and community that continues to find difficulties with a bureaucratically controlled, complex society that is more concerned about practical means and technological possibilities than about ultimate ends, meaning, and truth. Catholics, of course, are by no means alone in making these contemporary criticisms, but they come out of a tradition that has shaped these criticisms since the late eighteenth century.

Since the election of John F. Kennedy and the Second Vatican Council, Catholics more than ever before have entered into American public life. This transformation was symbolized most dramatically by the widespread attention given to the American bishops' pastorals on peace and the economy, both of which called for public conversation on, and criticism of, some contemporary social, political, and economic options in American society. The ecclesiastical and moral conflicts within contemporary Catholicism, the recent pastorals, and the three camps of contemporary reflection indicate that the Catholic convergence and controversy with the Enlightenment ethos have been transformed and redirected, but have not yet ended.

5

━━

Organizing the past

JACOB NEUSNER

THE ENLIGHTENMENT'S TIME

Accounting for the passage of time and disposing of the past for the Enlightenment yielded historical thinking. That meant three things: criticism of the allegations as to past events set forth by received writings; selection of consequential events; and organization of the selected events into patterns meant to demonstrate out of secular facts reasoned propositions, that is, the this-worldly explanation of the present out of the resources of the past. Imposed paradigms from heaven do not pertain; we can find our own way. The premises of historical thinking about time and especially past time, which are with us to this day, are then self-evident. The past is clearly differentiated from the present. An accurate knowledge of precisely what happened long ago bears self-evident meaning for the understanding of the present. For events, critically narrated, produce intelligible patterns, not chaos. The passage of time is read as linear, cumulative, and purposive; secular rationality substitutes for the teleology of revealed religion.

Enlightenment history's distinction between past and present is not the only indicator of historical modes of organizing experience. A further trait of historical thinking is the linearity of events, a sense for the teleology of matters, however the goal may find its definition. Past was then but leads to now. It is not now, but it guides us into the acute present tense and onward to the future. For what may happen is not to be predicted; linearity presupposes predictability, regularity, order—and therefore contradicts the unpredictability of the world. Historical study correlates this to that, ideas to events, always seeking reasonable explanation of what has come about. Its very premise is that of the Enlightenment, concerning the ultimate order awaiting discovery. History, then, forms a subset of the quest for order—a persuasive one that enjoys the standing of self-evidence.

The premise of history is that events, critically reconstructed and properly selected and ordered, yield an order that follows a rule. That governing premise accounts for the importance of critical history. History then, out of singular and onetime happenings, states social rules and laws to describe the orderly character of human events that explain how things now are and will come about. Historical thinking about the past, with its premises concerning the certainty of ordering events into meaningful patterns; the rationality of what was then to be called, and endowed with authority as, history; and above all the absolute separation between present and past time—these aspects of the Enlightenment presented an unprecedented approach to the course of human events. The language of organizing the past substituted the preface "History proves" for "God reveals."

Note the contrast to the received Judeo-Christian paradigm. The Hebrew Scriptures were gathered to impose on the past a meaningful pattern so as to answer an urgent question: What must Israel do to keep the Holy Land?[1] Those same Scriptures made their way into the West through the media of Judaism and Christianity, and both heirs recast the historical writings in an altogether different, ahistorical structure. The Enlightenment did not invent history; Scripture did. The Enlightenment, however, offered a mode of organizing the past to compete with the one that had long predominated in the West, the reading of Scripture's history that framed the Judaic and Christian reception of the Israelite past and defined the West's long-established mode of organizing time. So although the Enlightenment's formulation of a historical mode

---

[1]For an account of the character of history writing in the Hebrew Scriptures, see John van Seters, *In Search of History: Historiography in the Ancient World and the Origins of Biblical History* (New Haven: Yale University Press, 1983). The most important recent statement of how the Hebrew Scriptures were formed in response to the destruction of the Jerusalem Temple in 586 B.C. and as a systematic explanation thereof is David Noel Freedman's *The Unity of the Hebrew Bible* (Ann Arbor: University of Michigan Press, 1991). Note also Sara Mandell and David Noel Freedman, *The Relationship between Herodotus' History and Primary History* (Atlanta: Scholars Press for South Florida Studies in the History of Judaism, 1993). For corroboration from a completely different viewpoint, see Philip R. Davies, "In Search of Ancient Israel," *Journal for the Study of the Old Testament* (Sheffield), supp. ser. 148 (1993), who assigns this cogent and systematic work to the same period as does Freedman, though for different reasons. For the theological statement of the Hebrew Scriptures' historical mode of thought, see G. Ernest Wright, *God Who Acts: Biblical Theology as Recital* (Chicago: Regnery, 1952).

of thinking concerning the past represented a break with many centuries of thinking in a different way about the same matter, it could point to authoritative precedent in Scripture. The Hebrew Scriptures of ancient Israel ("the written Torah" to Judaism and "the Old Testament" to Christianity), all scholarship concurs, set forth Israel's life as history, with a beginning, middle, and end; a purpose and a coherence; a teleological system. All accounts agree that Scripture distinguished past from present, present from future, and composed a sustained narrative of one-time, irreversible events. All scholars maintain that, in Scripture's historical portrait, Israel's present condition appealed for explanation to Israel's past, perceived as a coherent sequence of weighty events, each unique, all formed into a great chain of meaning.

But that is not how through most of the history of Western civilization the Hebrew Scriptures were read by Judaism and Christianity. The idea of history, with its rigid distinction between past and present and its careful sifting of connections from the one to the other, came quite late onto the scene of intellectual life. Both Judaism and Christianity through most of their histories have read the Hebrew Scriptures in an other than historical framework. They found in Scripture's words paradigms of an enduring present, by which all things must take their measure; they possessed no conception whatsoever of the pastness of the past. Let us explore the full and detailed character of the paradigmatic approach to the explanation of Israel's condition, viewed (to state the negative side of matters) atemporally, ahistorically, episodically, and not through sustained narrative or its personal counterpart, biography, composed of connected, unique, irreversible events, in the manner of history.

Visually, we grasp the ahistorical perception in the union of past and present that takes place through representation of the past in the forms of the present: the clothing, the colors, the landscapes of the familiar world. That is mere anachronism, however, which history can tolerate. Conceptually, we understand the mode of receiving Scripture when we understand that, for "our sages of blessed memory" of Judaism, as far the saints and sages of Christianity, the past took place in the acutely present tense of today, but the present found its locus in the presence of the ages as well. That is something historical thinking cannot abide; furthermore, it contradicts the most fundamental patterns of explanation that we ordinarily take for granted in contemporary cultural life. Historicism has governed for two hundred years.

The paradigmatic conception of marking time differs so radically from our own that reading Scripture in the way, for nearly the whole of its reception, it has been read proves exceedingly difficult. Our conception of history forms a barrier between us and the understanding of time that defined the Judaic and the Christian encounter with ancient Israel. The givenness of the barrier between time now and time then yields for us banalities about anachronism, on the one hand, and imposes on us the requirement of mediating between historical fact and religious truth, on the other.

Whether or not Voltaire's heirs can be discovered in *flagrante-delicto*—in the very act of appealing to Scripture for authority—need not detain us; Voltaire's mordant wit would have disposed of them if they were. What is more to the point is that the Enlightenment's insistence on the possibility of ordering the past, accurately portrayed through critical study, into patterns yielding demonstrable rules for making sense of time and change conflicted at its foundations with the established Judaic and Christian way of thinking about the past. That way sorted out times past in accord with quite other premises. As a result, the Enlightenment's critical history—its insistence that we can discover through criticism what happened and that, when we do, we can find those rules of order and regularity that govern even now and therefore explain the present and point to the future—that insistence cut the West off from its long-established ways of interpreting its religious heritage of Scripture and tradition. Those ways of reading the past, encompassing the story of ancient Israel, took for granted the facticity of the sources and regarded as mere improvements and refinements the study of contradictions that for the Enlightenment and its heirs in romantic historicism required the complete rewriting of the past. These same modes of thought further denied the pastness of the past, on the one hand, and affirmed the presence of the past in the everyday world of the here and now, on the other. Rules from the past provided what no one needed, since the past and present flowed together into an eternal now.

That same hermeneutics did not entrust to the hands of the present or future the selection of events that made a difference; it began with a well-crafted account of what mattered; the lessons and meanings of the historical record emerged not out of the past at all. For the mode of thinking that predominated offered a different view of time, one that rejected the notion that the past and present could be distinguished from each other, but that also dismissed the conception of cyclicality as an alternative. If, however, I had to specify a single paramount point of difference between the Enlightenment's reading of the past and that of the Judaic and Christian reception of ancient Israel's history as set forth in Scripture, it is a different sense of order. The Enlightenment optimistically saw in events unfolding on their own, in a secular world, the possibility of finding order in chaos. The Judaic and Christian thinkers never imagined that, unguided by revelation, any mind could perceive order out of the chaos of the world. The certainty of the Enlightenment's faith in the possibility of order contrasts strikingly with the profound skepticism of the Judaic and Christian disbelief in an order other than God's.

The entire Judeo-Christian hermeneutical tradition, with its exegesis, has been lost. Two examples suffice to prove the point, both deriving from normative scholarship in Scripture today. The first, by George Ramsey, states as fact the premises of the Enlightenment's way of organizing the past and insists these govern in reading Scripture:

A major part of any course in Old Testament is the study of the history of Israel. . . . the fact that [the history of the Israelite people] constituted the context out of which the Scriptures of the Old Testament emerged gives it special significance. . . . How can we really appreciate the messages of the Old Testament authors unless we are familiar with the situations which produced them and to which they were addressed?[2]

The answer to Ramsey's question given by many centuries of Judaic and Christian exegetes of the Hebrew Scriptures is that without the intervention of secular history, we of holy Israel (like our counterparts in the Church of Jesus Christ) appreciate the messages of the Torah very well indeed—just as we have in the millennia since God gave us the Torah. Without the slightest familiarity with the situations that produced them and to which they are addressed, we have no difficulty whatsoever in appreciating the messages of Scripture. For Judaic and Christian believers through the ages take as premise that it is to us and to the faithful of all times and places that the ancient Israelite Scriptures were and are addressed. Present-day reading of the Hebrew Scriptures, however, takes for granted that exegesis begins in history, not theology. Statements such as Ramsey's show how present-day reading also has lost sight of the

[2]George W. Ramsey, *The Quest for the Historical Israel: Reconstructing Israel's Early History* (London: SCM Press, 1982), xxi.

quite other than historical approach to history and time that governs throughout the corpus of Judaic and Christian reading of Scripture.

The second, disingenuous affirmation of the Enlightenment's premises on the past comes to us in Baruch Halpern's proudly dismissive account of the Judaic and Christian position:

The confessional use of the Bible is fundamentally ahistorical. It makes of Scripture a sort of map, a single, synchronic system in which the part illuminates the whole, in which it does not matter that different parts of the map come from divergent perspectives and different periods. The devotee uses it to search for treasure: under the X lies a trove of secret knowledge; a pot of truths sits across the exegetical rainbow, and with them one can conjure knowledge, power, eternity. Worshipers do not read the Bible with an intrinsic interest in human events. Like the prophet or psalmists or, in Acts, the saint, they seek behind the events a single, unifying cause that lends them meaning and makes the historical differences among them irrelevant. In history, the *faithful* seek the permanent, the ahistorical; in time, they quest for timelessness; in reality, in the concrete, they seek Spirit, the insubstantial. Confessional reading levels historical differences— among the authors in the Bible and between those authors and church tradition—because its interests are life present (in the identity of a community of believers) and eternal.[3]

Halpern here characterizes—with a measure of jejune and immature caricature—that alternative to the historical reading of Scripture that both Judaism and Christianity selected and faithfully followed for eighteen hundred years, until the advent of historical thinking in the eighteenth century and its transformation of the powerful instrument of exegesis of Scripture in the nineteenth.

What is at stake is a different conception of time, one that recognizes no wall between past and present but formulates matters in a quite different manner. It is a way of understanding Scripture that in its context enjoyed the standing of self-evident truth and may now lay claim to a serious hearing for the simple reason that it provides a more plausible model than the historical one. The Enlightenment attack on the received hermeneutics took as its target the gullibility of the faithful that things really happened as Scripture says, when it can be shown that this is not so. Yet the issue is not the faithful's indifference to whether things really happened as they are portrayed; moreover, Halpern's term *timelessness* obscures the vastly different conception of time in the Judaic and Christian reception of ancient Israel's Scripture, especially its history.

[3]Baruch Halpern, *The First Historians: The Hebrew Bible and History* (San Francisco: Harper and Row, 1988), 3–4.

The point is that through nearly the whole of the history of Judaism and Christianity, a mode of reading Scripture predominated that today is scarcely understood and only rarely respected. In Halpern's view, it is characterized as "confessional" and dismissed as ahistorical. But "confessional" tells us only that practitioners of Judaism and Christianity approach Scripture with reverence and seek there to find what God told to humanity. The faith of Judaism and Christianity need not insist on the reading of Scripture as a single, synchronic system—but it does, so the pejorative descriptor *confessional* is both beside the point and accurate. The key to Halpern's uncomprehending caricature lies in the contrasts, with the climax being the term *insubstantial*: Militant, ideological historicism makes its complete and final statement in that word. Faith admittedly is in things unseen but not in what is insubstantial, not at all. Still, Halpern speaks for a century and a half of scholarship that has appealed to secular rules for reading the documents of religions that read the Hebrew Scriptures as the written Torah or the Old Testament.

The ahistorical premise of the Judaic hermeneutic serves to raise the question, What is it that instead of history organizes the past? Here we find an explicit rejection of the premises of historical thinking, that there is an order to events and that that order overcomes chaos and imparts meaning. The Torah is alleged in *Sifré to Numbers*, a fourth-century A.D. commentary, to portray the past in complete indifference to considerations of temporal order:

"And the Lord spoke to Moses in the wilderness of Sinai in the first month of the second year after they had come out of the land of Egypt, saying, ['Let the people of Israel keep the passover at its appointed time. On the fourteenth day of this month, in the evening, you shall keep it at its appointed time; according to all its statutes and all its ordinances you shall keep it.']" (Num. 9:1–14):
Scripture teaches you that *considerations of temporal order do not apply to the sequence of scriptural stories.* For at the beginning of the present book Scripture states, "The Lord spoke to Moses in the wilderness of Sinai in the tent of meeting on the first day of the *second* month in the second year after they had come out of the land of Egypt" (Num. 1:1).
And here Scripture refers to "the first month," so serving to teach you that *considerations of temporal order do not apply to the sequence of scriptural stories.* (Sifré to Num. LXIV:1.1)

At first glance, this allegation concerning the Torah's way of organizing the past is jarring. On reflection, however, we realize that Enlightenment history's premise—the self-evidence of the linearity of events (first came this, then came that, and this explains or causes that)—contradicts the everyday experience of humanity, in which chaos governs, whereas from history's perspective, order should reign. Sometimes "this" yields "that," as it should, but sometimes it does not. What happens in ordinary life does not yield events that relate to one another like pearls on a necklace, in proper procession. Life is unpredictable; if "this" happens, we cannot securely assume or predict that "that" must occur in sequence—at least, not in the experience of humanity. That is proved by the irregularity of events, the unpredictability of what, if this happens, will follow. If not the historical way of organizing the past, then how? Clearly, a different way of ordering the past provides the framework for the statement or the rabbinic document before us. To understand that different way, we have to step back and consider the various means by which we tell time, for history's linearity and order form only one kind.

Unlike history, Judaism and Christianity have taken into account the failure of linear logic, with its regularities and certainties and categorical dismissal of chaos. To show the rationality of this Judaic and also Christian approach, I point to a metaphor supplied by the mathematics of our own time. In its reading of Scripture, Judaism (along with Christianity) posits a world that may be compared to that of fractal shapes (in the language of mathematics), or paradigms, models, or patterns (in the language used here). These fractals or paradigms describe how things are, whether large or small, whether here or there, whether today or in a distant past or an unimaginable future. Fractal thinking finds sameness without regard to scale or time; it therefore makes possible the quest for a few specific patterns, which will serve this and that, hither and yon, because out of acknowledged chaos it isolates points of regularity or recurrence and permits us to describe, analyze, and interpret them.[4]

Paradigms describe the structure of being. They derive from imagination, not from perceived reality. They impose on the world their own structure and order, selecting among things that happen those few mo-

---

[4] I invoke the analogy of fractal mathematics only to introduce external evidence in support of my insistence on the rationality of paradigmatic thinking. In particular, I find points of analogy in fractals in the dismissal of considerations of scale, the admission of chaos into the data out of which order is selected, and the insistence that a few specific patterns are all we have, but that these serve in a variety of circumstances and can be described in a reliable and predictable way. The starting point is chaos, the goal, the discovery of order. The givenness, for historical thinking, of linearity then defines a different starting point, one of order, not chaos, and that strikes me as lacking all rationality, when measured against the perceived experience of humanity. Historical thinking forms the last remnant of the Enlightenment's optimism, and paradigmatic thinking offers a more plausible way of ordering the chaos of nature and society alike, which the twentieth century has established as a given.

ments that are eventful and meaningful. Paradigms form a conception of time different from the historical and define a conception of relationship different from the linear. Whether we draw our analogy from mathematics or from structures, the upshot is the same. To call the religious reading of Scripture ahistorical is both accurate and monumentally beside the point; that is only to say what it is not, rather than what it is. I claim it is paradigmatic thinking, not linear thinking, and here I shall describe precisely what that mode of thought is, so far as the Judaism of the dual Torah exemplifies how history and time give way to a different order of being altogether.

The Judaic mode of organizing the past makes its statement through a medium that explicitly rejects distinctions among past, present, and future and treats the past as a powerful presence, but the present as a chapter of the past and the future as a negotiation of not time but principle. A paradigm governs, with all events conforming to its atemporal rule. Consequently, the two conflicting conceptions of social explanation—the historical and the paradigmatic—appeal to two different ways of conceiving of and evaluating time. Historical time measures one thing; paradigmatic time, another—although both refer to the same facts of nature and of the social order. Paradigmatic time, in which there is no "earlier" or "later," corresponds to nature's time rather than history's time as framed in the Enlightenment's certainties.

TIMES

Nature marks time in its way. People living ordinary lives mark time in its manner. Each entity accommodates the limits of its existence—a rock, a person, a river. Geologic time takes as its outer limit the 5 billion years of earth's existence (the planet's "history"), whereas human time is marked out in units of, say, the seventy years of a human life, or the two, three, or four centuries of an empire's hegemony. Religion—in particular, Judaism and Christianity—intends to bridge the gap between creation's and humanity's time by speaking of time in aggregates that transcend the limits of historical, that is, human, time and extend outward to nature's time, that is, God's evanescent moment. Scripture makes explicit the contrast between humanity's time and God's, and the task of religion, mediating between two forms of time, defines the way in which Scripture is taken over by the paradigms that govern the Judaic and Christian readings thereof.

These fractals or paradigms describe how things are. We know those paradigms because, in Scripture, God tells us what they are; our task is to receive and study Scripture so as to find them to examine and study events so as to discern the paradigms; to correlate Scripture and time—whether present time or past time matters not at all—so as to identify the indicators of order, the patterns that occur and recur and (from God's perspective) impose sense on the nonsense of human events.

A paradigm forms a way of keeping time that invokes its own differentiating indicators, its own counterparts to the indicators of nature's time. Nature defines time as that span that is marked off by one spell of night and day, by one sequence of phases of the moon, or by one cycle of the sun around the earth (in the pre-Copernican paradigm). History further defines nature's time by reference to an important human event, such as a reign, a battle, construction or destruction of a building. So history's time intersects with, and is superimposed on, nature's time. Cyclical time forms a modification of history's time, appealing for its divisions of the aggregates of time to the analogy, in human life, to nature's time: The natural sequence of events in a human life is viewed as a counterpart to the natural sequence of events in solar and lunar time. Paradigms are set forth by neither nature (by definition) nor natural history (what happens on its own here on earth), by neither the cosmos (sun and moon) nor the natural history of humanity (the life cycle and analogies drawn therefrom). In the setting of Judaism and Christianity, paradigms are set forth in revelation; they explain the creator's sense of order and regularity, which is neither imposed on nor derived from nature's time, nor to be discovered through history's time. That is why to paradigmatic time, history is wildly incongruous, and considerations of linearity, temporality, and historical order are beyond comprehension. God has set forth the paradigms that measure time by indicators of an other than natural character: supernatural time, which of course transcends any human conception of time.

The paradigm takes its measures in terms not of historical movements or recurrent cycles but, rather, of atemporal units of experience, those same aggregates of time such as nature makes available through the movement of the sun and moon and the passing of the seasons, on the one hand, and through the life of a human being, on the other. A model or pattern or paradigm presents an account of the life of the social entity (village, kingdom, people, territory) in terms of differentiated events—wars and reigns, for example, or erecting a given building and destroying it—yet entirely out of phase with sequences of time. A paradigm imposed on time does not call on the day or month or year to accomplish its task. It will set aside nature's time altogether, regarding years and months as bearing a significance other than the temporal, sequential one posited by history (including cyclical time's history). Paradigmatic time views humanity's time as formed into aggregates out of phase with nature's time, as being measured in aggregates not coherent with those of the solar year and the lunar month. The aggregates of humanity's time are dictated by humanity's life, as much as the aggregates of nature's time are defined by the course of nature. Nature's time serves not to correlate with humanity's patterns (no longer humanity's time) but, rather, to mark off units of time to be correlated with the paradigm's aggregates.

In paradigmatic existence, time is not differentiated by events, whether natural or social. Time is differentiated in another way altogether, which so recasts what happens on earth as to formulate a view of existence to which any notion of events strung together into sequential history, or of time as distinguished by one event rather than some other, is less irrelevant than beyond comprehension. Rabbinic Judaism posits a different conception of existence, besides the historical one that depends on nature's and humanity's conventions of the definition and division of time. Rather, existence takes shape and acquires structure in accord with a paradigm that is independent of nature and the axioms of the social order: God's structure, God's paradigm, as our sages of blessed memory would call it, but in secular terms, a model or a pattern that in no way responds to the rules of nature or the social order. It is a conception of time that is undifferentiated by event, because time comprises components that themselves dictate the character of events—what is noteworthy, chosen out of the variety of things that merely happen. What is remarkable conforms to the conventions of the paradigm.

Since my exposition focuses on Judaism, let me begin to exemplify paradigmatic modes of organizing the past by first alluding to a foremost Christian exponent of the same mode of thought, Saint Augustine, who says: "We live only in the present, but this present has several dimensions: the present of past things, the present of present things, and the present of future things", "Your years are like a single day . . . and this today does not give way to a tomorrow, any more than it follows a yesterday. Your today is Eternity."[5] Turning from a Christian to a Judaic

[5]Cited by Jacques LeGoff, *History and Memory*, trans. Steven Randall and Elizabeth Claman (New York: Columbia University Press, 1992), 3, 13.

expression of paradigmatic thinking, we find the same attitude toward time past, present, and future. The Torah, the written part in particular, defines a set of paradigms that serve without regard to circumstance, context, or, for that matter, dimension and scale of happening. A small number of models emerged from Scripture, captured in the sets of Eden and Adam, Sinai and the Torah, the Land and Israel, and the Temple and its building, destruction, rebuilding. These paradigms serve severally and jointly, such as Eden and Adam on its own but also superimposed on the Land and Israel, Sinai and the Torah on its own but also superimposed on the Land of Israel. Of course, the Temple, embodying natural creation and its intersection with national and social history, could stand entirely on its own or be superimposed on any and all of the other paradigms. In many ways, then, we have the symbolic equivalent of a set of two-, three-, or even four-dimensional grids. A given pattern forms a grid on its own, one set of lines representing, for example, Eden, timeless perfection, in contrast to the other set of lines, Adam, temporal disobedience. But on that grid, a comparable grid can be superimposed, the Land and Israel being an obvious one; and on the two, yet a third and fourth, Sinai and Torah, the Temple and the confluence of nature and history.

In the following passage, which I regard as the single best formulation of paradigmatic thinking in the rabbinic documents of late antiquity, Israel's history is taken over into the paradigmatic structure of Israel's life of sanctification, and all that happens to Israel forms part of the structure of holiness built around cult, Torah, synagogue, sages, Zion, and the like. I excerpt and translate only a small part.

GENESIS RABBAH LXX: VIII.

2.　A. "As he looked, he saw a well in the field":

　　B. R. Hama bar Hanina interpreted the verse in six ways [that is, he divides the verse into six clauses and systematically reads each of the clauses in light of the others and in line with an overriding theme]:

　　C. " 'As he looked, he saw a well in the field': this refers to the well [of water in the wilderness, Num. 21:17].

　　D. " '. . . and lo, three flocks of sheep lying beside it': specifically, Moses, Aaron, and Miriam.

　　E. " '. . . for out of that well the flocks were watered': from there each one drew water for his standard, tribe, and family."

　　F. "And the stone upon the well's mouth was great":

G. Said R. Hanina, "It was only the size of a little sieve."

H. [Reverting to Hama's statement:] " '. . . and put the stone back in its place upon the mouth of the well': for the coming journeys. [Thus the first interpretation applies the passage at hand to the life of Israel in the wilderness.]

3.   A. " 'As he looked, he saw a well in the field': refers to Zion.

B. " '. . . and lo, three flocks of sheep lying beside it': refers to the three festivals.

C. " '. . . for out of that well the flocks were watered': from there they drank of the Holy Spirit.

D. " '. . . The stone on the well's mouth was large': this refers to the rejoicing of the house of the water-drawing."

E. Said R. Hoshaiah, "Why is it called 'the house of the water drawing'? Because from there they drink of the Holy Spirit."

F. [Resuming Hama b. Hanina's discourse:] " '. . . and when all the flocks were gathered there': coming from 'the entrance of Hamath to the brook of Egypt' (1 Kings 8:66).

G. " '. . . the shepherds would roll the stone from the mouth of the well and water the sheep': for from there they would drink of the Holy Spirit.

H. " '. . . and put the stone back in its place upon the mouth of the well': leaving it in place until the coming festival. [Thus the second interpretation reads the verse in light of the Temple celebration of the Festival of Tabernacles.]

5.   A. " 'As he looked, he saw a well in the field': this refers to Zion.

B. " '. . . and lo, three flocks of sheep lying beside it': this refers to the first three kingdoms [Babylonia, Media, Greece].

C. " '. . . for out of that well the flocks were watered': for they enriched the treasures that were laid upon up in the chambers of the Temple.

D. " '. . . The stone on the well's mouth was large': this refers to the merit attained by the patriarchs.

E. " '. . . and when all the flocks were gathered there': this refers to the wicked kingdom, which collects troops through levies over all the nations of the world.

F. " '. . . the shepherds would roll the stone from the mouth of the well and water the sheep': for they enriched the treasures that were laid upon up in the chambers of the Temple.

G. " '. . . and put the stone back in its place upon the mouth of the well': in the age to come the merit attained by the patriarchs will stand [in defense of Israel]. [So the fourth interpretation interweaves the themes of the Temple cult and the domination of the four monarchies.]

7.   A. " 'As he looked, he saw a well in the field': this refers to the synagogue.

B. " '. . . and lo, three flocks of sheep lying beside it': this refers to the three who are called to the reading of the Torah on weekdays.

C. " '. . . for out of that well the flocks were watered': for from there they hear the reading of the Torah.

D. " '. . . The stone on the well's mouth was large': this refers to the impulse to do evil.

E. " '. . . and when all the flocks were gathered there': this refers to the congregation.

F. " '. . . the shepherds would roll the stone from the mouth of the well and water the sheep': for from there they hear the reading of the Torah.

G. " '. . . and put the stone back in its place upon the mouth of the well': for once they go forth [from the hearing of the reading of the Torah] the impulse to do evil reverts to its place." [The sixth and last interpretation turns to the twin themes of the reading of the Torah in the synagogue and the evil impulse, temporarily driven off through the hearing of the Torah.]

Here we see the correlation of the structures of the social and cosmic order with the condition of Israel. In this abbreviated passage, paradigms take over the organization of events. Time is no longer sequential and linear. What endures is the structures of cosmos and society: prophets, Zion, Sanhedrin, holy seasons, and so forth. Clearly, one thing that plays no role whatsoever in this tableau is Israel's linear history; past and future take place in an eternal present.

As a medium of organizing and accounting for experience, history—the linear narrative of singular events intended to explain how and why things got to their present state—does not enjoy the status of a given. Nor does historical thinking concerning the social order self-evidently lay claim on plausibility; it is one possibility among many. Historical thinking presupposes order, linearity, distinction between time past and time present, and teleology, among data that do not self-evidently sustain such presuppositions. Questions of chaos intervene; the very possibility of historical narrative meets a challenge in the diversity of story lines, the complexity of events, the bias of the principle of selection of what is eventful, of historical interest, among a broad choice of happenings: why this, not that. Narrative history first posits a gap between past and present but then bridges the gap; why not entertain the possibility that to begin with there is none? These and similar considerations invite a different way of thinking about how things have been and now are, a different tense structure altogether.

The models or paradigms that are so discerned then pertain not to one time alone (past time) but to all times equally—past, present, and future. "Time" no longer forms an organizing category of understanding and interpretation. The spells marked out by moon and sun and fixed stars bear meaning, certainly, but that meaning has no bearing on the designation of one year as past, another as present. The meaning imputed to the lunar and solar marking of time derives from the cult, on the one side, and the calendar of holy time, on the other: seven solar days, a Sabbath; a lunar cycle, a new month to be celebrated, the first new moon after the vernal equinox, the Passover, and after the autumnal equinox, Tabernacles. Rabbinic Judaism tells time the way nature does and only in that way; events in rabbinic Judaism deemed worth recording in time take place the way events in nature do. What accounts for the difference between history's time and paradigmatic time as presented here is a conception of time quite different from the definition of historical time that operates in Scripture: the confluence of nature's time and history's way of telling time—two distinct chronographies brought together, the human one then imposed on the natural one.

SEASONS

In rabbinic Judaism the natural way of telling time precipitated celebration of nature. True, those same events were associated with moments of Israel's experience, the exodus above all. The language of prayer—for example, the Sabbath's classification as a memorial to creation and also a remembrance of the exodus from Egypt—left no doubt about the dual character of the annotation of time. But the exodus, memorialized through the solar seasons and the Sabbath alike, constituted no more a specific, onetime historical event, or part of a sustained narrative of such events, than any other moment in Israel's time, including the building and the destruction of the Temple. Quite the contrary, linking creation and exodus classified both in a single category; the character of that category—historical or paradigmatic—is not difficult to define: The exodus was treated as consubstantial with creation, a paradigm, not a unique event.

It follows that rabbinic Judaism's Israel kept time in two ways, and the time particular to Israel (in the way in which the natural calendar was not particular to Israel), through its formulation as a model instead of a singular event, was made to accord with the natural calendar, not vice versa. That is to say, just as the natural calendar recorded time that was the opposite of historical, because it was not linear and singular and teleological but reversible and repetitive, so Israel kept time with reference to events, whether past or present, that also were not singular, linear, or teleological. These were, rather, reconstitutive in the forever of here and now—not a return to a perfect time but a recapitulation of a model forever present. Israel could treat as comparable the creation of the world and the exodus from Egypt (as the liturgy commonly does, e.g., in connection with the Sabbath) because Israel's paradigm (not "history") and nature's time corresponded in character, were consubstantial and not mutually contradictory.

That consubstantiality explains why paradigm and natural time work so well together. Now, "time" bears a signification different from the natural one. It is not limited here to the definition assigned by nature, yet also not imposed on natural time but treated as congruent and complementary with nature's time. How so? Events—things that happen that are deemed consequential—are meaningful by a criterion of selection congruent in character with nature's own. To understand, we must recall the character of the Torah's paradigms: (1) Scripture manifested certain patterns that, applied to the chaos of the moment, selected out of a broad range of candidates some things and omitted reference to others. (2) The selected things then were given their structure and order by appeal to the paradigm, or described without regard to scale by the fractal, indifference to scale forming the counterpart to the paradigm's indifference to context, time, circumstance. (3) Some events narrated by Scripture emerged as patterns, imposing their lines of order and structure on happenings of other times. This yields the basis for the claim of consubstantiality: (4) Scripture's paradigms—Eden, the Land—appealed to nature in another form.

The upshot, then, I state with heavy emphasis: *The rhythms of the sun and moon are celebrated in the very forum in which the Land, Israel's Eden, yields its celebration to the Creator.* The rhythmic quality of the paradigm then compares with the rhythmic quality of natural time: not cyclical but also not linear. Nature's way of telling time and the Torah's way meet in the Temple: Its events are nature's; its story, a tale of nature too. Past and present flow together and also join in future time because, as in nature, what is past is what is now and what will be. The paradigms, specified in a moment, form counterparts to the significations of nature's time.

These events of Israel's life (we cannot now refer to Israel's "history"), or rather, the models or patterns they yielded, served as the criteria for selection—among occurrences of any time past, present, or future—of the things that mattered out of the things that did not matter: a way of keeping track, a mode of marking time. The model of paradigm that presented the measure of meaning then applied, whether to events of vast consequence or to the trivialities of everyday concern. Sense was where sense was found by the measure of the paradigm; everything else lost consequence. Connections were to be made between this and that, and the other thing did not count. Conclusions were to be drawn from the connection of this and that, and no consequences were to be imputed into the thing that did not count.

That is not an ideal way of discovering or positing order amid chaos; much was left, if not unaccounted for, then not counted to begin with. We cannot take for granted that the range of events chosen for paradigms struck everyone concerned as urgent or even deserving of high priority, and we also must assume that other Israelites, besides those responsible for writing and preserving the books surveyed here, will have identified other paradigms altogether. For those who accorded these books authority and self-evidence, however, the paradigm encompassing the things that did conform to the pattern and did replicate its structure excluded what it did not explain. It gave the sense that while chaos characterized the realm beyond consciousness, the things of which people took cognizance also made sense: a self-fulfilling system of enormously compelling logic. For the system could explain what it regarded as important and also dismiss what it regarded as inconsequential or meaningless, therefore defining the data that fit and dismissing those that did not.

The paradigm did not discern order and regularity everywhere—in the setting of these books, "everywhere" defied imagining—but in some few sets of happenings. These were, specifically, the sets that organized the past, together with contemporary experience, in an encompassing and coherent way. The scale revised both upward and downward the range of concern: These were not all of the happenings, but they were the ones that mattered—and they mattered very much. Realizing or replicating the paradigm, they uniquely constituted events, and that is why by definition these were the only events that mattered. Paradigmatic thinking about past, present, and future ignores issues of linear order and temporal sequence because it recognizes another logic altogether, besides the one of priority and posteriority and causation formulated in historical terms. Out of the things that matter, that same logic defines the connections of things, so forming a system of description, analysis, and explanation that consists in making connections between this and that, but not the other thing, and drawing conclusions from those ineluctable, self-evident connections.

How did paradigmatic thinking take the place of the modes of historical thinking that Scripture had authoritatively set forth? To frame the answer, I ask the question in this simple way: How was an event turned into a series, from something that happened once into something that happens? The answer, of course, lies in the correspondence (real or imagined) of the two generative events that sages of Judaism found definitive: the destruction of the Temple in 586 B.C., to which Scripture is devoted, and the destruction of the Temple in A.D. 70, which formed the defining moment for the Judaic system posited by "our sages of blessed memory." The singular event that framed their consciousness recapitulated what had already occurred. For they confronted a Temple in ruins, and, in the defining event of the age just preceding the composition of most of the documents surveyed here, they found quite plausible the notion that the past was a formidable presence in the contemporary world. Having lived through events they could plausibly discover in Scripture (Lamentations for one example, Jeremiah for another), they also found entirely natural the notion that the past took place in the present as well.

When we speak of the presence of the past, therefore, we raise not generalities or possibilities but the concrete experience that generations actively mourning the Temple endured. When we speak of the pastness of the present, we describe the consciousness of people who could open Scripture and find themselves right there, in its record—not only in Lamentations but also in prophecy and, especially, in the books of the Torah. Here we deal not with the spiritualization of Scripture but with the acutely contemporary and immediate realization of Scripture: once again, as then; Scripture in the present day, the present day in Scripture. That is why it was possible for sages to formulate out of Scripture a paradigm that imposed structure and order on the world they themselves encountered.

Since sages did not see themselves as removed in time and space from the generative events to which they referred the experience of the here and now, they also had no need to make the past contemporary. Sages in Judaism neither relived nor transformed onetime historical events, for they found another way to overcome the barrier of chronological separation. Specifically, if history began when the gap between present and past shaped consciousness, then we naturally ask ourselves whether the point at which historical modes of thought concluded and a different mode of thought took over produced an opposite consciousness from the historical one: not cycle but paradigm. For, it seems clear, the premise that time and space separated our sages of the rabbinic writings from the great events of the past simply did not win attention. The opposite premise defined matters: Barriers of space and time in no way separated sages from great events, the great events of the past enduring for all time. How then are we to account for this remarkably different way of encounter, experience, and consequent explanation?

Sages assembled in the documents of rabbinic Judaism, from the Mishnah forward, all recognized the destruction of the Second Temple in A.D. 70 and all took for granted that that event was to be understood by reference to the model of the destruction of the First. A variety of sources maintain precisely that position and express it in so many words—for example, the colloquy between Aqiba, a second-century sage of Judaism, and sages about the comfort to be derived from the ephemeral glory of Rome and the temporary ruin of Jerusalem. It follows that for "our sages of blessed memory," the destruction of the Second Temple marked not a break with the past, such as it had for their predecessors some five hundred years earlier, but rather a recapitulation of the past. Paradigmatic thinking began in the very event that precipitated thought about history to begin with, the end of the old order. But paradigm replaced history, because what had taken place the first time as unique and unprecedented took place the second time in precisely the same pattern and therefore formed of an episode a series. Paradigmatic thinking replaced historical thought when history as an account of irreversible, unique events, arranged in linear sequence and pointing toward a teleological conclusion, became implausible. If the first time around, history—with the past marked off from the present, events arranged in linear sequence, narrative of a sustained character serving as the medium of thought— provided the medium for making sense of matters, then the second time around, history lost all currency.

The real choice facing our sages was not linear history as opposed to paradigmatic thinking but, rather, paradigm as opposed to cycle. The conclusion to be drawn from the destruction of the Temple once again— once history, its premises disallowed, yielded no explanation—could have taken the form of a theory of the cyclicality of events. As nature yielded its spring, summer, fall, and winter, so the events of humanity or of Israel in particular could have been asked to conform to a cyclical pattern, in line, for example, with Qohelet's view in Ecclesiastes that what has been is what will be. But our sages did not take that position at all.

They rejected cyclicality in favor of a different ordering of events. They did not believe the Temple would be rebuilt and destroyed again, rebuilt and destroyed, and so on into endless time. They stated the opposite: The Temple would be rebuilt but never again destroyed. That stance represented a view of the second destruction that rejected cyclicality altogether. Sages opted for patterns of history instead of cycles because they retained the latter notion for the specific and concrete meaning of events that characterized Scripture's history, even while rejecting the historicism of Scripture. They maintained that a pattern governed, and the pattern was not a cyclical one. Here, Scripture itself imposed its structures, its order, its system—its paradigm. The Official History described in Genesis through Kings left no room for the conception of cyclicality. If matters do not repeat themselves but do conform to a pattern, then the pattern itself must be identified.

Paradigmatic thinking formed the alternative to cyclical thinking because Scripture, its history subverted, nonetheless defined how matters were to be understood. Viewed whole, the Official History indeed defined the paradigm of Israel's existence, formed out of the components of Eden and the Land, Adam and Israel, and Sinai, and then given movement through Israel's responsibility to the covenant and Israel's adherence to, or violation of, God's will, fully exposed in the Torah, which marked the covenant of Sinai. Scripture laid matters out, and our sages then drew from that layout conclusions that conformed to their experience. So the second destruction precipitated thinking about paradigms of Israel's life, such as came to full exposure in the thinking behind the Midrash compilations we surveyed. With the episode made into a series, the sages' paradigmatic thinking asked of Scripture different questions from the historical ones of 586 B.C. because those sages brought to Scripture different premises, drew from it different conclusions. In point of fact, however, not a single paradigm set forth by sages can be distinguished in any important component from the counterpart in Scripture—not Eden and Adam in comparison to the Land of Israel and Israel (the holy people), and not the tale of Israel's experience in the spinning out of the tension between the word of God and the will of Israel.

The contrast between history's time and nature's time shows that history recognizes natural time and imposes its points of differentiation on it. History knows days, months, and years but proposes to differentiate among them, treating this day as different from that because on this day such and such happened but on that day it did not. History's time takes over nature's time and imposes on it a second set of indicators or points of differentiation. History, therefore, defines and measures time through two intersecting indicators, the natural and the human. So the context in which "time" is now defined is first the passage of days, weeks, months, and years, as marked by the movement of the sun and the stars in the heavens, and second the recognition of noteworthy events that have taken place on specific occasions during the passage of those days and months and years. In contrast, paradigmatic time in the context of Judaism tells time through the events of nature, to which are correlated the events of Israel's life: its social structure, its reckoning of time, its disposition of its natural resources, and its history as well. That is, through the point at which nature is celebrated, the Temple, Israel tells time.

Predictably, therefore, the only history the sages deemed worth narrating—and not in sustained narrative even then—was the story of the Temple cult through days and months and years, and the history of the Temple and its priesthood and administration through time and into eternity. We now fully understand that fact. To begin with, the very conception of paradigmatic thinking as opposed to the historical kind took shape through deep reflection on the meaning of events: What happened before has happened again—to the Temple. Methods of telling time before gave way, history's premises having lost plausibility here as much as elsewhere. Now Israel would tell time in nature's way, shaping history only in response to what happens in the cult and to the Temple. There is no other history, because there is no history.

Nature's time is the sole way of marking time, and Israel's paradigm conforms to nature's time and proves enduringly congruent with it. Israel conforming to nature yields not cyclical history but a reality formed by appeal to the paradigm of cult and Temple, just as God defined that pattern to Moses in the Torah. Genesis begins with nature's time and systematically explains how the resources of nature came to Israel's service to God. History's time yielded an Israel against, and despite, history—as the Torah tells it, an Israel fully harmonious with nature. The paradigm then poses a question about creation: Why? So long as the Judaism unfolded by the sages in the Mishnah, Tosefta, Talmuds, and Midrash compilations governed, Israel formed itself in response to the eternities of nature's time, bringing into conformity the ephemerals of the here and now. That answers the questions, Why here? Why now? So what? When and where this Judaism lost its power of self-evidence, there history intervened; philosophy and theology, including normative law, gave way to narrative; and the lines of structure and order took a new turning.

REALIZATION

How does the paradigmatic mode of organizing the past come to realization? Just as the dance is the physicalization of music, and memory is the immediate realization of history, so the lived dream is the here-and-now embodiment of paradigm. The task of dance is to give physical form to music; of memory, contemporary formulation of the past; and of dream, immediacy and concreteness to the model. The marriage of music and motion yields dance, the monument and rite of commemoration yield history, and the serene sense of familiarity with the new yields the lived paradigm: Purim in Patagonia, exodus in America ("as if we were slaves to Pharaoh"). As essential to historical modes of thought as is memory, so critical to the paradigm that identifies event out of happenings and consequence out of the detritus of everyday affairs is the dream (in sleep) or the intuition (when awake). Then everything is changed. When the model takes shape and takes place in the acutely, radically present moment, past and future meet in neither past nor future but paradigm. Then the mode of thought through paradigm accomplishes its enchantment. Paradigm or pattern or model (I speak here only in metaphors, and any that serves will do), then forms an alternative to historical knowledge, a different way of thinking about the same things and responding to the same questions: O Lord, why? O Lord, how long?

People who see time in the framework of history, of past, present, and future forming distinct spells, experience the passage of time through the medium of memory. They look backward into an age now over and done with. Affirming that that was then and this is now, they evoke memory as the medium for renewing access to events or persons deemed formative of how matters should be conducted in the present moment. A religion that frames its statement out of the conception of historical time—onetime events, bound to context and defined by circumstance but bearing long-term effects and meaning—evokes memory as a principal medium for the recovery of sense and order out of the chaos of the everyday and here and now. By remembering how things were, or how they have been, moving beyond the barrier of the present moment, people institute a certain order. They develop a sense for the self-evident and sensible quality of matters.

Israelite Scripture certainly qualifies as a religion of memory. It both recognizes the pastness of the past and invokes its ineluctable power to explain the present. But what are we to make of the rabbinic Judaism that insisted on the presence of the past and the pastness of the present, instructing the faithful to view themselves, out of the here and now, as living in another time, another place: "Therefore every person must see himself or herself as slave to Pharaoh in Egypt," as the Passover Haggadah narrative reads. The same invocation of the present into the past also serves to convey the past into the here and now. Once a religious obligation imposes past on present, shifting the present into a fully realized, contemporary past, rites of commemoration give way to the reformulation of the ages into a governing paradigm that obliterates barriers of time as much as those of space. Rules of structure and order apply without differentiation by criteria of time or space. These rules constitute a paradigm. The paradigm not only imparts sense and order to what happens but also, and first of all, selects what counts and is to be counted. The paradigm is a distinctive way of marking time, telling time.

A religion that organizes experience by appeal to enduring paradigms, transcending time by discovering the present in the past, the past in the present, in a process that is reciprocal, will find no more use for memory than it assigns to the concept of "history." In the experience of paradigm, what medium in ordinary life corresponds to the medium of memory for history? The question phrased in this way produces an obvious answer. We compare ordinary affairs with an enduring paradigm in dreaming or free-ranging imagination or instinct, what is known through self-evidence and the ineluctable sense for what fits: before thought, besides thought, as much as through ratiocination. Nostalgia is to historical thinking what realized dream is to paradigmatic thought. The sages never looked back with longing, because they did not have to, nor did they look forward with either dread or anticipation; theirs was a different model for perceived experience from the one that distinguishes past from present, present from future, invoking the one to "make sense" of the next phase in differentiated time. Paradigms or models took over and replaced the sense of history with a different sort of common sense.

There we put together, in our mind's eye, in the undifferentiated realm of night—the age of sin and exile, to be specific—those patterns and models of experience that coalesce and endure, taking the paradigm of one set of generative experiences and imposing them on chosen moments later on. Dream and fantasy select, as much as history selects, out of a range of happenings, a few incidents of consequence, history's events, paradigm's models. But in dreaming there is no earlier or later, no now or then, no here or there. Things coalesce and disintegrate, form and reform in the setting of a few highly restricted images. In the realm of dreams, paradigms (of experience, real or imagined) come together, float apart, reassemble in a different pattern, unbounded by considerations of now or then, here or there.[6] Whatever is chosen out of the chaos of the everyday to be designated a pattern imposes its order and structure on whatever, in the chaos of the here and now, fits.

History strings together event after event, like cultured pearls matched with precision in a necklace. Paradigm's sea-nurtured pearls impose no order or natural sequence in ordered size; being made by nature, they do not match exactly. That is why when they are in one combination they make one statement; in another, a different statement. These paradigms, I maintain, correspond more precisely to human mediums for the organization of experience than does the historical model: The paradigm is how we live. The sages formed their conception of time from the materials of the everyday perceptions of people, for whom past, present, and future yield to the recapitulation of patterns of meaning formed we know not how. Dreams, fantasies, moments of enchantment, occasions or circumstances or places that invoke the model or fit it—these form the medium for the organization of experience. To experience, time bears no meaning, memory no message. But sages saw matters the way they did because they took the measure of history, not because they ignored it. They formulated another and different reading of history

---

[6]That explains the aesthetics of the theology of symbolic expression worked out in my *Symbol and Theology in Early Judaism* (Minneapolis: Fortress Press, 1991).

from the historical one; aware of the one, sentient of the other, they transcended history and cast off the bounds of time.

In dreaming, images form the counterpart to the paradigm's formulations: dream of Eden, dream of Land, nightmare of Adam, nightmare of Israel—and the waking at Sinai. In that dream world formed of the paradigms of Scripture matched against our own immediate contemporary experience, time stands still, its place taken by form. In the world of paradigms manifested in Scripture and defined in simple, powerful images by the documents of rabbinic Judaism, imagination asks of itself a different task from the one performed in a religion of history through the act of memory. Imagination now forms an instrument of selection out of the here and now of those particular facts that count, selection and construction out of the data of the everyday of a realm of being that conforms to the model that is always present, waiting to be discerned, and not recapitulated once again but realized as always, whenever. Seeing the dream in the setting of the everyday defines the task of imagination: not "let's pretend" but, rather, "look here." In that particular vision lies the power of this Judaism to make of the world something that, to the untrained eye, is scarcely there to be seen but, to the eye of faith, evokes the sense of not déjà vu or *temps perdu* but self-evidence.

I offer next an accessible contemporary example of that same mode of thought, so that the way "our sages of blessed memory" organized and explained experience will prove accessible and reasonable to the world of historical explanation that retains plausibility, even self-evidence, for us. Having begun with a metaphor borrowed from the mathematics of our own time to explain why I conceive as entirely rational the modes of thought of the rabbinic sages, I conclude by turning once more to mathematics for help in explaining the alternative to historical thinking represented in rabbinic Judaism's principal exegetical documents.

Specifically, because I have used the word "model" as interchangeable with "paradigm" or "pattern," I briefly discuss the use of the model in mathematics, the source for my resort to the same word and the mode of description, analysis, and interpretation of data for which it stands. My purpose is to render reasonable a mode of thought that until now has been dismissed, in Halpern's words, as "fundamentally ahistorical . . . insubstantial." It would be difficult, however, to find a more substantial, concrete, and immediate mode of addressing events and explaining the here and now than the paradigmatic: ahistorical, yes, and from one angle of vision atemporal, too, but far from insubstantial, and, in the context of natural time, profoundly time-oriented.

The paradigm forms a medium for the description, analysis, and interpretation of selected data: existence, rightly construed. In this, paradigmatic thinking forms a counterpart to that of the mathematics that produces models. Specifically, mathematicians compose models that, in the language and symbols of mathematics, provide a structure of knowledge forming a "surrogate for reality."[7] These models state in quantitative terms the results of controlled observations of data, and the observation that generates plausible analytical generalizations will serve. Seeking less the regularities of the data than a medium for taking into account several variables among a vast corpus of data, the framer of a model needs more than observations of fact, for example, regularities or patterns. What is essential is a structure of thought, which mathematicians call a "philosophy": "As a philosophy it has a center from which everything flows, and the center is a definition."[8] For a model, data alone, however voluminous, is insufficient. One needs some idea of what one is trying to compose—a model of the model: "Unless you have some good idea of what you are looking for and how to find it, you can approach infinity with nothing more than a mishmash of little things you know about a lot of little things."[9] So, in order to frame a model of explanation, we start with a model in the computer and then test data to assess the facility of the model; we may test several models, with the same outcome: the formation of a philosophy in the mathematical sense. The relevance of this brief glimpse at model making in mathematics is expressed in Norman Maclean's use of mathematics to give guidance on fighting forest fires:

> If mathematics can be used to predict the intensity and rate of spread of wildfires of the future (either hypothetical fires or fires actually burning but whose outcome is not yet known), why can't the direction of the analysis be reversed in order to reconstruct the characteristics of important fires of the past? Or why can't the direction be reversed from prophecy to history?[10]

Here the reversibility of events, their paradigmatic character, their capacity to yield a model unlimited by context or considerations of scale—

[7]Norman Maclean, *Young Men and Fire* (Chicago: University of Chicago Press, 1992), 257.
[8]Ibid., 261.
[9]Ibid., 262.
[10]Ibid., 267.

the principal traits of paradigmatic thinking—turn out to enjoy a compelling rationality of their own. Reading those words, we can immediately grasp what a service the models or paradigms served for "our sages of blessed memory," even though the sages lived many centuries before the creation of the mathematics that would yield models in that sense in which sages' paradigms correspond in kind and function to model explanation in present-day mathematics. Before us is a mode of thought that is entirely rational and the direct opposite of "insubstantial."

The essential aspect in the appeal to "paradigm" or "model" to explain how sages answered the same questions that, elsewhere, historical thinking admirably addresses is now clear. To use the term in the precise sense just stated, philosophy took the place of history in the examination of the meaning of human events and experience. Forming a philosophical model to hold together such data as made a difference, sages found ready at hand the pattern of the destruction of the Temple, alongside explanations of the event and formulations of how the consequences were to be worked out. And since the Temple represented the focus and realization of the abstractions of nature—from the movement of sun and moon to the concrete rhythm of the offerings celebrating these events, from the abundance of nature, the natural selection, by chance, and presentation of God's share on the altar—nature's time took over; history's time fell away. So the Enlightenment begat Hegel, and Hegel begat the conception of history that begat the hermeneutics, which, in scholarship on Scripture—the written Torah and oral Torah of Judaism, the Bible of the Old and New Testaments of Christianity—begat the historical certainties on the eternal verities of theology that today form the Enlightenment's no longer plausible legacy for organizing the past.

Part II

Enlightenment and representative figures

6

Puritanism and Enlightenment: Edwards and Franklin

JOHN E. SMITH

Neither Puritanism nor Enlightenment can be neatly defined, and yet we have no difficulty in recognizing both as distinctive and enduring strands in American thought and culture. We understand the power and the purpose of the Puritan tradition focused on the building of the New Jerusalem, and we likewise comprehend the concern of those figures we associate with the Enlightenment for building a new republic. What is not so clear is how these two outlooks stand in relation to each other. It is an easy matter to set them in opposition to each other, but that approach serves only to obscure the continuities that exist between them, and this remains true even if we allow that the points at which the two traditions diverge stand out more clearly than the similarities that connect them. I propose to approach our underlying topic through a device used to great advantage by Ralph Waldo Emerson and later revived by Josiah Royce, namely, an appeal to *representative* figures. Let us say that such a figure has what William James liked to call a "double-barrelled" character; on one side, the person *inherits* a set of beliefs, attitudes, and patterns of thought and, on the other, *reinterprets* this tradition in an original way so that it answers to the needs of the present and is given new life for the future.

I believe it would generally be admitted that Benjamin Franklin and Jonathan Edwards furnish excellent examples of representative men and that in the work of each we find a clear focus on our two traditions. Edwards inherited the Reformed faith as it had been transported to America, and he reshaped it through novel ideas of the will, understanding, and what he called affections, all coming together under the head of "experimental religion." Franklin was the heir to Roman law and Greek political philosophy as transmitted through the philosophy of John Locke and the British Whigs, so he had before him such ideas as a social contract, a republic, and natural and constitutional rights. Franklin put his original stamp on this political tradition by presenting it on the basis of prudence, common sense, and utilitarian practicality. In setting forth in brief compass what I take to be the significant contributions of both men, I shall not assume that their respective traditions were sealed off from each other, since there was much overlapping in both cases. Franklin retained a significant part of the "Puritan ethic" but replaced its religious foundations with the secular ideals of benevolence and service; moreover, he knew how to use the doctrine underlying the Puritan covenant theology to establish the idea of a secular commonwealth. As for Edwards, he was no stranger to Enlightenment thought—even in criticizing some of its ideas he showed that he was taking it seriously. He had studied Isaac Newton and had a definite interest in science; he was familiar with the writings of the British moral philosophers of the eighteenth century; and above all, he adapted the empirical philosophy of Locke in developing the theory of religious affections, through which he both defended and criticized the Great Awakening.

I issue one caveat in connection with the interpretation of the thought of both men from our present vantage point. In view of the current tendency to deny the reality of the past so that it can be reconstructed in terms of what often seem to be no more than personal preference and autobiographical interest, I would insist that the past be allowed to be just that, the *past*. Despite the familiar problems we confront in recovering the past, we must avoid the distortions of anachronism. In the present case, this means refusing to engage in the sort of misrepresentation I witnessed in a recent conference devoted to Edwards and Franklin, namely, aligning Edwards with current revivals of "evangelical religion" and placing Franklin under the banner of "secular humanism." Edwards would surely have been uneasy in the company of this new piety, not least because of the anti-intellectualism that pervades it. Franklin, likewise, would have resisted the incorporation of his deist convictions and his strenuous morality within this skeptical humanism. These facile identifications, moreover, not only serve to obscure the complexities of the situation but also establish at the outset a wall of separation between the two thinkers that makes it virtually impossible to see the features they share.

JONATHAN EDWARDS

Edwards's writings are far less known than those of Franklin, and where Edwards is familiar it is in the distorted image created by the wide circulation by anthologists of the Enfield sermon, "Sinners in the Hands of an Angry God," which, as Sydney Ahlstrom aptly puts it, has been for most Americans the only writing Edwards produced. The picture of Edwards as the preacher of hellfire has become fixed in the American imagination, and recounting the facts does not seem to dispel that view. Six hundred fully written sermons are among his surviving manuscripts, together with four hundred outlines, yet less than a dozen of them bear any likeness to the "Sinners" sermon. In addition, previous editions of Edwards's works failed to include a huge body of manuscript, especially the Miscellanies, with their more than thirteen hundred entries on theological and philosophical topics, and in any case these editions have fallen from sight. A fair and balanced view of Edwards will become possible only when all of his works have finally been published.

Edwards worked on many fronts and it is not surprising that his contemporaries found him enigmatic; for the most part the level of his thought and the scope of his accomplishments were beyond their own intelligence and experience. The opposition he encountered stemmed not least from the envy or *ressentiment* expressed in the dictum, well known in ancient Greece, "Let there be no one greatest among us," which often resulted in the banishment of the offender from the community.

One can detect at least five facets of Edwards's work as a scholar and minister of the gospel. He was a preacher of uncommon ability, combining rhetorical skill, exegetical competence, and logical order in the crafting of his sermons.[1] He was a polemicist who was inexorable in dealing with the controversies surrounding the revivals and issues of church polity. He was an apologist for Reformed doctrine, but many of

---

[1] There are about six hundred sermons in manuscript and fully written out to provide evidence for this judgment. Wilson Kimnach introduces the whole corpus and places Edwards's work in the context of the Puritan sermon tradition; see his introduction to Jonathan Edwards, *Sermons and Discourses 1720–1723*, ed. Wilson H. Kimnach, vol. 10 of *The Works of Jonathan Edwards* (New Haven: Yale University Press, 1992).

his fellow Calvinists found difficulty in understanding his philosophical approach and, of course, were uneasy over the importance he attached to the thought of Locke. He was a speculative thinker and engaged himself in determining the nature of Being, a concern that placed him in the tradition of theologians stretching from Augustine to Aquinas and beyond. This side of Edwards is best represented by *True Virtue, God's End in Creation*, an essay on the Trinity, the Miscellanies, and, not least, the essays *The Mind* and *Of Being*.[2] He was a sacred historian, as we see in his *History of Redemption*, which is remarkable for the grandeur of its scope and the force of imagination it represents.

The important point is that all of these five aspects are present in Edwards's work, and the curious fact is that concentration on any one of them can cause the others to disappear. One can read pages of his philosophical writings about the idea of Being and the consent of beings to Being, about the relations among affections, understanding, and will, about the proper meaning of virtue and the inherent good and scarcely be aware of the Edwards who argued for the transmission of original sin through Adam, or defended the Calvinist determinism against the views of the Arminians.

In order to make a large task manageable within our limits, I shall concentrate on how Edwards transformed his tradition through the idea of experiential religion, and the way in which he incorporated some features of the Enlightenment by emphasizing the need for understanding and critical thought in what he called divine things. More specifically, I focus attention on two main points. First is the appeal to experience and its aesthetic overtones, which led Edwards on to the original conception of religious affections and the idea that these are responses by the individual to a correct understanding of the nature of the object he or she is responding to. As will become clear, Edwards's insistence on the need for understanding enabled him to combat the uncontrolled emotionalism of evangelical religion and at the same time defend genuine affections against doctrinal rationalism. Second is the breadth of Edwards's vision, a feature I associate with the cosmopolitanism of the Enlightenment.

With respect to the first point, we must take note of two emphases that show themselves in Edwards's thought from the outset: the impor-

---

[2]See Jonathan Edwards, *Scientific and Philosophical Writings*, ed. Wallace E. Anderson, vol. 6 of *The Works of Jonathan Edwards* (New Haven: Yale University Press, 1980), and *Ethical Writings*, ed. Paul Ramsey, vol. 8 of *The Works of Jonathan Edwards* (New Haven: Yale University Press, 1989).

tance he attached to experience or what he called having "the sense of" something, and his appreciation of the beauty to be found both in every aspect of the natural world and in the Scriptures. It is certainly correct to trace the concern for experience to Edwards's study of Locke's philosophy, even if there is some disagreement about the extent of that influence.[3] The appreciation of the beauty of things, of harmony and proportion not only in nature but in the entire makeup of the sincere believer, belongs to Edwards's own experience. The Augustinian tradition in which Edwards stands had, to be sure, a powerful sense of the beauty of creation, as can be seen in Augustine's *De Ordine*, but Ahlstrom is absolutely right when he writes that "for [Edwards's] sense of nature's beauty, there is no precedent among his Puritan forefathers."[4]

The appeal to experience and the perception of beauty were closely connected in Edwards's mind. While walking in the fields in meditation, he tells us, "there came into my mind so *sweet* a *sense of* the glorious majesty and grace of God [that] after this, my *sense of* divine things gradually increased" (Italics added). An indication of the way he was to change the Puritan outlook through his larger vision of things appears early on in two of his best-known lecture-sermons, "God Glorified in Man's Dependence" (1731) and "A Divine and Supernatural Light" (1734). The subjects discussed in these two sermons are not the same; the former has to do with the absolute sovereignty of God and the latter

[3]Edwards found great inspiration in Locke's *Essay Concerning Human Understanding*, and he was deeply influenced by Locke's appeal to experience and the notion of a new simple idea that is beyond the human power to create. The nature and extent of that influence has been the subject of discussion since the appearance of Perry Miller's classic book, *Jonathan Edwards* (New York: Sloane, 1949). Miller was the first scholar to show Edwards's debt to Locke in some detail; he tended, however, to minimize the points at which Edwards modified or disagreed with Locke, and doubts arose as to whether Miller had exaggerated Locke's influence. We must bear in mind that those scholars approaching Edwards, in what now would be called reading him in a Calvinist context, were uneasy over the importance attached to Locke, who was generally described as a "mere deist." Since Miller's study there has been a subcurrent of thinking that Locke's thought could not have been that important to Edwards and that a reappraisal is in order. Discussions of the matter by Paul Ramsey and Wallace Anderson leave Miller's account largely intact, but both call attention to the points where Edwards dissented from Locke and went his own way. Here it is possible to do no more than indicate some points at issue. Edwards agreed with Locke that the "greater good" is what determines the will, but in his second edition, Locke introduced the idea of "felt uneasiness" as the motive and Edwards objected to that way of putting the matter; his reason is found in the different account he gave of the nature of pleasure and pain. For Edwards, both pleasure and pain are not properly called "ideas," because there is "an act of mind" in them and acts of the mind about its ideas are not "themselves mere ideas."
[4]Sydney E. Ahlstrom, *A Religious History of the American People* (New Haven: Yale University Press, 1972), 299.

with Edwards's version of the illumination doctrine—"In thy light, shall we see light"—but in both we find the same emphasis on experiencing, being aware of, and having a sense of the meaning of dependence and illumination. Edwards was well aware of the importance that was attached to doctrine in the Reformed tradition and he was not about to contest that emphasis. Those students who suppose, however, that he set doctrine in opposition to experience make a great mistake. On the contrary, Edwards sought to bring the two into the closest possible unity.[5] His concern was, rather, with those believers who could understand doctrine only in what he, following Locke at this point, called a purely notional sense that went no further than the grasp of the meaning of words in the dry light of understanding. Edwards demanded more; there must also be a sense of, an underlying experience of, what is expressed in doctrine. He fastened on to the idea that someone may know that honey is sweet without experiencing the taste itself, and he put this difference to the greatest possible use. Some illustrations from both sermons serve to establish the point. In declaring

[5]Edwards stood in the theological tradition begun by Augustine and carried on especially by such thinkers as Anselm and Bonaventure; its influence is also to be found in Aquinas, but in a different mode because he rejected the illumination doctrine, and in the Reformers, despite their antiphilosophical tendencies. According to this tradition of "faith seeking understanding," reason and faith work together with the aim of showing the intelligible character of the Christian doctrines. From Augustine to Aquinas, theology and philosophy were related through a continual dialogue; in fact, when reading Augustine it is often difficult to know when one ends and the other begins, and while Aquinas made a definite distinction between them, he sought to show that they do not contradict each other since both stem from God who is Truth. In the Enlightenment this harmony was disrupted in the sense that the metaphysical firmament that had so long served as a medium for theology was seriously undermined by the empirical skepticism of Hume and the critical philosophy of Kant. One consequence of this development was the search for a new medium through which to communicate theological ideas. On the assumption that metaphysics was no longer available for this purpose, attention was turned to morality, history, and political theory as new mediators. Much light is thrown on the entire problem if we take note of the efforts made in the past two hundred years since Kant's *Critique* to find a new medium—what I call a "firmament"—in place of metaphysics. We have seen the attempt to use morality and value judgments, history sacred and secular, the concept of *Existenz*, religious language, and more recently, sociology, literature, depth psychology, and liberation politics as means for relating religious insight to human life. The problem posed by any one of these alternatives should be obvious: unlike Being, no one of these limited aspects and dimensions of things can serve as a correlate for God. Edwards is unique in that he clearly stands in the Augustinian tradition, but he was greatly influenced by the empirical philosophy of the Enlightenment and he had an interest in scientific knowledge of the world that Augustine did not share. He did not, however, regard faith and reason as being in any essential opposition, but sought to hold them together within experience. It is for this reason that he approached every theological issue through Scripture and reason with special attention to the experience underlying both. He did not hesitate to correlate Being and God in his metaphysics, and he saw the relation between people and God as that of the "consent" of beings to Being in a cosmic order of harmony and beauty.

that all is from God and that humans are totally dependent on the divine power, Edwards writes:

However great and glorious the creature *apprehends* God to be, yet if he be *not sensible of* the *difference* between God and him, so as to *see* that God's glory is great, compared with his own, he will not be *disposed* to give God the glory due to his name. . . .
For there is included in the nature of faith, a *sensible acknowledgment* of *absolute dependence* [italics in original] on God. . . . Let us endeavor to obtain, and increase in, a *sensibleness* of our great dependence on God, to have an *eye* on him alone. (other italics added)

Furthermore,

He that is spiritually enlightened truly apprehends and *sees* it, or has a *sense* of it. He does not merely rationally believe that God is glorious, but he has a *sense* of the gloriousness of God *in his heart*. . . .
There is a twofold understanding or knowledge of good . . . that which is merely speculative or notional . . . and that which consists in the *sense* of the *heart*: as when there is a *sense* of the beauty, amiableness, or sweetness of a thing . . . thus there is a difference between having an *opinion*, that God is holy and gracious, and having a *sense* of the loveliness and beauty of that holiness and grace. (italics added)[6]

Upon this foundation, Edwards built the entire theory of religious affections and introduced the novel conception that there are reliable signs or marks that serve to distinguish genuine piety from counterfeit exaggerations and aberrations. Edwards's chief problem was posed by his belief that faith as doctrine is incomplete without fruition in felt experience, but at the same time he had to distinguish this experience from the emotional extravagances—seeing visions, hearing voices, and the like—marking the revivalism of his era. His strategy was to find a philosophical concept through which to express precisely the experiential element in faith, but also to connect it with an understanding that allows for rational control by the ideas found in the doctrine. That concept was the idea of "religious affections," an idea Edwards believed faithfully represented the biblical picture of the fruits of faith, although it stemmed from Locke's empiricism and from Edwards's original idea of an affection. The important point is that through this concept, Edwards aimed

---

[6]Quoted in Walter G. Muelder, Laurence Sears, and Anne V. Schlabach, eds., *The Development of American Philosophy: A Book of Readings*, 2d ed. (Boston: Houghton Mifflin, 1960); the page numbers for the respective selections are: "God Glorified," 22–23, and "Divine Light," 26.

to bring together both idea and the corresponding sense of its meaning in one experience.

What are religious affections? How do they figure in Edwards's proposal to use them as critical tests of genuine faith? With regard to the first question, two inveterate misunderstandings are to be avoided at the outset. First, affections are not emotions that stand in opposition to reason or thought; hence, the heart-versus-head dichotomy used by Edwards's opponents is totally misleading. Second, affections are not "passions," because affections presuppose an active subject; Edwards understood passions to be states in which the individual is simply overwhelmed and is, as he said, "less in its own command."[7] What affections are is best understood through the distinction between understanding—the capacity to discern, view, and judge things—and inclination—the power to approve or disapprove, accept or reject. In the mode of understanding, we are as spectators and are "in no way inclined" but have only a notional grasp of what we entertain. Passing out of this indifference, however, we find ourselves engaged in the way of attraction or aversion to the object of understanding. Edwards identified the affections with inclination and proposed to define as "will" those associated with overt action and to define as "heart" those associated with the mind— joy, hope, and so forth.

The affections, then, are the sensible exercises of inclination wherein the person is no longer indifferent to the object but is attracted toward it or turns away. The main feature of the analysis is that an affection is a response by and through the person to an object—God, Scripture, the neighbor—where that response is a function of two factors. First, and crucial, is a person's proper understanding of the nature of the object responded to, and second is the inclination of the heart or the dominant predisposition of that person. Genuine affections, far from being accidental or occasional emotional states that may arise from a "heightened imagination," as Edwards says, are essentially related both to what he calls a "spiritual understanding" in the mind of the person and to the fundamental inclination of that person as a unified whole. The essential connection of an affection with understanding and with inclination provides a basis for critical evaluation, something that is not possible when

[7]Jonathan Edwards, *A Treatise Concerning Religious Affections*, ed. John E. Smith, vol. 2 of *The Works of Jonathan Edwards* (New Haven: Yale University Press, 1959), 98 (hereafter cited as *RA*).

we are confronted with merely sporadic emotions unrelated to an understanding of their objects or to the person who experiences them.

"Critical evaluation" here involves several considerations, the first and clearest of which is the idea of establishing a set of signs or "distinguishing marks" denoting the actual presence and activity of the Spirit in the life of the individual. These "fruits of the Spirit"—love, faith, hope, peace, joy, humility, and holy practice—Edwards derived from the Bible, as can be seen from the text that he placed at the head of the first chapter of the *Affections*: "Whom having not seen, ye love; in whom, though now ye see him not, yet believing, ye rejoice with joy unspeakable, and full of glory" (1 Pet. 1:8). Edwards interpreted these fruits in terms of his concept of religious affections and held them up before the individual as criteria or tests for self-appraisal. The crucial question for a person was, Do I manifest these signs in my life and experience? This question was Edwards's most explicit prescription for "testing the spirits."

The more complex consideration in this regard was Edwards's proposal for testing the genuineness of these affections when, as he was fully and painfully aware, there are counterfeits and false affections, the tares among the wheat. His contention is that if we are confronted with emotions that have no essential connection with an idea or doctrine, there is no rational way to evaluate them, since they are bare or disconnected occurrences unrelated to the person's meaningful life. If, however, a genuine affection is one that arises *only* in connection with a proper understanding—a "spiritual understanding"—of the nature of the object to which the person is responding—God, Scripture, the beauty of holiness, the excellency of divine things, the harmony in nature—we have a criterion of judging the genuineness of affections. An understanding of the sort required is under the control of the Word and of experience and provides the key to the true nature of the reality that evokes the affection and to which it is directed. The Bible and doctrine derived from it serve as standards for critical evaluation.

Edwards, however, was not content with a profession of doctrine in its merely "notional form"; since the essence of true religion is in holy affections, it is essential that the fruits of the Spirit manifest themselves in personal experience. The presence of an idea in affection and the demand that it arise from a true understanding of the nature of its object were Edwards's criteria for assessment. Perhaps Edwards's original claim can be made clearer by contrast with the views of his opponents. Charles

Chauncy, minister of the First Church in Boston, was in favor of rational doctrine, but he would have no part of "heart religion" and thought of it in terms of emotion and imagination in opposition to reason.[8] Uncritical defenders of revivalism were in favor of emotional manifestations of religion, but they would not accept Edwards's tests. Edwards argued for both affections and critical evaluation. The proponents of heart religion gave unwitting testimony to the force of Edwards's criteria for appraising affections in their very rejection of them.

Having insisted that "Holy Affections are not heat without light, but evermore arise from some information in the understanding" (*RA*, 226), Edwards went on to analyze further the nature of this understanding and the role it performs in the person's experience. The first point is that an affection arising from the grasp of some beautiful form or lively idea without instruction in it, by which he means the doctrines of the gospel, is without spiritual significance. Second, the understanding that is essential is what he called a "spiritual" understanding and it is not the same as the understanding involved in human learning or the improvement of the mind. Spiritual understanding is the knowledge of the loveliness of divine things, and if that knowledge is the proper foundation of love itself, it can only be a knowledge of loveliness (*RA*, 271). A merely speculative knowledge or understanding, however, cannot apprehend or "know" this loveliness because it is without the sense of the heart or that first-person experience to which we refer when we say that only the one who has tasted the honey can "know" what the "sweetness" of it is and means. Here Edwards is bringing a sensible element into the dry light of understanding, which, however, remains understanding insofar as a genuine affection is never possible without the presence of an idea. "When the mind," he writes, "is sensible of the sweet beauty and amiableness of a thing, that implies a sensibleness of sweetness and delight in the *presence of the idea of it*" (*RA*, 272; italics added).

---

[8]No simple conception of an emotion devoid of any relation to thought can do justice to Edwards's novel and subtle idea of affections. Peter Gay—who endorses Chauncy over Edwards—makes the same mistake as his hero when he says, "Locke's psychology gave him useful material for understanding the quality of religious emotion." Apart from the fact that this declaration tells us nothing about this "quality" of religious "emotion," the use of the term *emotion* indicates a failure to grasp what Edwards was claiming. Edwards sometimes used *emotion* to indicate what he regarded as spurious in the revivals, but it is interesting that he could also use *affections* even in describing those he thought to be false (Peter Gay, "Jonathan Edwards: An American Tragedy," in *Jonathan Edwards: A Profile*, ed. David Levin [New York: Hill and Wang, 1969], 248).

Before turning to what I have called Edwards's cosmopolitanism, I must give some attention to the sign of genuine affections which he called "holy practice." As we have seen, Edwards's set of signs was meant not only to describe religious affections, but to test them. The importance he attached to the sign of holy practice can be gauged by the fact that it is discussed at far greater length than any other sign. Edwards was fond of saying, "It is easier to get 'em to talk like saints than to act like saints," a clear echo of Jesus' words, "Not everyone who saith 'Lord,' 'Lord,' but he that doeth my commandments" (*RA*, 383). In stressing conduct that issues from faith and the conviction of the heart, Edwards was taking a long step in the direction of bringing the Puritan consciousness out of the dark closet of introspection and soul-searching and into the light of behavior that all may see. Much as he valued the naked ideas immediately present to the mind, he was moving away from Locke's tendency to see experience only in terms of inner apprehensions of the mind (later expressed in F. H. Bradley's "What we experience is experience") and demanding instead that experience and faith must find overt expression in appropriate conduct. If the emphasis Edwards placed on holy practice signaled his turn away from Locke, it also pointed forward to the transcendentalists and, ultimately, to the pragmatists.

The new turn bespeaks something both deeper and subtler than that "ideas must have consequences." That, to be sure, was very much involved, since Edwards was as aware as were C. S. Peirce and William James that if ideas, beliefs, and convictions are left merely idling in the mind, they lose their motive force and are reduced to objects of contemplation. Like Edwards, the pragmatists saw practice as the "upshot" (Peirce's favorite term) of belief, its final discharge in human conduct. Although for Peirce, belief and doubt have different effects on the individual mind, both demand some form of expression and are not merely "mental" states locked up in themselves. Belief, says Peirce, leads to the establishment "in our nature [of] some habit which will determine our actions."[9] Like Edwards before him, Peirce calls habits "tendencies" or dispositions in the nature of the person to act in accordance with beliefs serving as a guide. Doubt, according to Peirce, has a different effect; it

[9] Charles Hartshorne and Paul Weiss, eds., *The Collected Papers of Charles Sanders Peirce*, (Cambridge, Mass.: Harvard University Press, 1931–35), 5:371 (hereafter cited as *CP*); references are to sections, not pages.

signals uneasiness and uncertainty and, if it is genuine doubt, it leads to inquiry aimed at settling belief.[10]

Edwards, however, went farther: Holy practice is a mark of sincerity in what the person really believes, an outward manifestation of the state of the heart seen only by God. The parallel with the pragmatists is striking; for them, belief is serious only when it remains in close touch with conduct consistent with that belief. Stating that one believes is not enough; action is required as the test of sincerity. Indeed, in Edwards's case, even the most passionate profession of faith in God would prove hollow if it did not issue in holy practice. Nor is this evidence meant to be chiefly a sign for others; it is a test of ourselves, since we may deceive our own selves with a faith that does not exist. Like Kierkegaard, Edwards insisted on "self-examination" or self-judgment in terms of the signs he discovered; the question is, Do I *do* the deeds that faith prescribes? Edwards was well aware of the discrepancy that all too often exists between a faith professed and our actual behavior; "If a man say, 'I love God,' and hateth his brother," says the writer of the First Epistle of John, "he is liar." This blunt pronouncement expresses precisely what Edwards means by the need for holy practice.

Now we may ask, Where does Franklin and indeed the Enlightenment as a whole fit into this picture? The answer is very nicely, if we take seriously Franklin's concern for projects that would benefit humanity—think of Poor Richard's passion for improvement—and the preoccupation of the philosophes with setting things right. In his most perceptive and too often neglected interpretation of the eighteenth century, Carl Becker writes: "Its characteristic note is not a disillusioned indifference, but the eager didactic impulse to set things right. *Bienfaisance, humanite*—the very words, we are told, are new, coined by the Philosophers to express in secular terms the Christian ideal of service." Becker goes on to list the projects of the Abbé de Saint Pierre—"Project for the Reform of Begging," "Project for Making Peace Perpetual in Europe"—and concludes, "It was at all events inspired by the same ideal—the Christian ideal of service, the humanitarian impulse to set things right."[11]

---

[10]With Descartes always in mind, Peirce inveighed against "paper" doubt, which begins and ends with "I doubt" as a mere declaration. "Do you call it *doubting*," he says, "to write down on a piece of paper that you doubt? If so, doubt has nothing to do with any serious purpose" (*CP*, 5:416). Doubt that does not lead to inquiry, like belief that does not lead to action, is idle and not real.

[11]Carl L. Becker, *The Heavenly City of the Eighteenth Century Philosophers* (New Haven: Yale University Press, 1932), 39–41.

Becker's brilliantly written and well-documented study is a much-needed corrective to the traditional picture of the Enlightenment as an age in which reason served as no more than a destructive force aimed at abolishing superstition, which usually meant religion. As Becker acknowledges, the philosophers had their own foibles: They preached toleration but could not tolerate priests; they were at once too credulous and too skeptical; they were cynical with the same fervor with which they denounced enthusiasm. But Becker says, "In spite of it all, there is more of Christian philosophy in the writings of the *Philosophes* than has yet been dreamt of in our histories. . . . I shall attempt to show that the *Philosophes* demolished the Heavenly City of St. Augustine only to rebuild it with more up-to-date materials."[12]

Turning now to the second point mentioned earlier, Edwards's cosmopolitanism, I illustrate rather than describe it, by introducing one of the most remarkable entries among the Miscellanies. Let me first anticipate an objection. Earlier, I attacked the identification of Edwards with the "Sinners" sermon, and now I am about to characterize him through a document that is much shorter. The justification for this procedure is that while the sermon is not representative, the entry on the millennium to follow is characteristic of Edwards's outlook and is by no means an idiosyncratic piece.

Those readers familiar with the pictorial and symbolic representations of the millennium in Western religious history know that the great majority of them concentrate on a martial figure; the army of God is to appear and overcome the forces of Satan, sin, and evil on a cosmic scale. There is nothing of this sort whatever in the text that follows, and, if I am not mistaken, it must come as a great surprise. Space will not permit an excursion into the intricacies of millenarian doctrine; it is sufficient to point out that Edwards thought of this event as falling within historical time, and, in fact, he was bold enough to suggest that it had begun in Northampton, Massachusetts! The text is entry 26 in the Miscellanies:

MILLENNIUM. How happy will that state be, when neither divine nor human learning shall be confined and imprisoned within only two or three nations of Europe, but shall be diffused all over the world, and this lower world shall be all over covered with light, the various parts of it mutually enlightening each other; when the most barbarous nations shall become as bright and polite as

[12]Ibid., 31.

England; when ignorant heathen lands shall be stocked with most profound divines and most learned philosophers; when we shall from time to time have the most excellent books and wonderful performances brought from one end of the earth and another to surprise us—sometimes new and wondrous discoveries from Terra Australis Incognita, admirable books of devotion, the most divine and angelic strains, from among the Hottentots, and the press shall groan in wild Tartary—when we shall have the great advantage of the sentiments of men of the most distant nations, different circumstances, customs and tempers; [when] learning shall not be restrained [by] the particular humor of a nation or their singular way of treating of things; when the distant extremes of the world shall shake hands together and all nations shall be acquainted, and they shall all join the forces of their minds in exploring the glories of the Creator, their hearts in loving and adoring him, their hands in serving him, and their voices in making the world to ring with his praise.

What infinite advantages will they have for discovering the truth of every kind, to what they have now! There will continually be something new and surprising discovered in one part of the world and another [because of] the vast number of explorers, their different circumstances, their different paths to come at the truth. How many instructive and enlightening remains of antiquity will be discovered, here and there now buried amongst ignorant nations![13]

This remarkable vision of a world community, not only of religion but also of science, definitely placed Edwards in the "modern" world. It is, moreover, noteworthy that none of his theological contemporaries thought in such global terms or had any of his prophetic insight into what the spread of knowledge might mean.

It might appear that Edwards's portrayal of the millennium in *Miscellany* 26 is no more than an adaptation of this episode in sacred history to the basic Enlightenment beliefs. Such a view, however, is far too simple and fails to take account of Edwards's attempt to show that these ideals provide insight into the way that God seeks to realize the divine purpose in history. This miscellany is preceded in Edwards's text by a discussion of the Four Beasts and the pouring out of the Vials as part of the prophecy in Revelation. Edwards identifies the beasts with the chariots or wheels of Ezekiel and the four standards of judgment—derived from the religious norms that guided the Israelites in the wilderness through which God implements his Providence; the wheels, in short, are the dynamic of history. The Bible, says Edwards, is deliberately dark and cryptic for the express purpose of driving people to seek understand-

---

[13]The entire collection, known as Miscellanies, was transcribed, dated, and edited by Thomas A. Schafer. These volumes are to be published in the Yale Edition. In the meantime, however, I can do no more than indicate the entries by number.

ing of the course of history through increasing knowledge of both God and the world.[14] Edwards specifically interprets the pouring of the Third Vial as a plea for the "enlightenment" of the Jesuits to cast off their unswerving loyalty to the pope, by which Edwards participates in the anticlericalism of many representatives of Enlightenment, but for vastly different reasons. He was obviously not rejecting religion on behalf of atheism but looking, instead, for a purification of Christianity in much the same way as the prophets of the Old Testament appealed ever and again to the religious and moral rigor of the nomadic period (the "wilderness") as the standard by which to judge the infidelity of the people and the idolatry of cultic practices that defiled the Temple.

A pointed example of Edwards's integration of progress in knowledge with biblical religion is found in the idea that God is at the beginning and the end of all things and that in between are the world and the course of history, through which God works to bring about his purpose. Our task is to plumb the secrets of the universe through knowledge so that Enlightenment becomes the effective means whereby humanity comes to know how God works in history. No more telling illustration of the bridge Edwards envisaged as spanning Providence and Enlightenment is to be found than in his description of the plight of the devil (*Miscellany* 48). The devil, he writes, has been frustrated and outsmarted over and over by the power of God, but the devil remains unenlightened and never learns the folly of his ways. Edwards, moreover, did not hesitate to construe the cosmic events foreshadowed in the Bible in terms of Newtonian science. The divine judgment represented by the great conflagration, for instance, mentioned by Isaiah (chap. 34) and reiterated in 2 Peter (3:12), is explained by Edwards in accordance with gravitational theory; God has only to withdraw his hand from the cosmic order and all parts of the universe would come together in one point and thus generate the heat necessary for the conflagration.

As Stephen Stein has pointed out, Edwards's conception of the millennium developed over time and was dependent on his continuing study of Revelation and his attempts to interpret the meaning of the familiar imagery—the Four Beasts, the Vials, and so forth.[15] Several ideas, how-

---

[14]We have a classic example of the idea that God withholds understanding and perception as a means of judgment and punishment in Isaiah 6:9–10, but at the same time it is clearly indicated that if the people were to see, hear, and "understand with their heart" they would be healed.

[15]See Jonathan Edwards, *Apocalyptic Writings*, ed. Stephen J. Stein, vol. 5 of *The Works of Jonathan Edwards* (New Haven: Yale University Press, 1977).

ever, persisted in Edwards's mind in writing about the millennium and
they serve to show that the passage previously cited is quite in accord
with his other pronouncements on the subject. One of these ideas is the
spread of divine light, of enlightenment in all parts of the world and an
increase in the knowledge of God. Edwards envisaged God pouring out
the vials of wrath on his enemies so that the memory of persecution and
martyrdom will fade in the future as the knowledge of divinity spreads.
It is clear that Edwards is applying to sacred history the central belief
of the Enlightenment in the salutary effects of the diffusion of knowledge
to all humanity. The second idea that, as Stein suggests, points to the
political aspects of the millennium is that despotism whether civil or
ecclesiastical will be done away with, and "liberty shall reign throughout
the earth."[16] Such liberty, however, will not be anarchy, because Edwards envisaged the existence of many forms of government, his favorite
model being that of the period of the judges who ruled over Israel before
the coming of the monarchy. The important point is that, whatever the
form, none shall be contrary to "true liberty." We may be inclined to
overlook the continuity of Edwards's thought and Enlightenment ideals
because of our tendency to see an opposition between the two traditions
that had not established itself in Edwards's time.

We might go even farther in the direction of underlining this continuity by taking note of Edwards's faith in the sovereign power of God,
on the one hand, and Edwards's habitual tendency to fasten on what he
found congenial or consonant with his thought from whatever source it
might come, on the other. Since God is working out his purpose in the
world, what better way to do so than through the spread of knowledge
to humanity. Edwards had no trouble in seeing the contribution of the
historical era we call the Enlightenment in such terms. If the power of
God is in it, then it works for the good regardless of any imperfections—
the tares among the wheat again.[17] Students of Edwards have often
called attention to his single-mindedness in dealing with the writings of
others. More often than not, he consulted other works for the purpose

---

[16]Ibid., 136.
[17]We need to remember how seriously Edwards took this figure in interpreting historical
developments, and there is no better example than the Great Awakening. He insisted
repeatedly that the presence of evil and error in the revivals does *not* prove that the Spirit
of God is absent or that the religious awakening is counterfeit. For Edwards all history
is a mixture of good and evil and he frequently found himself perplexed by the tension
between the long time needed for the accomplishment of God's purpose and God's power
to intervene at any time.

of finding support for his own ideas, with the result that he frequently cited passages that suited his purpose even if he disagreed with the author's main thesis. He seems to have followed this practice in approaching the Enlightenment as a whole. The point to remember is that we must not read later perceptions of a total opposition between Puritanism and the Enlightenment back into Edwards's time; that would be falsifying history.

Great men are also capable of making great mistakes, not least because they have more momentous opportunities to go wrong than the average person. Edwards illustrated the point with his ill-advised speculation that the millennium might begin in America, or, closer to home, Northampton. In a letter of 12 December 1743 to the Rev. Thomas Prince of Boston, Edwards wrote that "the beginning of this great work of God must be near," and added, "there are many signs that make it probable that this work will begin in America." Edwards subsequently had serious misgivings about this display of enthusiasm and wrote at the same time to the Rev. William McCulloch in Scotland with the following retraction: "It has been slanderously reported and printed concerning me, that I have often said that the Millennium was already begun, and that it began at Northampton . . . but the report is very diverse from what I have ever said."[18]

BENJAMIN FRANKLIN

Benjamin Franklin, or, more accurately, the image of Benjamin Franklin, has often appealed to the American public chiefly as an embodiment of the traits possessed by the typical American, whether as a matter of what we actually are or as a projection of what we would like to be, or, even further, what we would like others to think we are. Consider some features of his life and work, which, apart from any judgments about his political views, his attitude toward religion, or his moral precepts, must be acknowledged by anyone considering what sort of man he was.

To begin with, there was his versatility. Who cannot but stand in awe of the talents and energy of a person who could serve as a statesman, engage the savants of Europe, write essays on moral philosophy, make

[18]See Edwards, *Apocalyptic Writings*, 26, and idem, *The Great Awakening*, ed. C. C. Goen, vol. 4 of *The Works of Jonathan Edwards* (New Haven: Yale University Press, 1972), 71, 84–85, 560; also Miller, *Jonathan Edwards*, 318, for the part played by Charles Chauncy in embarrassing Edwards over the claim.

excursions into matters scientific, and busy himself with devising a means for heating houses in winter. As has often been noted, Franklin seemed to be nothing short of the universal, natural man so dear to the Enlightenment. Then there is his ingenuity, his capacity to invent and improvise and make do with whatever resources were at hand; he had no time to complain about his situation or to think of how much easier it would be if things were different. In addition, he was a model of independence, a forerunner of the self-made man who does everything on his own. This trait shines through even if we allow that Franklin's account of his humble beginnings and his frugal self-discipline was colored by afterthought. He preached and practiced common sense and prudence, and he had an uncanny sense of what was relevant for dealing with the matter before him. He understood what William James later emphasized when pointing out that even if we had the whole of knowledge before us, we would still need to determine what idea, fact, or theory is relevant to the problem we are trying to solve. And not least, Franklin had a realistic view of the human condition; he was more aware than many of his contemporaries of the human capacity for evil, greed, and injustice. As we see in his criticism of Samuel Johnson's moral philosophy, Franklin welcomed the idea of taking the whole truth into account, because this must include acknowledging not only our virtues but our evil tendencies as well, including the pride that places us above other creatures in the order of things.

I think it would be fair to say that, with the possible exception of the last trait—a stumbling block for inveterate optimists and those who regard sin as no more than ignorance or the result of a faulty education—a great majority of people would find the foregoing features enviable in the sense that they would like to find them exemplified in their own lives. It seems unlikely, however, if we were to draw a profile of Edwards, that the characteristics traditionally associated with his life and thought would strike many observers as enviable, and that says a great deal about our own values and outlook on life. It is, nevertheless, important not to lose sight of the one clear point of intersection between the two figures: their recognition of pride and pretension in the human constitution and the tendency to say, as was so candidly expressed by Augustine, "I liked to think that I was more myself in those features in myself of which I approved than in those of which I disapproved."[19]

[19]*Confessions*, trans. E. B. Pusey, Modern Library ed. (New York: Random House, 1949), 153.

Unlike Edwards who, despite his extensive correspondence with the Scottish divines of the time, lived his entire life in a small corner of New England, Benjamin Franklin was the best-known and most widely traveled man in his century. The remark of John Adams that Franklin's name was known to the people and governments throughout Europe is frequently quoted. Perhaps less well known is Goethe's description of Franklin as a man of "deep insight and emancipated outlook." In seeking to account for Franklin's wide influence, Herbert Schneider describes him as the "American incarnation of 'public spirit' " and calls attention to the selfless way in which he devoted himself to all that he undertook.[20] Franklin's writings were certainly widely read, but they were supplemented by his extensive activities, which his contemporaries saw as a living illustration of the principles he taught. Like David Hume in his own time and William James almost a century later, Franklin had an uncanny ability to make other thinkers appear to be caught in a thicket of confusing philosophical subtleties, while he alone was getting to the heart of the matter and expressing truth in plain common sense. As Schneider says, philosophers who know the complexity of moral philosophy from the time of Plato to the Utilitarians of the last century are offended by "the simplicity, almost simple-mindedness of Franklin's morality. . . . Surely there can be nothing profound in a doctrine which a Pennsylvania farmer could understand."[21]

Simple or not, Franklin's thought was to help bring about significant changes in the way people regarded God, themselves, and their life in the world. To begin with, he had much to do with the shift away from the emphasis on God's glory manifested in human dependence and God's wrath and toward a benevolent God. The situation was indeed ambiguous. Whereas in Edwards, the glory of God overshadows all else and is *the* end for which God created the world, the idea was gaining ground, under the aegis of deism and the optimism of the Enlightenment, that God is benevolent and is less interested in his own glory than in the happiness of his creatures. Franklin, though a believer in God's benevolence, laid less store in happiness than in humanitarianism, public service, and useful projects. He was, above all, opposed to the belief that God so arranged the world that unending human happiness is ensured.

Franklin saw this as a complacent and self-serving doctrine, and he attacked it with common sense, wit, and his realistic view of human

[20]Herbert W. Schneider, introduction to *Benjamin Franklin: The Autobiography*, ed. Herbert W. Schneider (New York: Liberal Arts Press, 1952).
[21]Ibid., xii.

nature in his *Dissertation on Liberty and Necessity, Pleasure and Pain.*
Franklin's attack was actually aimed at William Wollaston's version of
the happiness doctrine set forth in his *Natural Religion*, but Franklin
had an opponent closer to home in Samuel Johnson of King's College
(later Columbia University) whose book, *Ethica*, was patterned after
Wollaston's work. According to Johnson, God treats all beings according to truth, and hence he treats humans as beings created for happiness.
Johnson understood truth as meaning "the *whole* of our nature and
duration, as being sensitive and rational, social and immortal creatures."
Franklin was quick to seize on this holistic emphasis and pointed out
that a person is a "naturally *covetous* being" prone to appropriate the
property of others; this, says Franklin, "is Truth likewise," and a person
acts according to it when stealing something from another. It is clear
that he was bent not only on showing the self-serving character of the
happiness doctrine but also on bringing into view the whole range of
human propensities. If the whole is to be considered, he insisted, then
the evil tendencies must also be taken into account.[22]

   Franklin went even farther; he claimed that uneasiness or pain is also
an essential feature in the cosmic design and—vintage Franklin—that it
is "beautiful in its place!" Without the goad of pain, human beings
would be reduced to the condition "of statues, dull and lifeless." His
point goes beyond its obvious irony; Franklin's main aim was to expose
the pride expressed in the belief that human beings are a species "above
the rest of creation," a belief that he said would readily be accepted
because it flatters and seduces us.[23] As a parting shot, he said that if we
are to take the whole truth into account, we must face it, "though it
sometimes prove mortifying and distasteful."[24] Here Franklin clearly
joins hands with Edwards in going against the easy optimism of the
Enlightenment and the belief that humanity is unambiguously good at
heart.

   Franklin's conception of religion and his own religious convictions are
well known and have often been discussed, hence only a few comments
are in order. His classic statement occurs in the *Autobiography*:

I had been religiously educated as Presbyterian; and though some of the dogmas
of that persuasion, such as the eternal decrees of God, election, reprobation etc.,

---

[22]Herbert W. Schneider *A History of American Philosophy* (New York: Columbia University Press, 1946), 37–38.
[23]Ibid., 38–39.
[24]P. R. Anderson and M. H. Fisch, *Philosophy in America* (New York: Appleton-Century-
Crofts, 1939), 134.

appeared to me unintelligible, others doubtful, and I early absented myself from the public assemblies of the sect, Sunday being my studying day, I never was without some religious principles. I never doubted, for example, the existence of the Deity, that he made the world and governed it by his providence, that the most acceptable service of God was the doing good to man. . . . Though I seldom attended any public worship, I had still an opinion of its propriety and of its utility when rightly conducted.[25]

We readily recognize this view as expressing the natural religion of the Enlightenment, with perhaps a greater emphasis on doing good for humanity than was to be found in those thinkers who otherwise shared his view. Franklin regarded theological disputes as the sure means of making enemies. As he puts it in another section of the *Autobiography*:

We sometimes disputed, and very fond we were of argument . . . which . . . besides souring and spoiling conversation, is productive of disgusts, and perhaps enmities, with those who may have occasion for friendship. I had caught this by reading my father's books of dispute on religion. Persons of good sense, I have since observed, seldom fall into it, except lawyers, university men, and generally men of all sort, who have been bred at Edinburgh. I grew convinced that truth, sincerity, and integrity . . . were of the utmost importance to the felicity of life.[26]

Essentially, Franklin's view is one of humanitarianism coupled with the belief that morality suffices and that, as he tells us, being a good citizen is more important than being a good Presbyterian. We must not, however, overlook the fact that Franklin was not simply cutting religion adrift, so to speak, but was engaged rather in putting it on a utilitarian basis. He makes this clear in the following passage:

Revelation had indeed no weight with me, as such; but I entertained an opinion, that, though certain actions might not be bad, *because* they were forbidden by it, or good, *because* it commanded them; yet probably these actions might be forbidden *because* they were bad for us, or commanded *because* they were beneficial to us, in their own natures, all the circumstances of things considered.[27]

It is important to notice what is happening here; Franklin is referring to biblical commandments and prohibitions, but he is interpreting their authority in a new way. The basis of these judgments is not the divine fiat as such—decrees issued at God's own pleasure—but the wisdom of the God of benevolence who knows and declares what is best for hu-

---

[25]Schneider, *Benjamin Franklin*, 79.
[26]Ibid., 57.
[27]Ibid.

manity. For Franklin this is not the eternal happiness proposed by Wollaston and Johnson but, rather, God's concern for what will be most beneficial for people in their efforts to develop themselves and their nations in the world. I think it is not an exaggeration to say that in Franklin's view, God is concerned no longer only for the New Jerusalem, but also for helping make possible the larger community of human beings central to the Enlightenment vision and celebrated, as we have seen, in Edwards's conception of the millennium.

It seems correct to say, as many scholars have claimed, that Franklin was showing that, in addition to the traditional theological basis, the Puritan ethic had also a foundation in utility. Achievement in the world depends on adherence to certain precepts, and the evidence for their fitness is found in experience—Franklin's own as well as the colonies'. If we call this the "secularization" of traditional virtues, we must do so with a full awareness of the continuity that existed. Schneider makes this point when he writes: "Benjamin Franklin made the attempt to maintain the Puritan virtues in all their rigor, but to abandon entirely their theological sanctions."[28] The latter judgment is based largely on Franklin's statement that revelation carried no weight with him, but it does not alter the fact that the morality *was* preserved. This positive feature of Franklin's thought is not to be outweighed by the emphasis that has been placed on the negative aspects of the Enlightenment—skepticism, irreligion, and worldliness. The Puritan ethic was stern and rigorous, at least in principle, and, while Franklin's list of virtues may not appear as "stern" they are equally rigorous. What he demands is much like what James was to call the "strenuous" life, and it contains as small a place for sloth as any Puritan would allow. Although Franklin's list of virtues does not explicitly include faith, hope, and charity, his gamut from temperance to humility overlaps at certain points with the older ethic. What Franklin calls for in every case is self-discipline and the avoidance of excess; it is prudence at its best. The continuing question for the United States has been whether prudence is enough.

THE LEGACY OF EDWARDS AND FRANKLIN

We can—must—now ask, What is to be learned about ourselves and our own period from the ways in which we respond to and reinterpret

---

[28]Herbert W. Schneider, *A History of American Philosophy,* 2d ed. (New York: Columbia University Press, 1963), 41.

the two major thinkers we have been considering? It is highly significant that the most comprehensive, critical editions of the writings of Edwards and Franklin have been undertaken in this century; the first volume of *The Papers of Benjamin Franklin* appeared in 1959, and the initial volume in *The Works of Jonathan Edwards*, the *Freedom of the Will*, appeared in 1957.[29] The original impetus for both editions was much the same; there was a strong sense, on the one hand, of the importance of the voluminous writings of Edwards and Franklin as treasures of the American heritage and, on the other, of the awareness that all previous editions or collections of their works were neither comprehensive nor critical in the sense of meeting modern standards of accuracy in transcriptions and editing.

To take but one example, publishers of previous editions of Edwards paid little attention to his footnotes and simply reprinted paraphrases as if they were direct quotations, making no attempt to find accurate citations to replace such expressions as "Ch. I, towards the end." In both cases, it was felt that there could be no understanding of either thinker or an informed assessment of their contributions to American life and culture without reliable editions of all their available and authentic writings. The need was all the more urgent in view of the fact that both thinkers had become associated in the popular mind with but one of their best known works: *Poor Richard* in Franklin's case and "Sinners in the Hands of an Angry God" in Edwards's.

Although the publication of collected works is certainly a recognition of an author's importance, that recognition itself must have been evoked by the high quality of the thought manifested and the significance of the issues under discussion. Two major trends made their appearance in American cultural life during the two decades after World War II: One was a sharp increase of interest in the concerns of religion, and the other was a new and determined search for American origins. Both trends had an impact on the recovery of the thought of Edwards and Franklin. In those decades the theology of Paul Tillich was much discussed, especially his idea of the interplay between religion and culture and his interpretation of theological categories in terms of depth psychology. Reinhold Niebuhr's emphasis on the Christian doctrine of sin in the face of the

---

[29]Both editions have emanated from Yale University. For the background of the Franklin edition, see vol. 1 (New Haven: Yale University Press, 1959), xxi, and for a similar account of the Edwards edition, see vol. 1 (New Haven: Yale University Press, 1957), which contains Perry Miller's statement of the aims of the edition.

easy optimism about human nature that flourished in the decades between the two wars, and his prophetic pronouncements about politics
and world history in the light of his theology, had an enormous influence
not only on Protestantism but on the religious scene in general. Trans-
lations of Kierkegaard's theological works were published and widely
distributed, and the voluminous theology of Karl Barth was finding its
way into the major theological seminaries. The time was ripe for a rediscovery of Edwards.

The quest for the American past was under way at the same time; the
late 1940s and the 1950s saw the birth of American studies as an academic field and witnessed the establishment of editions to make available
the works of the founding fathers Jefferson, Adams, and Franklin, to
name but a few, and of later figures such as Woodrow Wilson. Edwards
figures in this development as well as in the revival of interest in religion.
With the recovery of his treatises, *Freedom of the Will*, *Religious Affections*, and his writings about the Great Awakening, it was no longer
possible to think of him as one more "Calvinist" who preached hellfire
and damnation. The depth of his philosophical acumen and the breadth
of his biblical and theological knowledge became apparent, as did the
fact that he was the greatest mind on the American scene up to the
emergence of Charles Peirce after the Civil War.

Although conservative, evangelical Protestantism has always laid
claim to Edwards, the curious fact is that the only critical edition of his
works was initiated not by evangelical scholars but by an intellectual
and literary historian, Perry Miller, who certainly had no special religious interest in bringing to light the true stature of Edwards. Miller saw
the scholarly task before him and, while those of us whom he brought
together to carry out the task were variously interested in religion, American church history, theology, literature and philosophy, there was no
sense of our having a common sectarian commitment to Edwards's version of Calvinism. It was the importance of Edwards and the originality
of his thought that motivated our work, combined with an increasing
awareness of how great a thinker he was when we took into account *all*
of his writings and not just such well-known pieces as the "Sinners"
sermon and the "Narrative of Surprising Conversions."

Miller was, and remains, something of an enigma; in addition to his
study of Edwards, he had probed deeply into the mind of New England
and, due to his voluminous reading, there were few scholars to match
him in knowledge of the theology, the church history and polity, the

social and religious practices, and the literature of New England from the days of the Mathers to the time of Emerson and beyond. Despite this intimate involvement in religious ideas especially, Miller, to use Royce's description of his own role as described in *The Problem of Christianity*, was neither an apologist for the faith nor a hostile critic, but an interpreter who seeks to bring to a contemporary audience an understanding of a past tradition. In this role, Miller was suspect in theological circles: What was this "secular" scholar doing expounding so assiduously the intricacies of Puritan theology when he had no avowed belief in it? Most of those for whom Puritanism was gospel truth, however, had not one-tenth of Miller's knowledge. Edwards was subject to a similar suspicion in his own time: What was he doing rubbing elbows with John Locke—"a mere deist"—while at the same time criticizing the hallowed Isaac Watts for his Arminianism?

More recently, Miller has been charged not only with exaggerating the influence of Locke on Edwards, but with reading him in a "modernist" mode, which seems to mean that Miller was merely trying to make Edwards interesting for the times. Miller certainly did not misrepresent the importance of Locke for Edwards, as subsequent scholarship has made clear; if he had a fault it was simply that he did not sufficiently emphasize the points at which Edwards dissented from Locke's position. As for the modernist reading, Miller had every right to it in view of Edwards's appeal to experience in religion, insistence on a philosophical theology, understanding of the new science and Enlightenment thought, and demand for critical, biblical scholarship. If, however, as has been suggested, Edwards must be read in a Calvinist rather than an Enlightenment context, there is no assurance that the "real" Edwards will be disclosed in this fashion. There is too much in Edwards that is original and not derived from the Reformed tradition: the emphasis on experience, beauty, and the sense of the heart; the idea of appraising piety through signs or distinguishing marks; the appeal to science and to the picture of the Newtonian universe, which formed the basis of his determinism.

Increasing current interest in Edwards, especially his appeal to people with diverse religious outlooks, may be understood as due to several features in the present climate of opinion. The most obvious, of course, is the resurgence of evangelical religion within Protestantism and the perception that Edwards's thought is important to that revival. This turn signals another important shift, namely, a tendency among evangelicals to break away from previous anti-intellectual attitudes that represented not only an opposition between "being touched by the Spirit" and "book learning," but also a reluctance to involve theology with "secular" learning. This new trend can be seen in the work of Mark Noll and others who are aware that taking Edwards seriously cannot be consistent with the evangelicalism of the past.

A second feature of the present situation is the spread of an ecumenical spirit that goes beyond the borders of denominations within Protestantism and extends to increased communication between Catholics and Protestants as well. Karl Rahner and Bernard Lonergan, for example, have attracted much attention in Protestant seminaries where Catholics are also studying such thinkers as Edwards, Reinhold and Richard Niebuhr, and Paul Tillich. Another feature is a new concern for the *experiential* dimension in religion—a sense that although doctrine is always essential for interpreting experience, doctrine points beyond itself in transforming the person.[30] As we have seen in Edwards's thought, religious faith is more than intellectual assent—the mere "notional" understanding—because it must finally reveal itself in love and purity of heart. William James's *Varieties of Religious Experience* had much to do with establishing the importance of experience, as did Kierkegaard's idea of "becoming subjective," and indeed the existential orientation as such has had a profound influence in this direction. One thinks here of Gabriel Marcel, Martin Buber, and Miguel de Unamuno, each of whom was working out a synthesis of experience and thought.

All these features of the present situation in religion—the revival of the evangelical spirit, the spread of ecumenical thinking, and the importance of experience—would help to explain why a thinker like Edwards is being rediscovered. If we ask why this did not happen sooner, the answer is to be found in the damage done by the dominant image of Edwards as the "fiery Puritan" based almost exclusively on the "Sinners" sermon which, as we have noted, was regarded for almost a century as the paradigm of Puritan thought and rhetoric. It is, to be sure, a brilliant piece of work, but it certainly provides neither a rounded nor a representative picture of the Edwards we know from the full range of his writings. The Edwards identified through that sermon, however, has been made to serve two important functions. On the one hand, he could

[30]See Vincent G. Potter, ed., *Doctrine and Experience: Essays in American Philosophy* (New York: Fordham University Press, 1988), for an exploration of this topic among several thinkers from Edwards to the present.

be portrayed as exhibiting those unhappy characteristics that anti-Puritans have invariably seen as the essence of Puritanism: self-righteousness in the judgment of hypocrites, depicting humanity as no more than a worm of depravity, invoking biblical literalism in the face of science and critical scholarship and spreading a God of anger from whom all mercy has departed, or, worse, a God whose mercy consists precisely in the damnation that sin merits. On the other hand, this image provided a way of distancing the American of good will, common sense, prudence, and reasonableness and the defender of justice and democracy from all for which Puritanism was supposed to stand. Of course, there are straw horses on both sides but, viewed in this light, we can understand why so much was invested in this picture of Edwards and how convenient it was for disposing of him and simultaneously congratulating the modern American who, as George Santayana said, is convinced "that he always has been, and always will be, victorious and blameless."[31]

From our present vantage point with its modern and postmodern overtones, we may gain insight into Edwards, Franklin, and the Enlightenment by focusing some perspectives on the nature of evil in human life and how it is to be confronted. Becker is surely correct in saying that there was a consensus about human nature among the major thinkers of the Enlightenment: "They knew, instinctively that 'man in general' is natively good, easily enlightened, disposed to follow reason and common sense; generous, humane and tolerant, more easily led by persuasion than compelled by force; above all a good citizen and a man of virtue."[32]

Kant, it is noteworthy, dissented from this view, although, as we shall see, not entirely. After calling attention to the ancient complaint that "the world lieth in evil," Kant goes on to speak of his own times: "More modern . . . is the contrasted optimistic belief, which indeed has gained a following solely among philosophers and, of late, especially among those interested in education—the belief that the world steadily (though almost imperceptibly) forges in the other direction, to wit, from bad to better."[33] In his typical thorough fashion, Kant finds that there is a propensity to good in human nature but also a propensity to evil, and he

---

[31]George Santayana, "The Genteel Tradition in American Philosophy," in Muelder, Sears, and Schlabach, *The Development of American Philosophy*, 173.
[32]Becker, *The Heavenly City*, 103.
[33]Immanuel Kant, *Religion within the Limits of Reason Alone*, trans. Theodore M. Greene and Hoyt H. Hudson (New York: Harper and Brothers, 1960), 15.

clearly regards the latter as the prevailing tendency. In discussing the thesis that people are evil by nature, he writes: "From what we know of man through experience we cannot judge otherwise of him, or, that we may presuppose evil to be subjectively necessary to every man, even to the best." But just as he had described a person's becoming a victim of ignorance and superstition (*Unmundigkeit*) as self-imposed and hence as subject to being overcome, he qualifies his judgment about radical evil by noting, "Yet at the same time it must be possible to *overcome* it [radical evil], since it is found in man, a being whose actions are free."[34]

We need not follow Kant's views farther; it is enough to say that his was the minority opinion and that the general consensus noted earlier is what was passed on to the Enlightenment in the United States. Two features of that general opinion proved to be of special importance; one was the tendency to think of evil in terms of ignorance, prejudice, and superstition, and the other, closely related, was an almost limitless faith in the power of education to overcome the ills of both individuals and society.

The attitudes of our classical American philosophers to either or both of these two features of Enlightenment wisdom not only are illuminating but present a study in contrasts. Peirce was emphatic in his condemnation of the "greed philosophy," as he called it, by which he meant the egoism and competitiveness of individualism, and he set his own philosophy of "evolutionary love" or *Agapism*—cooperation and community—against what he at other times called the "every man for himself" outlook. Although James had more individualism in him than Peirce found congenial, James was no less aware of the evil in the world and insisted that the religions of Buddhism and Christianity—in which the pessimistic attitude is most fully acknowledged and developed—are more realistic and comprehensive than what he called the religion of healthy-mindedness, which responds to failure, anxiety, wickedness, and even death with "Cheer up, it will all work out in the end."

Royce repeatedly insisted, in opposition to the widely held assumption that idealism must regard the evil in the world as mere appearance, that the "problem of Job" is among the most profound issues we face. In *The Problem of Christianity*, he put the doctrine of sin among the essential Christian ideas and described the "Hell of the irrevocable" in terms of the disloyal deed that can never be undone.

[34]Ibid., 27, 32.

Neither Peirce, James, nor Royce regarded the human capacity for evil as stemming merely from ignorance or faulty education. Here the contrast with Dewey is striking indeed. He accepted both Enlightenment features; he envisaged no radical evil in human nature, yet he had a robust and sustained faith in the power of education for resolving all human problems. In *A Common Faith* Dewey set aside the traditional problem of evil as an unfruitful inquiry and one that distracts us from what he regarded as the more important task of seeking to overcome *evils*. The shift of focus is typical of Dewey's concern to avoid "wholesale" questions, which he saw as too abstract to be managed, in favor of "retail" problems, which are specific and concrete, and to mark out a plan of the action to be taken to deal effectively with them. Confronting evils, then, becomes far more important than speculating about the existence and significance of evil as such. As regards education, one need not deny the importance of the contributions Dewey made to the reform of education at all levels in calling into question one of his cherished beliefs, namely, the redemptive power in the social sciences.

In many writings, Dewey diagnosed as one of the major problems of our culture the fact that the great achievements of the modern natural sciences had led to an undermining of the authority of religion and morality, thus creating a crisis in the culture. In acknowledging this problem, Dewey asked, What is to be put in the place of religion and morality? Although *A Common Faith* might suggest that the answer is to be found in his proposal to reconstruct the "religious" as basic to society, his more usual answer was to recommend the findings of the social sciences as the proper way to fill the void. Dewey was convinced that in his time the social sciences were in the same position as were the natural sciences in the sixteenth and seventeenth centuries; that is, they were breaking away from the pseudosciences and establishing themselves on a firm footing through the development of experimental method. Hence anthropology, sociology, psychology, and economics must overcome their "lag" behind the state of physics, chemistry, and other natural sciences and establish themselves on similar firm footing. When this has been accomplished, Dewey believed, the social sciences will find themselves in a position to provide the knowledge and guidance needed for resolving the problems of individuals and of the society at large.

At least two assumptions are implicit in Dewey's conception. The first is that human problems are largely of the sort that can be dealt with through warranted knowledge under the command of the instrumental intelligence; the second is that such knowledge can be communicated through education and thus provide us with a new source of values and ideals to make up for the decline of religion and traditional morality. The first of these assumptions is questionable, and the second is paradoxical. Clearly, there are problems in American society to which the findings of the social sciences are indeed relevant—health care and housing, poverty and economic opportunity, illiteracy and education, crime and punishment, to name but a few. But not all of what Dewey called the "problems of men" are of a sort to be dealt with by sociologists, economists, and anthropologists. When W. H. Auden described the situation prevailing at mid-century as the "Aspirin Age" he was pointing to human problems of a quite different order. Anxiety, insecurity, the sense of meaninglessness, failure of nerve, loss of faith either in God or in oneself, breakdown of community, and the loneliness of individualism—these were the ills he had in mind and, among other signs, the evidence of the burgeoning industry of psychoanalysis and psychiatric medicine in the succeeding decades proves his point. On this account alone, Auden was right in seeing that the underlying concern of millions of Americans was essentially religious and moral, a concern not to be dealt with by scientific knowledge alone. The proposal to have the social sciences perform the offices of religion and morality is paradoxical in view of the fact that when it was made by Dewey these sciences, in their effort to be "scientific," were declaring themselves to be "value-free." It is difficult to see how fields of inquiry so conceived could possibly accomplish the task assigned to them of filling the value void that Dewey described.

If, however, we are told that the foregoing account belongs to modernism and that such views have been eclipsed in the postmodern perspective, we shall have to consider that claim, albeit briefly, in the light of the questions put to the Enlightenment. To begin with, most of what passes for postmodernism is essentially aesthetic in orientation and not immediately concerned with moral and religious matters. Much depends on which thinkers one includes. If, for example, Paul Ricoeur were taken into account, there is no doubt that we have someone who is seriously and profoundly concerned with the many faces of evil in the human situation. His hermeneutic of suspicion is aimed at exposing ideology and unmasking self-deception through an interpretation and assessment of the work of Freud, Nietzsche, and Marx. Ricoeur, moreover, sees the important role of the religious dimension and is far from supposing—

as Richard Rorty, for example, does—that it may safely be ignored or that a substitute is to be found in some form of ironic stance toward things. Kierkegaard, though too early to be a postmodernist, was early enough to see that irony is an aesthetic category, one that signals a *distance* from the actual situation and not just the "standing back" necessary for gaining objective knowledge, but the disengagement, the abandonment of participation in a common human lot that accompanies looking at the human scene as if it were a play, a game, a performance, or a trick played on the benighted who are not sophisticated enough to know what is really going on.

The postmodern attitude, in short, lacks the one trait that is found in Edwards, Franklin, and the Enlightenment as a whole—not to mention modernism at all—a responsible seriousness in the face of the realities of the actual situation. Postmodernists often betray a frivolousness in their reluctance to express strong convictions about what is worth living for and in their tendency to make light of those who do hold such convictions. By contrast, both Edwards and Franklin, regardless of their differences, were similar in their *seriousness* about life and the entire gamut of human concerns. Here being serious stands in contrast not to having a sense of humor but, rather, to being frivolous and without respect for the duties and responsibilities thrust on us by the mere fact of being human. As Kierkegaard saw so clearly, the aesthetic stance of human existence has its own invaluable contribution to make, but only if it is not, so to speak, absolutized to the extent of excluding the ethical and the religious. For in that case the desire for self-gratification, whether sensual or intellectual, becomes parasitic on the rest of society. Thus it was said in the ancient world that the Epicureans could enjoy themselves as long as there were Stoics around to hold office and discharge the responsibilities of the polis.

Rorty, for example, tells us that he aims to establish literature at the center of the culture in much the same way that Dewey provided the rationale for the social sciences. In neither case, however, is this plan enough, because it does not speak to the religious concern or address the frightening problem of the widespread erosion of morality in contemporary society. Edwards, Franklin, and indeed the whole Enlightenment stand against the spirit of postmodernism. It is to them, not the pundits of deconstruction, that we should look for the resources needed to reorient the country. To paraphrase Reinhold Niebuhr: When we were a weak and struggling nation, we stood for ideals that inspired people and nations around the world, but when we became a world power our faith in those ideals seemed to fade and instead we set about the awesome task of playing God in history. Perhaps what is needed is to go forward by going back to our own tradition as defined by the development from Edwards to Franklin and beyond. Seen in this light, postmodernism represents no more than a regression.

7

Emerson's constitutional amending:
Reading "Fate"

STANLEY CAVELL

The essay "Fate" is perhaps Ralph Waldo Emerson's principal statement about the human condition of freedom, and about what Emerson calls the paradox that freedom is necessary; we might formulate this belief as the human fatedness to freedom. This leads to speaking of the human fatedness to thinking, since "Intellect annuls Fate. So far as a man thinks, he is free. . . . The revelation of Thought takes man out of servitude into freedom."[1] Could it be that the founder of American thinking, writing this essay in 1850—just months after the passage of the Fugitive Slave Law, the support of which by Daniel Webster we know Emerson to have been unforgettably, unforgivingly horrified by—was in this essay not thinking about the American institution of slavery? I think it cannot be.

Then why throughout the distressed, difficult, dense stretches of metaphysical speculation of "Fate" does Emerson seem mostly, even essentially, to keep silent on the subject of slavery, make nothing special of it? It is a silence that must still encourage his critics, both his admirers, such as Harold Bloom, and his detractors, such as John Updike, to imagine that Emerson gave up on the hope of democracy. But since I am continuing to follow the consequences of discovering in Emerson the founding of American thinking—the consequence, for example, that his thought is repressed in the culture he founded—the irony of discovering that this repressed thinking has given up on the hope and demand for a nation of the self-governing would be more than I could digest.

I was myself silent about this question of Emerson's silence when I

---

[1] Ralph Waldo Emerson, "Fate," in *Selections from Ralph Waldo Emerson*, ed. Steven E. Whicher (Boston: Houghton Miffin, 1957), 340–41.

wrote an essay in 1983 mostly on Emerson's "Fate," my first somewhat extended treatment of an Emerson text.[2] It seemed so urgent then to address the claim of Emerson as a philosophical writer, in principle imaginable as founding a philosophy for a nation still finding itself, that I recurrently hoped that Emerson had, for the moment of the essay "Fate," sufficiently excused or justified his silence in saying there, "Nothing is more disgusting than the crowing about liberty by slaves, as most men are." No sooner would I see this as an excuse or justification of silence, however, than it would seem empty to me, so that I could never appeal to it. Is not the statement that most men are slaves merely a weak, metaphorical way of feeling and of speaking, one that blunts both the fact of literal slavery and the facts of the particular ways in which we freely sell ourselves out? How is this conventional use of words essentially different from the sort of "shameful capitulation . . . to badges and names, to large societies and dead institutions" that had so chagrined Emerson in "Self-Reliance":

If malice and vanity wear the coat of philanthropy, shall that pass? If an angry bigot assumes this bountiful cause of Abolition, and comes to me with his last news from Barbados, why should I not say to him, "Go love thy infant; love thy woodchopper; be good-natured and modest; have that grace; and never varnish your hard, uncharitable ambition with this incredible tenderness for black folk a thousand miles off. Thy love afar is spite at home."[3]

Is it not news that high philosophy can be used to cover low practice, or that the love in philanthropy is tainted. Is Emerson so in doubt about the state of his own malice and vanity and anger and bigotry and charity and love that he has to clear them up before he can say clearly that he sides against slavery?

On 7 March 1854, Emerson delivered a lecture called "The Fugitive Slave Law," marking the fourth anniversary of Webster's decisive speech in favor of that legislation. Emerson's lecture reads as follows:

Nobody doubts that Daniel Webster could make a good speech. Nobody doubts that there were good and plausible things to be said on the part of the South. But this is not a question of ingenuity, not a question of syllogisms, but of sides. How came he there? . . . There are always texts and thoughts and arguments. . . . There was the same law in England for Jeffries and Talbot and Yorke to read slavery out of, and for Lord Mansfield to read freedom. . . . But the question which History will ask [of Webster] is broader. In the final hour when

[2]Stanley Cavell, "Emerson, Coleridge, Kant,"
[3]Ralph Waldo Emerson, "Self-Reliance," in Whicher, *Selections*, 150.

he was forced by the peremptory necessity of the closing armies to take a side,— did he take the part of great principles, the side of humanity and justice, or the side of abuse and oppression and chaos?[4]

So Emerson would avoid angry bigots incredibly varnishing their uncharitable ambition by taking the side against slavery afar, as well as avoid those at home who choose to read the law so as to take the side in favor of slavery. Both positions may count as "crowing about liberty by slaves," and his refusal of crowing (for or against) would perhaps be what strikes one as his essential silence on the subject in an essay on freedom paradoxically entitled "Fate." The suggestion is that there is a way of taking sides that is not crowing, however, a different way of having a say in this founding matter of slavery. If Emerson is who I think he is, then how he finds his way to having his say—whether, most particularly, he is serious in his claim that "so far as a man thinks, he is free"—is as fateful for America's claim to its own culture of thinking as its success in ridding itself of the institution of slavery is for establishing its claim to have discovered a new world.

We need to consider the writing—philosophical? political? religious?—style of the pent, prophetic prose of "Fate." Emerson speaks there (as well as later in the "Fugitive Slave Law") of taking a side. His formulation in "Fate" is of the capacity, when a man finds himself a victim of his fate—for example, "ground to powder by the vice of his race"—to "take sides with the Deity who secures universal benefit by his pain." This may seem the formulation less of a course of action than of inaction. Take Emerson's reference in his phrase the "vice of his race" (by which a person finds himself victimized) as specified in the description earlier in the essay of "expensive races—race living at the expense of race." But which vice does "expensive" suggest? The literal context of that predicate takes the races in question as the human race living at the expense of the races of animals that serve us as food: "You have just dined, and however scrupulously the slaughter-house is concealed in the graceful distance of miles, there is complicity, expensive races." It happens that we can produce evidence that this passage about human carnivorousness—and its companion human gracefulness, in keeping its conditions concealed from itself—is a parable about the cannibalism implied in living gracefully off other human races. The evidence

---

[4]Ralph Waldo Emerson, "The Fugitive Slave Law," in *Emerson's Complete Works*, vol. 11, ed. J. E. Cabot (1883).

comes from an early paragraph in Emerson's address "On Emancipation in the British West Indies," delivered in 1844, the tenth anniversary of that emancipation legislation. In Emerson's West Indies address he remarks that "from the earliest monuments it appears that one race was victim and served the other races," and that "the negro has been an article of luxury to the commercial nations"; furthermore, "language must be raked, the secrets of the slaughter-houses and infamous holes that cannot front the day, must be ransacked, to tell what negro-slavery has been."[5]

I propose to consider "Fate" pervasively, however—beyond the reach of the sort of textual intersection I just adduced—as a philosophical enactment of freedom, a parable of the struggle against slavery not as a general metaphor for claiming human freedom but as the absolute image of the necessary siding against fate toward freedom that is the condition of philosophical thinking; as if the aspiration to freedom is philosophy's breath.

Does not the sheer eloquence of the West Indies address compromise this proposal from the outset, with its demand to rake language and ransack slaughterhouses to tell of Negro slavery? Is not Emerson in "Fate"—the same man who in the earlier West Indies address confessed himself heartsick to read the history of that slavery—courting the danger of seeming to avoid the sickening facts of the slavery that continues not metaphysically afar but at home? What is he thinking of, whom is he thinking of when in "Fate" he says, "In the history of the individual there is an account of his condition, and he knows himself to be party to his present estate"? If the sentences of "Fate" are to be brought to the condition of slavery, are we to imagine this statement about the individual's knowing himself to be party to his estate to be said to the individual who is enslaved? What would prevent this announcement from constituting the obscene act of blaming the slave for his slavery?[6]

One implication of saying, "You know yourself party to your estate" (if it is not pure blame) is that you are free to leave it. John Brown might

[5]Ralph Waldo Emerson, "On Emancipation in the British West Indies," in *Works*, 11: 133, 134.
[6]My intermittent sense of this possibility, and of the fact that I had no satisfying answer to it, was brought home to me by a letter from Barbara Packer, whose book *Emerson's Fall: A New Interpretation of the Major Essays* (New York: Continuum, 1982) is indispensable to readers of Emerson, following a brief conversation between us concerning Emerson's politics. She writes in her letter of her sense of what I called the "obscene announcement" in "Fate" as something that she had yet to bring under control, and asked for my thoughts; that was about eighteen months ago—I am trying to collect them.

say something of the sort, without obscenity, to a person in the condition of enslavement, given that he would be saying, "I know the only way to exercise your freedom to leave your estate is to court death, and I'll court it with you." Walt Whitman might say something related, as in the remarkable "I Sing the Body Electric," in which he watches the man's body at auction and the woman's body at auction and declares his love for, his sameness with, the body and thus the soul of the slave. The absolute pain of the knowledge of American slavery is the knowledge that enslaved human beings persist with every breath in interpreting and preserving what a human existence can bear. But do we imagine that Emerson, like John Brown and Walt Whitman, has a way to bear the knowledge of that pain—he who is habitually supposed to have turned aside from the philosophically tragic sense of life?

Perhaps Emerson means only to say of Northerners, neither slaves nor slaveowners, that they are party to their own estate, meaning perhaps that they make themselves slaves to the interests of Southern slaveowners, who never even paid for them. But that is not exactly news. Emerson reports in the West Indies address that when "three hundred thousand persons in Britain pledged themselves to abstain from all articles of island produce . . . the planters were obliged to give way . . . and the slave trade was abolished."[7] Such responses to slavery as economic boycott are evidently not Emerson's business in "Fate." To whom, then, is he writing?

If "taking sides with the Deity" does not mean taking the right side in the crowing about slavery, the side Daniel Webster failed to take, what does it mean? Emerson suggests the choice concerns the fatefulness of the *way* sides are taken: "A man must ride alternately on the horses of his private and his public nature. . . . Leaving the daemon who suffers, he is to take sides with the Deity who secures universal benefit by his pain." The notion that the human being is the being who can take a representative (public) stance, and knows the imperative to the stance, is familiar and recurrent Emersonian ground; nothing is a more founding fact for him. I quote this Platonic image about riding alternately the horses of human nature to suggest that taking sides with the deity is a refusal to take sides in the human crowing over slavery. Emerson's taking sides with the deity, like and unlike the political extremity of Locke's appealing to heaven, is not exactly a call to revolution but a claim to

[7]Emerson, "On Emancipation in the British West Indies," in *Works*, 11:140, 141.

prophecy.[8] "Leaving the daemon who suffers" means leaving one's private, limited passions on the subject of slavery, be they for or against.

What is the alternative horse, the public expression of a beneficial pain (given in the absence of a constituted public, since so much of the human voice, the slave's voice, is unrepresented in that public)? The alternative is not venting one's pain but maintaining it; in the case of "Fate," it is writing every sentence in pain. It contains the pain of refusing human sides, shunning argument, with every breath. The time of argument is over. Where is pain's benefit? Is philosophy over?

At the opening of "Fate," Emerson writes: "We are incompetent to solve the times. . . . To me . . . the question of the times resolved itself into a practical question of the conduct of life." In "Fate" the question of the times—what Emerson calls in his opening "the huge orbits of the prevailing ideas" whose return and opposition we cannot "reconcile," and what he describes near his close by remarking, "Certain ideas are in the air"—is the question of slavery. The certain ideas in the air are emancipation and secession, issues producing the compromise of 1850, which concerned—besides the Fugitive Slave Act—the slave trade and the admission of territories into the Union with or without slaves. Setting out the terms for the "greatest debate in Congressional history," Henry Clay prefaces his resolutions of compromise by saying, "It being desirable, for the peace, concord and harmony of the Union of these States to settle and adjust amicably all existing questions of controversy between them, arising out of the institution of slavery, upon a fair, equitable and just basis"—and then follow eight paragraphs, each beginning "Resolved" or "But, resolved."[9] Emerson introduces "Fate" by speaking in his opening paragraph of our incompetence to *solve* the times and of *resolving* the question of the times; in the second paragraph he states that "the riddle of the age has for each a private solution"; and, continuing to reverse or recapture the word *resolved*, Emerson says in the middle of the essay, "Thought dissolves the material universe by carrying the mind up into a sphere where all is plastic"; and in the closing paragraphs he speaks of a "solution to the mysteries of human condition" and of "the Blessed Unity which holds nature and soul in perfect solution." This is not Henry Clay's imagined union.

Emerson is aware that, compared with Henry Clay's resolutions, his

[8]The reference is to Locke's Second Treatise.
[9]Henry Clay, in *Documents of American History*, ed. Henry Steele Commager (New York: Appleton-Century-Crofts, 1948), 319.

words about resolution and unity will sound, at first, private, not to say ethereal. He seems also to know that he is speaking with necessity ("Our thought, though it were only an hour old, affirms an oldest necessity") and with universality (being thrown "on the party and interest of the Universe [i.e., taking sides with the deity] against all and sundry; against ourselves as much as others"). According to Kantian philosophy, necessity and universality are the marks of the a priori, that is, of human objectivity; so if Emerson's claim is valid, it is the opposing party who is riding the horse of privacy, of what Emerson also calls selfishness, a quality he would equate with Henry Clay's use of the word *desirable*.

We must ask—since Emerson would also know that anyone can claim to be speaking in the interest of the universe and on the side of the deity—what the source is of his conviction in his own objectivity, his ability, as he puts it in the poem composed as an epigraph for "Fate," to read omens traced in air. I understand the source to be his conviction that his abilities are not exclusive, that he claims to know only what everyone knows.

Toward the close of the essay Emerson states, "The truth is in the air, and the most impressionable brain will announce it first, but all will announce it a few minutes later." He is not even claiming that he is announcing it first, since the truth that is in the air is also, always already, philosophy; it contains not just the present cries for freedom and union and the arguments against them, but perennial cries and arguments. This is surely the meaning of the gesture Emerson habitually enjoys making, of listing his predecessors and benefactors, the benefactors of the race, who are part of our air, our breath. The essay "Fate" cites the names of Napoleon, Edmund Burke, Daniel Webster, Kossuth; Jenny Lind; Homer, Zoroaster, Menu; Robert Fulton, Benjamin Franklin, James Watt; Copernicus, Isaac Newton, Pierre-Simon Laplace; Thales, Anaximenes, Empedocles, Pythagoras; Hafez, Voltaire, Christopher Wren, Dante, Columbus, Goethe, Hegel, Metternich, John Adams, John Caldwell Calhoun, Guizot, Sir Robert Peel, Mayer Rothschild, John Jacob Astor, Herodotus, Plutarch. As Emerson says: "The air is full of men."[10]

I associate the men in air with the birds in Emerson's epigraph poem:

---

[10]Emerson puts those words in quotation marks without saying who or what he is quoting. *Bartlett's Unfamiliar Quotations* contains the line "In the air men shall be seen" in a list of rhymed prophecies attributed to Mother Shipton, who was, according to the *Bartlett's* editors, a witch and prophetess fabricated in the seventeenth century.

"Birds with auguries on their wings" / [who] "chanted undeceiving things, / Him to beckon, him to warn." The "few minutes later" Emerson calculates between the first announcements of truth and, for example, his own impressionable announcements of it—which the world may measure as millennia but which are a few minutes of eternity—are essentially no more than the few minutes between our reading Emerson's pages (his wings of augury) and our announcing or pronouncing, if only to ourselves, what is chanted there. Like his great reader Thoreau, Emerson loves playing with time, that is, making time vanish where truth is concerned: " 'Tis only a question of time," he says casually a few minutes later in "Fate," as a kind of answer to the earlier and more portentous phrasing "the question of the times." In invoking casualness as one characteristic tone Emerson gives his prose, I am thinking of his characteristic association of that idea with the idea of causality; as if he misses no opportunity to show that we do not see our fate, because we imagine that it is extraordinary and "not yet," rather than ordinary and "already," as are our words.

Here are three successive sentences to this effect from "Fate" (341). First, "If the Universe have these savage accidents, our atoms are savage in resistance." That is, speaking philosophically, or universally, "accidents" are opposed to "necessities," and in thus implying that slavery is accidental, or arbitrary, and resistance to it necessary and natural, Emerson removes its chief argument. Second, "We should be crushed by the atmosphere but for the reaction of the air within the body." That is, the ideas that are in the air are our life's breath; they become our words; slavery is supported by some of them and might have crushed the rest of them; uncrushed, they live in opposition. Third, "If there be omnipotence in the stroke, there is omnipotence in the recoil." That is, every word is a word spoken again, otherwise there would be no words. Since recoil and aversion have been expressed only by breathers of words, mortals, their strokes may be given now and may gather together now—in a recoiling—all the power of world-creating words. The sentence introducing the three just cited asserts: "Man also is part of [Fate], and can confront fate with fate." Emerson's way of confronting fate, his recoil of fate, is in every word of his writing, for example, in every word of "Fate," each of which is a stroke, because a counterstroke, of fate. The power he claims for his words is precisely that they are not his, no more new than old. It is the power of the powerlessness in being unexceptional, or exemplary ("We go to Herodotus and Plutarch for examples of Fate; but we are examples"). This unavoidable power of exemplification may be named impressionability and seen to be responsibility construed as responsiveness, passiveness as receptiveness.

These are various ways of approaching the idea that the source of Emerson's conviction in what I called the objectivity (I might have called it the impersonality) of his prophesying, his wing-reading and omen-witnessing, lies in his philosophical authorship, a condition each of his essays is bound to characterize and authenticate in its own terms.

A characteristic of this authorship is announced in the opening paragraph of "Self-Reliance": "In every work of genius we recognize our own rejected thoughts; they come back to us with a certain alienated majesty." Even among those readers who know this sentence well, there is resistance in taking Emerson to be naming his own work as an instance of the work he is characterizing, resistance in reading that sentence about rejected thought as itself an instance of such a rejected thought coming back in familiar strangeness, so with the power of the uncanny. The mechanism of this rejection and return is, I suppose, that characterized by Freud as transference, a process in which another person is magnified by our attributing to him or her powers present in our repressed desires and who, putting himself or herself aside for the moment, gives us in useful form what we have shown ourselves unusefully to know. It is an interpretation of the mechanism of projection Kant calls the sublime, reading our mind's powers in nature, in the air. Emerson's authorship enacts with his reader a relationship of moral perfectionism in which a friend permits one to advance toward oneself, which may present itself, using another formulation of Emerson's, as attaining one's unattained self, a process that has always happened and is always to happen.

The word "majesty" reappears in "Fate," again in a context in which the presence of a "thought and word of an intellectual man [rouses] our mind . . . to activity": " 'This the majesty into which we have suddenly mounted, the impersonality, the scorn of egotisms, the sphere of laws, that engage us." A "sphere of laws" into which we have suddenly mounted, as if attaining a new standpoint, suggests Kant's Realm of Ends—call it the eventual human city—in which the reception of the moral law, the constraint by the moral imperative, expressed by an "ought," is replaced by the presence of another, like and unlike myself, who constrains me to another way—another standpoint, Kant says (Emerson says, transfiguring Kant, a new standard). This other of myself—

returning my rejected, my repressed, thought—reminds me of something, such as where I am, as if I had become lost in thought and stopped thinking. In "Experience," Emerson expresses finding the way, learning to take steps, as if to begin to walk philosophically, in the absence of another presence—more accurately, allowing himself to present himself to the loss of presence, to the death of his young son.[11] His description of his authorship in that essay takes the form of fantasizing his becoming pregnant and giving birth to the world and to his writing of the world, which he calls a new America and Being.[12] In "Fate" he is giving the basis of his authorship in the passage about riding alternately on the horses of his private and his public natures. Those horses are descendants of the horses he invoked in his essay "The Poet," where he named the Poet as one whose relation to language is such that "in every word he speaks he rides on them as the horses of thought."[13]

The idea here is that the words have a life of their own, over which our mastery is the other face of our obedience. Ludwig Wittgenstein in *Philosophical Investigations* affirms this sense of the independent life of words in describing what he does as "leading words back from their metaphysical to their everyday use," suggesting that their getting back (whatever that achievement is) is something they must do under their own power, if not quite or always under their own direction.[14] Alternating horses teaches the two sides of thoughts that objectivity is not a given but an achievement; *leading* the thought, allowing it its own power, takes a person to new ground.

The achievement of objectivity cannot be claimed for oneself, that is, for one's writing: "I would write on the lintels of the door-post, *Whim.* I hope it may be better than whim at last." But in the necessity for words, "when [your] genius calls [you]," you can only air your thoughts, not assess them, and you must.[15]

To Emerson's way of thinking, as to Wittgenstein's, ethics is not a separate field of philosophical study, but every word that comes from us, the address of each thought, is a moral act, a taking of sides, though not in argument. In Emerson's terms, the sides may be called those of self-reliance and conformity. In Wittgenstein's terms, the privacy and

[11]Ralph Waldo Emerson, "Experience," in Whicher, *Selections.*
[12]I have given my evidence for this statement elsewhere.
[13]Ralph Waldo Emerson, "The Poet," in Whicher, *Selections.*
[14]Ludwig Wittgenstein, *Philosophical Investigations.*
[15]Emerson, "Self-Reliance," in Whicher, *Selections.*

emptiness of assertion he calls metaphysical, and the dispersal of this empty assertiveness by what he calls "leading words back" is his image of thinking. It strikes me that the feature of the intersection of Emersonian with Wittgensteinian thinking that primarily causes offense among professional philosophers is less the claim to know peculiar matters with a certainty that goes beyond reasonable evidence (matters such as the location of the deity's side of the temptation to insistent emptiness), and less the sheer, pervasive literary ambition of their writing, but more the sense that these locations, diagnoses, and ambitions are in service of a claim to philosophical authorship that can seem the antithesis of what philosophical writing should be, a denial of rational or systematic presentation apart from which philosophy might as well turn itself into, or over to, literature, or perhaps worse.

The "worse" may be called esotericism, an effect both Emerson and Wittgenstein recognize in themselves. Wittgenstein recognizes it in his continuous struggle against his interlocutors, whose role sometimes seems less to make Wittgenstein's thoughts clearer than to allow him to show that his thoughts are *not* clear, and not obviously to be *made* clear: They must be *found* so. Emerson recognizes his esotericism in such a remark from "Fate" as "This insight [that] throws us on the party of the Universe, against all and sundry . . . distances those who share it from those who do not." But what is the alternative? At the close of "Experience," Emerson suggests that the alternative to speaking exoterically is speaking polemically (taking sides in argument), which for him, as for Wittgenstein, gives up philosophy and can never lead to the peace philosophy seeks. Hegel preceded Emerson in contrasting something like the esoteric with the polemical by considering the presentation of philosophy as a matter internal to the present state of philosophy. The dissonance between these thinkers and professional philosophers is less an intellectual disagreement than a moral variance in their conceptions of thinking, or perhaps I can say, in their conceptions of the role of moral judgment in the moral life, in the way each pictures "constraint."

If slavery is the negation of thought, then thinking cannot affirm itself without affirming the end of slavery. For thinking to *fail* to affirm itself is for it to deny the existence of philosophy. It is accordingly no more or less certain that philosophy will continue than that human self-enslavement will end. Philosophy cannot abolish slavery, and it can only call for abolition to the extent, or in the way, that it can call for thinking and can provide (adopting Kant's term) the incentive to thinking. The incentive Emerson offers is what I call his authorship, which works to attract our knowledge that we are rejecting, repressing thinking, hence the knowledge that thinking must contain both pain and pleasure (if it were not painful, it would not require repression; if it were not pleasurable, it would not attract it).

The linking of philosophical thinking with pain is expressed in an Emersonian sentence that seems a transcription at once of Plato and of Kant: "I know that the world I converse with in the city and in the farms is not the world I *think*" ("Experience"). To think of this other world, the Realm of Ends, is pleasure; to bear witness to its difference from the actual world of cities and farms is pain. Here perhaps, in this pleasure and pain, before the advent of an imperative judgment and before the calculation of the desirable, is the incentive of thinking that Kant sought. The pain is a function of the insight that there is no reason that the eventual world is not entered, not actual, and thus that I must be rejecting it and the existence of others in it, and the others must be rejecting my existence there.

From this point I continue with Emerson's understanding of the origination of philosophy as a feminine capacity. Toward the end of "Fate," Emerson writes: "The truth is in the air, and the most impressionable brain will announce it first, but all will announce it a few minutes later." He continues by claiming that "women, as most susceptible, are the best index of the coming hour. So the great man, that is, the man most imbued with the spirit of time, is the impressionable man," which seems to divine that the great man is a woman. The idea that philosophical knowledge is receptive rather than assertive, that it is a matter of leaving a thing as it is rather than taking it as something else, is not new and is a point of affinity between Wittgenstein and Heidegger. Emerson's thought here is that this characteristic makes knowledge difficult in a particular way, not because it is hard to understand exactly but because it is hard to bear. His suggestion, accordingly, is that something prepares the woman for this relation to pain, whereas a man must be great to attain it. I grant this point may be made stupidly. It may be used—perhaps most often is—to deny injustice done to women. I associate Emerson's invocation of the feminine with a striking remark of Hélène Cixous's, in which she declares her belief that whereas men must rid themselves of pain by mourning their losses, women do not mourn, but bear their pain.[16] The connection is that the better world we know not to exist, with no reason not to exist, is not a world that is *gone*, hence is not one to be mourned, but one to be borne, witnessed. The attempt to mourn it is the stuff of nostalgia. The closing of "Experience" reads: "Patience, patience, we shall win at the last"; until recently I had not understood this as the demand on Emerson's writing and on his readers to let the pain of his thoughts, and theirs, collect itself.

In 1983, in discussing "Fate," I did not speak of Emerson's philosophical authorship and esotericism or see the connection between Emerson's mode of thinking and his moral perfectionism, his constraint of his reader through his conviction in the magnified return of the reader's own rejected thoughts. It is as if in my desperation to show Emerson capable of rigorous, systematic thinking against the incessant denial of him as a philosopher, I felt I could not at the same time show his practice of thinking as one of transfiguring philosophy in founding it, finding it, for America. I could not *assume* his right to speak for philosophy.

My primary focus in that earlier encounter with "Fate" was on Emerson's use of the term *condition* and his relation of it to the term *terms* (meaning both words and stipulations) and *dictation*, which I claim shows Emerson turning Kant's *Critique of Pure Reason* on itself. He takes the *Critique*'s term *condition* in its etymological significance to be "speaking together," suggesting that the condition of the possibility of there being a world of objects for us is the condition of our speaking together; that is not a matter of our sharing twelve categories of understanding but of our sharing a language. Hence the task of philosophy is not to derive privileged categories but to announce the terms on the basis of which we use each term of the language.

Any term may give rise to what Wittgenstein calls a grammatical investigation, but beyond *condition* and its relatives, my earlier essay got just to the idea of *character* as meaning the fact of language, as well as the formation of an individual. Yet even that distance allowed me to summarize the essay's word by saying that character is fate and that the human is fated to significance, to finding it and to revealing it, and—as if tragically—fated to thinking or to repressing thinking. Emerson, the

---

[16]Hélène Cixous, as cited in Tania Modleski, "Time and Desire in the Women's Film," in Christine Glendhill, ed., *Home Is Where the Heart Is* (London: British Film Institute, 1987); and Stanley Cavell, "Postscript 1989" to "Ugly Duckling, Pretty Butterfly: Bette Davis and *Now Voyager, Critical Inquiry* (Winter 1990).

American who is repeatedly, famously, denied the title of philosopher
and described as lacking the tragic sense, writes an essay on freedom
entitled "Fate" and creates the mode of what we may perhaps call the
tragic essay.

If I now add the use of the term *constitution* in that essay to the words
whose terms I demand, Emerson's claim for his philosophical authorship
becomes unpostponable. Along with *condition* and *character*, other philosophical terms Emerson allows the reader to find unobtrusive are *possibility* and *accident, impression* and *idea. Constitution* appears in
"Fate" only a few times, but its placement is telling, and the essay's
array of political terms or projects magnifies its force. We have heard of
our being party to our estate, and a not especially obtrusive sentence
contains: "this house of man, which is all consent, inosculation and
balance of parts," where *consent* works to associate "balance of parts"
with "checks and balances" and "house" thus names each of the
branches of Congress. Here is an example of placement:

Jesus said, "when he looketh on her, he hath committed adultery." But he is an
adulterer before he has yet looked on the woman, by the superfluity of animal
and the defect of thought in his constitution. Who meets him, or who meets her,
in the street, sees that they are ripe to be each other's victim. (334)

In my earlier essay, I read this passage as the claim that most of what
we call marriage is adultery, not a thought original with Emerson. According to my hypothesis that every metaphysical claim in "Fate" about
freedom and its deprivation is to be read also in a social register, as
applying also to the institution of slavery, I read the phrase "defect of
thought in his constitution" as referring to the famous defect in the
Constitution of the United States concerning those persons who are in-
terminably unfree—a defect that adulterates our claim to have established a just and tranquil human society, corrupts it, makes it spurious.
I discuss the "defective" passage in depth later in this chapter.

From at least as early as "Self-Reliance," Emerson identifies his writing (what I am calling his philosophical authorship) as the drafting of
the nation's constitution, or as the amending of its constitution. When
he says in "Self-Reliance," "No law can be sacred to me but that of my
nature," he is saying no more than Kant had said—that, in a phrase
from "Fate," "we are law-givers" to the world of conditions and objects,
and to ourselves in the world of the unconditioned and freedom. But
the next sentence of "Self-Reliance" takes another step: "Good and bad

are but names readily transferrable to that or this; the only right is what is after my constitution; the only wrong that is against it." (The anticipation of Nietzsche's *Genealogy of Morals* is no accident.) "My constitution" seems uniformly to be understood by Emerson's readers as referring to Emerson's personal, peculiar physiology and as an expression of his incessant promotion of the individual over the social. Such an understanding refuses the complexity of the Emersonian theme exemplified by his saying that we are now "bugs, spawn," which means simultaneously that we exist neither as individual human beings nor in human nations, and also exemplified when, chastising himself for having given a dollar in charity out of conformity to pressure, he says that "one day I shall have the manhood to withhold" it, which means simultaneously that he will have entered into his humanity and that there will be a company of humanity to belong to, in just circumstances, who will not need charity.

The theme is fervently announced in Emerson's various formulations of the vision that the innermost becomes the outermost. In "The American Scholar": the scholar "is one who raises himself from private considerations and breathes and lives on [as if they were air] public and illustrious thoughts."[17] In "Self-Reliance": "To believe your own thought, to believe that what is true for you in your private heart is true for all men—that is genius," and specifically it is what in every work of genius comes back to us with the alienated majesty of our own rejected thoughts. Speaking what is "true for all men," which in "Fate" is "truth com[ing] to our mind," is an event of insight Emerson describes as our "suddenly expand[ing] to its [truth's] dimensions, as if we grew to worlds. [It is this insight that] throws us on the part and interest of the Universe . . . against ourselves as much as others." Throwing us "on the part . . . of the Universe," as if to say taking its part, reminds me of what Kant calls speaking "with the universal voice," which is the essential feature in making an aesthetic judgment. That activity demands or imputes or claims universal agreement with it—a claim made in the face of the knowledge that this agreement is in empirical fact not likely to be forthcoming. Moral judgment also speaks with—or rather listens to—what we might call the universal voice, in the form of the capacity to act under the constraint of the moral imperative, the imperative of the universal (of the universalizable).

---

[17]Ralph Waldo Emerson, "The American Scholar," in Whicher, *Selections*, 73.

Emerson is appealing to something of the kind in simply claiming as a fact that we can judge the constitution of the world and of the lives complicitous with it from a standpoint that "all and sundry" may be expected to find in themselves. The great difference from aesthetic and moral judgment is that the constitutional judgment demanding the amending of our lives (together) is to be found by each of us as a rejected thought returning to us. This mode of access to constitutional judgment seems no less well characterized by Emerson than moral or aesthetic judgments are by philosophers generally.

It is the appeal to what we have rejected, forgotten, or displaced that gives Emerson's (and Wittgenstein's) writing the feel of the esoteric, of work to whose understanding one is asked to convert. This is an obvious sign of danger for professional, university philosophy, and it should be. Emerson ought to have to make his way, to bear the pain of his arrogating his right to speak for philosophy in the absence of making himself curricular, institutionalizable, polemical. In other words, it does not follow from his institutionalized silence that he has failed to raise the call for philosophy and to identify its fate with the fate of freedom. The fact of his call's repression would be the sign that it had been heard. The apparent silence of "Fate" might become deafening.

The absoluteness of the American institution of slavery, among the many forms of human self-enslavement (hence the absoluteness of philosophy's call to react to it, recoil from it), is recorded in the sentence cited earlier from the West Indies address: "Language must be raked, the secrets of the slaughter-houses and infamous holes that cannot front the day, must be ransacked, to tell what negro-slavery has been." I address the idea of raking language as another announcement, in a polemical context, of Emerson's philosophical authorship of what cannot be undertaken polemically.

On the surface of the idea of raking language is a kind of Emersonian joke, namely, that we are to respond to the fact and be responsible to it; that the largely unquestioned form or look of writing is of being raked on a page, that is, racked in parallel straight lines; and then to recognize that bringing what writing contains to light, letting these words return to us, as if to themselves, to mount suddenly to their majesty, to the scorn of egotisms, is to let the fact of them rouse our mind to activity, to turn it to the air, perhaps to think that the fact of language is more telling than any fact uttered within it, as if every fact utters the fact of language. Against this fatedness to language and to character, against, that is, what I earlier called our condemnation to significance, it is we who are raked. To think of language as raking and recoiling is to think of it, although it may look tranquil, as aimed and fired at itself, as if the creature of conditions, fated to language, exists in the condition of threat, the prize of unmarked battles, where every horizon—where the air of words (of what might be said) gravitates to the earth of assertion (of what is actually said)—signifies a struggle between possession and dispossession, between speech and silence, between the unspeakable and the unsilenceable. (Here I am letting myself express a little the anguish I sense in Emerson's language in "Fate.")

The particular direction in the raking of language I emphasize now is its office in *telling*, which is to say, in counting and recounting— "tell[ing] what negro-slavery has been" is how Emerson put it—hence in telling every enslavement. One source of the word "raking" is the idea of reckoning or counting as well as recking, paying attention. Of the endless interest there may be in thinking of language itself as a matter of counting, I confine attention momentarily here to the connection between counting or telling and the writing of our constitution.

When in the second paragraph of "Experience" Emerson asks bleakly, "How many individuals can we count in society?" he is directing our attention back to the famous passage I alluded to earlier, the fifth paragraph of the Constitution of the United States: "Representatives and direct Taxes shall be apportioned among the several States which may be included within this Union, according to their respective Numbers, which shall be determined by adding to the whole number of free Persons, including those bound to service for a Term of Years, and excluding Indians not taxed, three fifths of all other Persons." The paragraph goes on to specify the calculation of democratic representation, and I find the comic invoking in "Fate" of the new science of statistics, in its attention to populations, to be another allusion to the "defect," the lack of philosophical necessity, in our constitutional counting. In the large we do not see how many we are; in the small we do not know, as Emerson puts it in "The American Scholar," whether we add up to what the "old fable" calls "one Man," as if we do not know whether any of us, all and each, counts. We are living our skepticism.

Emerson's simultaneous use of the idea of "my constitution" to name at once his makeup and the makeup of the nation he prophesies is a descendant of Plato's use of his Republic to name a structure of both the soul and the city. Socrates calls the Republic he and his friends have created "a city of words" and says that the philosopher will participate in the public affairs of only that city. I find Emerson's philosophical prose, his authorship, to earn something like Plato's description (a city of words) for itself—as I find Thoreau's *Walden* to do—and thus to imagine for itself the power to amend the actual city in the philosophical act of its silence, its power of what Emerson calls patience, which he seeks as the most active of intellectual conditions, the simultaneous turning away from and turning toward the city, Emerson's aversive thinking.

Nothing less would satisfy my craving for philosophy, but nothing so much creates my fears for it. I am aware that I have mentioned the name of Heidegger in these remarks but cited no word of his. Yet in my return here to Emerson's "Fate" and my sense of its tortured, philosophical silence about the tyranny of the institution of slavery—its effort to preserve philosophy in the face of conditions that negate philosophy—I am aware of a kind of preparation for some explicit coming to terms on my part with Heidegger's relation to the tyranny of Nazism, an explicitness I have, with growing discomfort, postponed over the years. Am I prepared to listen to an argument in Heidegger's defense that he was, after his public falling out of favor with the regime, attempting to preserve philosophy in the face of conditions that negate philosophy? If not, how am I prepared to understand (as in his 1936 lectures on Nietzsche and in his contemporaneous "Origin of the Work of Art") his call of a people to its historical destiny and his announcement of a form of the appearance of truth as the founding of a political order? Such questions press me now not only because of the oddly late and oddly stale recent accounts of Heidegger's extensive involvements with Nazism or the inundation of responses to these revelations by so many major philosophical voices of Europe but also because of the pitch of Nietzsche's absorption in Emerson's writing and of Heidegger's absorption or appropriation, in turn, of Nietzsche.

Only recently have I for the first time read all the way through Heidegger's lectures on Nietzsche, delivered from 1936 to 1940 and surely the most influential interpretation of Nietzsche to have appeared for serious philosophers in Europe. Emerson's presence in Nietzsche's thought as Heidegger receives it is so strong in certain passages that one has to say that Nietzsche is using Emerson's words, which means that Heidegger in effect, over an unmeasured stretch of thought, is interpreting Emerson's words. Here are two instances: In the second volume of the lectures' English translation, Heidegger notes that Nietzsche's "early thought . . . was later to become the essential center of his thinking."[18] Heidegger mentions two school essays of Nietzsche's, and in a footnote the translator mentions in passing that the essays exhibit the "influence" of Emerson and quotes two sentences from the longer of the essays, "Fate and History: Thought":

> Yet if it were possible for a strong will to overturn the world's entire past, we would join the ranks of self-sufficient gods, and world history would be no more to us than a dream-like enchantment of the self. The curtain falls, and man finds himself again, like a child playing with worlds, a child who wakes at daybreak and with a laugh wipes from his brow all frightful dreams.[19]

Compare this with a sentence from the penultimate paragraph of "Fate": "If we thought men were free in the sense that in a single exception one fantastical will would prevail over the law of things, it were all one as if a child's hand could pull down the sun." Nietzsche is not "influenced" by Emerson but is quite deliberately transfiguring Emerson, as for the instruction of the future. This happens both early and late. In the section from Book 3 of *Thus Spoke Zarathustra* called "The Convalescent," of which Heidegger's reading is among the high points of his opening set of Nietzsche lectures, Nietzsche says: "To every soul belongs another world; for every soul, every other soul is an afterworld."[20] In "Fate," we find: "The hero is to others as the world." The relation of transfiguration here is clearer the more one explores what Emerson means by the hero (who is in principle every soul) and his view of how souls touch.

So I am faced with the spectacle of Heidegger's, in effect, unknowingly facing certain of Emerson's words, guiding himself in those fateful years by signs from, all places on earth, the waste of America. How do I guide myself? Is it by the thought that since Emerson is the philosopher of freedom, I can, by means of his mediation through Nietzsche to Heidegger, in principle trust to our eventual success in showing Heidegger's descent into the allegiance with tyranny to be a lifelong aberration of his philosophical genius? Or must I guide myself by the thought that since Heidegger is so radically uncompromised, and since Emerson is

---

[18]Heidegger's lectures on Nietzsche, English trans., 2:134.
[19]Ibid.
[20]Friedrich Nietzsche, "The Convalescent," in *Thus Spoke Zarathustra*, Book 3.

thus mediated by philosophers of the powers of Nietzsche and Heidegger, it is not even certain that we will eventually succeed in showing Emerson's genius to be uncompromised by this mediation, so that the way of philosophy I care about most is *as such* compromised?

8

Lincoln and modernity

ANDREW DELBANCO

No matter how far we may have come from the old notion that history is made by presidents and generals, any meditation on the meaning of the Civil War must come to terms with the man whose election provoked it, whose directives and words drove it, and whose death seemed—to many—to redeem it. In the remarkable public-television series on the war, which for eleven hours in the fall of 1990 held nearly 20 million viewers, pictures of Abraham Lincoln were submerged among the thousands of images of death. From the campaign posters to the famous last photograph, in which the crack of the glass negative seems a premonitory head wound, Lincoln's image, usually kept central, was allowed in this case to recede from the foreground. Yet this extraordinary documentary, whose reception is itself a historical phenomenon of no little interest, has nevertheless furnished us with a new way to speak about Lincoln. He remains, I think, the key to understanding why the war still grips us.

What was called in his time "Mr. Lincoln's war" was the first war to be photographed, and the surviving images, which were frozen because the technology did not permit photographs of people or objects in motion, include a vast number of pictures of the dead. The television series—made by (and, I suspect, largely for) the generation that has come of age since the Vietnam War—proceeded with a relentless accumulation of these images: piles of amputated limbs, skeletons (living and dead) at Andersonville, skulls washed out of the soil by the rain at Fredericksburg. The visual meaning of the war has become a great *memento mori*, forcing on us the question (the filmmakers went again and again for an answer to Shelby Foote, arguably the writer most intimately acquainted with the choreography of death in the war) of why these men went willingly to die. Faced with this question, we pose another: How willingly? We are told of desertion rates and draft riots, and of rich men cheating death by buying substitutes. We hear of the young men's prewar illusions, and of the pernicious myths of chivalry and equestrian glory. But after Shiloh and Antietam and Chancellorsville these explanations take on a hint of pettiness. The questions persist: How could the generals, proclaiming their devotion to their men, order them to the slaughter? Why did the men go?

These questions are, I think, beyond answering because they are barely amenable to the methods we have for talking about our own past. This is not only because they involve inarticulate (sometimes illiterate) men, and all the usual problems of judging the relations between public ideology and the common person's belief. There is a certain embarrassment in such questions because they force us to confront an aspect of our civilization that we usually attribute to Asia or the Middle East—places where the "human wave" is a legitimate instrument of war because men there are willing to die for a transcendence that we deem credible only to the insane.

How did this happen in America? The very fact that this question is thinkable, and, since the television series, widely asked, confirms something we know about ourselves: that in the realm of belief we have become frantically impoverished.

The importance of Lincoln is that he saw this new world of unbelief—our world—coming. His life adumbrates the sea-change into modern culture, the banishment of what we now call religious superstition and the advent of a different kind of affliction—the collapse of any capacity to think or talk coherently about good and evil. Lincoln was the last public man in America, at least until Reinhold Niebuhr in the twentieth century, to address seriously, and without demagoguery or cynicism, the fear of living in a world of debilitating moral ambiguity.

THE CONTEST FOR THE PUBLIC MIND

When Thomas Jefferson died on 9 July 1826, Abraham Lincoln was a "friendless, penniless, uneducated boy working on a flatboat," several years away from achieving his first public office, the postmastership of

New Salem, Illinois.[1] By the late 1830s he had learned the trades of surveying and law, and had entered the state legislature as a Whig "internal improvements" man. His interests were growing beyond local affairs, and his conventional reverence for the founding fathers was unconventionally mixed with envy:

We, when mounting the stage of existence, found ourselves the legal inheritors of these fundamental blessings . . . of civil and religious liberty. . . . We toiled not in the acquirement or establishment of them—they are a legacy bequeathed us, by a *once* hardy, brave, and patriotic, but *now* lamented and departed race of ancestors. Their's [*sic*] was the task (and nobly they performed it) to possess themselves, and through themselves, us, of this goodly land; and to uprear upon its hills and its valleys, a political edifice of liberty and equal rights; 'tis ours only, to transmit these. . . . If they succeeded, they were to be immortalized; their names were to be transferred to counties and cities, and rivers and mountains; and to be revered and sung, and toasted through all time. . . . They succeeded. The experiment is successful; and thousands have won their deathless names in making it so. But the game is caught; and I believe it is true, that with the catching, end the pleasures of the chase.[2]

Lincoln spoke for his generation when he expressed this resentful awe. A thousand miles away in tradition-bound Massachusetts, Ralph Waldo Emerson, six years older, was voicing the same sentiment when he complained that there seemed to be no manly work left for his generation, that "our age . . . build[s] the sepulchers of the fathers."[3] Yet if Lincoln was expressing the political equivalent for his generation of what in the literary sphere has been called "the anxiety of influence," he was ahead of his counterparts in recognizing a more ominous feature of the bequest of the founding fathers.

Lincoln understood that he had inherited a defective nation, which had been patched and filled and cosmetically mended, but which, under stress, would break open again. It has been said by the cultural historian Lewis P. Simpson that for the founders "the supreme issue of the Revolution [had been] the efficacy of mind as the source and model of history, as opposed to a transcendent reference for order decreed by God." This is the bearing that gives to the founders their modernity. They seem

[1] Abraham Lincoln, *Speeches and Writings, 1832–1865*, 2 vols. (New York: Library of America, 1989), 1:106.
[2] Ibid., 28, 34.
[3] Ralph Waldo Emerson, "Nature" (1836) in *Selections from Ralph Waldo Emerson*, ed. Stephen E. Whicher (Boston: Houghton-Mifflin, 1957), 21.

closer to us than their Puritan predecessors—even those who lived into the eighteenth century—because they were beginning to apprehend "a world . . . which, being independent of any other worldly plan or scheme of meaning, has ceased to be a figura [*sic*] of anything extrinsic to itself and is sealed off against any transcendental ingress from without."[4] For them "the efficacy of mind" was not a doctrine as it is for us; it was, as Simpson says, an "issue," because the mind of the founders was divided against itself.

When Jefferson, whom Lincoln regarded as "the most distinguished politician in our history," looked into his own mind for a mirror of the republic, he saw (at least in his moments of honest self-reflection) something much like civil war. He struggled publicly with the irrefutable knowledge that the virtuous citizenry required of a republic could not be slaveowners. This knowledge was built into the very structure of Jefferson's Declaration of Independence, which argues a case that the American colonists themselves had been cruelly enslaved by a tyrannical king. Reading the Declaration, certain skeptical English readers were moved to ask, "How is it that we hear the loudest yelps for liberty from the drivers of Negroes?" Jefferson felt the force of this question.

In Jefferson's waning years his reasoning about slavery became more and more tortuous. The idea of an uncrossable geographical line between slave state and free, as established by the Missouri compromise of 1820, came to him "like a fire bell in the night," and stimulated him to offer the contorted warning that only the "diffusion [of the slaves] over a greater surface would make them individually happier, and proportionally facilitate the accomplishment of their emancipation, by dividing the burthen on a greater number of coadjutors." Jefferson was sure that "the hour of emancipation is advancing in the march of time. It will come . . . whether brought on by the generous energy of our own minds; or by the bloody process of St. Domingo." More and more doubting the former and bracing for the latter, he declared that "I tremble for my country when I reflect that god is just: [and] that his justice cannot sleep forever."[5]

Lincoln knew that Jefferson's personal civil war could not forever re-

---

[4]Lewis P. Simpson, *The Brazen Face of History: Studies in the Literary Consciousness in America* (Baton Rouge: Louisiana State University Press, 1980), xii, and Nathan A. Scott, Jr., *The Wild Prayer of Longing: Poetry and the Sacred* (New Haven: Yale University Press, 1971), 25.
[5]Thomas Jefferson, *Writings*, ed. Merrill Peterson (New York: Library of America, 1984), 289, 1345, 1734.

main an internal conflict within the American mind. This was because he understood the peculiar self-contradiction of American constitutionalism—that its government was based on a written prescription that could have no meaning apart from the successive acts of interpretation performed on it. Each generation of Americans was required to reinvent America, and Lincoln knew that his own generation was poised to do more than make refinements.

Towering genius . . . *scorns* to tread in the footsteps of *any* predecessor, however illustrious. It thirsts and burns for distinction; and, if possible, it will have it, whether at the expense of emancipating slaves, or enslaving freemen. Is it unreasonable then to expect, that some man possessed of the loftiest genius, coupled with ambition to push it to its utmost stretch, will, at some time, spring up among us?[6]

Although for mixed reasons of politics and principle Lincoln always dissociated himself from the radical abolitionists, this eerie prophecy was, as Edmund Wilson has remarked, Lincoln's prophecy of himself. His words (spoken in 1838 to a Lyceum audience at Springfield, Illinois) were a rehearsal for the great "House Divided" speech to be delivered twenty years later, in which he made more explicit his vision that the forces of emancipation and the forces of slavery were moving toward a collision. In later years he seemed, in retrospect, to have known that he himself would be the instrument of that catastrophe, even as he insisted that "I have no purpose, directly or indirectly, to interfere with the institution of slavery in the States where it exists."[7]

During the 1850s many of Lincoln's contemporaries—Whigs and Democrats alike—managed still to believe that such a confrontation between slave and free labor could be averted by the sheer abundance of land. Senator Lewis Cass of Michigan regarded westward expansion as the nation's "safety valve" through which the pent-up pressures of social conflict would be released. William H. Seward, first as senator from New York, then as secretary of state, harbored a pet scheme by which the secession of a few Southern states would be balanced by gaining from Britain some remaining territories in the North and West. Stephen Douglas, Lincoln's adversary in the debates of 1858, put forward a version of what might be called the western romance by treating slavery as a

[6]Lincoln, *Speeches and Writings*, 1:34–35.
[7]Lincoln made this statement frequently during his first campaign for the presidency, and quoted himself in his First Inaugural Address; see *Speeches and Writings*, 2:215.

minor distraction beside the real business of linking the coasts by freight-carrying railroads.

For Lincoln all these notions that the nation could be saved from confronting itself were delusion. It was as if a child were trying to outrun its shadow. Douglas's presumption that the physical climate of the contested Kansas and Nebraska territories would not suit slavery was nothing, Lincoln said, but "a palliation, a lullaby."[8] The problem of slavery expansion could not be tabled like a troublesome motion at a parliamentary meeting, or left, as Douglas would have it, to the morally indifferent processes of nature.

For one thing, the expansion of slavery was the desired object of a monstrous conspiracy that had begun with the Kansas-Nebraska Act, advanced with the election of James Buchanan, and culminated in the *Dred Scott* decision. After these events, all the talk about "popular sovereignty" was a sham. Any vote to exclude slavery from the territories would be judged, under *Dred Scott*, to be an unconstitutional violation of the property rights of slaveholders. President Buchanan had shown himself to be an enthusiastic enforcer of the will of the Supreme Court, and so the whole sordid business, Lincoln thought, was a plot to make slave property portable and secure. Under the sway of these precedents, slavery could never contract; like "a wen or cancer," it would only expand.[9]

Despite his metaphor of excisable disease, Lincoln would have preferred to let slavery die of its own accord rather than cutting it out. He always insisted, most emphatically in the address at the Cooper Institute that made him a truly national figure, that the founding fathers were not responsible for bringing slavery into the United States. They had, on the contrary, found it here, and had contrived every politically possible means to "place it where the public mind shall rest in the belief that it is in the course of ultimate extinction."[10] The question is not whether Lincoln's interpretation of history was reliable; the point is that his operative word was *belief*.

Lincoln was a pragmatist in the sense that he considered belief, not material interest, to be the heart of human affairs. In this way he was consistent with the founders, who were in many respects far advanced—though not so impressed as we are today by the novelty of our sophis-

[8]Ibid., 1:323.
[9]Ibid., 338.
[10]Ibid., 514.

tication—in recognizing the contingency of knowledge. Even at the high tide of Enlightenment, they were already expressing the modern sense of mind as an elusive consciousness, continually reshaping and reshaped, to which all phenomena must conform. Here is James Madison on the geography of the mind: "Sense, perception, judgment, desire, volition, memory, imagination are found to be separated by such delicate shades and minute gradations that their boundaries have eluded the most subtle investigations."[11] For Madison the representational process—whether political, literary, or linguistic—was a matter of continual adjustment of mind to the constructs of mind, between which no clear distinction could be drawn. Madison knew, as surely as we do, that the graphs and diagrams by which nature and mind are represented are merely inventions useful for keeping at bay a vertigo that ensues if one has no maps.

Lincoln inherited this attitude. He knew that belief encompasses reality and that, despite the rising prestige of science, there can be no firm division between knowledge and belief. Politics, to Lincoln, was a struggle for dominion over the world precisely because it was a contest for belief—for "the *attachment* of the people." If the people still believed in the ultimate extinction of slavery (as Lincoln insisted the slaveholder Jefferson had done), then the nation would not be in crisis. "I believe if we could arrest the spread, and place it where Washington, and Jefferson, and Madison placed it, it *would be* in the course of ultimate extinction, and the public mind *would*, as for eighty years past, believe that it was in the course of ultimate extinction. The crisis would be past." In fact the people were slipping into a state of unbelief, and Lincoln—like a revival preacher trying to save a man suspended by a filament over hell—stopped at nothing in his effort to reprieve them. He implied that the conspirators ("Stephen [Douglas], Franklin [Pierce], Roger [Taney], and James [Buchanan]") would not hesitate to revive the Atlantic slave trade: "For years, [Senator Douglas] has labored to prove it a sacred right of white men to take negro slaves into the new territories. Can he possibly show that it is *less* a sacred right to *buy* them where they can be bought cheapest? And unquestionably they can be bought *cheaper in Africa* than in *Virginia*." Lincoln pandered to fears of miscegenation ("The Judge regales us with the terrible enormities that take place by the mixture of races; that the inferior race bears the superior down. Why, Judge, if we do not let them get together in the

[11]James Madison, *Federalist* No. 37, 227.

Territories they won't mix there"); and he exploited the fears of malev-
olent conspiracy in high places. He played on the public's dread of a
new influx of Africans. He even implied that there was no reason that
slavery need be, in principle, restricted to Africans:

If A. can prove, however conclusively, that he may, of right, enslave B.—why
may not B. snatch the same argument, and prove equally, that he may enslave
A?—
   You say A. is white, and B. is black. It is *color*, then; the lighter, having the
right to enslave the darker? Take care. By this rule, you are to be slave to the
first man you meet, with a fairer skin than your own.
   You do not mean *color* exactly?—You mean the whites are *intellectually* the
superiors of the blacks, and, therefore have the right to enslave them? Take care
again. By this rule, you are to be slave to the first man you meet, with an intellect
superior to your own.
   But, say you, it is a question of *interest*; and, if you can make it your *interest*,
you have the right to enslave another. Very well. And if he can make it his
interest, he has the right to enslave you.

Lincoln was posing here, in the most intimate and frightening terms, a
question that Melville would ask more abstractly: "Who in the rainbow
can draw the line where the violet tint ends and the orange tint begins?"[12]

THE CORRUPTION OF LANGUAGE

The prose through which Lincoln built his constituency varies little between its private and public forms. Talking to himself in his notes, to
friends in his letters, or from the platform, he always insisted: "I am
not . . . capable of entering into a disquisition upon dialectics."[13] He presented himself on the stump in a way that is hard for us to recapture,
since the populist style in our time has been so degraded that most intellectuals refuse to think about it seriously. It has become merely vulgar,
in the debased sense of that word, although there is still the occasional
political figure in our time (Jimmy Carter, in his better moments, or Sam
Ervin, in his Big-Daddy seersucker suit) who comes self-consciously out
of this lineage. Its political style features the tall tale, as Lincoln loved
to tell and retell the story of the quality folks of Springfield who set the

[12]Lincoln, *Speeches and Writings*, 1:31, 514, 431, 433, 455, 303, and Herman Melville,
Billy Budd (1924), chap. 21.
[13]Lincoln, *Speeches and Writings*, 1:447.

wheels of justice in motion to convict three brothers of murder. No stone is left unturned in their search for the missing corpse:

Dr. Merryman found two hairs, which after a long scientific examination, he pronounced to be triangular human hairs, which term, he says includes within it, the whiskers, the hairs growing under the arms and on other parts of the body; and he judged that these two were of the whiskers, because the ends were cut, showing that they had flourished in the neighborhood of the razor's operations.[14]

This was Lincoln's version of the plain style, which he quite consciously offered as relief from the "bombastic parades" of Senator Douglas.[15] If it was a frequently comic style (the murder victim, whose hairs Dr. Merryman so proudly identified, turns up alive and well), this was because it expressed Lincoln's instinct that the rituals of genteel culture are, as a rule, absurd. It is important to recognize the centrality to the Lincoln legend of this sort of humor. Even the apocryphal stories, which constitute a large part of Lincoln's continuing mythic presence in American life, tend to represent him as the twinkling-eyed iconoclast, the bad boy (like Mark Twain's Huck and Tom) who exposes the triviality of most people's commitments. I remember as a child reading about how young Abe lifted a local boy upside down in the Lincoln house and had him stomp muddy footprints across the ceiling. Abe is, of course, all innocence when his mother gets home—and though he confesses to having violated the rules of household cleanliness, he shows himself in the end to be the best of all mothers' sons.

Reading Lincoln is a reminder that all humor is at bottom satiric—an attack on the pieties that constitute culture. The plain style was not only an instrument of laughter, however; it was also an expression of faith that beyond the decorative or critical uses of language are still higher uses. "A man's power," as Emerson put it, "to connect his thought with its proper symbol, and so to utter it, depends on the simplicity of his character, that is, upon his love of truth and his desire to communicate it without loss."[16] This was Emerson's way of decrying what Melville later called "citified" language—words that have become chiefly the means of self-display and instruments of hypocrisy. Lincoln agreed. He thought that Americans were increasingly unable to com-

---

[14]Ibid., 71. Lincoln came close to having to fight a duel with Merryman, who was incensed at the account of his gullibility.
[15]Ibid., 459.
[16]Emerson, "Nature," 33.

municate without loss their sense of the founding principles of the republic. He wrote and spoke in a tradition that originated with the Puritan revolt against High-Church homiletics, the tradition that declares (in a phrase from the Bay Psalm Book, 1640) that "God's altar needs not our pollishings."[17]

For Lincoln, God's altar was the Declaration of Independence. It was "the sheet anchor of the republic," and it was being "soiled and trailed in the dust" by the likes of Douglas. Its irreducible truth was what Melville called "our divine equality," which could be once again revealed if it were "wash[ed] white in the spirit, if not the blood, of the Revolution." Calling for this revelation in the language of Apocalypse, Lincoln conceded only a little to the racists: "Certainly the negro is not our equal in color—perhaps not in many other respects; still, in the right to put into his mouth the bread that his own hands have earned, he is the equal of every other man, white or black."[18] It was as simple as that.

The integrity of the self was the cornerstone of Lincoln's religion. As his greatest eulogist, Walt Whitman, put it,

after the rest is said . . . it remains to bring forward and modify everything else with the idea of that Something a man is . . . standing apart from all else, divine in his own right, and a woman in hers, sole and untouchable by any canons of authority, or any rule derived from precedent. . . . The radiation of this truth is the key of the most significant doings of our immediately preceding three centuries, and has been the political genesis and life of America.[19]

[17]Melville, *Billy Budd*, chap. 2.
[18]Ibid., 328, 339–40, 478, and Herman Melville, *Moby-Dick* (1851), chap. 26.
[19]Walt Whitman, "Democratic Vistas," in *Whitman: Complete Poetry and Selected Prose*, ed. James E. Miller (Boston: Houghton Mifflin, 1959), 464. This deification of the self sometimes serves to justify an insidious relativism, as when Emerson remarks in his journal that "Lidian grieves aloud about the wretched negro in the horrors of the middle passage; and they are bad enough. But to such as she, these crucifixions do not come. They come to the obtuse & barbarous to whom they are not horrid but only a little worse than the old sufferings. They exchange a cannibal war for a stinking hold. They have gratifications which would be none to Lidian" (Joel Porte, ed., *Emerson in His Journals* [Cambridge, Mass.: Harvard University Press, 1982], 169). The early Lincoln occasionally comes close to a similar solipsism, by which the reality of another's suffering can be evaded: "By the way, a fine example was presented on board the boat for contemplating the effect of condition upon human happiness. A gentleman had purchased twelve negroes in different parts of Kentucky and was taking them to a farm in the South. They were chained six and six together. A small iron clevis was around the left wrist of each, and this fastened to the main chain by a shorter one at a convenient distance from the others; so that the negroes were strung together precisely like so many fish upon a trot-line . . . yet amid all these distressing circumstances, as we would think them, they were the most cheerful and apparently happy creatures on board" (*Speeches and Writings*, 1:74).

This, for Lincoln, was the truth that language must not be allowed to obscure. Like the later pragmatists, he conflated transcendence with the self. To engage in misrepresentation, as Douglas was doing with his chant of "popular sovereignty," was to desecrate this truth. It was to blaspheme.

"Popular Sovereignty" is to be labelled upon the cars in which he travels; put upon the hacks he rides in; to be flaunted upon the arches he passes under, and the banners which wave over him. It is to be dished up in as many varieties as a French cook can produce soups from potatoes.[20]

In Lincoln's portrait of Douglas there is a touch of the ridiculous Old-World potentate—like Charlie Chaplin's version of Il Duce in *The Great Dictator*. The Senator's supporters "have seen in his round, jolly, fruitful face, post offices, land offices, marshalships, and cabinet appointments, chargeships and foreign missions, bursting and sprouting out in wonderful exuberance ready to be laid hold of by their greedy hands."[21] And what is the essence of this man beneath the posturing?

Does Judge Douglas, when he says that several of the past years of his life have been devoted to the question of "popular sovereignty," and that all the remainder of his life shall be devoted to it, does he mean to say that he has been devoting his life to securing to the people of the territories the right to exclude slavery from the territories? If he means so to say, he means to deceive; because he and every one knows that the decision of the Supreme Court, which he approves and makes especial ground of attack upon me for disapproving, forbids the people of a territory to exclude slavery. This covers the whole ground, from the settlement of a territory till it reaches the degree of maturity entitling it to form a State Constitution. So far as all that ground is concerned, the Judge is not sustaining popular sovereignty, but absolutely opposing it.[22]

We would nowadays call this passage an act of deconstructive criticism; it takes one of Douglas's signifiers, the term *popular sovereignty*, and shows that it refers to nothing outside itself. It exposes what we now call the self-referentiality of language. But Lincoln did not need such a vocabulary to make the point. "The corruption of man," Emerson had

[20]Lincoln, *Speeches and Writings*, 1:463.
[21]Ibid., 461.
[22]Ibid., 463–64. "Under the Dred Scott decision," Lincoln declared, " 'squatter sovereignty' squatted out of existence, tumbled down like temporary scaffolding—like the mould at the foundry served through one blast and fell back into loose sand—helped to carry an election, and then was kicked to the winds" (ibid., 429).

said twenty years before, "is followed by the corruption of language."[23]
Douglas was well advanced in both.

THE RENEWAL OF BELIEF

The reason that such a politician as Douglas could prosper, Lincoln
thought, was that the people were no longer capable of noticing when
words became instruments of deceit. Americans were suffering from a
collective memory loss; they would not recognize their own authentic
speech if they heard it. They had arrived at the place where amnesia and
aphasia meet—a silent place that was filled with the sound of Douglas,
droning.

This, I think, is why Lincoln sounds so often in his own speeches like
the tireless history teacher repeating the lesson. History had become
veiled and muted and arcane, so must be learned anew. The chain of
national memories was showing its vulnerability to time, and to be without memory was to be susceptible to alien fables.

I do not mean to say, that the scenes of the revolution *are now* or *ever will be*
entirely forgotten; but that like every thing else, they must fade upon the memory
of the world, and grow more and more dim by the lapse of time. . . . Those
scenes, in the form of a husband, a father, a son or a brother, a *living history
was* to be found in every family—a history bearing the indubitable testimonies
of its own authenticity, in the limbs mangled, in the scars of wounds received,
in the midst of the very scenes related—a history, too, that could be read and
understood alike by all, the wise and the ignorant, the learned and the unlearned.
But *those* histories are gone. They *can* be read no more forever. They *were* a
fortress of strength; but, what invading foemen could *never do*, the silent artillery
of time *has done*; the levelling of its walls. They are gone.[24]

This is the same analysis that led Emerson to remark (in the same year)
that "historical Christianity has fallen into the error that corrupts all
attempts to communicate religion," that "men have come to speak of
the revelation as somewhat long ago given and done, as if God were
dead." When Emerson mused that "if the stars should appear one night
in a thousand years, how would men believe and adore; and preserve
for many generations the remembrance of the city of God," he was

[23]Emerson, "Nature," 33.
[24]Lincoln, *Speeches and Writings*, 1:35–36.

driven by the same desire as Lincoln—that Americans should once again have the capacity for wonder.[25]

Another way to put this—to borrow a term made famous by Robert Bellah—is to say that Lincoln was determined to find a way to revive America's "civil religion."[26] Although Bellah derived his phrase directly from Rousseau, Lincoln himself had spoken in the Springfield Lyceum address of "political religion," by which he meant the equality principle of the founders. Twenty years before the debates with Douglas, he considered this principle already attenuated in the minds of a citizenry who had neither participated in nor been witness to the struggle by which it had been earned. He knew that the great political problem in the early republic had been to devise and maintain a symbolic system—flag, music, popular myths and fictions, regular political rituals, sacralization of the landscape through public monuments—on which the nation could subsist and flourish. These symbols, which were now largely in place, had to command the allegiance (or what Lincoln called "the attachment") of the people more powerfully than any competing symbol system, including Christianity itself.

By mid-century Christianity in America was a weakened competitor of the civil religion because of what was becoming an unbridgeable division within itself that ran along sectional lines. John Brown (whom Melville, invoking the old language of providential signs, called "the meteor of the war") crossed the Potomac with murderous vengeance on his mind and claimed that he was patterning his life on the martyrdom of Christ. At the same time, in the South, Christianity produced a "distended emphasis on sentiment, charity, and love utterly uncharacteristic of the society in which it was propounded."[27] If Christian slaveowners refrained from whipping their chattel, it was less out of charity than out of concern to maintain their resale price by keeping their bodies free of leather-cuts—the marks of recalcitrance. And so they paddled them instead. A few years before the Lincoln-Douglas debates, Harriet Beecher Stowe invented a Christian slaveowner named Augustine who went through the world wearing a Mephistophelian smile.

Yet civil religion was losing its battle for the "attachment of the peo-

---

[25]Ralph Waldo Emerson, "Divinity School Address," in Whicher, *Selections*, 106, and idem, "Nature," 23.
[26]Robert Bellah, "Civil Religion in America," in *Beyond Belief: Essays on Religion in a Post-traditional World* (New York: Harper, 1970), 168–89.
[27]Jon Butler, *Awash in a Sea of Faith: Christianizing the American People* (Cambridge, Mass.: Harvard University Press, 1990), 147.

ple"—not, perhaps, to Christianity, but to the centrifugal effects of greed—to the new religion of capitalism. The idea of the integral self was, to be sure, invoked by both sides of the slavery debate: Lincoln used it on behalf of "free white people" whose ownership of their own labor was threatened by slave competition; Douglas and Taney used it on behalf of slaveowners whose property rights were, they said, sacred. This internecine conflict left republican politics in the same attenuated state as organized Christianity. The American belief system was breaking apart because of its own internal stress. Lincoln's genius was to recognize this crisis and to draw for its resolution on the people's residual belief in the sacredness of the self.

Any such statement about the relation between the judgments of leaders and the convictions of ordinary people requires us to acknowledge that one of the most difficult projects of the historical imagination is to inquire into the popular mind. Here one must speak provisionally. There are, however, tantalizing hints that may, eventually, be assembled into a convincing picture of Lincoln's age. Lawrence Levine has recently made the interesting remark that the Oedipus plays failed to hold the stage in nineteenth-century America because "Sophocles seemed guilty of determinism—an ideological stance nineteenth-century Americans rejected out of hand."[28] In this context—the repugnance of the determinist worldview for ordinary Americans—it is not surprising to find diaries of Civil War veterans suggesting that "nothing to me would appear more degrading . . . than to be dragged into the army as a conscript." The voluntarism of the act makes the difference between a coward and a man.[29]

Free-soil politics, then, was not merely a politics of fear. The very idea of slavery was a violation of what may be called the republican theodicy.

---

[28]Lawrence Levine, *Highbrow/Lowbrow: The Emergence of Cultural Hierarchy in America* (Cambridge, Mass.: Harvard University Press, 1988), 41.

[29]Bell Irvin Wiley, *The Life of Billy Yank: The Common Soldier of the Union* (Baton Rouge: Louisiana State University Press, 1952), 38. The illusory nature of this distinction is, of course, the theme of the best-known novel of the Civil War, Stephen Crane's *The Red Badge of Courage* (1895). Another way to sense the internal strain within antebellum culture is to pay attention to popular literary forms such as drama. In the years of Lincoln's youth, for example, a favorite theatrical experience for many Americans was the Indian play—popular dramatic spectacles performed by traveling acting troupes who played out the bloody conflict between British and Indians, inviting their audiences into the delicious paradox of split allegiance. Stage Indians were, after all, the virtuous victims of British rapacity, and could be cheered for their stoic resistance to the imperialists. But even as the audience applauded their pluck, it was also applauding their doom. Lincoln himself had served as a militia captain in the Black Hawk Indian War.

Degradation and social failure had to be understood in antebellum America—even before Protestant self-reliance combined with greed to create the frantic atmosphere of the Gilded Age—as self-wrought punishments. If you were at the bottom of the ladder, you had gotten yourself there. Slavery, as an inherited and racially determined condition, was at odds with that principle. Despite widespread racism in the free states as well as in the South, there was a deep antipathy to slavery in the very constitution of the American self. It sprang from the same sources as did antimonarchism. For "middling" whites, it was the same emotion—aimed downward rather than upward—as the hatred of a social order based on primogeniture or any other form of advantageous inheritance. Whether it transmitted wealth or servitude, inherited status was un-American.

Lincoln's shrewdness was to tap these dormant beliefs for use as political resources. In doing so, he performed what Emerson deemed the poet's work: "Man . . . watches for the arrival of a brother who can hold him steady to a truth until he has made it his own." Lincoln crystallized inchoate truths within the popular mind into an ideology—the free-soil politics of the Republican Party. Yet he had limited success; he was a minority president, and his real triumph in revitalizing the civil religion may be said to have awaited his death. He seems, moreover, to have known this. Consider the many intimations by his friends and colleagues that he anticipated his own death, and even welcomed it. He seemed reluctantly to know that a new holy war would be required to restore what he regarded as the faith once delivered to the saints. Like Emerson, Lincoln recognized that the gospel was being recited, if at all, by rote. "The idioms of his language," said Emerson of Christ, "and the figures of his rhetoric have usurped the place of the truth; and churches are not built on his principles, but on his tropes."[30] Substitute Jefferson or Clay for Christ and we have a Lincolnian sentiment.

One reason that Lincoln has remained such a dominant figure in the American heroic procession is that subsequent generations, including our own, only suffer more intensely from the affliction which Lincoln identified among his contemporaries: a sense of estrangement from the founding American experience. The last living witnesses to the Revolution were disappearing by the outset of the Civil War, and as Lewis Simpson has recently remarked, "the living chain of connection with the

[30]Emerson, "The Poet," 226; "Divinity School Address," 105.

Civil War era is [now] dissolving as the last generation to know living voices from that time grows old." Though we have seen in our own time plenty of organized carnage, only the great war against fascism has injected into the culture its own enduring myths and symbols. Even that war is now subject to ferocious demystification (notably in a recent book by Paul Fussell that narrates it as a sequence of senseless butcheries).[31] At the same time, we are witnessing the reorganization of Europe under the direction of people who are, for the most part, free of any personal memory of World War II. Lincoln's sense of time as the solvent of cultural memory is not arcane to us.

Lincoln believed that a culture, like a person, has only a limited amount of negative capability. If he was lonely among politicians in making this judgment, he had company among the nation's intellectuals. He was no less than the incarnation of what Melville imagined in *Moby-Dick* (1857): an "ungodly godlike man" who acknowledged of himself that the "path to my fixed purpose is laid with iron rails, whereon my soul is grooved to run." Death-obsessed, gaunt, sleepless, like Melville's Captain Ahab, he was "always wakeful"—pacing all night and emerging hollow-eyed but unswerving in the morning. He, like Ahab, had his "bigotry of purpose." If Ahab had an auger hole bored into the deck wherein he could pivot on his wooden leg and survey his crew, and weld their will to his own, Lincoln suspended habeas corpus and jailed his political opponents if he sniffed appeasement of the rebellion in their speeches. If Ahab declares that "the white whale . . . tasks me; heaps me; I see in him outrageous strength, with an inscrutable malice sinewing it. That inscrutable thing is chiefly what I hate; and . . . I will wreak that hate upon him,"[32] for Lincoln there was an equivalent object of hate:

This declared indifference [on the part of Senator Douglas], but, as I must think, covert real zeal, for the spread of slavery, I cannot but hate. I hate it because of the monstrous injustice of slavery itself. I hate it because it deprives our republican example of its just influence in the world; enables the enemies of free institutions with plausibility to taunt us as hypocrites; causes the real friends of freedom to doubt our sincerity; and especially because it forces so many good men among ourselves into an open war with the very fundamental principles of

[31]Lewis P. Simpson, paper delivered at the Modern Library Association convention, Washington, D.C., December 1985, and Paul Fussell, *Wartime: Understanding and Behavior during the Second World War* (New York: Oxford University Press, 1989).
[32]Melville, *Moby-Dick*, chaps. 16, 37, 29, 36.

civil liberty, criticizing the Declaration of Independence, and insisting that there is no right principle of action but self-interest.[33]

Finally, Lincoln knew, as Ahab did, that "to accomplish his object [he] must use tools; and of all tools used in the shadow of the moon, men are most apt to get out of order."[34] There was something in Lincoln not only reminiscent of Ahab's monomania, but even prophetic of Aleksandr Solzhenitsyn's Stalin—the obsessed man who, walled inside his besieged capital, will save his country at any cost. To save it meant to arrest its descent into a world where it seemed impossible to imagine anything worth dying for.

LINCOLN'S CONCEPTION OF EVIL

The secret of Lincoln's power was his recognition that his people were starved for belief. He understood that the companion of belief is a capacity to recognize the reality of evil. If the essence of religious faith is the idea of transcendence, it is a concept that contains within itself—as in its two Latin elements (*trans*, beyond or over, and *scandere*, to climb or to scale)—the idea of its opposite: limitation, boundedness, the thing to be transcended. As John Wesley is said to have remarked, "No devil, no God." The one idea cannot fully exist without the other; each requires its opposite to be intelligible. In most formulations, especially when put to political use, the distinction between the two halves of the meaning of transcendence is clear. In the speech of most politicians there is no interchange between the sacred and the profane, no ambiguity of border between the virtuous and the damned. Especially in wartime, how many leaders (even those we call statesmen) speak generously of their enemies?

Lincoln certainly used the nationalist sentiment for political advantage. "Surely, if our evil passions must find vent," Melville had written when the sectional crisis was building, "it is far better to expend them on strangers and aliens, than in the bosom of the community in which we dwell."[35] Lincoln knew this. Despite his high rhetoric of Union and Manifest Destiny, however, he seemed also to know that when transcendence becomes a political ideology, it invests a culture with a defi-

---

[33]Lincoln, *Speeches and Writings*, 1:315.
[34]Melville, *Moby-Dick*, chap. 46.
[35]Herman Melville, *Typee* (1846), chap. 27.

nition of itself that is based more and more on some form of exclusionary classification—on xenophobia, on racism, ultimately on hate. This he refused.

Some historians have credited (or blamed) him for the emergence of American nationalism, which aimed the exclusionary impulse mainly outward, thus protecting the culture against internal disintegration. But Lincoln had an integrative rather than a classifying mind. He was obsessed with the idea of Union, but his vision of Union was like Whitman's catalogues of human variety—without beginning or end, and certainly without the possibility of ever being fully realized in worldly form. In his style and in his political commitments Lincoln celebrated the democratic chaos of individual truths that constitute a free society. In this sense, too, he was a pragmatist.

He was, in other words, that rare politician who resists the inclination of the collective mind to condemn the world outside itself. He thought the Union should have room within it for the starkest oppositions, including the apparently incompatible races of black and white. In their fruitful conflict they would work out something like truth—not an end point, but a process.

One problem with contemplating Lincoln in our time is the difficulty of reconciling this capacious quality of mind with his drive to extend the dominion of his controlling idea. To do this, we have to consider what we might call Lincoln's implicit metaphysics, which brings us to the most remarkable feature of his imagination. Lincoln's conception of evil was, I think, entirely privative. Free of the Manichaean vision, he had no devils. He had only a kind of *horror vacui*, a revulsion at the absence of the good—good being, to his mind, Union. Unlike William Seward, unlike the old cotton Whig Edward Everett, who ran against Lincoln and then shared the platform with him at Gettysburg (where Everett excoriated the Satanic enemy before Lincoln spoke quietly about consecrated ground), unlike Salmon P. Chase and the ferocious Charles Sumner—Lincoln was capable of inhabiting the mind of the Southerner. And from within that mind he understood that freedom and slavery were not only incompatible in two halves of the nation, but were finally incompatible for those who tried to will them into partnership in the South. He said to the nation (never restricting his remarks to any particular region) what Hinton Rowen Helper had been saying to Southern whites who did not own slaves: that slavery was a threat to all free labor, to all free people. Lincoln had not forgotten that Jefferson and Madison and Washington were Virginians.

His breadth of mind is clearest in the Gettysburg Address, in which no enemy is ever mentioned. The speech builds on the word *dedicate*, which is used in varying form four times, and rises to a greater and greater sense of bound humility and transcendent possibility. The verbs with which Lincoln frames the main body of his message, "endure" and "perish," are intransitive. They depend on no resistant object for their meaning. The force of the whole is not to inspire or maintain enmity, but to foster a new measure of positive devotion to the principle invoked by the opening invocation of Genesis—the equality principle of the Declaration. This is a universalist vision, and one that posits no Satan. It is Augustinian in the sense that the only evil it understands—with a singleness of purpose that is both appalling and sublime—is the evil of incompleteness.

With the Gettysburg Address in mind, we may find it almost poignant that Lincoln was amazed at "the theory of the general government being only an agency, whose principals are the States." This idea, he wrote to Everett (who had attacked it at length in his own speech at the battlefield), "was new to me." What Lincoln is confessing here is a constitutional blindness to the basic secessionist argument "that the States have retained their separate existence as independent and sovereign communities in all the forms of political existence through which they have passed," an argument John C. Calhoun, among others, had put forward years before.[36] Lincoln, in effect, refused to face the fact that to some Americans the United States no longer existed. He could not countenance the idea that the nation had been signed into being as if by an abrogable treaty.

To have entered into dialogue with persons of such an opinion would, for Lincoln, have been tantamount to surrendering to a kind of nihilism. It would have been to permit a merely functional, utilitarian concept of the state and to conceive of it as merely an instrument for ancillary purposes. Such a conception of the Union had a beginning and could have an imaginable end—as it did in the mind of Seward and others who entertained without horror the idea of a new nation without the South.

[36]John C. Calhoun, "Disquisition on Government and a Discourse on the Constitution and Government of the United States," in *The Works of John C. Calhoun*, ed. Richard Cralle (1855), 1:117.

Something like this account of Lincoln's religion has been given be-fore—by commentators ever since Alexander Stephens, vice president of the Confederacy, said that for Lincoln the Union had risen to the sub-limity of religious mysticism. For Edmund Wilson, Lincoln's political religion marked the beginning of a kind of statist mania, about which Wilson grumbled all his life as it evolved into the meddlesome New Deal, and which he associated with the carnivorous nationalisms of the twen-tieth century. There is, too, an undeniable force in Richard Hofstadter's tragic view of Lincoln as the man who unwittingly prepared the way for the Gilded Age—its gluttony for land, for cheap and disposable labor, for foreign conquest.

While respecting the tough-mindedness of such views, I have tried to put a different emphasis on Lincoln's fervor. If Lincoln appropriated the language of religious passion to achieve his political ends, he did so, I think, because he found insufficient, for conceptual as well as rhetorical purposes, the Enlightenment traditions that had descended to him. He spoke advisedly of "the mystic chords of memory" because he recog-nized the limits of rationalist discourse for animating human beings.

A way to test this proposition is to try to make a composite portrait of Lincoln by pulling together the Enlightenment elements of American political history that were available to him. He spoke the natural-rights vocabulary of the founders. He invoked the old idea of self-disciplined republican virtue when he appealed to "the feelings of the best citizens." In his attacks on the "piece of machinery" that Douglas, Buchanan, and Taney fashioned out of Kansas-Nebraska and *Dred Scott*, Lincoln en-gaged in what Richard Hofstadter called "the paranoid style" of Amer-ican politics—a style that has since been traced back to the British Commonwealthmen of the seventeenth century. In his insistence that it is "the abundance of man's heart, that slavery extension is wrong; and [that] out of the abundance of his heart, his mouth will continue to speak," Lincoln showed himself to be committed to the idea of a "moral sense" (a phrase he liked)—which American moralists derived from the Scottish Common Sense school of Francis Hutcheson. Lincoln can, in other words, be seen as a vessel into which all the major streams of American political tradition flow.[37]

[37]Lincoln, *Speeches and Writings*, 1:334; Gordon S. Wood, *The Creation of the American Republic, 1776–1787* (New York: Norton, 1972); J. G. A. Pocock, *The Machiavellian Moment: Florentine Political Thought and the Atlantic Republican Tradition* (Princeton: Princeton University Press, 1975); Richard Hofstadter, *The Paranoid Style in American*

Yet something is missing from this composite portrait. What is absent is Lincoln's essence: his faith. He was not religious in any conventional sense; he had even been harassed in one of his early campaigns by a Methodist circuit-rider who posted handbills accusing him of infidelity.[38] Never a churchgoer, he was not given to uttering pious platitudes of the sort that we expect from politicians. Yet he restored a religious fervor to the Enlightenment traditions that he had inherited—traditions that converged in the concept of the autonomous self—and renewed them as a living force in American politics. "I look for the new Teacher," Emerson wrote in the same year that Lincoln announced his arrival on the national political scene, "that shall follow so far those shining laws; that he shall see them come full circle; shall see their rounding complete grace; shall see the world to be the mirror of the soul."[39]

Lincoln regarded his life as a mission to achieve this unity of world and soul. Like religious prophets before him, he believed in the possibility of obliterating the expanse of history that separated the fallen present from the holy moment at which the gospel had first been delivered. This, I think, is why the Gettysburg Address is written in a kind of perpetual present tense. "Four score and seven years ago" the world began, and all time before and since has been eclipsed. Near the end of his life, in the great Second Inaugural Address, Lincoln spoke in biblical accents again:

It may seem strange that any men should dare to ask a just God's assistance in wringing their bread from the sweat of other men's faces; but let us judge not that we be not judged. The prayers of both could not be answered; that of neither has been answered fully. The Almighty has His own purposes. "Woe unto the world because of offences! for it must needs be that offences cometh!" If we shall suppose that American Slavery is one of those offences which, in the providence of God, must needs come, but which, having continued through His appointed time, He now wills to remove, and that He gives to both North and South, this terrible war, as the woe due to those by whom the offence came, shall we discern therein any departure from those divine attributes which the

---

Politics and Other Essays (New York: Knopf, 1958); Bernard Bailyn, *The Ideological Origins of the American Revolution* (Cambridge, Mass.: Harvard University Press, 1967); and Garry Wills, *Inventing America* (New York: Vintage, 1978).

[38] For Lincoln's reply to the charges, see *Speeches and Writings*, 1:139. "My wife has some relatives in the Presbyterian and some in the Episcopal Churches," Lincoln wrote in 1843, "and therefore, whereever [sic] it would tell, I was set down as either the one or the other, whilst it was every where contended that no christian ought to go for me, because I belonged to no church, was suspected of being a deist, and had talked about fighting a duel" (idem, 107).

[39] Emerson, "Divinity School Address," 115–16.

believers in a Living God always ascribe to Him? Fondly do we hope—fervently do we pray—that this mighty scourge of war may speedily pass away. Yet, if God wills that it continue, until all the wealth piled by the bond-man's two hundred and fifty years of unrequited toil shall be sunk, and until every drop of blood drawn with the lash, shall be paid by another drawn with the sword, as was said three thousand years ago, so still it must be said "the judgements of the Lord, are true and righteous altogether."[40]

These sentences are an uncanny reprise of Jefferson's warning that God's justice will not sleep forever.

For Lincoln the suspension of the divine spirit in human affairs, which would sooner or later be lifted, expressed itself as the intolerable inhibition of the self. Again, he spoke in unison with Emerson: "The only sin is limitation."[41] In this sense he brought to a climax both Enlightenment and romantic individualism—a tradition whose reputation has lately fallen on bad times and is now more often blamed for the cruelties of the free market, the prestige of technology, and the exploitation of nature than it is credited with the liberation of the self. (The postmodernist vocabulary has, in fact, more or less relinquished the word "self" as an intelligible term and substituted the word "subject," with its implications, both grammatical and political, of passivity and dependence.) As writers like Hofstadter and Wilson lamented thirty and forty years ago, Lincoln, in obliterating the slave power, released the pent-up energies of what would become the capitalist giant of the modern world. But he also bequeathed to us something of inestimable value in his recognition that no one could be free in a society where anyone was enslaved. By completing Jefferson's thought, he healed the American mind, and at the end of his life he made a start toward closing the rift that had opened in American society largely as a result of his actions. It would seem that the first step—emancipation—was not the hardest.

William James (in a phrase that finely registers his sense that reality exists somewhere between subjectivity and the objective world) said that great people are those "individuals whose genius was . . . adapted to the receptivities of the moment [and who] became ferments, initiators of movement . . . or destroyers of other persons, whose gifts, had they had free play, would have led society in another direction."[42] Lincoln was such a man. And so he remains long after his death, because in one

[40]Lincoln, "Second Inaugural Address," in *Speeches and Writings*, 2:687.
[41]Emerson, "Circles" (1840), 169.
[42]William James, "Great Men and Their Environment," in *The Will to Believe and Other Essays in Popular Philosophy and Human Immortality* (New York: Dover, 1960), 227.

important respect his "moment" cannot be said to have passed. He identified for his time and ours the most difficult challenge in American history—a history unique in the West because it came to self-consciousness in the age of Enlightenment. What Lincoln faced, and faced up to, was the challenge of retaining a sense of evil in a posttheistic world—and doing so without resorting to demons.

9

Stuck between debility and demand:
Religion and Enlightenment traditions
among the pragmatists

HENRY SAMUEL LEVINSON

THE ORIGINATING PRAGMATISTS
AS POST-ENLIGHTENMENT THINKERS

My aim in this essay is to give rough characterizations of the originating
pragmatists, of the Enlightenment movements that provided a broad
context for the emergence of their views, and of some steps the pragmatists took to distance themselves from certain excesses and mistakes
they judged the Enlightenment to have suffered or made, especially the
transcendental turn Kant gave to Enlightenment philosophy, a turn that
eventually provoked pragmatist rejection and revolt in the late nineteenth century.[1] My eventual aim will be to show a diversity of ways in
which contending and contentious pragmatists upheld certain Enlightenment traditions and abandoned others in their efforts to reflect on
circumstances allowing humanity to flourish in the bright, sometimes
blinding, light of inevitable human finitude.

If we focus on the decade when pragmatism was in the making—the
years, say, between James's Berkeley address entitled "Philosophical
Conceptions and Practical Results" in 1898 and Horace Kallen's "Pragmatism and Its Principles" in 1911—we find three philosophers originating the movement: William James, George Santayana, and John
Dewey. Despite telling differences among their views from the start,
James, Santayana, and Dewey seemed to circle their philosophical wag-
ons around a cluster of five basic positions. They pictured knowledge as

[1]Thanks are due to Derek Krueger, Charlie Orzech, Ben Ramsey, and Mary Wakeman for
various helpful criticisms of this chapter.

nonfoundational inquiry; reason as nontranscendent and nontranscendental criticism; every sort of thought or language as expressive, poetic, or imaginative; every part of existence—paradigmatically personal life— as contingent or historical; and philosophy itself as reflection on problems of human finitude rather than as a search for first principles or for the really real.[2]

Did these originating pragmatists maintain or dismantle Enlightenment traditions? Surely it is barely imaginable to find a philosophical niche for all of these five starting points, at least altogether, prior to the Enlightenment. This is the case no matter how we slice the celebrations of natural human capacity that emerged politically, socially, technologically, and intellectually in the eighteenth century, along with the birth pangs of the modern North Atlantic republics.[3] In order to get pragmatism off the ground, among other things we need to recognize the achievements of such Enlightenment figures as John Locke, David Hume, Thomas Reid, and Immanuel Kant. We need to have acknowledged, that is, the sorts of liberal psyches that thinkers like these modeled—whereby selves *own* or *have* webs of belief—in order to make way for James's

[2]This characterization of the originating pragmatists adds Santayana to the typical portrait given by historians of philosophy in the United States, and drops, or at least evades, C. S. Peirce and the more doubtable Josiah Royce. I quote Santayana more liberally than the others in an effort to show why I think he should be brought into the fold, rehearsing here the extended argument that I give in *Santayana, Pragmatism and the Spiritual Life* (Chapel Hill: University of North Carolina Press, 1992). James, of course, would claim the paternity of C. S. Peirce on behalf of pragmatism from day one, even though the older polymath's project was fundamentally architectonic and transcendental, and even when the mentor continuously blushed in embarrassment and upbraided the student for all his category mistakes and "psychologisms" as a result of failing to capture what Peirce took to be the centrality of mathematics and symbolic logic to philosophy. I acknowledge Peirce's efforts to distance himself from pragmatism, and see him as (what he once called himself) an ingenious "triadomaniac." For my rough-and-ready view of Peirce, see "Religious Philosophy," in *The Encyclopedia of the American Religious Experience*, ed. Charles H. Lippy and Peter W. Williams, 3 vols. (New York: Scribner, 1988), 2:1189–206. In my view, Josiah Royce was desperately trying to change most of the subject when he called his own architectonic, transcendental, and foundationalist philosophy "Absolute Pragmatism" on the grounds that he, along with Peirce and James, construed beliefs as plans of action. For my sketch of Royce, see "Josiah Royce," in *A Companion to American Thought*, ed. Richard Wightman Fox and James Kloppenberg (Cambridge, Mass.: Basil Blackwell, forthcoming). Of course there are significant, perhaps decisive, lessons the originating pragmatists learned from Peirce about why and how to counter representationalism; there are certain resemblances between Roycean idealism and the pragmatisms I characterize here; and there are certainly parallels between Royce and Peirce that could stand a good deal more investigation.

[3]I find Henry F. May's fourfold characterization of kinds of Enlightenment—moderate, skeptical, revolutionary, and didactic—as persuasive as any. It certainly allows us to see both the similarities and dissimilarities among, say, James, Hume, Paine, and Stewart. See May, *The Enlightenment in America* (New York: Oxford University Press, 1976).

liberal, democratic psyche, whereby selves *are* webs of belief. We need to have recognized the privileges of the natural sciences along with the profundities of human sentiment, cracking the constraints of sacred revelation. We need to have linked up history not just with memory, witness, and testimony, but with theories and techniques by which to transform these things into material evidence. We need to be able to place any claim in jeopardy, no intellectual holds barred. We need to have developed moral fiber out of the intertwined strands of human autonomy, personal assertion, political rights, and social obligations. Last but not least, we need to have identified ourselves as responsive and responsible citizens actively supporting liberal republican or democratic republican institutions.[4]

If we want to understand pragmatism, in other words, there is no going back to medieval (or even Renaissance or dogmatic Reformation) conceptions of soul, or to ecclesiastical or royal censorship of science or poetry on behalf of Holy Writ or church doctrine, or to the just-so providential histories of court mentors, or to the patronizing pieties of pastors eager to guard their unwary flocks from their own curiosity, or to authoritarian ethics, or to the illiberal sorts of society that let such notions and institutions flourish.

But just as surely, it is hardly appropriate to see the originating pragmatists as leftover eighteenth-century Enlightenment figures. The pragmatists tried to prune back excesses, uncover blind spots, and block paths leading to cul-de-sacs on the philosophical trails blazed by their various Enlightenment forefathers. The originating pragmatists are already four steps removed from various shadows cast by the Enlightenment or (sometimes distorted) memories of it. First, their acceptance of Hegel's assault on Enlightenment foundationalisms, along with his attack on Kant's appearance-reality distinction, puts them one step beyond the eighteenth-century Age of Reason. Second, their participation in romantic, especially Emersonian, raids on Enlightenment scientisms removes them another pace. Third, their consent to Darwin's disrobing of essentialisms and concomitant metaphysical-biological teleologies often maintained in the Enlightenment sets them three large steps away. Fourth, finally, and just as decisively, the pragmatists are separated from

---

[4]Those institutions include, for example, freedom of conscience, freedom of speech, free universities, a free press, free and fair markets, the social and political tolerance of diverse reasonable conceptions of the good and consequently reasonable voluntary associations, and the political rule of common or constitutional law.

somewhat misleading memories of the Enlightenment, if not by its best minds—memories linked to recollections of the Reign of Terror and, probably, their own recent Civil War—by their own perduring Reformed Protestant suspicions about human hubris. They distrust Enlightenment tendencies to endorse Promethean visions of human self-sufficiency and the consequent capacity of humankind to do what Westerners previously thought only God could accomplish: redeem a radically fallen world by graciously inspiring moral regeneration and assuring true cosmic balance or harmony, thus creating a new heaven and a new earth.

Certainly, that last Reformed Protestant misgiving focused on pride had not been entirely lost on Enlightenment thinkers. Most of them, in fact, had continued to assume that being Protestant and enlightened could constitute two sides of the same thoughtful character. Yet just as unquestionably, combining the enthusiastic celebration of natural human capacity with Protestant dismay about inalienable human sin had suggested hobgoblins of inconsistency overwhelming enough to haunt even—perhaps especially—the largest minds. Throughout the Age of Enlightenment, the failure to comprehend personal turns from evil to good, and then again a perceived dissonance between doing well and being well, plagued headier Enlightenment promissory notes about humanity's ability to achieve the highest good on its own terms and under its own steam.[5]

Whether the pragmatists continued or discontinued Enlightenment traditions in regard to this last set of spiritual issues is a judgment call that depends on the particular figures we investigate. We surely find the pragmatists preoccupied with many of the same moral or spiritual disparities and discrepancies that boxed-in visions of the best and the

---

[5]Even in Revolutionary America and France—perhaps with Jefferson the greatest of the exceptions—it turns out that few eminent intellectuals found satisfactory ways to embrace wholeheartedly the view that the True and the Good and the Beautiful could be reached through the sole use of faculties and the practice of methods at work in the natural sciences (the textbook caricature of Enlightenment ideology). Thus I find Giles Gunn's characterization of "the key to the difference between Protestant Christianity and the Enlightenment" both telling and somewhat misplaced. Gunn sees the issue as "the question of whether relief of the human estate is dependent on powers that originate in, and derive their authority from, realms of experience beyond the boundaries of its own agencies and capacities or, rather, from realms of experience within them." As I see things, especially in the American colonies and through the national period, this is a question that particularly pestered self-described Enlightenment Protestant Christians, a problem that certain Protestants had with themselves rather than with critics situated definitively outside the faith. See Giles Gunn's essay in this volume, Chapter 2.

brightest of their eighteenth-century foreparents. What can be suggested is that the pragmatists tried to make better headway on comprehending these problems of human finitude by snipping the scientistic, representationalist, foundationalist, essentialist, and existentialist growths that they pictured eating away at Enlightenment gains from the inside out.

THE ORIGINATING PRAGMATISTS
AS KANT'S PATRICIDAL CHILDREN

Kant is the crucial case in point, not only for honing in on this historically inescapable aspect of the Enlightenment, but also for coming to grips with the problems and promises exhibited by its pragmatic grandchildren in American philosophy. Kant, we now understand, exhibited the pathos of the Enlightenment by essentially admitting that his own critical philosophy could account neither for the "radical evil" that he thought cursed humankind, nor for the moral regeneration he claimed was somehow humanly possible (if only with divine aid), nor for the summum bonum to which he pinned his religious aspirations. At crucial points, Gordon E. Michalson has shown us, Kant folded his transcendental cards and tried to check opponents by relying on the traditional Christian language of "original sin," "rebirth," and "new creation" to account for human debility and the promise of moral and spiritual transformation.[6]

Recognizing this move by Kant not only muddles more usual portraits of him as the champion par excellence of unbridled autonomous reason (the kind presumably deployed quite apart from traditional sources of authority) but also complicates the current standard understanding of his impact on the pragmatists. It flusters a prevailing caricature of Kant as relying on "reason alone," by showing his willingness (indeed self-described need) to employ the testimony of the most traditional sources of moral and spiritual authority in Christendom in order to account for the human predicament and prospect.

Michalson's revisionary work on Kant also reveals lines of thought positively *linking* Kant's religious philosophy to the pragmatists who were largely responsible for dismantling his big transcendental machine. James (in, for example, *The Varieties of Religious Experience* and *Pluralistic Universe*), Santayana (in, for example, *The Life of Reason* and

---

[6]Gordon E. Michalson, *Fallen Freedom: Kant on Radical Evil and Moral Regeneration* (Cambridge: Cambridge University Press, 1990).

Realms of Being), and Dewey (in, for example, *A Common Faith* and *Art as Experience*) took up the same double concern for moral regeneration and the slip between moral perfection and spiritual salvation that Kant had pursued in *Religion within the Limits of Reason Alone*. Like him, they did so in ways that presumed some variant of the liberal psyche, gave science and sentiment their due, linked historical claims to evidence, made criticism open-ended, construed morality in terms of a dynamic relation between autonomy and obligation, and embraced the security of liberal institutions.

Even more particularly, like Kant, the pragmatists remained preoccupied with the ways that the freedom of liberal psyches could enslave itself morally and spiritually; and they identified the character of human well-being in basically aesthetic terms. For Kant as for the pragmatists, it was one (morally necessary) thing to obey the moral law and another (ultimately aesthetic) thing to experience the grace of divinity. For both Kant and the pragmatists, beauty was to duty as grace was to law.[7]

Realizing all this may appear, at least partially, to confirm the widely held view that Murray Murphey, and then his student Bruce Kuklick, have been arguing for the past twenty-five years: that the Cambridge pragmatists (and I believe we could add Dewey to the list in light of Kuklick's *Churchmen and Philosophers*) were "Kant's children." The picture is far more complicated, however, than the Murphey-Kuklick narratives suggest. Murphey and Kuklick have argued that the pragmatists took up a broadly Kantian project, and so an Enlightenment tradition, in that they all tried "to construct an epistemology adequate for both science and religion and one which would insure the active constructive role of the mind while yet affording a solid basis for empirical knowledge."[8]

So far, so good? Not really. The trouble with the Murphey-Kuklick

---

[7]I have shown elsewhere (e.g., in *Santayana*) that other Protestant Enlightenment figures, for example, Jonathan Edwards, also expressed variants of the aesthetic spirituality exhibited by Kant. We have many good reasons to claim that the pragmatists actually inherited aesthetic spirituality through the generation of natural supernaturalists for which Emerson is eponymous. On the other hand, there is little evidence one way or the other that they read or were influenced directly by Kant's *Religion within the Limits of Reason Alone*. My argument in this chapter does not demand this direct link.

[8]Murray Murphey, "Kant's Children: The Cambridge Pragmatists," *Transactions of the C. S. Peirce Society* 4 (1968): 3–33. See also Bruce Kuklick, *The Rise of American Philosophy* (New Haven: Yale University Press, 1977), and idem, *Churchmen and Philosophers: From Jonathan Edwards to John Dewey* (New Haven: Yale University Press, 1985). See my review of *Churchmen*, which criticizes what I call Murphey's school of thought, in "Fathers and Sons," *Religious Studies Review*, April 1987, pp. 114-17.

view is that it claims too little and too much. It claims too little because the pragmatists also—and more particularly—tried to give something like Kant's "autonomous freedom" its due while yet implicating it, in much the same manner that Kant had, in humankind's most vexing moral weaknesses. Moreover, as Kant had, the pragmatists characterized perfect well-being in ways that relied on a "nonmoral element" which, again like Kant (and other Enlightenment figures such as Jonathan Edwards), turns out specifically to be aesthetic.

The Murphey-Kuklick view of the pragmatists as Kant's children claims too much because once James, Santayana, and Dewey reject the transcendental turn with which Kant is eponymous, terms like *epistemology, science, religion,* and *empirical knowledge* fail to mean anything like what Kant had in mind when using them. If James, Santayana, and Dewey were Kant's children, surely they were patricidal rather than piously filial.

Put another way, once we admit the pragmatists' acceptance of the contingent and historical character of existence, once we take into account their animus toward the metaphilosophical position that philosophy can be placed on the secure path of a rigorous science capable of breaking through historical variation and change, along with their rejection of foundationalism, scientism, representationalism, essentialism, and existential arrogance, it makes more sense to construe these pragmatists as trying to forge something that looks more like present-day cultural criticism than transcendental idealism, old-time epistemology, or Kant's critical philosophy. It makes more sense to describe them as fashioning a model of the way we hang together all the ways in which we hang things together—a synoptic picture of our intellectually active life—capacious enough to pay all the compliments due the arts and sciences along with every other sort of rational human activity (including religious ones), than it does to picture them constructing something as singular as a distinctive theory of knowledge. It makes more sense to characterize them as "insuring the active constructive role of the mind while yet affording" broad-ranging meditation on the nonhuman conditions that render mentality possible, along with reliable reflection on a diversity of problems and difficulties that surpass our physical, intellectual, and moral capacities, than it does to describe them as providing, more narrowly, "a solid basis for empirical knowledge."[9]

[9]Murphey, "Kant's Children," 34.

Even when we pursue the striking similarities between Kant and the pragmatists on the issues of moral regeneration and the tensions between beauty and duty or grace and law, which I am about to do in a little more detail, we end up being even more impressed by the ways and means the pragmatists used to transform philosophy from the sort of "science" Kant wanted into an art that would have caused Kant to turn over in his proverbial grave. We will be far less sanguine than Murphey and Kuklick about the suggestion that, somehow, the pragmatists tried to make the world safer for Kantian philosophical stratagems.

REHEARSING KANT'S TRANSCENDENTAL TURN

Ernest Gellner surely captured the gist of a widely held current opinion about the pathos of Kant's project when he noted that "the great irony of [his] critical philosophy is of course that it is simultaneously inspired by two fears which, superficially, one might expect to make each other redundant. The first fear is that the mechanical vision does *not* hold; the second fear it that it *does*. The first fear is for science, and the second for morality."[10] Kant's architectonic philosophy is built to solve this apparent *double* double bind. In other words, Kant tries to design a discipline that saves its practitioners, on the one hand, from being damned if they do accept the mechanical vision and damned if they don't and, on the other hand, from being damned if they do accept moral freedom and damned if they don't.

Gellner's account of the origin of Kant's critical philosophy begins with Kant aiming to calm his twin fears by placing philosophy on the secure path of a rigorous science. This discipline, Kant claimed, would cure reason of pretentious claims to transcendent knowledge both by determining the necessary (transcendental) conditions for the possibility of any experience or observation and by demonstrating the concepts and claims required to render morality intelligible. Kant was still part of a culture that presumed a sharp distinction between *scientia*, which establishes invariant truths, and *opinio*, which firms up—as best people can under turbulent circumstances—convictions about topics subject to time and chance. He still assumed that the point of philosophy *as a science* was to show how fixed mind knows the fixed world according to fixed

[10]Ernest Gellner, *The Legitimation of Belief* (Cambridge: Cambridge University Press, 1974), 185.

principles of understanding or knowledge, and knows it in a way that allows it to achieve the highest good, which is also fixed.

Second, Kant attempted to render this sort of rigorous scientific philosophy *transcendental*. Here, Kant's scheme/content distinction was paramount. In Kant's diagnosis, previous efforts to show how fixed mind knew fixed nature according to fixed principles all suffered from attempts to identify rock-bottom matters of fact about God's Nature and the Moral Law. By turning to matters of fact, philosophers had sought solid ground where only quicksand was available: hence Kant's "Copernican Revolution." The point of philosophy, Kant thought, is to establish the foundations of scientific and moral inquiry, but observations of matters of fact are contingent, so they cannot provide the elements for grounding philosophical constructions. What previous philosophers have failed to realize is that the building materials for which they had been searching are hardwired into mind itself. The stuff of philosophy is formal, not factual; structural, not empirical; necessary, not contingent; a priori, not based on observations. Kant claimed that philosophy establishes the invariant and invariable scheme that mind brings to experience, the constitutive forms of thought without which any empirical observation or moral decision would remain impossible. Kant's transcendental turn handed over issues of factual content to the empirical sciences, with the claim that philosophical success—foundational reason and knowledge—lay in demonstrating the fixed *forms* of mind that know fixed *forms* of nature, according to fixed *formal* principles and categories of knowledge or understanding, in a way that would carry with it realization of the *formal conditions* of the highest good.

Third, Kant readily assimilated the traditional Platonic-Christian picture—revised and augmented, to be sure—relating the self to the world, in his efforts to pull off this philosophical venture. That depiction had distinguished the true (freely virtuous) self from the fallen (body-obsessed) self. It had divided the world of appearance from eternal reality. In addition, it had suggested that human well-being depended on clearing away the fallen from the true or freely virtuous self in a (divinely organized or instituted) manner that allowed the true, freely virtuous self to break through the apparent world to eternity (or, as Kant put it, to the noumenal world) in order, eternally, to be truly and freely itself.

Finally, Kant developed an ingenious strategy to limit knowledge to the phenomenal world and to deny knowledge of the noumenal world,

simultaneously to secure the empirical sciences on unshakable foundations and to make room for a rational faith that let people understand
themselves morally and gave them the capacity to make moral decisions
with certainty, to boot. Kant's "reason" came packaged two ways: People deployed their theoretical reason to warrant true *representations* of
phenomena apodictically; they engaged their practical reason procedur-
ally to sanction morally good *decisions* that (Kant claimed) could be
shown to have universal application or persuasive force. They had no
capacity to *know* anything about the noumenal realm, which in Kant's
view, transcends the natural or phenomenal world. Kant tried to turn
this veil of ignorance to good use, however, by showing that, where
knowledge was impossible, belief might still remain a rational requirement: In his view, the demands of intelligibility or the views required to
make reasonable sense of moral life compelled people personally to believe specific things about the noumenal realm that lay beyond their ken.

In particular, Kant claimed, practical reason bound me to believe personally in its own pure postulates, namely, that I am (noumenally) free,
that the (noumenal) world is divinely ordered, and that I may look forward to a (noumenal) life that is immortal. Without these postulates of
pure practical reason, Kant would try to argue, moral life fails conceptually to cohere: Practical reason requires these particular religious beliefs because, without them, moral thinking becomes incoherent or
absurd. These religious beliefs, to be sure, are part of reason's hardwir-
ing; they depend on no traditional or any other source external to reason
for their authorization.

Now, there is method in the madness to which I have subjected you
by making you jump through all these Kantian hoops (and there are, of
course, lots more). Only by vaulting through them could we come close
to understanding what Kant had in mind by "constructing an epistemology adequate for science and religion which would insure the active
constructive role of mind while yet affording solid grounds for empirical
knowledge."[11]

Unpacking these notions in a Kantian way carries all the commitments
the pragmatists reject. Kant's effort to place philosophy on the secure
path of a rigorous science shows his scientism, or the view that science,
among all the methods and manners of human conduct, is the privileged
approach to issues of human well-being. His distinction between nou-

[11]Murphey, "Kant's Children."

menal and phenomenal worlds displays a commitment to essentialism, or the view that behind appearance resides the really real. His construal of science as making it possible to mirror the way things empirically are exhibits representationalism, or the notion that there are conditions that obtain which make verisimilitude the quality that, in turn, makes some statements true and others false. His transcendental turn designs yet another foundationalism, or the claim that the only reason or knowledge that is genuinely sound and safe from skeptical attack is firmly grounded in necessary and indubitable truths. His picture of human freedom as somehow noumenally located (whatever that could mean) outside (whatever that could mean) the natural world virtually invents existentialism, or the view that, one way or the other, we individually make ourselves and are responsible for doing so.

KANT'S FALLEN FREEDOM AND AESTHETIC SPIRITUALITY

One more relatively close look at Kant will help to clarify the philosophical seas on which the pragmatists sailed as well as the course(s) on which they settled because, as I have suggested already, two key intuitions linked the two parties in ways that render their differences all the more salient: Both Kant and the pragmatists recognized that moral life was bedeviled by what Michalson has called "fallen freedom, " and both parties contended in similarly aesthetic ways with their common Protestant judgment that all the well-doing in the world failed to secure the well-being for which people yearned.

It is over fallen freedom and aesthetic (rather than moralistic) spirituality that the Gellner-Murphey-Kuklick accounts of Kant and his connection with the pragmatists begin to crash on interpretive shoals. According to those accounts, one might think that once Kant had split the difference between the mechanical vision underpinned by theoretical reason and the moral freedom secured by practical reason, and then had curbed the pretensions of religious belief by redesigning it as internal to ethics, Enlightened Western culture could sail smoothly into its brave new world. Not so.

Michalson has identified the heart of the problem with this commonplace sketch of Kant's project. When Kant's fourth critique, *Religion within the Limits of Reason Alone*, is taken into account, it turns out that "freedom is more fundamentally in conflict with itself than it is threatened by a mechanistic universe," or put yet another way, "what makes us human is our ability to oppose not only the ends imposed on us by nature [i.e., sensuous inclinations], but also the ends that our own reason would freely give to itself [i.e., by autonomously embracing a basic maxim which subordinates duty or moral incentives to such inclinations, motivated by self-love]."[12] In Kant's view, constructed with the conceptual tools of his transcendental criticism, we corrupt our own wills in a way that, apparently anyhow, makes it impossible for us to change our own hearts.

In other words, Kant stood opposed to other, more healthy-minded Enlightenment options for understanding our moral and spiritual predicaments. He could not accept Leibniz's instrumental view of evil, which suggested that we conceive of it as serving some "purpose of the whole," leaving the universe better off with evil than without it. Nor could he embrace Rousseau's environmentalist idea of it, which blamed evil on ignorance or on social institutions alone, leaving individuals heteronomous and, so, on Kant's grounds, incapable of moral action. Augustinian pietist that he was, Kant tried to safeguard moral reasoning by asserting that it was precisely the autonomous individual who *chose* to ground his maxims in a basic way that subordinated duty to maxims of self-interest. Through that choice, freedom fell: Human will corrupted or enslaved itself.[13]

Overall, Kant's *Religion* leaves us with the following picture of our moral predicament, which "wobbles," as Michalson puts it, between two historical epochs: between something close to orthodox Protestant notions of original sin and the need for gracious and divine assistance, on the one hand, and, on the other, something close to avant-garde nineteenth-century existentialist notions of freedom along with the moral world that it constructed (or destroyed) on its own. In particular the construal of the human spiritual predicament that Kant gave in *Religion* involves the following claims:

1. Humankind has an "original predisposition to good" but "a natural propensity to evil" (21–27).

---

[12]Michalson, *Fallen Freedom*, 10.
[13]By calling Leibniz's and Rousseau's options healthy minded, I do not mean better. Rather, I follow James's distinction between "healthy-minded" and "sick-souled" religions. In James's view, the healthy-minded person sees the natural course of things as fundamentally sound, whereas the sick-souled person perceives "something wrong about us as we naturally stand" (see James, *The Varieties of Religious Experience* [Cambridge, Mass.: Harvard University Press, 1985], 51–53, 93–98). To James, at least, ironically the healthy minded are deluded and the sick souled are spiritually honest and perceptive.

2. Radical evil is "innate" but is "brought upon us" by our own freedom (28, 33, 38).

3. We are morally obliged to deliver ourselves from radical evil, even though "it is *inextirpable* by human powers" (32).

4. We must "make ourselves" good again, but divine aid "may be necessary" for us actually to become good (40).[14]

Let's flesh these claims out a little:

1. We are originally predisposed to good in the sense that we finite rational animals have the capacity to make our moral selves virtuous before we actually do. But we have a natural propensity to evil because, although we cannot help having sensuous inclinations—we are animals—and although deviating from the moral law is not predetermined—we are free—all rational animals do in fact so deviate, even though we do not know why or how, since freedom, being noumenal, exists behind a veil of ignorance.

2. This complex picture apparently demands, for Kant, the construal of evil as innate, meaning something like universal or invariable, though not necessary, because we bring it on ourselves because, from the standpoint of practical reason, we are (noumenally) free.

3. Because we are responsible for actualizing our potential for evil, we are accountable for not suppressing this propensity, and we are obliged to overcome it. We cannot do so on our own, however, "since extirpation could occur only through good maxims, and cannot take place when the ultimate subjective ground of all maxims is postulated as corrupt."[15]

4. We thus find ourselves "impelled to believe in the cooperation or management of a moral Ruler of the universe, by means of which alone this goal can be reached," all the while recognizing that "what God may do, whether indeed *anything* in general, and if so *what* in particular should be ascribed to God" remains the "abyss of a mystery."[16]

THE NONMORAL ELEMENT OF KANT'S "HIGHEST GOOD"

From Kant's point of view, of course, comprehending our spiritual problems was even more complex than the foregoing argument, because

[14]Michalson, *Fallen Freedom*, 8. Original references are to Immanuel Kant, *Religion within the Limits of Reason Alone*, trans. Theodore M. Greene and Hoyt H. Hudson (New York: Harper Torchbooks, 1960).

[15]Kant, *Religion*, 32.

[16]Ibid., 130.

within the framework of his critical philosophy, the religious question was not simply whether I have the ability—on my own—to transform my self-corrupted will into a genuinely virtuous one (and so do what I ought to do). The religious question for Kant was the query about what I can *hope*. It concerned the chance of salvation and pertained to what Kant calls "the highest good." Even if autonomous human freedom, or some other agency outside it, could resolve the conflict it had with itself, the "highest good" or well-being was not constituted by moral activity alone. Reformed Christian that he was, Kant claimed that well-being exceeds well-doing as grace exceeds law. Well-being, Kant claimed, occurs when happiness is in proportion to virtue. It is specifically that aesthetic quality of being in general, that symmetry or proportionality between virtue and happiness, which constituted salvation or consummate harmony for him. For Kant, people might stand in need of something like grace, or benign and voluntary supernatural cooperation, to overcome the moral blockage with which, he thought, freedom ineluctably presents itself in this actual moral universe. On his grounds, however, people surely remained incapable of structuring the cosmos on their own in the specifically aesthetic way that would render happiness proportional to virtue, as the Kantian concept of the highest good demanded. That Kant simply *assumed* that the cosmos is structured in the requisite way indicates the depth of what Michalson calls his "metaphysical trust," his "deep sense that, when moral striving is viewed as a totality . . . we ultimately discover something like fairness and correct proportion as features of the universe."[17]

According to Kant, then, there was a firm distinction between moral life per se, which depends on doing duty for duty's sake, and the religious hope that relies on nonmoral conditions of symmetry or correct proportion between virtue and happiness for satisfaction. As Michalson points out, for Kant, "the spectre of an unhappy person of great virtue [is] distressing and deeply poignant . . . [but] hardly threatens the moral status of the person in question."[18] Nevertheless, unhappiness out of proportion to virtue does preclude salvation or the highest good. On these Kantian grounds, religious belief about salvation could not be *reduced* to moral action, even if it underscored the fact that all I (possibly) can and must do on behalf of salvation is be virtuous; the nonmoral

[17]Michalson, *Fallen Freedom*, 19.
[18]Ibid., 24.

condition of proportionality between virtue and happiness must be met.[19]

Thus for Kant, people are, in Michalson's words, "stuck between debility and demand" twice over—once between freedom and its virtually inevitable tendency to attack its own moral potential, and then again between (conceivably perfect) well-doing and consummate well-being.[20] Kant left resolution of the first bind opaque to transcendental criticism or analysis; indeed, he left it as mysterious as Christian Scripture does. His metaphysical trust might seem to obviate the second bind, but only by relying on—what was for him at any rate—vicious reasoning: He assumed that, because the requisite symmetry exists, there must be divine agency. He could do this, however, only after arguing that because we must assume divine agency, we can believe in the requisite symmetrical order. From the standpoint of Kant's own transcendental criticism, such circularity was intolerable.

PRAGMATISTS AND THE RELIGIOUS DEMAND

Among the originating pragmatists, James was the first to take up the sort of spiritual double whammy that had so preoccupied Kant. In the 1880s, in an effort to sum up his father's religious thought and explicitly begin formulating his own, James had indicated, first, that there is something wrong about us as we naturally stand: "The sanest and best of us are of one clay with lunatics and prison inmates." He had reflected, second, that moral achievement or the realization of well-doing lay constantly dogged by a lack of well-being. Well-being, he said, was the "object of the religious demand," a call "so penetrating that no consciousness of such occasional and outward well-doing as befalls the human lot can ever give it satisfaction."[21] So again, in James's reading, humanity seemed stuck between debility and demand twice over. It ap-

---

[19]This is the case even though much of *Religion* appears to urge such a reduction. Despite the fact that the claim adheres to traditional Christian theological narratives, nothing conceptual per se in *Religion* demands that the agency causing moral regeneration be identical with the agency causing cosmic harmony (a point Michalson may miss).

[20]I cannot tell whether Michalson himself explicitly drew the inference I draw, that is, that Kant multiplies human debility in a way that calls for grace squared, so to speak (see Michalson, *Fallen Freedom*, 73). But the "Kant" he reveals surely begs for this sort of solution. The fact that I use Michalson's phrase for my chapter title gives some sense of my great debt to his work.

[21]William James, *The Literary Remains of Henry James* (Upper Saddle River, N.J.: Literature House, 1970), 118.

peared to him that answering the question of whether somebody was morally committed, or rather criminally or insanely committable, apparently depended on something like a matter of luck. It seemed, further, that answering the question of whether somebody who was morally committed ever experienced the well-being he or she sought depended on conditions appearing just as random or chancy. Finally, James characterized well-being in terms of a sense of fittingness or harmony, much as Kant had depicted the highest good in terms of proportionality or symmetry.[22]

Santayana, already James's student when his mentor began reflecting in print on moral binds and the religious demand, followed suit. By the 1890s, he had placed issues of moral regeneration and the slip between well-doing and well-being at the heart of his philosophical concerns, and had described well-being as grounded in the sense of beauty. For Santayana, people were invariably blinded from perspectives, letting them treat others as moral ends rather than as means, and stood constantly in need of some process of ongoing self-transcendence for the requisite moral enlightenment. In his view, however, even ethical perfection could not clinch well-being: To love life was to find it lovely, to experience religious fulfillment or consummate well-being was to "love life in the consciousness of impotence," and to have that sort of awareness involved, among other things, honestly confronting inalienable creatureliness without blinking; that is to say, it involved meditating no holds barred on the limits of human physical, intellectual, and moral capacity.[23]

Dewey, too, would make these "problems of men"—the issues of moral regeneration and the gratuitous aesthetic quality of well-being—crucially his own. Beginning with the work he would publish as the *Outlines of a Critical Theory of Ethics* (1891) and *The Study of Ethics: An Outline* (1894), he brought together his interests in the logic of moral judgment, his psychological account of human conduct, and his efforts to naturalize Hegelian self-realization ethics to comprehend transformations from selfishness to social solicitude.[24] Furthermore, his natural-

---

[22]See my *Religious Investigations of William James* (Chapel Hill: University of North Carolina Press, 1981), esp. chap. 2, for a discussion of James's aesthetic spirituality.

[23]See, e.g., George Santayana, *Winds of Doctrine* (New York: Harper Torchbooks, 1957), 43, as well as my *Santayana*, esp. chaps. 1–4.

[24]The best critical exposition of Dewey's concern with moral transformation is Robert B. Westbrook, *John Dewey and American Democracy* (Ithaca: Cornell University Press, 1991), especially its characterization of Dewey's "Good Democrat," 151–66.

ized Hegelian stance in ethics, which identified the good with the whole or the fitting, led him to celebrate the creation and enjoyment of works of art (in a very broad sense) as fostering a consummate experience in which

> we are, as it were, introduced into a world beyond this world which is nevertheless the deeper reality of the world in which we live in our ordinary experience. We are carried out beyond ourselves to find ourselves. I can see no properties of such an experience save that, somehow, the work of art operates to deepen and to raise to great clarity that sense of an enveloping undefined whole that accompanies every normal experience. This whole is then felt as an expansion of ourselves. . . . Where egotism is not made the measure of reality and value, we are citizens of this vast world beyond ourselves, and any intense realization of its presence with and in us brings a peculiarly satisfying sense of unity in itself and with ourselves.[25]

If the originating pragmatists followed Enlightenment forefigures like Kant in their preoccupation with moral metamorphosis and aesthetic spirituality, they tipped basic Enlightenment assumptions about the traditional problem of the one and the many on their edge by tracing out the ramifications of Darwin's decisively natural-historical approach to humankind, thought, and being. In the process, they transformed boundary conditions for the fields of philosophy.

Whereas Enlightenment thinkers analyzed how fixed mind knows fixed nature according to fixed principles of knowledge, in order to clarify how these things essentially stayed the same despite the appearance of change, the pragmatists tried to determine how changing and variable humans interacted with changing and variable environments by acting in changing and variable ways, exhibiting changing structures and variable degrees of intelligence. In their view, the point (scientific, moral, spiritual, aesthetic, or otherwise) was not to establish the invariable essence of anything. The point, rather, was to ponder how things—not only zoological species but such things as concepts and characters, diverse traditions and distinctive temperaments—maintain continuity and coherence in light of all the real changes they undergo, especially how humans keep the sort of constancy and cohesion that enables them to flourish materially, morally, and spiritually.

Indeed, this Darwinian transformation of the problem of the one and the many rested at the heart of the pragmatists' indictment, not just of Kantian or Enlightenment philosophy but of the entire philosophical

---

[25]John Dewey, *Art as Experience* (New York: Capricorn, 1958), 195.

tradition in the West. One example is James's startling affirmation that philosophy has been on "a false scent ever since the days of Socrates and Plato." Those Greeks, he claimed, were largely responsible for making philosophy a lasting but peculiar footnote to their own odd visual metaphors by teaching that

what a thing really is is told us by its *definition* [that] reality consists of essences, not of appearances, and that the essences of things are known whenever we know their definitions. So far we identify the thing with a concept, and then we identify the concept with a definition, and only then, inasmuch as the thing is whatever the definition expresses, are we sure of apprehending the real essence of it or the full truth about it.[26]

James's line of thought did for thinking and concepts what Darwin had already done for coral reefs and orchids (and James himself had already done, in a more pervasive way, for the psyche, in *The Principles of Psychology*). It stopped people from denying, for example, that a human baby with six fingers on one hand, or without the normal genitals, or with a tail, or deaf and dumb, was human because the child did not fit the proper definition, hence concept, hence truth. "It is but the old story," James complained, "of a useful practice first become a method, then a habit, and finally a tyranny that defeats the end it was used for. Concepts, first employed to make things intelligible, are clung to even when they make them unintelligible."[27] This is the intuition that began to leverage the pragmatists' rejection of Kant's transcendental turn and let them reshape their understanding of the problems and promise of human life in post-Darwinian ways.

REJECTING KANT'S BIG TRANSCENDENTAL MACHINE

The pragmatists dismantled Kant's architectonic work by arguing for, and then affirming, the following Darwinlike claims:

1. Human beings are (variable and plastic) intelligent animals that are born into and die out of (variable and plastic) natural environments.

2. Intelligence—reasoning, knowing, calculating, obligating, and all—is a particular functional quality of animals living *in* such a world, not some stuff existing apart from living animals or external to the world

---

[26]William James, *A Pluralistic Universe* (Cambridge, Mass.: Harvard University Press, 1977), 132, 99.
[27]Ibid., 99. See my *Religious Investigations*, 248–57, for the impact of this diagnosis on James's religious investigations.

in which they are situated. If this is so, however, then there is no good motive or reason for distinguishing between noumenal and phenomenal worlds from the standpoint of understanding sense or nonsense. Nor is there a philosophical motive for picturing knowledge as dependent on linking internal mind to the external world. Hence the task of epistemology—to overcome skepticism about the external world by establishing foundational knowledge of it—is initially (though not yet decisively) undercut. Finally, if reasoning and knowing are practical activities, then Kant's distinction between theoretical and practical reason collapses.

3. What gives human intelligence a degree of distinction among the other animals is a singular coping mechanism: (variable and plastic) human languages, which let human beings express themselves, that is, communicate beliefs and desires (including the ability to communicate beliefs and desires about beliefs and desires), not (primarily at any rate) any particular likeness or correspondence between human intelligence construed as a substance and some other, even finer substance. But if language is a coping mechanism, mirroring may be no more than one of many functions, and representationalism is initially (though not yet decisively) weakened.

4. Then it follows that people *are* (mainly learned, though surely revisable) webs of belief and desire. With respect to those webs, there is no explanatory power added by invoking some inner self which *owns* them or *has* them. If this is so, Enlightenment models of the psyche, either shaping or molded by the sort of philosophical liberalism that accompanies possessive economic, political, moral, and spiritual individualism, are abandoned for expressive social individualism.

5. Likewise abandoned are the varieties of existential liberty that depend on liberal, possessive individualist, models of psyche. This is so because, as Santayana puts it:

At the level of complexity at which thought and laughter are possible, to exist means to be distinctly organized, localized, contrasted with other things, and conditioned by them. It means to have a mock freedom only; freedom to exert oneself spontaneously in one way, but no freedom to exert oneself otherwise or not at all or under different circumstances or with another result. In order to live without control and absolutely ungoverned, as the spirit thinks it lives, it must be controlled by an organism that governs itself. In other words, it cannot be anarchical, but must be inwardly, precisely, and irretrievably governed.[28]

[28]George Santayana, *Dominations and Powers* (New York: Charles Scribner's Sons, 1951), 241.

The point is not that historical entities are inevitably predetermined or determined in ways that foreclose options or, in the case of human life together, preclude responsible conduct. The point, to the contrary, is that historical beings, including human beings, are determinable *chances* in transaction with other determinable chances, developing as they may, rather than any way they wish or will.

6. Beliefs and desires are (variable and plastic) tools for environmentally situated action or interaction or transaction, not primarily mirrors of anything. If this is so, then representationalism loses its raison d'être.

7. The beliefs and desires with which people identify themselves serve various purposes and are more or less entrenched. Like all other historical entities, they are inherited or born, they are subject to change, and they decease. Indeed, there is no particular sort of belief or desire that carries invariable privilege over all the other sorts; and there are no firm distinctions among those beliefs that count as true as a matter of necessity, those that count as true as a matter of fact, and those that count as matters of commitment randomly related to truth function. If no particular sort of belief carries invariable privilege, however, then scientism is ridiculous (along with other pretensions like moralism, aestheticism, pietism, and theologism). If holism reigns, if the view that reasons, beliefs, and desires hang together or hang one another holds, if beliefs and desires are indeed spun together continually in weblike fashion, then foundationalisms, including Kant's transcendental turn, are decisively impugned.

8. The world only comes in one (developmentally open-ended) edition which is natural-historical, not two editions (one fixed and deluxe, the other variable and discounted). If so, there is no philosophically defensible motive to invoke any noumenal-phenomenal distinction, and more generally, essentialism is weakened.

9. In the world of natural history, which is the only world there is, entities are characterized in terms of their family resemblances, not natures behind or below or apart from those resemblances. If this is so, then essentialism is decisively weakened.

10. Humankind cannot flourish without artful human-environmental transactions. But nothing that people do on their own can suffice to secure well-being, because people are dependent on environmental conditions over which they have no control and for which they cannot be held responsible. That means that well-being exceeds well-doing; it also

means that well-being is gratuitous. Yet whether the extravagance and gratuity of well-being demands or even suggests the view that intentionally benign superhuman power is at work in the cosmos to secure what people themselves cannot, the way Kant had claimed, is still an open question, and one that divides James from Santayana and Dewey.

PRAGMATIC PHILOSOPHY AND THE MORAL LIFE

The pragmatists tore down Kant's noumenal-phenomenal distinction and the veil of ignorance regarding personhood that was sewn into it. Sure, understanding of ourselves and others was fallible and corrigible, often mysterious enough to be vexing, but not utterly out of reach. The pragmatists pictured reasoning as an activity occurring in the world, not simply as a visual representation of it, and not simply in the mind. They argued that theory was a human practice and that human practice was theory-laden, so that no sharp theoretical/practical contrast held water, and also so that any sort of knowledge was a sort of skill. They dismantled the sharp break between necessary and contingent truth, claiming, as Santayana phrased it, that "necessity is a conspiracy of accidents."[29] They maintained that thought was a poetic or imaginative process that allowed people to cope, even at wit's end and death's door. They contended that appreciative and open-ended criticism was central to this process. They noted that criticism had better be open-ended because the world and everything in it, as James put it, was subject to boiling over; hence the quest for certainty was irrelevant and the sufficiency of intelligence and spirit became the desideratum. The pragmatists moderated the existential heroism of their romantic predecessors by declaring that if people were chances to make things better or worse, which they surely were, they were also inevitably dependent on the rest of the world.[30] They were finite creatures: born, nurtured, culturally shaped, spontaneously variable, so possibly original in some direction or other, and mortal.

What, then, of Kant's spiritual double whammy? What happened to fallen freedom and the tensions between law and grace in the hands of the originating pragmatists? How did they contend with the vexing is-

---

[29]George Santayana, *Realms of Being* (New York: Charles Scribner's Sons, 1942), 291.
[30]I owe my characterization of pragmatism as an alternative to existential heroism, rather than as a variation of it, to Bennett Ramsey, *Submitting to Freedom: The Religious Vision of William James* (New York: Oxford University Press, 1992), 77–102.

sues of moral transformation and an all-too-apparent disproportion between justice and destiny?

There is no one answer to these questions, because the originating pragmatists were far from monolithic. James, for example, gave us pragmatic accounts of moral and religious experience that focused primarily on social individuals, sometimes even more decisively on what he called "individual men in their solitude."[31] Santayana's pragmatism was far more institutional, concentrating on cultural and social forms that made up "the life of reason," that is, that fostered both private and public well-being.[32] Dewey's pragmatism transformed moral and religious philosophy, at least primarily, into social and political policy formulation (informed by an aesthetic account of experience, especially at its best).

A few points can be made about a common view that the three originating pragmatists held on issues concerning moral life. First, the sole and sufficient reason why something is good is that it is felt to be good; somebody exhibits a felt desire for it. Second, there are many and diverse actual felt desires. This line of thought suggests that

someone cannot truly grasp the fact that something is a value for someone without it becoming something of a value for oneself. Such a grasp coincides with imaginative reproduction of the way things look to the other, and this necessarily brings with it the associated conations. From this it follows that the more one grasps the ideal colors in which things look to others the more one will take as one's aim the joint realization of as many of these values as possible in a single harmony. The essential point is that nothing anyone values is condemned as such, only, at most, as the realization of other values.[33]

In this view, moral transformation is occurring as and when somebody imaginatively reproduces the way things look to others, including the associated felt intentions or objectives that others maintain. This involves, as James put it, willingness to "let go" of one's own wish and will or, as Santayana said, the willingness "not to will, but to understand the lure and suffering in all willing."[34] For all three pragmatists, moral life together demanded a "metanoia," a conversion, a metamorphosis or

---

[31]James, *Varieties*, 34.

[32]See George Santayana, *The Life of Reason; or, The Phases of Human Progress*, 5 vols. (New York: Scribner's, 1905–6). For my account of it, highlighting its pragmatism, see *Santayana*, chap. 5.

[33]Timothy Sprigge, "The Distinctiveness of American Philosophy," in *Two Centuries of Philosophy in America*, ed. Peter Caws (Totowa, N.J.: Rowman and Littlefield, 1980), 207–8, makes these claims about James, Royce, and Santayana, not Dewey. I doubt Sprigge would dispute the addition.

[34]See James, *Varieties*, e.g., 110–14. See Santayana, *Realms*, 731.

turning momentous enough to let "me" identify myself "not with my-self" but, rather, as one of us (however "we" identify ourselves).[35] Such a turn was, biographically speaking, tantamount to being "born into another life," a profound shift of attention or interest or felt desire that, in moments of transport if only in such moments, detached "us from each thing with humility and humour, and attach[ed] us to all things with justice, charity, and pure joy."[36]

This pragmatic construal of moral transformation clipped one of Kant's conundrums in the bud. Certainly the rest of nature threatened the part of nature exhibited by human freedom, but it did not have to wait for the invention of Newtonian mechanics to do so or for people to explain why: suffering, absurdity, and natural evils were each and all as old as weeds, and more or less as explicable.

Moreover, there was something utterly stilted about Kant's sharp dis-tinction between morality and prudence, or the realms of responsibility and desire, because responsibility was constituted by desire—"our" de-sires. In the pragmatic view, building a durable moral character was a matter of fashioning and maintaining some natural inclinations rather than others, not the carpet bombing of any and all natural inclinations by transcendental virtue.

Leaving aside Kant's nature-freedom conflict (as much as possible at any rate), the pragmatists still found friction between freedom and free-dom that is genuinely or practically problematic. Kant had never ques-tioned the actuality of moral transformation, but his own conceptual tools had blocked "critical" analysis of moral generation or regeneration (and he had invoked the Christian language of divine intervention and human rebirth where and when it did). This was so for three reasons. First, Kant's picture of moral life as a conflict between duty and desire left persons bifurcated in multiple ways—free on one side of a divide, natural on the other; unknowable when free on one side, determined, and so not free, to any extent knowable on the other; selfishly desirous on the one side, virtuously desire-suppressed on the other. Second, be-cause he maintained the view that the essential or noumenal self stayed the same despite phenomenal changes, Kant assumed what I would call

---

[35]The metanoia Santayana calls for does not, then, ultimately lead to embracing only the orientation of the other who I am not, but to adopting an orientation that tries to ac-commodate both our concerns as much as possible.

[36]This phrasing is actually Santayana's: see, e.g., Santayana, *Realms*, 741, 745, 778, 827; but see also James, *Varieties*, 41–47, and Dewey, *Art as Experience*, 195.

the saturated integrity of human personality: I mean he pictured a person governing herself either by the basic maxim of duty or the basic maxim of self-interest as solidly identical, the way, say, a piece of red-dyed ice is solidly red. He had no conceptual way to show how the "same identical person" could autonomously, and so morally, change her conceptually formed moral identity through any employment of the rules of reason, any more than he had a conceptual way to show how red ice could remain the same while clearing itself up. Third, Kant designed a rule-obedient analysis of reason. To be reasonable was to determine one's life according to rules, and it appeared impossible to him to generate a rule book for good out of a rule book for evil (or vice versa).

Once the pragmatists seized the genuine genius of the Darwinian revolution, however, Kant's transcendental criticism fell down like a house of cards in ways that had far-reaching consequences for the analysis of moral life. According to the pragmatists, morality emerged out of sentimental sentience, and the sort of individually responsible conduct on which it depended was as describable as anything else. Personalities could maintain continuity and coherence in light of all the real changes they underwent; sometimes, to be sure, changes had such all-encompassing consequences for identity that it made literary sense to call the alterations revolutionary.[37] Reason, James said, was the sentiment people felt as or when they solved their problems. It was a form of sentimental life bent on harmony, Santayana and Dewey agreed, not a set of rules. It depended on modeling, imagining, entertaining, rehearsing, and imitating certain virtues, habits of heart and soul and might, far more than it boiled down to doing things according to some rule book.

From this vantage point, people certainly could, and often did, freely enslave themselves to racks of "care, doubt, pain, hatred and vice" that distracted them from the life of solicitous mutuality so central to liberal democratic culture.[38] Indeed, as all three pragmatists pointed out, "the moral consecration of the *status quo*," as Dewey put it, often blinded people from the very desires of others that made life worth living as

---

[37]In addition, personalities sometimes fall apart, no longer able to maintain continuity or coherence.

[38]Santayana, *Realms*, 673. For commitments to mutualist ethics, see William James, "The Moral Philosopher and the Moral Life," in *The Will to Believe and Other Essays* (Cambridge, Mass.: Harvard University Press, 1979); Santayana, *Life of Reason*, 3:214–16, 221; and John Dewey, e.g., *Ethics* (New York: H. Holt, 1908), *The Middle Works* (Carbondale: Southern Illinois University Press, 1982), 5:259, and "The Psychology of Social Behavior" (1914), in *Middle Works*, 7:404.

those others understood themselves.[39] James went so far as to claim that people must often become practically irresponsible or worthless in order to cure such blindness and open themselves up to the "world of impersonal worths."[40] Santayana, pledging allegiance to Hermes the interpreter, urged people to appreciate the innocence of the things they hated and the clearness of the things they frowned on or denied in order to free themselves from their own voluntarily embraced concerns.[41] In each of these cases, we find originating pragmatists fleshing out, at least from a particularly moral angle, what is involved in willing not to will, where freedom actually finds itself propitiously divided against itself.

James and Santayana articulated their views of the moral life in ways that did not blink tragedy, whereas Dewey's seemed all too Pollyannaish to some. For James, because one's moral power almost inevitably involved the frustration of another's, "some part of the ideal must be butchered" in the quest for mutual wholeness.[42] Santayana argued that the ultimate moral ideal "must have taken all interests into consideration; it must be universally representative." To do this meant "to intend, as far as possible, to secure the particular good which that particular interest looks to, and never, whatever measures may be adopted, to cease to look back on the elementary impulse as upon something which ought, if possible, to have been satisfied, and which we should still go back and satisfy now, if circumstances and the claims of rival interests permitted." Both these thinkers admitted what Kant's metaphysical trust could not: the texture of "the soul and . . . society" was antinomial, constituted by conflicts of interests "all of which cannot be satisfied altogether."[43] Dewey made no such assumptions nor drew such conclusions. Without significant argumentation on the point, he maintained a sort of optimism that was virtually a naturalistic equivalent to Kant's metaphysical trust. In any case, all three originating pragmatists zeroed in on conflicts of freedom with itself as constituting the very heart of moral life. Each of them could have affirmed the ancient Talmudic injunction that although it is not required of one to complete the work, neither is one free to

[39]Dewey, Art as Experience, 348.
[40]William James, Talks to Teachers on Psychology and to Students on Some of Life's Ideals (Cambridge, Mass.: Harvard University Press, 1983), 141.
[41]George Santayana, Soliloquies in England and Later Soliloquies (Ann Arbor: University of Michigan Press, 1967), 263.
[42]James, "The Moral Philosopher," 155–56.
[43]Santayana, Life of Reason, 3:214–16.

desist from it: There will always be a gap between debility and moral demand.

VARIETIES OF PRAGMATIC RELIGION

At the same time, the originating pragmatists affirmed the view that well-being exceeds well-doing, much as Kant had claimed that virtue fails to secure happiness. Relying on his metaphysical trust in a manner that was circular, Kant invoked divine power along with faith in an ever-lasting time span to secure the requisite proportionality.

The originating pragmatists divided most notably over the issue of how James's "religious demand" could be satisfied. James himself investigated exceptional mental states and the testimony of religious founders and converts in his effort to persuade people that there were superhuman powers at work in the world to help people experience consummate harmony, or salvation, when they could not help themselves. On his reading of this testimony, people remained stuck between debility and religious demand as long as they hemmed themselves in with anxious self-consciousness and calculating rationality. When they let go of self-consciousness and the effort to push things through on their own, when—as Bennet Ramsey puts it—they submitted to freedom, individuals often enough experienced help from unseen others apparently at play in their subliminal consciousness.[44] Indeed, James invoked the "subliminal self" in his effort to transform religious testimony into evidence for his conclusion that it was "objectively and literally true" that "the conscious person is continuous with a wider self through which saving experiences come."[45]

Santayana could not accept James's argument concluding with this "objective and literal truth," accusing his mentor of falling victim to the sort of vicious intellectualism James had done so much to uncover as preposterous. Santayana gladly admitted that spiritual transformations of the requisite sort occurred, but he argued that invoking divinity to account for these developments carried no more explanatory force than dormative power did for sleep. He complained that James, along with his whole Protestant culture, suffered from "the natural but hopeless

[44]See Ramsey, *Submitting to Freedom*, 77–102.
[45]James, *Varieties*, 405; see also Levinson, *Religious Investigations*, part 2.

misunderstanding of imagining that poetry in order to be religion, in order to be the inspiration of life, must first deny that it is poetry and deceive us about the facts with which we have to deal."[46]

Kant certainly had been on the right track when he had invoked the Gospels to account for moral and spiritual transformation. He had done so with an unhappy conscience, a lot of angst, and not a little proud piety, however, because relying on Scripture seemed to him to weaken his transcendental armor. So much the worse, Santayana thought, for Kant's critical philosophy. Kant, like James after him, had assumed that religion was meant to be realistic, literal, explanatory, and obligatory.

Santayana argued, to the contrary, that religion was "another world to live in" that was not transcendent or postmortem but, rather, cultural: Religion was imaginative, socially unrealistic, seriously playful, symbolic, optative, and better off religiously and pragmatically for being all of these things.[47] If diverse religions were indispensable to cultures—and Santayana thought they were—this was because religious fictions and festivities provided cultural locations for people to change their lives in moral and spiritual ways that brought experiences of consummate joy. When people experienced that "sense of beauty" in their lives, "the reign of duty gives place to the reign of freedom, and the law and the covenant to the dispensation of grace."[48] People remained stuck between debility and religious demand as long as they clung to their false notions about the pragmatic possibilities of poetry and kept their religious imaginations at bay.

Dewey demurred from James's account of religious experience for essentially the same reasons Santayana did. He also objected to Santayana's construal of religious Scripture as a sort of poetry and religious ritual as poetry in motion that permitted not only cultural bonding but an experience of liberation from incessant concerns of the self. I think he did so mainly because he thought, at any rate, that he knew his Protestant, iconoclastic, literal-minded, moralistic culture could never embrace the sort of pragmatic religious naturalism that averted hopeless misunderstanding. I think he knew at least that *he* could not. Dewey was no Mr. Mardi Gras.

To the contrary, Dewey urged people to pour all the fervor they had

---

[46]George Santayana, *Interpretations of Poetry and Religion* (Cambridge, Mass.: MIT Press, 1989), 71–72.
[47]Santayana, *Life of Reason*, 3:6.
[48]George Santayana, *The Sense of Beauty* (New York: Charles Scribner's Sons, 1896), 19.

once devoted to religious creeds, codes, cults, and exclusive communities into the cultural life of strong liberal democracy. He distinguished between religious and religiousness. He argued that whereas religions amounted to the four *cs*—creed, code, cult, community—which, he claimed, were inevitably informed by superstition and fanaticism, religiousness denoted a "quality of experience" accompanying "any activity pursued in behalf of an ideal and against obstacles and in spite of threats of personal loss because of conviction of its general and enduring value.[49] Dewey concluded that people would remain stuck between debility and demand so long as they confused religions with religiousness.

There are sharp, at points insurmountable, differences among these pragmatic options for comprehending tensions between grace and law: James's "crass" or "piecemeal" supernaturalism,[50] Santayana's festive "world to live in," and Dewey's "common faith" in the life and institutions of American democracy. But they were all motivated by the perception that well-being exceeds well-doing. They all depended on an account of extraordinary, abnormal conduct that defies the typical bounds of reason, the moral status quo, the organization of the workaday world, and conflicting interests. They all invoked an aesthetic appreciation of indefinite others, if not the Other (inevitably essentialistic in concept). Thus they all continued to avow the aesthetic tradition of spirituality and the principle that beauty is to duty as grace is to law.

PRAGMATISM AND ENLIGHTENMENT TRADITIONS

In the end, then, can we determine whether the pragmatists maintained or dismantled Enlightenment traditions? We certainly can; indeed, in a rough way, we have already done so. The story reads like most family romances, not only full of affection and avowal, but also filled with aggression, even with a couple of attempted homicides thrown in for good measure. This much we can say: James, Dewey, and Santayana tried to topple scientism, essentialism, foundationalism (including rulebook rationalism and rock-bottom empiricism), representationalism, existentialism, the cult of saturated integrity, and the prevailing old-time assumption that chance was inevitably trouble and that certainty was all to the good. That stance pitted them against some Enlightenment ten-

---

[49]John Dewey, *A Common Faith* (New Haven: Yale University Press, 1934), 27.
[50]This is what James himself called his position, in *Varieties*, 520.

dencies, and when it came to Kant's transcendental turn, they tried to kill it.

The originating pragmatists, however, celebrated science without scientism, coherence without essentialism, inquiry without foundationalism, reason without representationalism, responsibility without existentialism, health and sanity and honesty and honor without saturated integrity, chance without chaos, and sufficiency without certainty.

Moreover, the pragmatists avowed these things pledged to the view— the view that sits at the heart of the modern democratic republics which emerged with the Enlightenment—that finite, sentient, needy, mortal creatures could work away at the construction of a life of mutual solicitude, even if their eventual and inevitable impotence kept them from ever completing the task. Finally, they did so with the understanding that, even when our chances at satisfying wish and will go bust—even at wit's end—a personal joy in life alone and in life together might still well up within us, making life a little more divine as long as it lasts.

10

0▬▬▬▬▬▬▬▬▬▬▬▬▬▬▬▬▬▬▬▬▬▬▬▬0

Wallace Stevens, T. S. Eliot, and
the space between them

DENIS DONOGHUE

Reading *The Phenomenology of Mind*, I come at length if not at last upon a passage I think I understand. Hegel has been administering cold but not equally cold comfort to believers and philosophes. His official theme is *Aufklarung*, Enlightenment as we agree to call it, and for many pages he has been personifying Enlightenment and belief and scolding each in turn: They do not know themselves; they cannot recognize their mutual bearing. Having set them apart and brought them together, he settles for making the contrast between them a contrast within Enlightenment itself:

Since belief is without content and cannot continue in this barren condition, or since, in getting beyond finitude, which is the sole content, it finds merely the empty void, it is a sheer longing: its truth is an empty beyond, for which there is no longer any appropriate content to be found, for everything is appropriated and applied in other ways.

Belief . . . has in fact become the same as enlightenment—the conscious attitude of relating a finite that inherently exists to an unknown and unknowable Absolute without predicates; the difference is merely that the one is enlightenment satisfied, while belief is enlightenment unsatisfied. It will yet be seen whether enlightenment can continue in its state of satisfaction; that longing of the troubled, beshadowed spirit, mourning over the loss of its spiritual world, lies in the background.[1]

I should not have thought it possible for Enlightenment to continue long in its state of satisfaction, but I have heard Richard Bernstein and two or three equally sensitive scholars declaring that they are indeed content.

G. W. F. Hegel, *The Phenomenology of Mind*, trans. J. B. Baillie (New York: Harper, 1967), 588–89.

It seems strange, after two world wars, genocides in Russia, Poland, Germany, Austria, and Colombia, technologically accomplished slaughter in Hiroshima and Nagasaki, the gas chambers in Auschwitz. I thought the Enlightenment promised that such acts would cease. I am not blaming our modern philosophes for these or other deeds, but I remain bewildered by their insistence on the adequacy of Enlightenment thinking.

Hegel's account of Enlightenment and belief is invidious to both parties, though on balance an adept of the Enlightenment would feel justified rather than disgraced. A believer is bound to take it hard to be pushed into Enlightenment in the end and allowed to retain mainly the dignity of his or her dissatisfaction. Perhaps the distinction is merely an opportunism, but I am persuaded that there are men and women of goodwill who would accept it. I assume that such people, adepts of a satisfied Enlightenment, would explain themselves somewhat in these terms: I am an individual. I have the use of my faculties and notably of my reasoning capacity. I take full responsibility for the exercise of my mind and for whatever I do in that light. No external authority, church or state, has my allegiance unless I choose, day by day, to give it. If I exhibit benevolence toward other people, it is because I choose to act in that way. I do not kill other people; I decide, day by day, not to kill them. I conduct my life as a "permanent creation of myself in my autonomy"—the pertinent phrase I find in Michel Foucault's "What Is Enlightenment?"[2] If other people act on different reasons or no reason that I can see, so much the worse for them and perhaps for me.

It hardly matters whether I have characterized these adepts justly or caricatured them; it is enough that I point to a certain motive, indeed a prejudice, and mark its provenance in American life. It is an active force whenever Americans feel that life is their oyster, that at any moment they can make a fresh start, hit the road. Franklinism is another name for it, but the name is inaccurate; Franklin had a wider culture and a more complex sense of life than he is regularly given credit for. The motive I am describing comes into political life when Americans cannot understand why other people evidently do not want to live like Americans. The ideology of America as "Redeemer Nation" depends on thi

---

[2]Michel Foucault, "What Is Enlightenment?" in *The Foucault Reader*, ed. Paul Rabinov (Harmondsworth: Penguin, 1984), 44.

prejudice and also on the still-deeper prejudice by which reality is taken to be the scientific account of it, or the positivist's version of it.

Exemplars of Enlightenment unsatisfied are more interesting folk. Hegel calls them believers, but only because they are not fully at home within the Enlightenment. They probably believe just as much as anyone else, but their beliefs are likely to be theologically unexacting; no church is low enough for them. Sometimes they take pride in their atheism, but they are not, in practice, immune to credences just as unaccountable as any theism. Reviewing Bertrand Russell's *What I Believe*, T. S. Eliot professed himself "amazed at Mr. Russell's capacity for believing. . . . St. Augustine did not believe more."[3] As for pragmatism, which thinks itself superior to beliefs and independent of them, Eliot pointed out that the pragmatist believes his or her own doctrine in a sense that is not pragmatic but absolute. The error of pragmatism is "to treat certain other concepts, like 'usefulness' or 'success', as if they had the absoluteness denied to truth."[4] It is wrong to believe professed unbelievers when they insist that they are unbelievers: They merely act on beliefs they are not in a position to justify. Those who belong to what Hegel calls the unsatisfied Enlightenment believe just as much as the pope does, but they take pleasure in claiming that they, unlike the pope, have chosen the objects of their faith. The claim is, I suspect, bogus. The main difference between the pope and Wallace Stevens is that the pope does not claim to have invented, or deduced from his private desires, the articles of his belief. This is precisely what Stevens claims, and he is self-deceived in the claim, since most of what he claims to have invented he has inherited from a certain philosophic tradition.

No matter. The satisfied inheritors of the Enlightenment claim that their reasoning power gives them unmediated access to truth and that they may therefore dispense with all the official mediations—traditions and myths, especially those myths that speak of an accredited origin from which meaning is derived. The unsatisfied ones are those who try to walk in the presumed light of reason, find themselves disappointed, and deal with the disappointment as best they can. Usually they deal with it by retaining the terminology of Enlightenment and making it, if they can, more flexible, more responsive. This device, when practiced in

[3]T. S. Eliot, "The Preacher as Artist," *Athenaeum* (28 November 1919): 1,252.
[4]T. S. Eliot, "A Contemporary Thomist," *New Statesman* (10 December 1917): 312.

Europe, is called romanticism; when practiced in America, it is called transcendentalism, and Emerson and Thoreau are regarded as its saints. Devotees no longer speak of reason—Stevens mocked that capacity as "Reason's click-clack"—but of vision or imagination.

Stanley Cavell, who represents Enlightenment unsatisfied in a style that mourns over the loss of its spiritual world, tries to redeem his enlightened vocabulary by speaking not of knowledge but of acknowledgment. A disappointed man, he has made disappointment his theme. In *In Quest of the Ordinary*, he speaks of romanticism as

working out a crisis of knowledge, a crisis I have taken to be (interpretable as) a response at once to the threat of skepticism and to a disappointment with philosophy's answer to this threat, particularly as embodied in the achievement of Kant's philosophy—a disappointment most particularly with the way Kant balances the claims of knowledge of the world to be what you may call subjective and objective, or, say, the claims of knowledge to be dependent on or independent of the specific endowments—sensuous and intellectual—of the human being.

This in turn, Cavell says, "perhaps means a disappointment in the idea of taking the success of science, or what makes science possible, as an answer to the threat of skepticism, rather than a further expression of it."[5]

I have been referring to European romanticism and American transcendentalism as attempts to go beyond the Enlightenment or to take the harm out of it by exceeding its characteristic terms. For the moment, that is, I have been taking Hegel at one or two of his words and construing a certain story as if it were still one of the stories of the Enlightenment. But I do not set this procedure against the other way of interpreting the same evidence, which is to take it as evidence of the "secularization of inherited theological ideas and ways of thinking" in England, France, Germany, and therefore the United States in the middle of the nineteenth century. The phrase just quoted comes from M. H. Abrams's *Natural Supernaturalism: Tradition and Revolution in Romantic Literature* (1971), where the case it implies is made.[6] Either we construe the case of transcendentalism (to hold with that) as one of unsatisfied Enlightenment and a device to cope with the disappointment

---

[5]Stanley Cavell, *In Quest of the Ordinary* (Chicago: University of Chicago Press, 1988), 52.
[6]M. H. Abrams, *Natural Supernaturalism: Tradition and Revolution in Romantic Literature* (New York: Norton, 1971), 12.

Cavell describes, or we see it as a "translation downward" of fundamental terms in theology and religion. I am sure it makes a difference: In the first version, disappointment is likely to be incorrigible, since the extension of the terms of Enlightenment is bound to appear opportunistic. Cavell is not convincing when he speaks of acknowledgment as a further mode of knowledge and not a departure from it. In the second case, there is likely to be a conviction of bad faith if the terms of faith are smartly secularized: In practice—by which I mean in the diverse practices of Wordsworth, Coleridge, and Emerson for the most part— there is honest recognition that much has been sacrificed to obtain the easier certitudes.

In commoner practice, the question comes to this: Is Christianity compatible with Enlightenment thinking? If it is not, so much the worse for Christianity. If it is, or might be, is it still Christianity?

THE QUESTION OF CHRISTIANITY

The issues between Eliot and Stevens—not that they ever debated them—concern reason, faith, and authority. I want to approach them by reading a book that raises these issues in ways hardly to be looked for in poetry. Josiah Royce's *The Problem of Christianity* (1913) at least puts the main question clearly: What is the essence of Christianity, the particular understanding or vision of the world, such that a "modern man" may believe it and live according to its light?

I shall mention only those parts of *The Problem of Christianity* that bear on the question of knowledge and belief, and then I shall turn to our poets. Royce emphasizes that he is not concerned, as William James was, with the particular religious experiences of individuals. "My main topic," he says, "is a form of social religious experience, namely, that form which, in ideal, the Apostle Paul viewed as the experience of the Church."[7] Some readers may feel that Royce is giving the shortest of shrifts to Jesus, since he is merely the one who founded an institution far more important than himself. Royce is concerned with Christianity, in its historical manifestation, only at the moment in which it becomes, mainly through Paul, a spiritual and social community. The basis of this community is not, according to Royce, its shared "imitation of Christ,"

[7]Josiah Royce, *The Problem of Christianity* (1913), 2 vols. (Hamden, Conn.: Archon Books, 1967), 1:xv.

but the multiple acts of interpretation which constitute its social existence. To clarify this point, Royce uses C. S. Peirce's system of signs and the mediating idea, or "third," of which Peirce made so much (more about this later). The gist of Royce's argument, then, is that a community is founded on the will to interpret.

By emphasizing this will in Peirce's terms, Royce can assure himself that when he comes to believe something, what he believes will be compatible with the procedures not only of reason but of natural science and logic. As a Darwinian, Royce accepted notions of evolution and progress with a degree of buoyancy now hard to credit: he found it easy, apparently, to believe that the human race has been the beneficiary of education to the point at which he can project a fictitious entity called "modern man" and endow him with exemplary capacities:

> For by the "modern man" most of us mean a being whose views are supposed to be in some sense not only the historical result, but a significant summary, of what the ages have taught mankind. The term "modern man" condenses into a word the hypothesis, the postulate, that the human race has been subject to some more or less coherent process of education. The modern man is supposed to teach what this "education of the human race" has taught to him. The ages have their lesson. The modern man knows something of this lesson.[8]

(Readers of Stevens will recognize some features of Royce's "modern man" in the "major man" of Stevens's *Notes toward a Supreme Fiction*, to be discussed later.)

It is not surprising that Royce, making so little of the life, death, and resurrection of Christ, concludes:

> Let your Christology be the practical acknowledgement of the Spirit of the Universal and Beloved Community. This is the sufficient and practical faith. Love this faith, use this faith, teach this faith, preach this faith, in whatever words, through whatever symbols, by means of whatever forms of creeds, in accordance with whatever practices best you find to enable you with a sincere intent and a whole heart to symbolize and to realize the presence of the Spirit in the Community. All else about your religion is the accident of your special race or nation or form of worship or training or accidental personal opinion, or devout private mystical experience,—illuminating but capricious. The core, the center of the faith, is not the person of the individual founder, and is not any other individual man. Nor is this core to be found in the sayings of the founder, nor yet in the traditions of Christology. The core of the faith is the Spirit, the Beloved Community, the work of grace, the atoning deed, and the saving power of the loyal life. There is nothing else under heaven whereby men have been saved or can

[8]Ibid., 17–18.

be saved. To say this is to found no new faith, but to send you to the heart of all true faith.[9]

I quoted this passage mainly to indicate what a short step it would take to reach the churchless Church, the beliefless Belief of Robert Bellah, who took the title, and much else, of his famous book from a line of Stevens's poem "Flyer's Fall": "dimensions in which / We believe without belief, beyond belief."

PAGAN STEVENS

I propose to refer briefly to two poems by Stevens, starting with "Sunday Morning," his most celebrated poem and the one in which he first addressed, explicitly if not justly, the experience of wanting to believe.

Stevens said that "Sunday Morning" is "not essentially a woman's meditation on religion and the meaning of life. It is anybody's meditation. . . . The poem is simply an expression of paganism, although, of course, I did not think that I was expressing paganism when I wrote it."[10] Formally, it is a poem of eight stanzas, fifteen lines each, which proceeds by "free indirect narrative." That is, a woman's thoughts on a Sunday morning, when she might well have gone to church, resolve themselves from time to time into words and are scolded, in effect, by the narrative voice for wanting more than paganism. Despite the secular comforts of her life, she thinks of Christ, "the dark / Encroachment of that old catastrophe," and is immediately rebuked for having such thoughts, for giving the bounty of her consciousness to the dead. The narrative voice is somewhat disingenuous in saying that the woman should be just as well satisfied by the thought of pungent fruit and the beauty of the earth as by thought of heaven:

> Divinity must live within herself:
> Passions of rain, or moods in falling snow;
> Grievings in loneliness, or unsubdued
> Elations when the forest blooms . . . [11]

These, Stevens says, are the "measures destined for her soul." Perhaps they are, but it seems wicked to demand that she be totally fulfilled in them and that they constitute her entire spiritual life.

[9]Ibid., 2:428–29.
[10]Holly Stevens, ed., *Letters of Wallace Stevens* (New York: Knopf, 1966), 250.
[11]Wallace Stevens, *Collected Poems* (London: Faber and Faber, 1955), 67.

The third stanza seems to allow for more. It refers to Jove and his descent to love, an allegory that gives human life at least partial access to divinity:

> Jove in the clouds had his inhuman birth.
> No mother suckled him, no sweet land gave
> Large-mannered motions to his mythy mind.
> He moved among us, as a muttering king,
> Magnificent, would move among his hinds,
> Until our blood, commingling, virginal,
> With heaven, brought such requital to desire
> The very hinds discerned it, in a star.
> Shall our blood fail? Or shall it come to be
> The blood of paradise? And shall the earth
> Seem all of paradise that we shall know?
> The sky will be much friendlier then than now,
> A part of labor and a part of pain,
> And next in glory to enduring love,
> Not this dividing and indifferent blue.[12]

Stevens refers to Jove again, in an essay called "Two or Three Ideas," where somewhat puzzlingly he speaks of the gods not "in their religious aspects but as creations of the imagination." Puzzling because generally Stevens thinks of the gods as creations of the imagination and as nothing else:

When we think of Jove, while we take him for granted as the symbol of omnipotence, the ruler of mankind, we do not fear him. . . . To speak of the origin and end of gods is not a light matter. It is to speak of the origin and end of eras of human belief. And while it is easy to look back on those that have disappeared as if they were the playthings of cosmic make-believe, and on those that made petitions to them and honored them and received their benefits as legendary innocents, we are bound, nevertheless, to concede that the gods were personae of a peremptory elevation and glory. It would be wrong to look back to them as if they had existed in some indigence of the spirit.[13]

So in "Sunday Morning" mention of Jove is enough to make Stevens feel some misgiving, not about his humanism but about its premature identification with a taste for coffee and oranges.

In the fourth stanza, for the first time, the woman is allowed to be heard:

---

[12]Ibid., 67–8.
[13]Wallace Stevens, "Two or Three Ideas," in *Opus Posthumous*, ed. Samuel French Morse (New York: Knopf, 1957), 205–6.

She says, "I am content when wakened birds,
Before they fly, test the reality
Of misty fields, by their sweet questionings;
But when the birds are gone, and their warm fields
Return no more, where, then, is paradise?"

The reply to this is, in effect, that no paradise according to any of the accredited mythologies—Christian, Greek, Roman, Arabic, or any other—"has endured / As April's green endures." The woman is not convinced by it: "She says, 'But in contentment I still feel / The need of some imperishable bliss.' " The answer, this time, is that "Death is the mother of beauty." The inevitability of one's death intensifies one's experiences and makes up for their transience, an admonition Stevens's poem entrusts to a Keatsian rhetoric of heartbreaking authority. Imperishable bliss would soon become tedious because it would lack the character we crave, that of change. However we imagine paradise, it would be a mere repetition of the same.

In the seventh stanza Stevens seems to reach for the peremptory glory that he ascribed to the cult of Jove and the ancient gods, but he now projects it toward some future occasion of worship—with a difference. The worshipers are to chant their devotion to the sun, "Not as a god, but as a god might be." The difference seems to be that the worshiped force is an object not of belief but of pure imagination. The energy of the ritual will come from one's identification with the natural world, the winds, the trees, the lakes.

In the last stanza, the woman does not speak in her own voice, but she hears a voice:

She hears, upon that water without sound,
A voice that cries, "The tomb in Palestine
Is not the porch of spirits lingering.
It is the grave of Jesus, where he lay."

Stevens's answer to this message is that our only life is the life we know, the planet on which we live, an "old chaos of the sun":

We live in an old chaos of the sun,
Or old dependency of day and night,
Or island solitude, unsponsored, free,
Of that wide water, inescapable.
Deer walk upon our mountains, and the quail
Whistle about us their spontaneous cries;
Sweet berries ripen in the wilderness;

And, in the isolation of the sky,
At evening, casual flocks of pigeons make
Ambiguous undulations as they sink,
Downward to darkness, on extended wings.

This, too, gorgeous as it is, merely brushes the woman's misgiving aside; there is to be no talk of Jesus, or of resurrection, or of immortality.

SUPREME FICTION

In the essay "Two or Three Ideas," Stevens says that "in an age of disbelief, or, what is the same thing, in a time that is largely humanistic, in one sense or another, it is for the poet to supply the satisfactions of belief, in his measure and in his style."[14] He does not mean that he wants poets to recover the old beliefs; not at all. Poets are to appease one's desire to believe and they are to do this by working out the unlimited possibilities of the "increasingly human self," which is in any case all there is.

It is as if Stevens had anticipated Jürgen Habermas and gone beyond his program, as if he retained the project of Enlightenment but proposed to pursue it by recourse not to reason but to imagination. Significantly, and perhaps inevitably, he retains the hierarchical terms of Christianity, but "translates them down," turning God into a human being, according to the formula of the late poem "Final Soliloquy of the Interior Paramour": "We say God and the imagination are one." Other equations or substitutions follow. Christ becomes a person, merely, like any other. The church becomes the fellowship of one's mind with other minds, or with a few notable minds, as in certain poets and philosophers. Prayer becomes not an elevation of the soul to God in praise, but verbal brooding on nearly any theme that occurs; hence Stevens's favorite form, variations on a theme having to do with reality and the imagination. Where Christianity speaks of truth or revelation, Stevens speaks rather of fictions, structures devised by acts of an individual imagination. The ideal form of such fictions is what Stevens calls a Supreme Fiction; it is his version of theology. Instead of the Christian sacraments, Stevens works out the possibilities of a few leading ideas, not because they are or may be true but because they are poetic, beautiful, or perhaps sublime. In

[14]Ibid., 206.

that sense Stevens may be called a post-Christian poet—not because Christianity has died, which is evidently not the case, but because the structure of Stevens's desires is that of Christianity, the validity of which institution he no longer accepts.

It would be a serious error of judgment, and certainly of tact, to try to turn Stevens into a philosopher. He liked reading philosophy and used it for five-finger exercises. He was a poet, not a philosopher, and the poetic character of his poems is not the same as the character, whatever that may be, of the ideas he mulled over. Beyond an uncertain point, it is misleading even to advert to these ideas; they are no more than raw material with which he worked and to which he gave the acute attention of an amateur. It is clear, nonetheless, that a certain paradigm is useful to a reader of Stevens's poems, and may be at worst a working hypothesis. It may be better than that, if only because Stevens's poems offer evidence of it at every point.

The paradigm goes as follows: We live in a place that we have not made; therefore it is not our own. The sky is an indifferent blue. Our only capacity is consciousness: We think ourselves into the distinctive form of being which we call human being. But it may be possible to continue with those acts of consciousness to the point at which we have transformed the world into ourselves. At that point we would be in no respect inferior to the gods, or to the Christian God in whom we no longer believe. Poetry is the form of a consciousness turned toward that project and, ideally, capable of carrying it forward if not of carrying it out. If it could be done, the poet would be "major man."

Before I quote from *Notes toward a Supreme Fiction* the passage in which this paradigm is most explicit, I want to refer to a comment on Hegel that Royce includes in *The Problem of Christianity*. It is by R. H. Mackintosh:

Christianity receives (according to Hegel) absolute rank, but at the cost of its tie with history. For only the world-process as a whole, and no single point or person in it, can be the true manifestation of the Absolute. . . . Thus, when Hegel has waved his wand, and uttered his dialectical and all-decisive formula, a change comes over the spirit of the believer's dream; everything appears to be as Christian as before, yet instinctively we are aware that nothing specifically Christian is left. . . . When once the Gospel has been severed from a historic person, and identified with a complex of metaphysical ideas, what it ought to be called is scarcely worth discussion; that it is no longer Christianity, is clear. . . . The proposed identification of the Christian faith with the ontological theory that God and man are one,—God the essence of man, man the actuality of God,—is an utterly hopeless enterprise, which the scientific historian cannot take seriously.[15]

I quoted this passage—especially those last sentences—because the project it describes is close to Stevens's, although Stevens undertook it not on behalf of Christianity or with any zeal to save the Christian revelation but, rather, to claim for humanity the attributes of God. The project is, as I understand it, an extreme version of idealism, according to which consciousness is deemed to account for the whole of one's experience.

Here, then, is the passage from *Notes toward a Supreme Fiction*:

> The first idea was not our own. Adam
> In Eden was the father of Descartes
> And Eve made air the mirror of herself,
>
> Of her sons and of her daughters. They found themselves
> In heaven as in a glass; a second earth;
> And in the earth itself they found a green—
>
> The inhabitants of a very varnished green.
> But the first idea was not to shape the clouds
> In imitation. The clouds preceded us
>
> There was a muddy centre before we breathed.
> There was a myth before the myth began,
> Venerable and articulate and complete.
>
> From this the poem springs: that we live in a place
> That is not our own and, much more, not ourselves
> And hard it is in spite of blazoned days.
>
> We are the mimics. Clouds are pedagogues.
> The air is not a mirror but bare board,
> Coulisse bright-dark, tragic chiaroscuro
>
> And comic color of the rose, in which
> Abysmal instruments make sounds like pips
> Of the sweeping meanings that we add to them.[16]

I should emphasize that this passage reveals Stevens in only one of his moods, even if it is one of the most suggestive and far-reaching; it is not meant to be a culmination. It does mark what I have called his project, but chiefly the difficulties it has to face. Stevens seems to have accepted, as Royce did, Peirce's system of Firstness, Secondness, and Thirdness, where Firstness is the conception of being or existing independent of anything else; Secondness is the conception of being relative to, or in

[15]Royce, *The Problem of Christianity*, 2:331–32.
[16]Stevens, *Collected Poems*, 383–84.

reaction with, something else; and Thirdness is the conception of mediation, whereby a first and a second are brought into relation.[17] According to Stevens's parable, Adam and Eve were the first humanists, because—like Descartes—they conceived the world in their own terms and practiced the attribute of reason in doing so. They made a second earth by construing the first in terms most favorable to themselves. They founded the Enlightenment. In the meantime, things have become more difficult; it is hard to see the air as mirror of oneself. There is too much evidence that the constituents of reality are opaque. In *The Necessary Angel* Stevens endorses an argument he found in an essay by the philosopher H. D. Lewis:

Mr. Lewis says that poetry has to do with the matter that is foreign and alien. It is never familiar to us in the way in which Plato wished the conquests of the mind to be familiar. On the contrary, its function, the need which it meets and which has to be met in some way in every age that is not to become decadent or barbarous, is precisely this contact with reality as it impinges upon us from outside, the sense that we can touch and feel a solid reality which does not wholly dissolve itself into the conceptions of our own minds. It is the individual and particular that does this.[18]

I take this passage as expressing Stevens's scruple not about his project but about the empty ease with which it might seem to be achieved. If, as in Peirce's account of idealism, the idealist is one who deems the psychical law alone as primordial and the physical law as derived and special, it is always a question how the deriving is done, and what is the status of the particulars derived. That we add our own sweeping meanings is not to be disputed, unless the claim is made in extravagant terms.

But it is a strange if not extravagant feature of Stevens's project that, having reduced God to human, the poet should not be content with the reduction: He at once sets about trying to recover the loss and to add it, however implausibly, to humanity's capacity. In a letter of 12 January 1943 to Hi Simons, who had enquired about a later passage in *Notes toward a Supreme Fiction*, Stevens wrote: "The trouble with humanism is that man as God remains man, but there is an extension of man, the leaner being, in fiction, a possibly more than human human, a composite human. The act of recognizing him is the act of this leaner being moving in on us."[19] I take it that this notion of a composite human, a more than human

[17]Charles S. Peirce, *Values in a Universe of Chance*, ed. Philip P. Wiener (New York: Doubleday, 1958), 158.
[18]Wallace Stevens, *The Necessary Angel* (New York: Knopf, 1951), 96.
[19]Stevens, *Letters*, 434.

human, is a conceit good enough to cut a dash in the poem but, outside the poem, good for nothing but mystification. Of course it could be said that Stevens is merely imagining a fabulous creature, as predecessors imagined the Minotaur and other hybrid creatures, to express the inexpressible, or even as sages from Longinus to Boileau, Edmund Burke, and Kant posited the sublime as a category of inner disturbance for which nothing reasonable but something formidable nonetheless could be said. Stevens's attempt to ascribe such experiences not even to a genius but to a composite figure is bold: It seems to require us to believe in such a thing.

ELIOT AND BELIEF

When we consider Eliot's writings in relation to knowledge and belief, we come on far more ambiguous, if not far more complex, evidence than we had anticipated. It is well known that Eliot entered into communion with the Anglican Church in 1927 and that the particular traditions, within Christianity, which touched him most are sufficiently indicated by naming Saint Augustine, Dante, the English medieval mystics (especially Juliana of Norwich), Saint John of the Cross, and Pascal. It would be reasonable to assume, however, that the English Protestant divines meant much to him: that is true, and his admiration for Lancelot Andrewes and George Herbert in particular is on record. But it is beginning to be clear—especially in Jeffrey Perl's *Skepticism and Modern Enmity*—that Eliot did not regard philosophy as an adjunct or a set of prolegomena to belief. He was never much taken with the project of the Enlightenment or with the ambition of coming to truth by philosophic reasoning. In a letter of 6 January 1915 to Norbert Wiener, Eliot wrote that philosophy was "chiefly literary criticism and conversation about life":

> The only reason why relativism does not do away with philosophy altogether, after all, is that there is no such thing to abolish! There is art, and there is science. And there are works of art, and perhaps of science, which would never have occurred had not many people been under the impression that there was philosophy.[20]

At Harvard University, Eliot at least entertained an interest in many philosophic traditions, with perhaps a particular affection for Buddhist writings. He regarded the history of metaphysics, in any Western sense, as mostly a record of vanity. Much as he admired Aristotle, he thought

---

[20]Quoted in Jeffrey M. Perl, *Skepticism and Modern Enmity: Before and after Eliot* (Baltimore: Johns Hopkins University Press, 1989), 66.

that he had set metaphysics on an erroneous track, in quest of "being unconditioned":

It is only the persistent faith in a difference between thought and reality which prevents Aristotle from explicitly handling metaphysics as the investigation into the ultimate meaning of thought as expressed in the forms of language. He conducts himself as if he were analysing things and not ideas.[21]

Not that the damage could now be undone. Eliot worked up enough interest in metaphysics to complete a dissertation called "Knowledge and Experience in the Philosophy of F. H. Bradley," and he remained at least interested in Bradleyan idealism. But the unpublished manuscripts that Jeffrey Perl has studied—mostly Eliot's essays for Royce's seminar at Harvard—show that, so far as Eliot took a position at all, it was that of skepticism or conventionalism. The merit of skepticism or conventionalism was that it regarded truth as the coherence of all the available terms within a limited field of discourse. In his work on Bradley, Eliot attacked epistemology for its assumption "that there is one consistent world . . . and that it is our business to find it." In a paper on Kant and agnosticism, Eliot wrote: "Knowledge is only knowledge when 'taken internally.' If you contemplate knower and known from the outside, what you find is *not* simply knower and known, but a peculiar complex of existents, and knowledge fades into ontology. Hence to know we must begin with *faith*."[22]

It seems clear that Eliot did not believe that the royal way to faith was by starting with knowledge. As in other experiences of life, one starts with a vague or acute feeling of discontent, and tries to ease the distress by whatever means. Pascal was one whose conduct in this regard Eliot found most edifying:

Above all, he was a man of strong passions; and his intellectual passion for truth was reinforced by his passionate dissatisfaction with human life unless a spiritual explanation could be found. . . . The Christian thinker . . . proceeds by rejection and elimination. He finds the world to be so and so; he finds its character inexplicable by any non-religious theory: among religions he finds Christianity, and Catholic Christianity, to account most satisfactorily for the world and especially for the moral world within; and thus, by what Newman calls "powerful and concurrent" reasons, he finds himself inexorably committed to the dogma of the Incarnation.[23]

Eliot did not claim, of course, that this process solved all problems or subsumed them in an untroubled faith. Again, Pascal was his exemplar:

[21]Ibid., 71.
[22]Ibid., 68.
[23]T. S. Eliot, *Selected Essays* (London: Faber and Faber, 1963), 407–8.

Pascal, as the type of one kind of religious believer, which is highly passionate and ardent, but passionate only through a powerful and regulated intellect, is in the first sections of his unfinished Apology for Christianity facing unflinchingly the demon of doubt which is inseparable from the spirit of belief.[24]

It is not enough to say of Eliot's Christianity that the dogma of the Incarnation and the deeply apprehended sense of original sin were crucial. No single element in Christianity was more crucial than any other; since Eliot believed that "you must either take the whole of revealed religion or none of it."[25] The consideration that made the project of the Enlightenment appear shoddy to him was his distrust in unaided reason, which he derided as the inner voice so cherished by Middleton Murry. "The possessors of the inner voice," Eliot said, "ride ten in a compartment to a football match at Swansea, listening to the inner voice, which breathes the eternal message of vanity, fear, and lust."[26] More urbanely, Eliot regretted that the Protestant bishops at the Lambeth Conference in 1930 placed so much reliance "upon the Individual Conscience": "Certainly, anyone who is wholly sincere and pure in heart may seek for guidance from the Holy Spirit; but who of us is always wholly sincere, especially where the most imperative of instincts may be strong enough to simulate to perfection the voice of the Holy Spirit?"[27]

In his later years, wisely or not, Eliot became a social critic, writing about religion, education, and politics, defining culture, and proposing the idea of a Christian society. The enemy was always what he called secularism, an inability or a refusal to understand "the primacy of the supernatural over the natural life."[28]

FAITH AND FORM

Many passages in Eliot's poetry rebuke the Enlightenment project. In some of them, the rebuke is implicit; in others, explicit, as in "The Dry Salvages," where such optimistic notions as those of development and evolution are regarded as mere stratagems for disowning the past. That poem should be set beside a section in "East Coker" in which Eliot pours

[24]Ibid., 411.
[25]Ibid., 413.
[26]Ibid., 27.
[27]Ibid., 374.
[28]Ibid., 398.

cold water on any assumptions, popular or not, about knowledge and
experience:

> There is, it seems to us,
> At best, only a limited value
> In the knowledge derived from experience.
> The knowledge imposes a pattern, and falsifies,
> For the pattern is new in every moment
> And every moment is a new and shocking
> Valuation of all we have been. We are only
>   undeceived
> Of that which, deceiving, could no longer harm.
> In the middle, not only in the middle of the way
> But all the way, in a dark wood, in a bramble,
> On the edge of a grimpen, where is no secure
>   foothold,
> And menaced by monsters, fancy lights,
> Risking enchantment. Do not let me hear
> Of the wisdom of old men, but rather of their folly,
> Their fear of fear and frenzy, their fear of possession,
> Of belonging to another, or to others, or to God.
> The only wisdom we can hope to acquire
> Is the wisdom of humility: humility is endless.[29]

In a full consideration of this passage, it would be well to place beside
it the earlier poem "Animula" and the later passage in "Little Gidding"
in which a familiar compound ghost makes a stringent comment on the
wisdom of experience. Even by way of a brief gloss, one should remark
that the crux of the matter is "pattern." In Eliot's poetry generally, the
word "pattern" marks a moment in one's moral life that may be genuine
or specious. In "East Coker" the trajectory from experience to the
knowledge derived from it, and then to the pattern that knowledge imposes is specious because its certitude is premature. Knowledge should
not be so sure of itself as to think that it has taken full possession of
the past and may now embody that possession in a pattern. A pattern
is indeed necessary, but only one that is troubled with itself and turned,
in fright as much as in hope, toward a future in which it may or may
not be verified. This is the force of "pattern" in Eliot's "Burnt Norton":

> Words move, music moves
> Only in time; but that which is only living

[29]T. S. Eliot, *Collected Poems 1909–1962* (London: Faber and Faber, 1963), 199.

Can only die. Words, after speech, reach
Into the silence. Only by the form, the pattern,
Can words or music reach
The stillness, as a Chinese jar still
Moves perpetually in its stillness.[30]

This is as close as Eliot can come—as close as he is willing to come, to
try to come closer being an impertinence—to "the meaning"; it cannot
be a meaning enforced with the confidence of a mind utterly sure of
itself. The passages I quoted from his essay on Pascal should have made
that limitation clear enough. Silence is, in Eliot's later poetry, the act of
faith, the "awful daring" of the soul's surrender to God.

DARK ENLIGHTENMENT

With the example of Eliot before us, it would be absurd to stay with
Hegel's account of the Enlightenment, or to think that the concept of
Enlightenment can house both Enlightenment and belief. Belief, as we
use the word in describing Eliot's poetry from "Ash Wednesday" to
"Little Gidding" as poetry of belief, cannot be contained within any
feasible account of the Enlightenment as a system of values or axioms.
Not that opposition to Enlightenment is exerted only by Christians—
many of the people who oppose the Enlightenment agree on nothing
else. Think of Eliot's Christian poems, and then of William Blake's *Four
Zoas*, D. H. Lawrence's *Women in Love*, Michael Polanyi's *Knowing
and Being*, Michael Oakeshott's *On Human Conduct*, Marjorie Grene's
Knower and the Known, F. R. Leavis's *Nor Shall My Sword*, the last
with its reference to "our technologico-Benthamite world" and the
"blind enlightened menace." No, we are not, all of us, men and women
of the Enlightenment; there is no such consensus.

So where are we? So far are we from enjoying a consensus on being
men and women of the Enlightenment that each of us is entirely free to
reconsider the program that goes by that name. It may be that the whole
project that includes eighteenth-century Enlightenment and nineteenth-
century romanticism and transcendentalism has come to an end. Habermas has argued, in *The Philosophical Discourse of Modernity* (1987),
that "the paradigm of the philosophy of consciousness is exhausted."[31]

[30]Ibid., 194.
[31]Jürgen Habermas, *The Philosophical Discourse of Modernity*, trans. Frederick Lawrence
(Cambridge, Mass.: MIT Press, 1987), 296.

He has reached this conviction after a remarkably just and perceptive analysis of Kant, Hegel, Schiller, Nietzsche, the Frankfurt school, Husserl, Heidegger, Derrida, Bataille, and Foucault. I do not see how his account of the philosophy of consciousness, in which these philosophers have played major and diverse roles, can be much faulted. Consciousness obviously includes the "reason" of the Enlightenment and claims to go beyond it, so it is the subject-based character of philosophy that comes under Habermas's scrutiny. I am not sure about his own proposal, that philosophy, having abandoned the philosophy of consciousness, should take up a different plan, that of achieving "mutual understanding between subjects capable of speech and action."[32] As Mahatma Gandhi is said to have responded when asked what he thought of Western civilization, "It would be nice." Habermas assumes that the language in which the communications he favors would take place is translucent, equally available to all its speakers, given ordinary goodwill. But Jean-François Lyotard is right in saying that language is like a highly complex archipelago, involving regimes of discourse so different—descriptive, prescriptive, evaluative, and so forth—that they are opaque to the program Habermas has in view.

I should remark, not at all by the way, that even if philosophers were to abandon the philosophy of consciousness, as Habermas recommends, the validity of individual consciousness and introspection would in no respect be undermined. Nor would Stevens's poetry, as a case in point, be invalidated. We would read it as if it turned episodes of individual consciousness into experiences that might be shared; which is pretty much the way we read it now. The only difference Habermas's program would make to my reading of Stevens is that I would not assume, as I have tended to, that a subject-based poetry is bound to have the privilege I have been giving to a subject-based philosophy. Habermas is not as forthcoming about this as I would like him to be. His descriptions of the communication he recommends are bound to have their main resonance in social and political action, but his would be a Pyrrhic victory if it required the devaluation of inwardness. There is no need to posit a philosophy of inwardness and to find some means of moving from subject to object and therefore to a decent politics. It is enough if my subjectivity is allowed for in a correspondingly generous politics and linguistics. Emmanuel Levinas is entirely right to say, in *Totality and*

---

[32]Ibid., 298.

Infinity, that "the inner life is the unique *way* for the real to exist as a plurality," and again that interiority constitutes an order in which "what is no longer possible historically remains always possible."[33] It would be wicked to remove that possibility or try to make people feel ashamed of themselves for resorting to it. The soliloquy is an entirely respectable form of expression; it does not entail a refusal of communicative practice.

Indeed, it is in Levinas rather than in Habermas that one finds the necessarily radical change of heart. If one accepts Habermas's argument, as on the whole I do, about the exhaustion of the metaphysics of being and knowledge, ontology and epistemology, then Levinas's *Totality and Infinity* and *Otherwise than Being* are the books to read. Levinas proposes not only to set aside the fixation on ontology and epistemology, on being, the same, the one, totality, and the claims of power they enforce, but also to ground philosophy itself on the primordial imperative of ethics. "Ethics precedes ontology," Levinas maintains.[34] The great meditation, in *Totality and Infinity*, on the "face" and the recognition its coming into view entails is the ground of our beseeching, from which we may indeed begin.

[33]Emmanuel Levinas, *Totality and Infinity*, trans. Alphonso Lingis (Pittsburgh: Duquesne University Press, 1969), 58.
[34]Emmanuel Levinas, *Collected Philosophical Papers*, trans. Alphonso Lingis (Dordrecht, The Netherlands: Martinis Nijhoff, 1987), 183.

Part III

The end of the Enlightenment?

11

The Enlightenment is not over

SCHUBERT M. OGDEN

In responding to the question, Is the Enlightenment over? I understand that I am also to outline my view of the current relations between the Enlightenment heritage and the heritage of religious thought. The purpose, then, is to advance the overriding aim of recovering the relations between these two heritages as they have played out in the course of U.S. history, so as to illuminate the nation's present cultural situation and to approach something like an overview of its problems.

With this in mind, I want to defend a negative answer to the question: No, the Enlightenment is not over, not least because the struggle for and against it continues and must continue within the religious communities themselves as well as within the secular communities of our society and culture. I argue for this answer not from my standpoint as a religious believer and a practicing Christian but from my own viewpoint as an academic, and thus as a specialist in religious studies and a Christian systematic theologian. If this distinction strikes you as odd, I respectfully suggest—for reasons that will become clear—that this itself may be relevant evidence for my answer to the question.

I need to say a few words about what I understand by the two principal terms of our discussion: *the Enlightenment heritage* and *the heritage of religious thought*. So used, the word "heritage" is like its synonym "tradition" in that it can have two different senses. On the one hand, it can have a descriptive sense in which it refers indiscriminately to whatever in fact is passed down or handed on as belonging to the Enlightenment or to religious thought respectively, while, on the other hand, it can have a normative sense in which it refers discriminately only to what by right ought to be passed down or handed on as belonging to one or the other of these two traditions. Both senses of the word are obviously important in the terms of our discussion. Given my assignment and viewpoint, however, I shall be using "heritage" for the most part with its normative meaning when speaking both of the Enlightenment heritage and of the heritage of religious thought, or as I shall say hereafter, simply the religious heritage, on the assumption that thought is certainly involved in the witness borne by a religious community even if it hardly exhausts such witness.

So far as my understanding of *the religious heritage* is concerned, I take it to refer normatively to what I as a Christian theologian understand to be normative religious tradition. Thus it means not only what I understand to be formally normative for the Christian religion, but everything else religious insofar as it substantially agrees with this formal norm, whether or not it has been passed down or handed on as belonging to the Christian tradition.

As for what I understand by *the Enlightenment heritage*, it, too, I take primarily in its normative sense. Insofar as I shall use it descriptively, however, I shall take it to refer to all that has in fact been passed down or handed on as belonging to the Enlightenment, whether or not its claim to belong is valid, given a normative meaning of the term. Just as not everything that purports, or is purported, to belong to the religious heritage may be able to make good on its claim, given a normative understanding of religion, so not everything that purports, or is purported, to belong to the Enlightenment heritage may be able to sustain its claim, assuming a normative understanding of the Enlightenment.

How, in a normative sense, is the Enlightenment to be understood? My answer to this question, which I consider crucial to my argument, is this: the Enlightenment is to be understood normatively as the consistent affirmation of the unique authority of human reason over all other putative authorities. By *human reason* I mean our capacity not only to make or imply various kinds of claims to validity but also, and above all, to validate critically all such claims as and when they become problematic by appropriate kinds of discourse or argument involving appeal in one way or another to common human experience. Thus from the standpoint of the Enlightenment, no claim to validity is valid or invalid simply because someone makes or implies it by what she or he thinks, says, or does. No matter what the claim is or who the claimant may be, whether or not it is valid can be determined only by critically validating it; this means, finally, only by discourse or argument somehow grounded in our common experience simply as human beings. By its very nature, then, the Enlightenment is a challenge to all traditional authorities, however venerable and in whatever field of society and culture, secular as well as religious.

It is just here, however, that we must be careful to avoid some possible misunderstandings. According to Hans-Georg Gadamer, "It is the general tendency of the enlightenment not to accept any authority and to decide everything before the judgment seat of reason. Thus the written tradition of scripture, like any other historical document, cannot claim any absolute validity."[1] The problem with this statement, however, is that it collapses two important distinctions: between not accepting any authority and accepting no authority without reason and between being able to claim absolute validity and being able validly to claim such validity. If I am right, it is no part of the normative meaning of the Enlightenment either simply to reject any authority or to deny the possibility of a tradition's claiming absolute validity. Its point, on the contrary, is that acceptance of an authority or of a tradition's claim to absolute validity needs to be critically validated by reason and experience. The counterpart misunderstanding is that the Enlightenment's negative prejudging of the past is but the other side of its positive prejudging of the present. Thus Mark Noll gives us to understand in his chapter that the Enlightenment lives on in, among other places, the commitment of the Protestant modernist Left to the "shifting norms of university discourse" and the group's desperate eagerness "to baptize the latest in secular trends." Here again, we need to be careful of the distinction between what may in fact be done in the name of the Enlightenment and what may with right lay claim to its name. If the whole point of the Enlightenment is that all claims to validity need to be critically validated as and when they become problematic, then it would be as irrational and contrary to its meaning simply to privilege the present as simply to deprive the past. In both cases, there would be an inconsistent appeal to authority, in that something other than reason and experience would be mistaken to validate our claims.

If this is the normative meaning of the Enlightenment, however, what does and does not belong to its heritage must be understood accordingly. This means that the heritage of the Enlightenment includes, in the first place, everything passed down or handed on as belonging to it that

---

[1] Hans-Georg Gadamer, *Truth and Method* (New York: Crossroad, 1989), 242.

consistently affirms the unique authority of human reason over all other supposed authorities. Beyond this, it may also be taken to include, in the second place, or by implication, anything that has been thought, said, or done insofar as its claims to validity can still be critically validated by the appropriate kind of discourse or argument and appeal to experience. On the other hand, the Enlightenment heritage includes nothing—not even things that have been passed down or handed on as belonging to it—that either denies reason's unique authority or affirms it only inconsistently, or whose claims to validity can no longer be critically validated by reason and experience.

To accept this understanding, however, is to see at once why the Enlightenment is anything but over and why its heritage continues to grow right up to the present moment. Of course, there is much in the Enlightenment heritage considered descriptively that definitely is finished and done with. The obliviousness to the persistence of human evil and the naive faith in inevitable progress that have only too often accompanied affirmation of reason's authority have long since been exposed for what they are by the bitter facts of world history. In a somewhat different way, the tendency of champions of the Enlightenment to identify reason with what are, after all, only certain of its uses, and hardly the most fundamental or important, has now given way to more careful analyses of human thought and speech. But if I am right, none of these developments provides the least reason for thinking that the Enlightenment heritage considered normatively now belongs to the past. On the contrary, they are clear cases of reason's correcting reason, or of reason's continuing self-criticism, in the face of ongoing experience and by way of appropriate discourse or argument.

It is also true that at the present time there are certain movements, secular as well as religious, that are outspokenly anti-Enlightenment, even in what I would understand to be the normative meaning of the words. In one way or another, they expressly question or deny the unique authority of human reason over all other supposed authorities. In the case of some of these movements, however, one finds less the opposition to reason, period, and more the opposition to Reason so as to make room for reason—to adapt a distinction from Richard Rorty's polemic against Philosophy in the name of philosophy.[2] It is at least

---

[2]Richard Rorty, *Consequences of Pragmatism: Essays, 1972–1980* (Minneapolis: University of Minnesota Press, 1982), xiii–xvii.

questionable whether this may not be yet another, perhaps subtler case of reason's criticizing reason, and thus as much a continuation of the Enlightenment heritage as an abandonment of it. In the case of other such movements, however, there is no question about the Enlightenment's being repudiated. This is particularly obvious in religious movements invoking the supreme authority of Scripture or appealing at some point or other to what Mark Noll speaks of as "the self-authenticating character" of religious proposals.

Embattled as it now is, the consistent affirmation of reason's authority is still to be heard on the American scene, and there is every prospect of the Enlightenment heritage's continuing indefinitely into our national future. Not the least reason for saying this is provided by perhaps the most important recent development in the history of religion in America. I refer to what Robert Wuthnow has called, in the titles of two of his latest books, "the restructuring of American religion" and "the struggle for America's soul."[3] Since roughly World War II, the historical divisions in the United States between the several religions, confessions, and denominations have all been increasingly relativized by another and very different kind of religious division. Prepared for to some extent by the earlier split between fundamentalists and mainstream religious believers, this more recent division is between conservatives, or, in the Protestant churches, evangelicals, on the one side, and liberals, on the other. Cutting across all traditional religious communities, it accounts for the fact that persons in one denomination or confession, or even religion, may find themselves closer in matters of belief and practice to certain persons in another such group than to many of the fellow members of their own religious community.

According to Wuthnow, a principal reason for this growing gap between religious orientations has been "rising levels of education": "The better educated typically adopted more liberal and relativistic belief patterns and favored active engagement in social issues; the less well educated followed more traditional lines in belief and practice and came increasingly to focus on issues of personal morality."[4] This development implies, clearly, that the present polarization between religious liberals and conservatives is a continuation of the struggle for and against the

---

[3]Robert Wuthnow, *The Restructuring of American Religion: Society and Faith since World War II* (Princeton: Princeton University Press, 1988), and idem, *The Struggle for America's Soul: Evangelicals, Liberals, and Secularism* (Grand Rapids, Mich.: Eerdmans, 1989).
[4]Wuthnow, *The Struggle for America's Soul*, 16.

Enlightenment, for and against the consistent affirmation of reason's unique authority even in matters of faith and morals.

Of a piece with this struggle within the religious communities is a deepening controversy over how theology should be understood and practiced. There are, of course, many facets to this controversy, and we must be careful not to oversimplify it. But behind such a well-known case as *Charles E. Curran v. The Catholic University of America* are two sharply different positions on what theology is all about. On the one side is the more traditional position, according to which theology is of direct service to the witness of the religious community, and so, being itself a form of this witness, is properly subject to the norms of the community and the institutional church. This is so, moreover, even when theology is undertaken as an academic discipline in a properly academic institution. On the other side is the expressly revisionary position that holds that, although theology's service to the community's witness is real, it can never be more than indirect, since theology is distinct from witness precisely in being critical validation of the claims to validity that witness makes or implies. As such, however, theology can and should be developed as a properly academic discipline on a par with every other and, therefore, subject to identical norms of academic freedom and institutional autonomy. I submit that the controversy now going on in most if not all of our religious communities between these opposed views of theology is as clear evidence as one could expect to find that the Enlightenment is not over and that the struggle for and against it continues within these very communities.

If this struggle undoubtedly continues, my own view is that it also must continue—for the sake of the religious heritage no less than for the sake of the Enlightenment. I contend that it belongs to the very nature of a religion to make or imply a claim to unique authority. Insofar as it is the truth about human existence become explicit in a primary form of culture, a religion is authorized by the primal source of all authority in ultimate reality itself. If a religion can thus claim unique authority, it can do so only because it also claims to be true—and true not in some utterly different sense from that in which anything else is true, but in essentially the same sense, in that it, too, can be verified in some way or other by common human experience and reason. Far from denying reason's unique authority, then, a religion implicitly affirms it. It affirms both the right and the responsibility of reason to validate critically all claims to validity, including its own claims to truth and unique authority.

I realize, naturally, that this is not the only view of religion and reason and that it requires a justification that I cannot provide here. But if it can be defended, as I am confident it can, the struggle for the Enlightenment and thus for the unique authority of reason even in religion is a struggle not against the religious heritage but for it. Indeed, continuation of the religious heritage in America is as dependent today as it has always been on the Enlightenment heritage's also being continued.

12

Modernity, antimodernity, and postmodernity
in the American setting

DAVID TRACY

Insofar as the American moderate and didactic Enlightenment continues to inform our discussions of knowledge and religious belief, it now informs those discussions in very general terms indeed, namely, in the assumption that we can and should trust our ordinary practices of reason, especially such practices as conversation and argument. In fact, we should trust these practices more than we trust any particular theory of rationality. This choice of practice over theory may also possess a certain fidelity to the American form of the Enlightenment itself as distinct from those other forms of the European Enlightenment that were more theoretically and epistemologically concerned.

These latter epistemological hopes for a full-fledged theory of rationality have come on bleak days. At the same time similar difficulties have, perhaps not surprisingly, come on the liberal and reformist traditions in the mainstream churches and synagogues. That the United States has become postmodern as a culture, as some French commentators like Jean Baudrillard suggest, seems to me at best controversial. But a substantial proportion of the American academy, including the academy in religious studies, has in fact become distrustful of the epistemological and theoretical versions of the Enlightenment in favor of one or another anti-Enlightenment version of what has come to be known as postmodernity.

In addition, a singular resurgence of antimodernity (meaning anti-Enlightenment in philosophies like Alasdair MacIntyre's or like the Yale school of antiliberal or postliberal theologies) has invaded all the disciplines and all the religions and theologies. In such a parlous situation, the question of belief and the relation of belief to religious knowledge

328

in its peculiarly American forms from the founders' time to the present is a far more difficult question today than it was even fifteen years ago. An irony of our situation that would have surprised even Reinhold Niebuhr, that prepostmodernist lover of American ironies, is that the American practical-didactic Enlightenment now finds some of its strongest defenders among religious thinkers—especially those thinkers committed to the liberal heritage in theology and to the constructive rather than purely analytical heritage in philosophy of religion. Perhaps some further reflection on these essentially contested categories—modernity, antimodernity, postmodernity—in our present American intellectual situation may help to clarify the context for questions of knowledge and belief.

First, modernity. The debates on the nature of modernity continue, seemingly without end. Much of the present debate is focused on the relation of a philosophical theory of rationality and a social theory of modernity. In Jürgen Habermas (who through his work on C. S. Peirce and John Dewey has become a kind of honorary American thinker), this discussion is a fruitful one. For without trying to link the many philosophical debates on rationality to some historical and also social-scientific or historical theory of modernity, our present philosophical and theological debates on the relation of faith and reason or knowledge and belief can quickly become ahistorical or purely formal.

Just how problematic some contemporary philosophical discussions of rationality have become can be shown by recalling the many contextualist positions that seem barely distinguishable from hard relativism or, more modestly, radical historicism. These present forms of contextualism can seem to suggest that any attempt to defend the Enlightenment, in either the American practical version or, a fortiori, some European theoretical version, is now in serious jeopardy. That would be the case for someone like Richard Rorty, who claims to be the heir of the pragmatist heritage yet believes (unlike Dewey) that our democratic ethos is defensible along ethnocentric but not philosophical lines. Moreover, when the subject of religion comes up, Rorty's entire response seems to be: Let us change the subject.

Awaiting the collapse of all radically historicized notions of reason like Rorty's is positivism, the last modern defender of ahistorical notions of reason. Positivism is now usually construed as a spent force intellectually. We should all be realistic enough to realize, however, that culturally positivism is as powerful a force as ever. For the modern positivist, there is truly no rational way to discuss what the American founders thought could be discussed rationally—the good life, the call to happiness, the need for meaning in history and time. The earlier great liberal pragmatists—such as William James, with his generous call to a radical pluralism; Dewey, with his persuasive account of the democratic ethos implied in a nonpositivistically construed understanding of scientific inquiry; Josiah Royce, with his sense of community, interpretation, and tragedy—can also now seem questionable as resources in an intellectual culture so radically contextualist in one understanding of reason. On the other hand, the recent intellectual alliance between revised forms of pragmatism and revised forms of hermeneutics seems to offer a genuine hope for reason, including a hope for new defenses of the pragmatic-hermeneutical American Enlightenment. Even that hope could become too easily a hope of reason alone, however, if that hope were not related to the social realities (as Habermas argues) of a dominantly scientific and technological culture.

For modernity for some thinkers has become what modernity seemed most to oppose and fear—one more tradition. The honest concern of many modern thinkers can reveal a general pathos, namely, that the forces for emancipation (and surely such emancipatory forces were set loose by the Enlightenment in the great modern bourgeois revolutions) may now seem to be entrapped in purely technical notions of reason from which there can seem no honorable exit: no exit and no ethics; above all, no genuine politics; and, just as tellingly for the concerns of this volume, no genuine conversation on religion that could be called reasonable. This surely would be a pathetic end to the American practical experiment in relating the Enlightenment and religion.

Against these purely contextualist scenarios rest the modern truths which the American Enlightenment thinkers and their successors have tried to defend—today in the revised forms of both hermeneutics and pragmatism. The reality of reason is communicative in conversation and argument. The hope of reason is also alive in all the new countermovements toward a dominantly technoeconomic realm, as well as in the drive toward a cultural pluralism and a genuine political democracy undivorced from concerns for economic democracy. In that sense, we are not trapped in Weber's iron cage.

Still, we can witness all our emancipatory traditions increasingly colonized by the forces of the technoeconomic social system. The technoeconomic realm does not hesitate to use its power to level all memory, including the memory of reason in the American Enlightenment. To remove memory is to decrease the possibility of all resistance, all difference, and, ultimately, all hope, including religious hopes. In such a situation religion inevitably becomes purely privatized, just as art becomes marginalized, and the classics of every culture—including the classics of the American tradition of Enlightenment—become mute. Even the public realm, the last true hope of reason in its modern Western and especially American forms, can become merely technicized.

Considering the alternatives (including the possibilities of intellectual mystification and social and intellectual oppressions in both church and society—oppressions against which the Enlightenment honorably fought), achievements of the American Enlightenment must be defended: an endangered democratic ethos, the classic middle-class virtues, the cultural and religious pluralism of our modern societies. These Enlightenment achievements also deserve theological defense when they are in danger of destruction either from within or from new opponents.

The first among these new opponents may be named with another essentially contested concept: the antimodern. It must be bluntly stated that religious fundamentalism cannot be taken as an intellectually serious theological option, any more than can secularist positivism—a position that it so ironically resembles epistemologically. But religious fundamentalism's social and historical power, again like positivism, is real and growing. Its significance is as a movement of troubled human beings whose sense of community and meaning in history is deeply threatened. Surely fundamentalism is a phenomenon that merits respect and attention from all theologians.

The nonfundamentalist versions of anti-Enlightenment theologies merit not merely human but full intellectual respect: in evangelical, but not fundamentalist, Christian theologies; in Roman Catholic traditional theologies as distinct from the traditionalism of Archbishop Marcel Lefebvre; in the great resurgence of Islamic thought as distinct from that of Ayatollah Khomeini and others; in the retrieval of Jewish traditions across almost all the forms of Judaism, including Reform Judaism. Some of this anti-Enlightenment religious revival is a profound and, in many ways, heartening phenomenon. For the antimoderns persuasively argue that we cannot know the present without respect for memory and tradition. They know instinctively that a subject without community and tradition can soon become little else than the modern individual rendered historyless and passive. In these terms, anyone can see the folly of the radical Enlightenment's wholesale attack on the concept of tradition. The antimodern thinker, like MacIntyre, can sense the unreality of the assumed universalism in some forms of Western liberal social-evolutionary schemes applied to history. She or he knows the wasteful and complacent obstruction of the rich resources of the tradition, including Enlightenment tradition. The antimodern thinker knows the need to retrieve those resources in our perilous times, if any tradition is to maintain any identity.

It is interesting to observe how the central issue always becomes the issue of identity in these antimodern positions. Thus the emergence in contemporary theology of honorable postliberal positions such as that of the new Yale school, or the new sectarian insistence on pure witness, or the insistence of so many Catholic theologians (starting with Joseph Cardinal Ratzinger) that perhaps after all it is Bonaventure and not Aquinas who provides the best model for Catholic theologies. The difficulty here is that, hermeneutically, Christianity and Judaism are always memories that turn as fiercely against themselves as against any other pretensions to triumph.

To defend tradition and community is, at least for Jews and Christians, to defend that disturbing and often self-judging prophetic memory. To become historically minded is to seize that memory for the present and to recall the past as finally subversive of the status quo. As Walter Benjamin insisted, every great work of civilization is at the same time a work of barbarism. Any defense of tradition or community that will not face that insight will not help much. The prophets knew that. So did the self-critical American Enlightenment: a position grounded in the self-correcting notion of reason—the secular counterpart and heir of the prophetic, self-critical heritage.

The final model is sometimes named postmodern. Postmoderns typically claim to expose such illusions of modernity as the unreality of the notion of presence as well as the concept of the present time as "modern." Above all, they challenge the unreality of the modern, purely autonomous, individualistic subject as self-grounded. Like all achievements, postmodernity is not without its ambiguities. Positively, to expose the illusory belief in pure presence of many forms of modern foundationalist thought is no small achievement. Some forms of modernity did attempt to ground themselves in themselves. Some forms of modernity since Descartes seemed to long to build for themselves foundations in a consciousness deceptively pure and an identity deceptively secure.

As the postmoderns strive to clarify, the modern self, unfortunately for its foundationalist pretensions, must also use language. Thereby, the very self-deconstructing, nongrounding play of the signifiers in all language will ensure that the transcendental significance of the modern self-grounding subject will never find the pure identity, that clear and distinct self-presence, it seeks. Modernity cannot achieve the totality it seems always to grasp at—once confidently, now desperately.

Through such typically postmodern gestures of reflection as deconstruction and genealogical analysis, postmoderns also act. Their best postmodern acts are acts of resistance: minimally, resistance to any complacency in the modern self-image; resistance to any concept of the present moment as "modernity," which bears only an illusion of pure presence; resistance, above all, to an alinguistic and finally ahistorical consciousness, resistance to what Michel Foucault nicely names "more of the same." Like Foucault, many of the postmoderns strive to rewrite the "history of the present." At their best, the postmoderns make modernity seriously question its most basic beliefs. They write the history of modernity in such a manner that formerly forgotten, even repressed others of the modern tradition and of the American tradition—hysterics, the mad, the mystics, the dissenters, avant-garde artists, whole marginalized traditions—are allowed to speak and disrupt the usual narratives of both knowledge and belief. In that sense, there is no surprise that the principal categories become otherness, difference, and excess, as alternatives to what is claimed to be the deadening sameness, the desire for totality, the false security engendered by the project of modernity. Nietzsche arrives anew in the United States, but he comes not as the old existentialist Nietzsche of Walter Kaufmann and others; rather, Nietzsche's second American coming is as the new, radically rhetoricized French Nietzsche who can help all postmoderns laugh at the abyss of indeterminacy.

In its theological forms the best postmodern thought can help one recover the mystical strands of the traditions of belief: in Christianity, the radically apophatic tradition from pseudo-Dionysius through Erigena and Meister Eckhart; in Judaism, the cabalistic traditions; in American thought, Emerson and his present descendants—a more apophatic Emerson, perhaps like Stanley Cavell's.

With some notable exceptions, the postmodern thinkers feel free to deconstruct the history of past and present rather than to actualize a concrete political-ethical hope. They wish to deconstruct the status quo in favor of a fluxus quo. Yet they cannot do so without further reflection on the ethical-political import of their own enterprise. There is an ethic of resistance implied in all postmodern thought, but that ethic is sometimes one that runs against the grain of postmodern reflections on the impossibility of any determinateness. How can resistance be secured without some agent—not, to be sure, the false self-grounding subject of modernity, but perhaps the responsible self of the great prophets and the far more modest notion of the self as agent of the practical-hermeneutical American Enlightenment?

In sum, the present questions of knowledge and belief in the American intellectual situation cannot avoid the complexities and frequent confusions in the conflicting interpretations of naming our situation as modern, antimodern, or postmodern. The traditions of both reason and religion are deeply affected, as the different contributors to this book have shown, by that debate over naming our present. It is no longer possible, as moderns hoped, to find a consensus on either reason or religion, on either knowledge or belief, much less on their complex interrelationships. Insofar as this volume has shown some of the full range of modern, antimodern, and even postmodern options, it has contributed to a clarification of both reason and religion as each is variously understood by some of the descendants of the American Enlightenment.

13

Are we beyond the Enlightenment horizon?

RICHARD J. BERNSTEIN

The Enlightenment has always aimed at liberating men from fear and establishing their sovereignty. Yet the fully enlightened earth radiates disaster triumphant.
Max Horkheimer and Theodor Adorno, *Dialectic of Enlightenment*

In our efforts to find ways to include voices of marginalized groups, one might expect helpful guidance from those who have argued against totalizing and universalistic theories such as those of the Enlightenment.
Nancy Hartsock, "Foucault on Power: A Theory for Women?"

The problems of modern moral theory emerge clearly as the failure of the Enlightenment project.
Alasdair MacIntyre, *After Virtue*

The contexts of the claims in this chapter's three epigraphs, the agendas of the authors making them, even the meanings of the word "Enlightenment" differ radically, yet there is one characteristic they share. Each of these authors does not hesitate to speak of the Enlightenment as if it were a unified whole with a common essence. The polemical force of these controversial claims presupposes that the reader grasps what is meant by the Enlightenment (or the Enlightenment project). Unfortunately, this figure of speech has become all too common, especially among critics of the Enlightenment. This reification is the beginning of our difficulties and tends to obscure what should be a prior question: What are we really talking about when we speak of the Enlightenment?

We may well agree with Michel Foucault when, in his own essay dealing with Immanuel Kant's famous essay *Was ist Aufklärung?* (1784), he declares that this is "a question that modern philosophy has

335

not been capable of answering, but that it has never managed to get rid of, either."[1] For heuristic purposes, I want to distinguish three ways in which we may understand this question before we even attempt to answer it.

First, we may consider it a historical question requiring the skills of a historian for a proper answer. Even though historians disagree about what constitutes the "age of Enlightenment" we can turn to some of the representative thinkers of the latter part of the eighteenth century. If we do this, however, we soon discover that the thinkers of the age of Enlightenment disagree about the most fundamental issues; *disagree* is too weak a term. Their claims not only conflict, they are logically incompatible. Consider, for example, what is frequently taken to be the most central concept of the Enlightenment—reason. When, to use Wittgenstein's expression, we "look and see," we discover striking differences in what is meant by *reason*, what are its characteristics, and what are its moral consequences. Suppose we focus on Hume, Kant, and Condorcet. David Hume's skeptical intent is to expose the narrowness of reason—to show how little reason by itself can achieve. Reason is neither sufficient to justify our belief in necessary causal connections nor sufficient to justify our moral convictions. For Kant, however, even though reason is limited, and we cannot hope to achieve knowledge of what transcends the limits of possible experience, we can give a transcendental rational deduction of the categories, including causality. Furthermore, he argues that practical reason is the exclusive ground of the categorical moral imperative. Condorcet thinks of reason in still a different way. For him, it is a dynamic force working itself out in the course of human history. Although reason may be subject to temporary setbacks, it will triumph in the course of history and bring about universal justice, liberty, equality, and happiness. If we pursue the details of these various philosophies, we discover that what each of them means by reason differs—and their differences are deeply embedded in these different philosophical orientations. The point I want to emphasize is that if we look and see, we will be extremely wary of facile universal claims about the Enlightenment. There is no single platform, no set of substantive claims, no common essence that the thinkers of the age of Enlightenment share.

[1]Michel Foucault, "What Is Enlightenment?" in *The Foucault Reader*, ed. Paul Rabinow (New York: Pantheon, 1984), 32.

Second, it may be objected that to emphasize the diversity of incompatible and even incommensurable claims made by thinkers in the age of Enlightenment is to miss the point and the rationale for speaking of the Enlightenment. For the concept of the Enlightenment is an "ideal type"—an artificial construct—which is not to be confused or identified with the views of any single historical individual. This brings me to the second way of understanding the question, What is Enlightenment? The construction or invention of ideal types is necessary if we are to classify, explain, and criticize historical and social developments. Such constructs are used to identify a set of attitudes and beliefs, a frame of mind or *mentalité* that may even have different historical embodiments. For example, this is the way Horkheimer and Adorno use the concept of Enlightenment. They argue that the Enlightenment designates a set of distinctive attitudes and fears that are already implicit in the origins of Western rationality and are prefigured in Homer's portrayal of Odysseus.

I do not think there is anything intrinsically wrong with constructing such ideal types, but I do want to emphasize that the construction of such ideal types requires us to confront a new set of questions. What is the justification for the specific ideal types constructed? What do they really illuminate (and obscure)? Why are certain features emphasized and others relegated to the background? What *work* are these ideal types doing? When we try to answer these questions, we discover that the variety of ideal types of the Enlightenment reveal the explicit and implicit projects of those who employ them. Hence, to grasp what is meant in the three epigraphs we need to uncover the unspoken presuppositions of Horkheimer, Adorno, Hartsock, and MacIntyre to understand why they characterize the Enlightenment in such a contentious manner.

This brings me to a third way of understanding the question, What is Enlightenment? We may call this the reception problem. We may focus our attention on the historical vicissitudes of the ways in which the Enlightenment has been understood in different cultural settings and at different times. For example, why is it that in an American context, the Enlightenment is not primarily understood as being antireligious (although it is considered antidogmatic), whereas in France the antireligious and anticlerical aspects of the Enlightenment are typically stressed? How is one to explain why not so long ago the Enlightenment was associated with the inspiring ideals of modernity—equality, justice, liberty, emancipation—whereas today, for many critics of the Enlightenment, it evokes images of totality, totalitarianism, and even terror? One could write an intellectual history of the past two hundred years by focusing on the changing understandings and valorizations of the Enlightenment.

The reason I stress these different ways of understanding the question, What is Enlightenment? is not only to highlight the complexities, ambiguities, and treacheries in attempting to answer the question. My primary reason is a concern with our present situation. For we are living through a period when Enlightenment bashing has become the sport of intellectuals. In this era, which Richard Rorty has characterized as the "posties"—poststructuralist, postmetaphysical, postmodern, post-Enlightenment—the line that separates counter-Enlightenment, anti-Enlightenment, and post-Enlightenment stances has become very thin. It is not surprising that when Habermas suggested in 1981 that there were hidden affinities between old-style conservative counter-Enlightenment thinkers and new-style "radical" post-Enlightenment thinkers, he touched a sensitive intellectual nerve and triggered a heated debate that still continues.[2] There is something deeply ironic about the recent "postmodern" Enlightenment bashing. One of the pervading characteristics of the postmodern mood is its antiessentialism and its celebration of differences, fragmentation, and irreducible plurality that defy totalization and universalization. Yet in the railing against the Enlightenment, postmodernism tends to mimic what it is presumably attacking. Too frequently there is a glib tendency to essentialize and universalize—to suppress and ignore differences when characterizing the Enlightenment. It is doubly ironic, with all the postmodern talk about exclusion and marginalization, that the Enlightenment comes to play the role of the Other, which is itself to be damned and marginalized.

The substantive thesis I want to advance is that rather than think we are living through a time when there has been (or should be) a complete break with the Enlightenment, we should realize Western intellectuals are all willy-nilly products of the Enlightenment. An Enlightenment horizon still defines the ways in which we think and act. The so-called post-Enlightenment moment is best understood as a variation on the Enlightenment legacy itself. Many of the conflicting strands that mark

[2]Jürgen Habermas, "Modernity versus Postmodernity," *New German Critique* 22 (1981): 3–14.

the *historical* Enlightenment are still with us. They form the matrix for our deepest aspirations and anxieties. I do not think we can even understand the sharpest criticisms of the Enlightenment unless we understand how these criticisms themselves are parasitic on Enlightenment ideals. It was Kant who declared that "our age is, in especial degree, the age of criticism, and to criticism everything must submit."[3] If we think of criticism as an *Aufgabe*—a task and obligation—that is never completed, then even those who engage in criticizing the historical Enlightenment are not breaking with the Enlightenment but, rather, fulfilling its promise in novel ways. Oxymoronically, we might say *our* age is one of postenlightenment Enlightenment.

None of this is intended to deny what has become all too evident in the twentieth century: that the Enlightenment legacy is radically ambiguous. Employing the privileged metaphors of the historical Enlightenment—lightness and darkness—we have become painfully aware of the dark underside of the Enlightenment legacy. Max Weber's thesis about the growth and spread of *Zweckrationalität* (instrumental rationality), which so deeply affects all aspects of our cultural, social, and personal lives; Georg Lukács's analysis of the increasing reification of bourgeois society; Martin Heidegger's reflections on the supreme danger of *Gestell* (enframing); Michel Foucault's microanalyses of the disciplinary society and the emergence of biopower; the Frankfurt school's critique of the "administered society"—all can be read as attempts to elicit the ambiguous legacy of the Enlightenment and its dark consequences. The question remains, How are we to respond in a responsible manner to these multifarious critiques of the ambiguities of the Enlightenment legacy?

In order to begin to answer this question and to support my thesis that we are still thinking and acting within the horizon of the conflicting strands of this Enlightenment legacy, I want to insolate a few major motifs in the American appropriation of the Enlightenment, especially as they have been transformed in the American pragmatic tradition. I begin with the antitotalistic and skeptical impulse initiated by Enlightenment thinkers, one that has been taken up in the pragmatic conception of fallibilism. It seems strange that many postmodern critics of *the* Enlightenment characterize it as totalistic when in fact many of the most powerful arguments against all closed systems of totalities were worked

---

[3]Immanuel Kant, *Critique of Pure Reason*, trans. Norman Kemp Smith (New York: Macmillan, 1965), preface.

out by the thinkers of the age of Enlightenment. When I speak of the skeptical impulse, I am not referring to what philosophers call "episte-mological skepticism"—the doctrine that casts doubt on all knowledge claims. Rather, I mean the growing realization that all claims of indub-itability, absolute certainty, and incorrigibility are suspect. One way of understanding Hume's moderate skepticism is as an endeavor to expose the pretensions of reason itself, to show how little reason can justify by itself and how little we can know with certainty. For Hume, all of our knowledge of "matters of fact" is probable and subject to contingency. It makes no sense to speak of a closed totality.

I do not want to deny that there were some Enlightenment thinkers who tended to deify reason. A much more important and lasting con-sequence of the Enlightenment, however, is the demythologizing of rea-son and the rejection of all forms of dogmatism. This suspicion of claims to absoluticity provides the background for the pragmatic conception of the fallibilism of all inquiry. All knowledge claims are always subject to critical revision and modification. It was Peirce who most rigorously thought through the meaning and consequences of fallibilism and who argued there are no absolute epistemological beginnings or endings of inquiry. There are no absolute foundations for knowledge. C. S. Peirce challenged and sought to deconstruct the metaphor of a foundation that had shaped so much of traditional and modern philosophy. He sought to replace the metaphor of a foundation with the fertile metaphor of a cable. In philosophy, as in the sciences, we ought to "trust rather to the multitude and variety of its arguments than to the conclusiveness of any one. Its reasoning should not form a chain which is no stronger than its weakest link, but a cable whose fibers may be ever so slender, provided they are sufficiently numerous and intimately connected."[4]

This fallibilistic theme, which can be traced back to the historical En-lightenment, is probed and developed by all the "classical" pragmatists, including C. S. Peirce, William James, John Dewey, and George H. Mead. Moreover, there is a continuity between the classical pragmatists and such contemporaries as W. V. O. Quine, Wilfrid Sellars, Hilary Putnam, and Richard Rorty. Dewey generalized this theme when, in his devastating critique of the "quest for certainty," he exposed the hidden complicity between epistemological certainty and moral certainty. The

---

[4]Charles Sanders Peirce, *Collected Papers*, ed. Charles Hartshorne and Paul Weiss, 6 vols. (Cambridge, Mass.: Harvard University Press, 1932–35), 5:265.

core of fallibilism is succinctly expressed by Sellars when he declares that "empirical knowledge, like its sophisticated extension science, is rational, not because it has a foundation, but because it is a self-correcting enterprise, which can put any claim in jeopardy, though not all at once."[5] The reason why I stress this fallibilistic, antifoundational legacy of the Enlightenment is because it is neglected—even suppressed—by those who caricature the Enlightenment as totalistic and totalitarian. Habermas is right when he suggests that Heidegger, Adorno, and Jacques Derrida (like many of today's postmodern figures) write as if

> they were living in the shadow of the "last" philosopher, as did the first generation of Hegelian disciples. They are still battling against "strong" concepts of theory, truth and system that have belonged to the past for over a century and a half. . . . They believe they have to tear philosophy away from the madness of expounding a theory that has the last word.

They neglect, distort, and suppress the fact that "the fallibilistic consciousness of the sciences caught up with philosophy, too, a long time ago."[6]

Closely intertwined with the growth of fallibilism is the appropriation of the Enlightenment conception of critique. If all inquiry, in whatever domain, is fallible, then all claims must be exposed to open public criticism. Again, it was Peirce who first elaborated the idea of the critical community of inquirers whose ongoing task is to subject all theories and hypotheses to relentless criticism. Criticism must be dialogical, where there is open and free communication, and where participants nurture the communal habits and dispositions required to engage in the practice of criticism. Although Peirce first elaborated this ideal of a critical community of inquirers, it was Dewey who drew out the political and moral consequences of the ideal for an understanding of democracy as a moral ideal. Dewey thought that one of the greatest dangers of his time was the "eclipse of the public"—a public space in which human beings would be properly educated in order to engage in reciprocal argumentation and criticism. Thus, contrary to the caricature of the Enlightenment as advocating a closed totalistic system of knowledge, the essential

---

[5] Wilfrid Sellars, "Empiricism and the Philosophy of Mind," in *Minnesota Studies in the Philosophy of Science*, vol. 1, ed. Herbert Feigl and Michael Scriven (Minneapolis: University of Minnesota Press, 1956), 300.
[6] Jürgen Habermas, *The Philosophical Discourse of Modernity*, trans. Frederick Lawrence (Cambridge, Mass.: MIT Press, 1987), 408.

and intrinsic openness of inquiry and experience is one of its most enduring contributions.

Furthermore, for the pragmatists, this understanding of inquiry and experience deeply influenced their understanding of ourselves in the world. They categorically rejected the idea that we are beings-in-the-world who are completely determined by laws and structures working behind our backs. They were just as relentless, however, in their criticism of any form of naive voluntarism—that we can determine our destinies by imposing our will on the world. I stress this because another misguided caricature of the Enlightenment is that it deified the human will to master, manipulate, and control reality. What is most vital for the pragmatic appropriation of the Enlightenment is the conception of the world as the place of open possibilities where human beings can play a role in ameliorating human suffering and rectifying injustices by the active use of "reflective intelligence." The radical contingency of the world in which we find ourselves is a source of possible failure and tragedy, as well as a source of opportunities—opportunities to make a difference in our destinies.

Another target of attack by postmodern critics of the Enlightenment has been its emphasis on universality. Here too, however, there is a tendency to distort and to smooth out complexities. Particularity, singularity, and difference are pitted against universality. Presumably, in their obsession with universality, Enlightenment thinkers suppressed differences and violated the singularity and integrity of marginalized groups. I do not want to deny that frequently, when Enlightenment thinkers spoke of humanity or Man, they were really referring to white, male property owners. We need to expose and criticize sexist and racist biases wherever we find them, but to leave the matter here is to be guilty of a one-sided distortion, for the universalistic thrust of Enlightenment thinkers can be understood in another way. It is the practical demand that all groups and individuals should have equal rights and should be treated with equal respect. Every human being—in Kant's words—has inviolable dignity. The concrete actualization of human freedom and dignity set an agenda for a democratic republic in which all share and participate. When the Enlightenment is legitimately criticized for betraying the ideals it professed, this is not a post-Enlightenment critique but, rather, an immanent critique that highlights the disparity between professed ideals and social reality. The point can be made in another way. When postmodern critics protest against the silencing of other voices, the failure to respect the otherness of the other, and the ways in which groups have been marginalized, they are not really objecting to the universal practical demands of Enlightenment thinkers but, rather, emphasizing the ways in which these ideals have been betrayed and undermined. This even becomes evident in postmodern critics like Rorty and Jean-François Lyotard, because they project a utopia in which the universal agonistic play of different forms of life, vocabularies, and language games becomes embodied in everyday practices.

Because this volume is concerned with the relation between the Enlightenment and religious life, I want to say something about the pragmatic attitude toward religion. Earlier, I claimed that although the Enlightenment in the United States has always been antidogmatic, it has not been primarily antireligious. It is well known that it was William James who popularized the term *pragmatism* (although he generously acknowledged Peirce as the founder of pragmatism). It is less well known that in his famous paper "Philosophical Conceptions and Practical Results" (1898), where James introduced pragmatism, he was primarily concerned to show its relevance for testing our religious convictions. As James initially understood the pragmatic principle, it means that

if there were any part of a thought that made no difference in the thought's practical consequences, then that part would be no proper part of the thought's significance.... There can be no difference which doesn't make a difference.... The whole function of philosophy ought to be to find out what definite difference it will make to you and me, at definite instants of our life, if this world-formula or that world-formula be the one which is true.[7]

To illustrate what he means, James focused on the controversy between materialism and religion in order to show the significant practical consequences of our religious convictions. The context in which James was working out his understanding of pragmatism was one in which it could be employed to clarify the meaning and truth of religious experience.

James was not alone in exploring the relations between pragmatism and the varieties of religious experiences. Even the more tough-minded Peirce, in his more speculative papers, sought to develop a religiously oriented theory of Evolutionary Love, and he elaborated a neglected argument for God. Dewey was more indifferent to religious concerns than either Peirce or James. As Bruce Kuklick has effectively

---

[7]William James, "Philosophical Conceptions and Practical Results," in *Collected Essays and Reviews,* ed. Ralph Barton Perry (New York: Longmans, Green, 1920), 413.

demonstrated, however, Dewey himself was deeply influenced by his religious Congregational upbringing. Late in his career, Dewey elaborated his own version of a common faith. Nevertheless, the pragmatists did accept that strand in the Enlightenment legacy (exemplified by Kant) that insisted that any adequate conception of religion must itself be open to rational criticism. None of them wanted to exclude the role that religion can play in human experience.

I want to conclude by discussing one of the deepest anxieties that has been bequeathed to us by the Enlightenment—an anxiety that is still very much with us and has become much more poignant. Although I have objected to facile universal claims about the Enlightenment, this does not mean that we cannot make responsible, well-grounded generalizations. Even though there are internal conflicts and complexities, most Enlightenment thinkers did object to any and all appeals to authority other than those that could be warranted by human reason and experience. This stance does have significant consequences for "justifying" our basic ethical and political norms, because it means giving up all attempts to ground such norms on transcendent principles. Nevertheless, most of the Enlightenment thinkers did think we could displace such transcendent grounding or heteronomous appeals to authority with an immanent grounding. They were not nihilists or relativists in the current senses of these concepts. I think Habermas is essentially right when he writes, "Modernity can and will no longer borrow criteria by which it takes its orientation from the models supplied by another epoch; it *has to create normativity out of itself.* Modernity sees itself cast back upon itself without any possibility of escape."[8]

After two hundred years of relentless criticism, we have become much more dubious about this project—about how and whether it is even possible "to create normativity out of itself," about how and whether we can justify ethical and political norms and the norms of critique itself. What sometimes seems so paradoxical about postmodern thinkers is that although they assume a radical stance of critique, it is never quite clear whether there are any nonarbitrary standards of critique. Critique in the name of what? There are those like Habermas and Karl-Otto Apel who argue that it is possible—and indeed necessary—to give an immanent, rational, communicative justification of the norms of theoretical and practical argumentation without relying on bad foundationalism. In

[8]Habermas, *The Philosophical Discourse of Modernity,* 7.

this respect, they are quite close (as they both acknowledge) to the American pragmatists. Of course, there are also those who are deeply skeptical that such a project is still viable. Yet even Derrida says, "I cannot conceive of a radical critique which would not be ultimately motivated by some sort of affirmation, acknowledged or not."[9] What precisely is being affirmed and why? As I read the dialectic of postmodernity, after the evolving negative and skeptical themes, there has been a return to the pressing questions the Enlightenment posed: How can we justify the projects of critique? How can we today justify or warrant our primary affirmations, our ethical and political norms? We all know there is no consensus about how to answer these questions. The questions do not disappear, however; they keep returning to haunt us as the repressed returns. I said that our doubts and anxieties have become more urgent and poignant—especially in view of our sensitivity to the ambiguous legacy of the Enlightenment. Even these doubts were already present in the historical Enlightenment. They were already present in Denis Diderot's *Rameau's Nephew* (1762)—one of the most important texts of the Enlightenment.

We cannot turn to the eighteenth century to solve our problems and alleviate our anxieties. Nevertheless, we can recognize both the continuity of our concerns with those of the Enlightenment and our indebtedness to it. For the aspirations, dreams, hopes, doubts, conflicts, and anxieties of the Enlightenment still form the horizon within which we continue to struggle with these questions.

[9]Jacques Derrida, "Dialogue with Jacques Derrida," in *Dialogues with Contemporary Continental Thinkers*, ed. Richard Kearney (Manchester: Manchester University Press, 1984), 118.

Contributors

WILLIAM M. SHEA is Professor of American Religious Thought and Chairman of the Department of Theological Studies at Saint Louis University. A Woodrow Wilson Center Fellow in 1986–87, he is the author of *The Naturalists and the Supernatural* (1984) and the editor of *The Struggle over the Past: Fundamentalism in the Modern World* (1993).

PETER A. HUFF is Assistant Professor of Theology at Saint Anselm College. He is the author of *Trace of the Fugitive Gods: Allen Tate and the Catholic Revival* (forthcoming).

RICHARD J. BERNSTEIN is Vera List Professor of Philosophy and Chair of the Department of Philosophy, Graduate Faculty, at the New School for Social Research. His books include *The New Constellation* (1992) and *Beyond Objectivism and Relativism* (1983).

PATRICK W. CAREY is Associate Professor of Theology, Marquette University. His books include *The Roman Catholics* (1993), *Orestes A. Brownson* (1991), *People, Priests, and Prelates: Ecclesiastical Democracy and the Tensions of Trusteeism* (1987), and *An Immigrant Bishop* (1979).

STANLEY CAVELL is Professor of Philosophy at Harvard University. He is the author of *Philosophical Passages: Wittgenstein, Emerson, Austin, and Derrida* (1994) and *A Pitch of Philosophy: Autobiographical Exercises* (1994).

ANDREW DELBANCO, Professor of English at Columbia University, is the author most recently of *The Death of Satan: How Americans Have Lost the Sense of Evil* (1995). His previous books include *The Puritan Ordeal* (1989) and, as editor, *The Portable Abraham Lincoln* (1992).

DENIS DONOGHUE holds the Henry James Chair of English and American Letters at New York University. He was Professor of Modern English and American Literature at University College, Dublin; University Lecturer in English at Cambridge University; and Fellow of King's College, Cambridge. His many books are mainly about eighteenth-, nineteenth-, and twentieth-century English, Irish, and American literature. Donoghue is a former Guest Scholar of the Woodrow Wilson Center.

GILES GUNN, Professor and Chair, Department of English, University of California, Santa Barbara, is the author of *Thinking across the American Grain*

(1992), *The Culture of Criticism and the Criticism of Culture* (1987), and *The Interpretation of Otherness* (1979).

JAMES T. KLOPPENBERG, Associate Professor of History at Brandeis University, is the author of *Uncertain Victory: Social Democracy and Progressivism in European and American Thought, 1870–1920* (1986), which was awarded the Merle Curti Prize by the Organization of American Historians, and a coeditor, with Richard Wightman Fox, of *A Companion to American Thought* (1995).

HENRY SAMUEL LEVINSON is Professor and Head of Religious Studies, University of North Carolina at Greensboro. His books include *Santayana, Pragmatism, and the Spiritual Life* (1992), *The Religious Investigations of William James* (1981), and *Science, Metaphysics, and the Chance of Salvation: An Interpretation of the Thought of William James* (1979).

JACOB NEUSNER is Distinguished Research Professor of Religious Studies, University of South Florida; Visiting Professor of Religion, Bard College; member of the Institute for Advanced Study, Princeton; and life member of Clare Hall, Cambridge University.

MARK A. NOLL is McManis Professor of Christian Thought at Wheaton College, the author of *Princeton and the Republic, 1768–1822* (1989), and coeditor of *Evangelicalism: Comparative Studies of Popular Protestantism in North America, the British Isles, and Beyond* (1994).

SCHUBERT M. OGDEN is University Distinguished Professor Emeritus, Southern Methodist University. His books include *Is There Only One True Religion or Are There Many?* (1992) and *On Theology* (1992).

JOHN E. SMITH is Clark Professor Emeritus of Philosophy at Yale University and General Editor of the Yale Edition of *The Works of Jonathan Edwards*. His books include *Quasi-Religions* (1994), *Jonathan Edwards* (1992), *America's Philosophical Vision* (1992), and *Purpose and Thought* (1978).

DAVID TRACY is affiliated with the Divinity School at the University of Chicago. He is the author of *Plurality and Ambiguity* (1987) and *The Analogical Imagination* (1985).

Index

Abrams, M. H., 302
Absalom, Absalom! (Faulkner), 69, 74
Adams, George Burton, 116
Adams, Henry, 59, 68, 115–16; on
  metaphor changes, 65–66; *The
  Education of Henry Adams* by, 60
Adams, John, 34, 104, 213, 218
Adler, Felix, 20
Adorno, Theodor, 337, 341
Adventures of Huckleberry Finn, The
  (Twain), 59
Aeterni Patris (Leo XIII), 148
affections, 202–5
agape, agapism, 49, 222
Agee, James, 68; *Let Us Now Praise
  Famous Men* by, 80
Age of Reason, 130, 135, 137, 272
Age of Reason, The (Paine), 133
Agrarians, Southern, 59
Ahab, 262; consciousness of, 76–78
Ahlstrom, Sydney, 197
Aids to Reflection (Coleridge), 111
Albion's Seed (Fischer), 30
Aldrich, Thomas Bailey, 58
America as "Redeemer Nation," 300–301
American Catholic Philosophical
  Association, 152
American Economic Association, 37
Americanism, 142–45
American Novel and Its Tradition, The
  (Chase), 64
American Republic, The (Brownson), 141
"American Scholar, The" (Emerson), 241
American Tragedy, An (Dreiser), 66
Ames, William, 97
anabaptism, 119
Anglican Church, 32, 312
"Animula" (Eliot), 315
"Annabel Lee" (Poe), 57
Antifederalists, 33
antifoundationalism, 13, 119

antimodernism, 150–51, 153, 328–29,
  332
Apel, Karl-Otto, 344
apologetics, Catholic, 131–35, 146
Aquiba, 183
Archer, Isabel, 69
Aristotle, 96–97, 99–100, 148, 312–13
Arminianism, 219
Art as Experience (Dewey), 275
Ashbery, John, 85; *Self-Portrait in a
  Convex Mirror* by, 81
"As I Ebb'd with the Ocean of Life"
  (Whitman), 86
atheism, 74
Auden, W. H., 224
Augustine, Saint, 175, 200n5, 212; *De
  Ordine* by, 199
authority, 29, 89; Catholicism and, 128–
  29, 134–35, 139, 142; Franklin on,
  215–16; reason and, 8, 322–25
Autobiography (Franklin), 74, 214–15
autocracy, 29
autonomy, 5, 8, 129
Awakening, The (Chopin), 71
Ayer, Alfred, 22

Babbitt, Irving, 68
Bacon, Francis, 97
Baldwin, James, 66, 68
Baptists, 95
Barlow, Joel, 75
Barth, John, 81
Barth, Karl, 218
Barthelme, Donald, 81
Bataille, Henry, 317
Baudrillard, Jean, 328
beauty and experience, 199–200
Becker, Carl, 206–7, 221; *The Heavenly
  City of the Eighteenth-Century
  Philosophers* by, 23
Beecher, Lyman, 35

being, 318. *See also* consciousness
Being There (Kosinski), 81
belief(s), 3–4, 18, 27–28, 44, 51, 205,
  308, 316, 333; Christianity and, 303–4;
  Eliot on, 312–14; knowledge and, 39–
  40, 334; Lincoln on, 252–53, 263;
  pragmatism and, 272, 288–89
*Belief and Disbelief in American
  Literature* (Jones), 67
Bell, Daniel, 47
Bellah, Robert, 48, 259, 305; *Habits of
  the Heart* by, 47
Benjamin, Walter, 332
Berger, Peter, 158
Berkeley, George, 120–22
Bernstein, Richard, 299
Berryman, John, 53, 74
Beulah (Evans), 72–73
Bible, 208–9. *See also* Scriptures
Bill of Rights, 33
Bishop, Elizabeth, 85
Blake, William, 316
Blessed Rage for Order (Tracy), 160
Bloch, Ruth, 32
Bloom, Harold, 227
Bonaventure, Saint, 200n5, 332
Boston College, 152
Boudinot, Elias, 94
Bradley, F. H., 205
Bradstreet, Anne, 85
Brazen Face of History (Simpson), 67
Brinton, Crane, 54
Brodhead, Richard, 59
Brooks, Van Wyck, 62
Brown, John, 230–31, 259
Brownson, Orestes, 16–17, 135, 148; *The
  American Republic* by, 141; "An Essay
  in Refutation of Atheism" by, 141;
  "Philosophy of the Supernatural" by,
  141; on role of church, 136–40
Brown University, 95
Buber, Martin, 220
Buchanan, James, 252–53, 266
Buchanan, Tom, 66
Burden, Jack, 67–68
"Burnt Norton" (Eliot), 80, 315–16
Bushnell, Horace, 21, 109, 116; "Dogma
  and Spirit" by, 109–10; *God in Christ*
  by, 110; on science, 111–13
Butler, Jon, 34

Calhoun, John C., 265
Calvin, John, 96
Calvinism, 31–32, 59–60, 68, 93n16, 198,
  218; legacy of, 63–64, 76

capitalism, 34, 136, 260
Carroll, John, 16, 130, 132–34
"Cask of Amontillado, The" (Poe), 57
Cass, Lewis, 251
Cather, Willa, 66
Catholicism, 5–6, 19, 39, 156–64, 220,
  331; American, 13, 15–17, 90, 125–26,
  129–31, 143–45; apologetics and, 131–
  35, 146; community and authority in,
  128–29, 134–35, 139, 142; education
  and, 150–53, 157; European, 146–47;
  neo-Thomism and, 147–56; and
  Protestantism, 142–43, 149–50;
  rationalism and, 126–27, 146; reason
  and, 132–34; romantic, 135–42;
  theology in, 153–54, 332
*Catholicism and Modernity:
  Confrontation or Capitulation*
  (Hitchcock), 158
Catholic Theological Society of America,
  153
Catholic University Bulletin, 145
Catholic University of America, 144–45,
  150–52
Catholic Worker Movement, 153, 155
Cavell, Stanley, 82–84, 86–87, 303, 333;
  In Quest of the Ordinary by, 302
"Chambered Nautilus, The" (Holmes), 58
Channing, William Ellery, 67
Charlotte Temple (Rowson), 71
Chase, Richard, 64
Chase, Salmon P., 264
Chauncy, Charles, 31, 203–4
Chavez, Cesar, 39
Cherry, Conrad, 110
Chopin, Kate, 71
Christianity, 33, 66, 72, 91, 101, 102,
  106, 166–67, 175, 191, 333; American,
  259–60; Augustinian, 31–32;
  communion and, 136–37; Eliot on,
  312–14; Emerson on, 258–59;
  humanitarian reform and, 35–36,
  identity and, 85–86; knowledge and
  belief in, 303–4; role of, 120–21, 140–
  41; Scriptural history and, 168–70,
  172–74; universal, 137–38. *See also*
  Catholicism; Protestantism
Christmas, Joe, 70
Church, 142; role of, 136–41. *See also*
  Catholicism; Christianity; Protestantism
Church and the Age, The (Hecker), 141–
  42
Churchmen and Philosophers (Kuklick),
  275
civil rights movement, 39

Civil War, 37, 247–48
Cixous, Hélène, 238–39
Clark, J. C. D., 32
Clay, Henry, 232–33
Coffin, William Sloane, 39
Coleridge, Samuel Taylor, 303; *Aides to Reflection* by, 111
colleges, 95, 104–5, 115
colonial era, 54, 101–2
Columbiad, The, 75
Columbia Literary History of the United States, 67
Commager, Henry Steele, 93
Common Grace, 122–23
Common Faith, A (Dewey), 42, 223, 275
Common Sense, Scottish, 18, 33, 54, 58, 64, 98–99, 115, 266; and American Enlightenment, 95, 107–8
Commonweal (magazine), 16, 153
communion, 136–39
community, 8, 128–29, 332
Compson, Quentin, 67, 74
Condorcet, Marquis de, 56n10, 336
Congregationalism, 95
Connecticut Wits, 75
Connell, Francis J., 154
Conquest of Canaan, The, 75
consciousness, 77–79, 333; in literature, 79–81; philosophy of, 316–18
Constantine, Emperor, 66
constitution, Emerson on, 240–43
Constitution, U.S., 33–34
Contingency, Irony, and Solidarity (Rorty), 44
Cooper, James Fenimore, 67
Cooper, John M., 151
Cooper Institute address (Lincoln), 252
Coquette, The (Foster), 71
Cornell University, 115
Corrigan, Michael, 142n30
cosmopolitanism, 205, 207
Cotton, John, 96
counternarrative, feminist, 70–73
Country of the Pointed Firs, The (Jewett), 71
Critical Legal Studies, 89
critical path, 9
critical theory, 89
criticism, 8–9, 89, 140, 145, 271; feminist literary, 70–73; institutionalizing, 10–11
Critique of Pure Reason (Kant), 239
Crying of Lot 49, The (Pynchon), 81
Cultural Contradictions of Capitalism, The (Bell), 47
cultural scarcity, 82–83

culture, 2, 35, 50
Curan v. The Catholic University of America, 326

Darrow, Clarence, 74
Darwin, Charles, 140, 112, 272, 286–87; *On the Origin of Species* by, 111
Davidson, Cathy N., 71
Dawson, Christopher, 151
Day, Dorothy, 39, 153
"Deacon's Masterpiece; or, The Wonderful 'One-Hoss Shay,' The" (Holmes), 58
Declaration of Independence, 55, 250, 256
Declaration on Religious Freedom, 156
Decline and Fall of Radical Catholicism (Hitchcock), 158
deconstruction, 89
deism, 97, 121
democracy, 34–35, 43, 108
De Ordine (Augustine), 199
Derrida, Jacques, 317, 341, 345
Descartes, René, 206, 332
"Descent into the Maelstrom, A" (Poe), 57
"Design" (Frost), 74
desire(s), 288–89
Dewey, John, 2, 5, 7, 9, 20, 22, 28, 40, 224, 329, 340–41; *Art as Experience* by, 275; *A Common Faith* by, 42, 223, 275; on language, 45–46; on moral life, 293–94; *Outlines of a Critical Theory of Ethics* by, 285; as pragmatist, 11–12, 270, 276, 285–86, 291, 297; *The Public and Its Problems* by, 43; *Reconstruction in Philosophy* by, 43; on religion, 42–44, 47–48, 50, 296–97, 343–44; *The Study of Ethics: An Outline* by, 285
Dickinson, Emily, 68, 74, 85
Diderot, Denis, 56n10, 74; *Rameau's Nephew* by, 345
Diggins, John, 36
Dignitatis Humanae, 156
Dissertation on Liberty and Necessity, Pleasure and Pain (Franklin), 214
"Diving into the Wreck" (Rich), 80
"Divinity School Address" (Emerson), 10
dogma, 109–10, 159
"Dogma and Spirit" (Bushnell), 109–10
Douglas, Stephen, 251–53, 256, 260, 266; Lincoln on, 257–58, 262–63
Douglass, Ann, 72
Douglass, Frederick, 68
dreams, 187–89
Dred Scott decision, 252, 257n22, 266
Dreiser, Theodore, 66

"Dry Salvages, The" (Eliot), 314
Dulles, Avery, 16–17, 159–61, 163
Dutch Reformed Church, 119, 195–96
Dwight, Timothy, 75

"East Coker" (Eliot), 314–15
Eckhart, Meister, 333
Eclipse of Biblical Narrative, The (Frei), 19
economy of cultural scarcity, 82–83
education, 9, 32, 65, 95, 142, 222, 224,
   341–42; American, 143–44; Catholic,
   150–53, 157; in moral philosophy, 104–
   5; religion and, 325–26; seminary, 148,
   220
Education of Henry Adams, The (Adams),
   60
Edwards, Jonathan, 6, 9, 17–18, 31–32,
   58, 93n16, 95, 97, 103, 107–8, 120,
   124, 195–96, 225; affectional theology
   of, 110–11; and evangelicalism, 218–20;
   Freedom of the Will by, 217–18; on
   God, 121–23, 209–11; *God's End in
   Creation* by, 198; *History of
   Redemption* by, 198; and Locke, 198–
   201, 205, 219; *The Mind* by, 198;
   Miscellanies by, 207–8; *The Nature of
   True Virtue* by, 98; *Of Being* by, 198;
   philosophy of, 196, 199–211, 275n7;
   on Puritanism, 61–62, 220–21;
   Religious Affections by, 218; "Sinners
   in the Hands of an Angry God" by,
   217
Eliot, T. S., 6–7, 68, 301, 312;
   "Animula," by, 315; "Burnt Norton"
   by, 80, 315–16; "The Dry Salvages" by,
   314; "East Coker" by, 314;
   "Knowledge and Experience in the
   Philosophy of F. H. Bradley" by, 313;
   "Little Gidding" by, 86, 315
Elliot, Walter, 146n42; *The Life of Father
   Hecker* by, 147
Ellison, Ralph, 66; *Invisible Man* by, 74
Elsie Venner (Holmes), 58
Ely, Richard T., 37–38
emancipation, 268
Emerson, Ralph Waldo, 61, 68, 82, 85,
   136, 195, 245–46, 249, 257, 268, 333;
   "The American Scholar" by, 241;
   "Divinity School Address" by, 10;
   "Experience" by, 243; "Fate" by, 6–7,
   10, 227–28, 230–39, 242, 244; "The
   Fugitive Slave Law" by, 228–29; on
   language, 242–43; "On Emancipation in
   the British West Indies" by, 230;
   philosophical authorship of, 239–41;
   "The Poet" by, 236; on religion, 258–

59; "Self-Reliance" by, 228, 235, 240–
   41; on slavery, 227–33, 237–38, 240,
   242; transcendentalism of, 302–3
"Emperor of Ice Cream" (Stevens), 74
England, John, 130–34
Enlightenment, 195, 332; American, 2–3,
   7–8, 28, 31–33, 88–89, 113–14, 328,
   331; defining, 55–56, 335–38; Eliot on,
   314–16; heritage of, 63–64, 66–67, 321–
   27, 338–45; literature and, 57–60, 67–
   68; Protestantism and, 53–54, 56, 90–92,
   95, 102, 118–20; and religion, 5–6, 11,
   14–15, 31–33, 53–54, 57–60, 68–69,
   126, 303; Scottish, 98–103, 107–8
Erigena, John Scotus, 333
esotericism, 237, 239
"Essay in Refutation of Atheism, An"
   (Brownson), 141
essentialism, 280
Ethica (Johnson), 214
ethics, 236–37, 318
Europe, 127, 146–47, 302
evangelicalism, 4–6, 20, 34–35, 90–91,
   99, 109, 123–24, 198; Edwards and,
   218–20
Evans, Augusta Jane, 72–73
events, Judaic ordering of, 180, 183–84
Everett, Edward, 264
evil, 15, 37; Kant on, 221–22, 281–82;
   Lincoln on, 263, 269; nature of, 221–
   23; William James on, 222–23
evolution, 111–12, 304
Evolution and Dogma (Zahm), 145
experience, 205; and beauty, 199–200;
   and faith, 201–2
"Experience" (Emerson), 243

faith, 48–49, 133, 267, 316; and
   experience, 201–2; and knowledge, 50,
   313
fallibilism, 340–41
"Fall of the House of Usher, The" (Poe),
   57
"Fate" (Emerson), 6–7, 10, 227–28;
   themes in, 229–40, 242, 244
Faulkner, William, 67–68, 80; *Absalom,
   Absalom!* by, 69, 74; *Light in August*
   by, 70
Fay, Daisy, 66
Federalist Papers, The, 34
Federalists, 33
Feidelson, Charles, 76
feminism and literature, 70–73
Fenton, Joseph, 154
Ferguson, Adam, 31
Ferguson, Robert A., 55

Feuerbach, Ludwig, 22
fictions, Stevens on, 308–12
Fiering, Norman, 100–101, 122
Filmer, Robert, 103
"Final Soliloquy of the Interior Paramour" (Stevens), 308
Fink, Leon, 37
"Fire and Ice" (Frost), 74
First Amendment, 33–34
Firstness, 310–11
First Vatican Council (Vatican I), 130–31, 146
Fischer, David Hackett, 30
Fitzgerald, F. Scott, 66–67
"Flyer's Fall" (Stevens), 305
Foote, Shelby, 247–48
Fordham University, 152
Foster, Hannah, 71
Foucault, Michel, 300, 317, 333, 335–36, 339
Four Zoas (Blake), 316
Fox-Genovese, Elizabeth, 72–73
fractals, 172–74
France, 16, 33, 102, 127, 133, 146–47, 150
Frankfurt school, 317, 339
Franklin, Benjamin, 6, 32, 54, 62, 68, 94, 195, 206, 218, 225, 300;
Autobiography of, 7, 214–15; *Dissertation on Liberty and Necessity, Pleasure and Pain* by, 214; papers of, 217; philosophy of, 196, 211–16; *Poor Richard's Almanack* by, 217
Franklinism, 300
freedom, 5, 49, 139, 162, 280–81
Freedom of the Will (Edwards), 217–18
free will, 97
Frei, Hans, 19
Freneau, Philip, 75
Freud, Sigmund, 161, 224, 235
Frost, Robert, 52–53, 68, 74, 85; "The Most of It" by, 80
Fugitive Slave Law, 6–7, 10, 227, 232
"Fugitive Slave Law, The" (Emerson), 228–29
fundamentalism, 18, 20, 91, 117
Fussell, Paul, 262

Gadamer, Hans-Georg, 323
Gandhi, Mohandas K. (Mahatma), 317
Gatsby, Jay, 66–67
Gaudium et Spes, 156
Gay, Peter, 89, 93, 115–16, 204n8
Geertz, Clifford, 89
Geisteswissenschaften, 27
Gellner, Ernest, 277
Genealogy of Morals (Nietzsche), 241

genteel tradition, 59
Gestell, 339
Gettysburg Address, 265, 267
Gigot, Francis E., 145
Gilded Age, 37
Gioberti, Vincenzo, 138, 141n27
Gleason, Philip, 149
God, 278; concepts of, 114–15, 121–23, 200–201; Edwards on, 121–23, 209–11; Franklin on, 213–16
God and Intelligence in Modern Philosophy (Sheen), 152
God in Christ (Bushnell), 110
God's End in Creation (Edwards), 198
Godwin, William, 54, 94
Goethe, Johann Wolfgang von, 89, 213
"Gold Bug, The" (Poe), 57
Gothicism, 57
grace, 122–23
Great Awakening, 31, 71, 98–99, 101, 196, 210n17, 218
Great Britain, 102, 109
Great Exposition (Paris), 65
Great Gatsby, The (Fitzgerald), 66–67
Greenfield Hill, 75
Greenstone, J. David, 36
Gregory XVI, Pope, 16
Grene, Marjorie, 316
Griffiths, Clyde, 66
Grimm, Percy, 70

Habermas, Jürgen, 11, 46, 48, 308, 318, 329, 338, 341, 344; *The Philosophical Discourse of Modernity* by, 316–17
habits, 205–6
Habits of the Heart (Bellah), 47
Halpern, Baruch, 170–71, 189–90
Hamilton, Alexander, 104
happiness doctrine, 213–14
Hart, Hornell, 91
Hartford Appeal, 160
Hartley, David, 57
Harvard University, 95
Hatch, Nathan, 100
Hauerwas, Stanley, 119
Hawthorne, Nathaniel, 57–58, 64, 67; *Mosses from an Old Manse* by, 63; *The Scarlet Letter* by, 68, 70
Heavenly City of the Eighteenth-Century Philosophers, The (Becker), 23
Hecker, Isaac, 16–17; *The Church and the Age* by, 141–42; on Enlightenment ethos, 135, 137
Hegel, George Wilhelm Friedrich, 22, 191, 272, 285–86, 300, 317; *The Phenomenology of Mind* by, 299

Hegelianism, 43
Heidegger, Martin, 10, 22, 244–46, 339, 341
Helper, Hinton Rown, 264
Hemingway, Ernest, 68, 80; *In Our Time* by, 66
hermeneutics, 168–69, 191, 330
"Hightoned Old Christian Woman, A" (Stevens), 74
Hill, Christopher, 92–93
historicism, 18, 167–68, 171
history, 1, 46, 145; paradigmatic, 172–75, 188–189; role of, 115–16, 165–68; in Scriptures, 168–74, 176–79, 182–86, 189, 191
History of Redemption (Edwards), 198
History of the Warfare of Science with Theology (White), 115
Hitchcock, James, 17, 159, 163; works of, 158
Hobbes, Thomas, 103
Hodge, Charles, 109, 112–13
Hoffman, Daniel, 77
Hofstadter, Richard, 266, 268
Hogan, John, 145
Holbach, Baron d', 54
Holmes, Oliver Wendell, 58
Hook, Sidney, 20
Hope Leslie (Sedgwick), 71
Howe, Daniel Walker, 35, 106
Howells, William Dean, 58, 59
humanism, 196, 308, 311–12
Humanist Manifestos, 20
humanitarianism, 213, 215
humanity, 105–6
Hume, David, 22, 31, 54, 56n10, 74, 94, 200n5, 213, 271, 336, 340
Husserl, Edmund, 317
Hutcheson, Francis, 31, 94, 97, 99, 102–5, 266; *System of Moral Philosophy* by, 103
Hutchinson, Anne, 85

idealism, 97
identity, 85–86
imperialism, 100–102
individualism, 5, 29, 45, 127–28, 134, 241, 268
In Our Time (Hemingway), 66
In Quest of the Ordinary (Cavell), 302
intellectualism, 128, 295
intelligence, 10–11, 142, 287–88
Invisible Man (Ellison), 74
Ireland, John, 142–43
Ishmael, 67; consciousness of, 76–78

"I Sing the Body Electric" (Whitman), 231
Israel: history of, 167–69; paradigmatic concepts of, 176–86
Italy, 146

Jackson, Jesse, 39
James, Henry, 58, 68, 85; *The Portrait of a Lady* by, 69
James, William, 5, 7, 21, 28, 43, 49, 78–79, 81, 85, 195, 205, 213, 268, 281n13, 290, 330, 340; on evil, 222–23; on moral life, 291–94; "Philosophical Conceptions and Practical Results" by, 270, 343; *Pluralistic Universe* by, 40, 274; as pragmatist, 11, 40, 271–72, 276, 284–85, 287, 297, 343; *The Principles of Psychology* by, 40, 287; on religion and knowledge, 42, 44, 295, 303; *The Varieties of Religious Experience* by, 40–41, 220, 274; *Will to Believe* by, 40
Jefferson, Thomas, 3, 49, 54, 56n10, 94–95, 218, 250–51, 268
Jesuits, 146, 148n44
Jewett, Sarah Orne, 71
John Paul II, Pope, 17
Johnson, Samuel, 97, 107, 212; *Ethica* by, 214
John XXIII, Pope, 17
Jones, Howard Mumford: *Belief and Disbelief in American Literature* by, 67; *O Strange New World* by, 67
Judaism, 6, 18–19, 166–67, 191, 331; paradigms and, 175–89; Scriptural history and, 168–74; time in, 178–86. *See also* Torah

Kallen, Horace, 270
Kansas-Nebraska Act, 252, 266
Kant, Immanuel, 7, 9, 22, 200n5, 235–36, 238, 241, 296, 313, 317, 336, 339, 342; *Critique of Pure Reason* by, 239; on evil, 221–22, 281–82; metaphysics of, 294–95; on moral life, 292–93; pragmatism of, 270–72, 274–77, 290; *Religion within the Limits of Reason Alone* by, 275, 280–82; on spirituality, 282–84; transcendentalism of, 270, 274–75, 277–80, 289, 298; *Was ist Aufklärung?* by, 335
Kaufmann, Walter, 333
Kazin, Alfred, 66
Kerby, William, 145
Kierkegaard, Søren, 218, 220, 225
King, Martin Luther, Jr., 39

Kneeland, Abner, 74
Knights of Labor, 37
Knower and the Known (Grene), 316
Knowing and Being (Polanyi), 316
knowledge, 3–4, 9, 27, 50, 318, 340; and belief, 39–40, 334; and education, 224, 341–42; Eliot's views on, 312–14; Kantian, 278–79; pragmatists' view of, 270–71, 276; and religion, 41–44, 109–10, 303–4; scientific, 111–12
"Knowledge and Experience in the Philosophy of F. H. Bradley" (Eliot), 313
Koch, Adrienne, 93
Kohlmann, Anthony, 132, 134
Komonchak, Joseph, 130
Kosinski, Jerzy, 81
Kuhn, Thomas, 27; *Structure of Scientific Revolutions* by, 89
Kuklick, Bruce, 116, 275–76, 343–44; *Churchmen and Philosophers* by, 275
Kulturkampf, 117

Lambeth Conference, 314
Lamentabili sane exitu (Pius X), 16
language, 271; Emerson on, 242–43; Lincoln and, 254–57; role of, 45–46
Lawrence, D. H., 62, 77; *Women in Love* by, 316
Leatherstocking, 67
Leavis, F. R., 316
Lefebvre, Marcel, 331
Leibniz, Gottfried Wilhelm, 281
Leo XIII, Pope: and *Aeterni Patris,* 148; and *Testem Benevolentiae,* 147
Leroux, Pierre, 136
Let Us Now Praise Famous Men (Agee), 80
Levinas, Emmanuel, 11; *Otherwise than Being* by, 318; *Totality and Infinity* by, 317–18
Levine, Lawrence, 260
Lewis, H. D., 311
liberalism, economic, 108
liberty, 16, 141, 154–55, 210
Life of Father Hecker, The (Elliott), 147
Life of Reason, The (Santayana), 274
Light in August (Faulkner), 70
Lincoln, Abraham, 7, 12–13, 247–48, 260, 269; on belief, 252–53, 263; on Douglas, 257–58, 262–63; and language use, 254–57; life role of, 267–68; politics of, 261, 266; religiosity of, 36–37; on self, 256–57; on slavery, 37, 49, 252–54, 264–65; on state of the nation, 249–51

Lindsay, Vachel, 68
Lippmann, Walter, 19
literature, 225; consciousness in, 79–81; Enlightenment and religion in, 57–60, 67–70, 72, 74–77; feminist criticism of, 70–73; pragmatism in, 81–87; religious skepticism in, 74–75
Literature and Theology in Colonial New England (Murdock), 61–62
"Little Gidding" (Eliot), 86, 315
Locke, John, 31, 54, 56n10, 93, 97–98, 100, 196, 271; Edwards and, 198–201, 205, 219
Lonergan, Bernard, 10–11, 90, 159, 161, 220
Longfellow, Henry Wadsworth, 58
Louvain, 150
Lowell, Robert, 66, 68
Lukács, Georg, 339
Luther, Martin, 96
Lyotard, Jean-François, 343

McCulloch, William, 211
MacIntyre, Alasdair, 27, 90, 332, 337
Mackintosh, R. H., 309–10
Maclean, Norman, 190
Madison, James, 33, 49, 50, 95, 104, 253
Malebranche, Nicholas, 120–22
manifest destiny, 75, 108, 263
Marcel, Gabriel, 220
Maritain, Jacques, 150; *True Humanism* by, 153
Marquette University, 152
Marx, Karl, 22, 161, 224
mathematics, paradigms in, 189–91
Mather, Cotton, 97
Maurin, Peter, 153
May, Henry F., 54, 56n9, 73–74, 93
Mayhew, Jonathan, 31, 54
Mead, George H., 340
Melville, Herman, 63, 67–68, 87, 254–55, 263; *Moby-Dick* by, 67, 75–77, 262; *Pierre* by, 74
memory, 186–87
Mennonites, 119
Mercier, Désiré, 150
metanoia, 291–92
metaphor, 65–66
metaphysics, 61, 98, 148, 294–95, 312–13
methodism, 119
Meyer, D. H., 106
Michalson, Gordon E., 274, 280–81, 283–84
Michel, Virgil, 151–53
Middle Atlantic region, 31–32

Mill, John Stuart, 22
millennialism, 101; Edwards on, 207–10
Miller, Perry, 61, 218–19; *The New England Mind* by, 60, 62
Mind, The (Edwards), 198
Mirari vos (Gregory XVI), 16
Miscellanies (Edwards), 207–8
Moby-Dick (Melville), 67, 75–78, 262
models, 189–91. *See also* paradigms
Moderate Party, 98–99
"Modern Age as a Chapter in the History of Christianity, The" (Rendtorff), 23
modernism, 2, 12, 21, 224; Catholic, 143–47, 151
Modernity, 17, 19–20, 249, 330, 333, 337–38, 344; Catholicism and, 156–64
Modern Schoolman (journal), 152
Molineaux, Robin, 67
Monroe Doctrine, 75
Montesquieu, Baron de la Brède et de, 31–32, 56n10
Moore, Marianne, 68
Moore, R. Laurence, 91
morality, 41, 106, 110, 235–37, 278, 283
moral life, pragmatism and, 290–95
moral philosophy, 97–98, 104–5, 108n62; Hutcheson's, 103–4
More, Paul Elmer, 68
Morgesons, The (Stoddard), 71
Mosses from an Old Manse (Hawthorne), 63
"Most of It, The" (Frost), 80
Mounier, Emmanuel, 153
"Murders in the Rue Morgue, The" (Poe), 57
Murdock, Kenneth, 61–62
Murphey, Murray, 275–76
Murray, John Courtney, 130, 154–55, 162
Murry, Middleton, 314
Mysterious Stranger, The (Twain), 59

Narrative of Arthur Gordon Pym, The (Poe), 74
National Education Association, 142
nationalism, 264, 266
naturalism, 2–3, 19, 42–43, 143, 146
Natural Religion (Wollaston), 214
Natural Supernaturalism: Tradition and Revolution in Romantic Literature (Abrams), 302
nature, 88n1, 98, 148, 278, 281; Judaic concepts of, 175, 191; and religion, 96–97, 133; and theism, 122–23; time in, 179–80, 185–86

Nature of True Virtue, The (Edwards), 98, 198
Nazism, 244
Necessary Angel, The (Stevens), 311
neo-orthodoxy, 39
neo-Thomism, 6, 90, 130n5; in America, 147–56
New Critics, 59
New Deal, 38, 266
New England, 31, 34, 60–61, 218–19
New England Mind, The (Miller), 60, 62
New Humanists, 59
New Scholasticism, The (journal), 152
Newton, Isaac, 31, 54, 93, 97–98, 100, 103, 105, 196
New York Review, 145
Niebuhr, H. Richard, 2, 47, 220
Niebuhr, Reinhold, 2, 39, 217–18, 220, 225–26, 248, 329
Nietzsche, Friedrich Wilhelm, 10, 22, 46, 161, 224, 244, 317, 333; *Genealogy of Morals* by, 241; *Thus Spoke Zarathustra* by, 245
Nor Shall My Sword (Leavis), 316
Notes toward a Supreme Fiction (Stevens), 304, 310–12
Notre Dame, University of, 152

Oakeshott, Michael, 316
O'Connor, Flannery, 68
Of Being (Edwards), 198
Old Testament, 167, 209
"On Emancipation in the British West Indies" (Emerson), 230
On Human Conduct (Oakeshott), 316
On the Origin of Species (Darwin), 111–12
orthodoxy, 20–21
O Strange New World (Jones), 67
Otherwise than Being (Levinas), 318
Ottaviani, Alfredo, 154
Outlines of a Critical Theory of Ethics (Dewey), 285
Oxford Companion to American Literature, 67
Oxford movement, 135

Pace, Edward, 150–51
paganism of Wallace Stevens, 305–8
Paine, Thomas, 3, 31, 54, 56n10, 94; *The Age of Reason* by, 133
Papers of Benjamin Franklin, The, 217
paradigms, 65–66; history and, 172–75, 188–89; and Judaism, 175–89; in religion, 187–88; role of, 189–91; in

Scriptures, 176–79; time and, 168, 172–76
Park, Edwards A., 111
Parker, Theodore, 68
Parkman, Francis, 68
Pascal, Blaise, 313–14
Pascendi dominici gregis (Pius X), 16, 147
Pastoral Constitution on the Church in the Modern World, 156
Peirce, Charles Sanders, 21, 78, 205–6, 218, 304, 310, 329, 340–41; on evil, 222–23; as pragmatist, 271n2, 343
Pelagianism, 133, 147
Perkins, William, 96
Perl, Jeffrey, 313: *Skepticism and Modern Enmity* by, 312
phenomenology, 40
Phenomenology of Mind, The (Hegel), 299
Phillips, Wendell, 68
"Philosophical Conceptions and Practical Results" (W. James), 270, 343
Philosophical Discourse of Modernity, The (Habermas), 316–17
Philosophical Investigations (Wittgenstein), 236–37
philosophy, 196, 271; Becker's, 206–7; Edwards's, 197–211; Emerson's, 240–41; as feminine, 238–39; and neo-Thomism, 149, 152–55; Peirce's, 205–6; as science, 277–78; and slavery, 237–38
"Philosophy of the Supernatural" (Brownson), 141
physics, Newtonian, 98, 103
Pierce, Franklin, 253
Pierre (Melville), 74
Pius IX, Pope, 146; and *Quanta cura,* 16; and *Syllabus errorum,* 16
Pius X, Pope; and *Lamentabili sane exitu,* 16; and *Pascendi dominici gregis,* 16, 147
Plantinga, Alvin, 119
Plath, Sylvia, 66
Plato, 243–44
pluralism, 16, 81, 331; Catholicism and, 157–64
Pluralistic Universe (W. James), 40, 274
Poe, Edgar Allan, 57, 67, 74
"Poet, The" (Emerson), 236
Poirier, Richard, 84–85, 87
Polanyi, Michael, 159; *Knowing and Being* by, 316
politics, 32–33, 36, 85–86, 108n62, 136; American, 300–301; free-soil, 260–61; Lincoln on, 253–55, 266; religion and, 3–4, 39, 44, 47–49

Poor Richard (Franklin), 217
Pope, Alexander, 31
Porter, Katherine Anne, 68
Portrait of a Lady, The (H. James), 69
positivism, 120n92, 140, 329–31
post-Enlightenment, 12
postfoundationalism, 5, 12, 21, 40, 51
postmodernism, 12, 21, 224–25, 328, 332–34, 342–43
poverty, 82–83
power, 66, 89, 139–40
pragmatism, 7, 11–12, 14, 19, 89, 205, 298, 330, 342; American, 79–80; and belief, 272, 288–89; concerns of, 273–74; Darwin and, 286–87; of Dewey, 11–12, 270, 276, 285–86, 291, 297; and intelligence, 287–88; Kantian, 270–72, 274–77, 290; in literature, 81–87; moral life and, 290–95; origins of, 270–73; religion and, 273, 295–97, 343–44; of William James, 11, 40, 271–72, 276, 284–85, 343; of Santayana, 270, 271n2, 276, 285, 290–91, 293–94, 297
"Pragmatism and Its Principles" (Kallen), 270
Prince, Thomas, 211
Princeton University, 95
Principles of Psychology, The (W. James), 40, 287
Problem of Christianity, The (Royce), 222, 303–5, 309
progressivism, 37–39
Protestantism, 2, 5–6, 17–19, 21, 30–31, 33, 63, 110, 220, 314; American, 93–94, 107–8; Aristotelian, 99–100; and Catholicism, 142–43, 149–50; Enlightenment and, 53–54, 56, 90–92, 95, 102, 118–20; God and, 114–15; Hawthorne and, 57–58; intellectual life of, 117–18; literature and, 69–71; pragmatism and, 273, 295–96; progressivism and, 37–39; science and, 111–13, 115, 117
"Provide, Provide" (Frost), 74
Public and Its Problems, The (Dewey), 43
public life, 5, 11, 164, 213
Pudd'nhead Wilson (Twain), 59
Puritan ethic, 196, 216
Puritanism, 28, 68–69, 96–97, 195; defining, 92–93; Edwards on, 61–62, 220–21; influence of, 60–62, 219
Putnam, Hilary, 340
Pynchon, Thomas, 66; *The Crying of Lot 49* by, 81

Quanta cura (Pius IX), 16
Quine, W. V. O., 340

Rahner, Karl, 159, 161, 220
Rainbow Coalition, 39
Rameau's Nephew (Diderot), 345
Ramsey, Bennet, 295
Ramsey, George, 169–70
Ramus, Peter, 99
rationalism, 2, 5, 51, 109, 117, 162, 339;
    Catholicism and, 126–27, 146; and
    religion, 28–29, 35
Ratzinger, Joseph Cardinal, 332
Rauschenbusch, Walter, 38–39; *A
    Theology for the Social Gospel* by, 37
"Raven, The" (Poe), 57
Rawls, John, 27
realism, 38–39, 104
Realms of Being (Santayana), 275
reason, 2, 14, 35, 48, 136, 271, 278, 281,
    317; ambiguity of, 9–10; and authority,
    8, 322–25; autonomous, 97, 127;
    Catholic views of, 132–34; pragmatism
    and, 290, 293; religion and, 279, 326–
    27
Reconstruction in Philosophy (Dewey),
    43
Recovery of the Sacred, The (Hitchcock),
    158
"Redeemer Nation," 300–301
reform, 37; humanitarian, 35–36
Reformation, 30, 95–96, 98
Reid, Thomas, 54, 94, 102, 271
religion, 1–2, 29–30, 108n60, 196, 217,
    261; American Revolution and, 54–55;
    civil, 259–60; and consciousness, 78–79;
    Dewey on, 42–44, 47–48, 50, 296–97,
    343–44; and education, 325–26;
    Emerson on, 258–59; and
    Enlightenment, 5–6, 11, 14–15, 31–33,
    53–54, 57–60, 68–69, 126, 303; and
    First Amendment, 33–34; Franklin on,
    214–15; heritage of, 23–24, 321–22;
    and knowledge, 41–44, 109–10, 303–4;
    and life, 153–55; and literature, 69–70,
    72, 74–77; nature and, 96–97, 133;
    paradigmatic thought in, 187–88;
    politics and, 3–4, 39, 44, 47–49;
    pragmatism and, 273, 295–97, 343–44;
    rationalism and, 28–29, 35; reason and,
    279, 326–27; role of, 224–25;
    Santayana on, 295–96; science and, 32,
    35, 41; society and, 139–40; tolerance
    and restraint of, 49–51. *See also*
    Catholicism; Christianity; Judaism;
    Protestantism; theology

*Religion within the Limits of Reason
    Alone* (Kant), 275, 280–82
religiosity, 34–35, 38–39; Lincoln's, 36–
    37; William James's, 40–42
Religious Affections (Edwards), 218
"Remarks on a National Literature"
    (Channing), 67
Rendtorff, Trutz, 23
Republic (Plato), 243
republicanism, 33, 47, 108
Republican Party, 261
revivalism, 12–13, 95, 125–26, 201
revolutions: American, 54–55, 102;
    French, 16, 33, 127, 133
Reynolds, David S., 74
Rich, Adrienne, 80
Ricouer, Paul, 224–25
Rinehart the Runner, 74
Rising Glory of America, The, 75
"River of Rivers in Connecticut, The"
    (Stevens), 86
Robinson, Edwin Arlington, 68
romanticism, 109–10, 302; Catholicism
    and, 135–42
Rorty, Richard, 22, 29, 45, 83, 225, 324,
    329, 338, 340, 343; *Contingency,
    Irony, and Solidarity* by, 44
Rousseau, Jean-Jacques, 54, 56n10, 94,
    281
Rowson, Susanna, 71
Royce, Josiah, 21–22, 78, 195, 223, 330;
    The Problem of Christianity by, 222,
    303–5, 309
Rush, Benjamin, 32
Russell, Bertrand, 22; *What I Believe* by,
    301
Ryan, John A., 145

sages: historical perceptions of, 182–89;
    paradigmatic thought of, 187–88
Saint Louis University, 152
Santayana, George, 7, 11–12, 221, 288;
    The Life of Reason by, 274; as
    pragmatist, 270, 271n2, 276, 285, 290–
    91, 293–94, 297; on religion, 295–96
Satolli, Francesco, 150
Scarlet Letter, The (Hawthorne), 68, 70
Schiller, Ferdinand, 317
Schneider, Herbert, 213
scholasticism, 152
science, 43, 106, 145, 149, 279;
    philosophy as, 277–78; and
    Protestantism, 111–13, 115, 117; and
    religion, 32, 35, 41
Scotland: Enlightenment in, 98–103. *See
    also* Common Sense, Scottish

Scriptures, 208–9; Hebrew, 166–67; historical organization in, 168–74, 176–79, 182–86, 189; structure of, 168–71; time concepts in, 179–86
Second Inaugural Address (Lincoln), 267–68
Second Vatican Council (Vatican II), 16–17; impact of, 125, 156–58
"Secret of Stars, The" (Holmes), 58
secularism, 2–3, 6, 15, 39, 47–48, 145–46, 302
Sedgwick, Catherine, 71
self, 63, 82, 85, 206; integrity of, 256–57
Self-Portrait in a Convex Mirror (Ashbery), 81
"Self-Reliance" (Emerson), 228, 235, 240–41
Sellars, Wilfrid, 340–41
Seward, William H., 251, 264–65
Sexton, Anne, 66
Shaftesbury, Lord, 97
Sheen, Fulton J., 152
Shields, Thomas E., 151
Sidney, Algernon, 31
Simms, William Gilmore, 64
Simpson, Lewis P., 249–50, 261–62; *Brazen Face of History* by, 67
sin, 97, 198, 217–18
"Sinners in the Hands of an Angry God" (Edwards), 217
Skepticism and Modern Enmity (Perl), 312
slavery, 6–7; Emerson on, 227–33, 237–38, 240, 242; issue of, 250–52, 260–61; Lincoln on, 37, 49, 252–54, 264–65
Smith, Adam, 56n10, 94
Smith, Henry Boynton, 111
Smith, H. Shelton, 110
Smith, James Ward, 108n60, 123
Smith, John E., 42–43
Smith, Samuel Stanhope, 105–6
Smith, Wilson, 106
"Snow Man, The" (Stevens), 80
social change, 30
social contract, 196
social order, 175, 261
social sciences, 223–24
society, 139–40, 330–31, 339
Socrates, 243–44
Sot-Weed Factor, The (Barth), 81
Sources of the Self (Taylor), 49
South, 31–32, 264–65
Southern Agrarians, 59
Spalding, John Lancaster, 141–44, 146n42
spirituality, Kant on, 282–84

Stedman, Edmund Clarence, 58
Stein, Stephen, 209–10
Stephens, Alexander, 266
Sterne, Laurence, 58
Stevens, Wallace, 6–7, 19, 68, 83, 85, 301, 317; "Emperor of Ice Cream" by, 74; on fictions, 308–12; "Final Soliloquy of the Interior Paramour" by, 308; "Flyer's Fall" by, 305; "A Hightoned Old Christian Woman" by, 74; *The Necessary Angel* by, 311; *Notes toward a Supreme Fiction* by, 304, 310–12; "The River of Rivers in Connecticut" by, 86; "The Snow Man" by, 80; "Sunday Morning" by, 305–8; "Two or Three Ideas" by, 306, 308
Stewart, Dugald, 54, 94
Stoddard, Elizabeth, 71
Stout, Harry, 33
Stowe, Harriet Beecher, 259; *Uncle Tom's Cabin* by, 71–72
Structure of Scientific Revolutions (Kuhn), 89
Study of Ethics: An Outline, The (Dewey), 285
subjectivism, 89–90, 127–28
Sumner, Charles, 264
"Sunday Morning" (Stevens), images in, 305–8
supernaturalism, 41
Supreme Fiction, Stevens on, 308–12
Syllabus errorum (Pius IX), 16
Synod of Dort, 53–54
System of Moral Philosophy (Newton), 103

"Tamerlane" (Poe), 57
Taney, Roger, 253, 260, 266
Tanner, Tony, 69–70
Taylor, Charles, 50; *Sources of the Self* by, 49
technoeconomics, 330–31
Temple, 182–84, 191
Testem Benevolentiae (Leo XIII), 147
theism, 122–23
theodicy, 15, 260. *See also* evil
Theological Studies (journal), 153
theology, 2, 5n6, 21, 119, 200n5, 302, 331; affectional, 110–11, 156–64; antimodernism in, 328–29; Catholic, 153–54, 332; role of, 39, 326; science and, 112–13, 145; twentieth-century, 217–18
Theology for the Social Gospel, A (Rauschenbusch), 37
Thirdness, 310–11

Thomas Aquinas, Saint, 120n93, 200n5, 332
Thomism, 152
Thoreau, Henry David, 68, 82, 85, 302
Thought (journal), 152
Thus Spoke Zarathustra (Nietzsche), 245
Tillich, Paul, 217, 220
time: historical organization of, 165–67; memory and, 186–87; paradigmatic, 168, 172–76; in rabbinic Judaism, 178–86; scriptural organization of, 170–72
Tocqueville, Alexis de, 36
Tompkins, Jane, 71
Torah, 167, 169, 191; organization of, 171–73, 176–79; paradigms in, 180–82, 184; time concepts in, 185–86
Totality and Infinity (Levinas), 317–18
Tracy, David, 16–17, 28, 90, 161–63; *Blessed Rage for Order* by, 160
tradition, 331, 333
transcendentalism, 10–11, 61, 135; American, 302–3; Kant's, 270, 274–75, 277–80, 289, 298
Trilling, Lionel, 59
True Humanism (Maritain), 153
Turner, James, 35, 114, 120, 123
Twain, Mark, 68, 59
"Two or Three Ideas" (Stevens), 308

"Ulalume" (Poe), 57
Unamuno, Miguel de, 220
unapproachability, 82, 83
unbelief, 114, 248
Uncle Tom's Cabin (Stowe), 71–72
union, 37, 263–65
Unitarianism, 95, 132, 136
unity, 155–56
Updike, John, 227
Usher, Roderick, 67

Varieties of Religious Experience, The (W. James), 40–41, 220, 274
Vatican I. *See* First Vatican Council
Vatican II. *See* Second Vatican Council
Very, Jones, 68
Virginia Statute for Religious Freedom, 49
Voltaire, 31, 54, 56n10, 74, 93–94, 168

Warner, Charles Dudley, 58
Warner, Susan, 71
"War Prayer, The" (Twain), 59
Warren, Robert Penn, 67–68
wars, 38, 247. *See also* Civil War; revolutions, American
Was ist Aufklärung? (Kant), 335
Watts, Isaac, 219
Weber, Max, 48, 339
Webster, Daniel, 227–28, 231
welfare state, 38
Wesley, John, 95, 263
westward expansion, 251–52
Wharton, Charles Henry, 133
What I Believe (Russell), 301
Whigs, 31, 35–36, 196, 104
White, Andrew Dickinson, 115
Whitefield, George, 95
Whitehead, Alfred North, 42
Whitman, Walt, 85, 87, 256; "As I Ebb'd with the Ocean of Life" by, 86; "I Sing the Body Electric" by, 231
Whittier, John Greenleaf, 58
Wide, Wide World, The (Warner), 71
Wiener, Norbert, 312
Williams, Michael, 153
Will to Believe (W. James), 40
Wilson, Edmund, 59, 251, 266, 268
Wilson, James, 32
Wilson, John F., 33–34
Wilson, Woodrow, 218
Witherspoon, John, 93, 99, 105–6
Wittgenstein, Ludwig, 239; *Philosophical Investigations* by, 236–37
Wollaston, William, 214
Wolterstorff, Nicholas, 119
Women in Love (Lawrence), 316
Wood, Gordon, 104
Wordsworth, William, 303
Works of Jonathan Edwards, The, 217
Wundt, Wilhelm, 150

Yale University, 95
Yoder, John Howard, 119

Zahm, John, 145
Zweckrationalität, 339